# SEA CHANGE

## FINE AND DECORATIVE ART

## IN ST IVES 1914-1930

David Tovey

## ABOUT THE AUTHOR

David Tovey was born in 1953 and was educated at his father's preparatory school, Tockington Manor, near Bristol, and at Clifton College, before reading Jurisprudence at Pembroke College, Oxford. After twenty years as a solicitor, he returned to University in 1996 to read History of Art and is now an independent art historian, specializing in Cornish Art. His particular interest in St Ives art derives from the fact that his great-grandfather, William Titcomb, was one of the early settlers in the colony. Since 2000, he has curated several exhibitions and written numerous books on Cornish art. In particular, he published in 2003 a history of the first 25 years of the St Ives Society of Artists (1927-1952), entitled *Creating A Splash*, and curated the resultant exhibition, which toured six venues during 2003-4. Then, in 2008, he was lead Curator of *Dawn of a Colony*, a joint exhibition staged by Tate St Ives and Penlee House Gallery & Museum, Penzance, which reviewed art in St Ives from 1811 to 1914, and published two extensive histories to accompany these shows. His last book was a Social History of the colony. He lectures widely on Cornish representational art, particularly to members of the National Association for Design and Fine Arts Societies. His previous books include:-

*George Fagan Bradshaw - Submariner and Marine Artist - and the St Ives Society of Artists*
(Wilson Books, 2000 ISBN 0953836304)

*W.H.Y.Titcomb : A Newlyner from St Ives*, dealing with the years 1858-1908
(Wilson Books, 2003 ISBN 0953836320)

*W.H.Y.Titcomb : Bristol, Venice and the Continental Tours*, covering the years 1909-1930
(Wilson Books, 2003 ISBN 0953836312)

*Creating A Splash - The St Ives Society of Artists - The First Twenty-Five Years (1927-1952)*
(Wilson Books, 2003 & 2004 ISBN 0953836347)

*St Ives Art pre-1890 - The Dawn of the Colony*
(Wilson Books, 2008 ISBN 9780953836352)

*Pioneers of St Ives Art at Home and Abroad (1889-1914)*
(Wilson Books, 2008 ISBN 9780953836369)

*St Ives (1860-1930) - The Artists and the Community - A Social History*
(Wilson Books, 2009 ISBN 9780953836376)


First published in 2010 by
WILSON BOOKS
11-13 Mill Bank, Tewkesbury, Gloucestershire, GL20 5SD
(01684 850898) Email : dwt4@talktalk.net

Copyright - D.C.W.Tovey

All rights reserved. No part of this publication may be reproduced, stored in a retrieval system, or transmitted in any form or by any means, electronic, mechanical, photocopying, recording or otherwise, without the prior written permission of the publisher.

A catalogue record for this book is available from the British Library.

ISBN for this paperback edition
9780953836383

Printed and bound in England by
R.Booth Print, The Praze, Commercial Road, Penryn, Cornwall TR10 8AA

# SEA CHANGE : FINE AND DECORATIVE ART IN ST IVES 1914-1930

## CONTENTS

| | | |
|---|---|---|
| AUTHOR'S NOTE | | 6 |
| ABBREVIATIONS | | 6 |

CHAPTER

1. SEA CHANGE — 7

2. WAR
   - 2.1 The American invasion of 1914 — 15
   - 2.2 The outbreak of hostilities — 16
   - 2.3 Outdoor sketching restrictions — 17
   - 2.4 Casualties — 18
   - 2.5 Borlase Smart's War - 'Vimy Ridge to the Somme' — 19
   - 2.6 George Bradshaw's paintings of submarine warfare — 28
   - 2.7 Dazzle Painting - The St Ives connection — 28
   - 2.8 The Naval paintings of William Parkyn — 30
   - 2.9 Other depictions of the War — 31
   - 2.10 War poetry — 31

3. FRESH FACES DURING DARK DAYS
   - 3.1 Displaced artists — 33
   - 3.2 The experimental figure paintings of Frances Hodgkins — 33
   - 3.3 The symbolist works of Emile Fabry — 44
   - 3.4 The colourful and decorative watercolours of Louis Reckelbus — 52
   - 3.5 The swansong of Frances Lloyd — 54
   - 3.6 The brief but productive visit of Dirk Smorenberg — 57
   - 3.7 Claude Francis Barry and Louis Sargent — 59
   - 3.8 Robert Langley Hutton - "a universal favourite" — 66
   - 3.9 Marcella Smith and Helen Stuart Weir — 68
   - 3.10 Some other American visitors during Wartime — 71
   - 3.11 Other visitors during the War years — 73

4. THE OLD GUARD
   - 4.1 Introduction — 77
   - 4.2 Moffat Lindner — 77
   - 4.3 Fred Milner — 84
   - 4.4 Arthur Meade — 88
   - 4.5 Farewells — 89
   - 4.6 Other elderly painters — 92

5. LEADING LIGHTS IN THE TWENTIES
   - 5.1 All Change — 93
   - 5.2 Charles Simpson — 93
     - 5.2.1 Charles Simpson's Wild Bird Series — 96
     - 5.2.2 Charles Simpson's seagulls — 97
     - 5.2.3 Charles Simpson's ducks — 100
     - 5.2.4 Charles Simpson's landscapes and marines — 102
     - 5.2.5 Charles Simpson's figure paintings — 105
     - 5.2.6 Charles Simpson's depictions of the fishing seasons — 108
     - 5.2.7 Charles Simpson and 'El Rodeo' — 112
   - 5.3 The portraits of Ruth Simpson — 114

|  |  |  |  | |
|---|---|---|---|---|
| | 5.4 | | Robert Borlase Smart | 116 |
| | | 5.4.1 | Borlase Smart's depictions of Old St Ives and Old Plymouth | 116 |
| | | 5.4.2 | Borlase Smart's depictions of 'England's Wooden Walls' | 118 |
| | | 5.4.3 | Borlase Smart's early marine paintings | 120 |
| | | 5.4.4 | Borlase Smart and the inspiration of Venice | 123 |
| | | 5.4.5 | Borlase Smart's departure and return | 123 |
| | 5.5 | | John Park | 123 |
| | 5.6 | | The figure paintings and portraiture of Arthur Hayward | 129 |
| | 5.7 | | The watercolours of Alfred Bailey | 130 |
| | 5.8 | | Other male artists | 132 |
| | 5.9 | | Other female artists | 140 |
| 6. | **TEACHERS AND PUPILS** | | | |
| | 6.1 | | Introduction | 143 |
| | 6.2 | | The classes of Frances Hodgkins | 143 |
| | 6.3 | | Edith Collier's finest hour | 149 |
| | 6.4 | | The Simpson School of Painting | 152 |
| | 6.5 | | Arthur Hayward's 'St Ives School of Painting' | 157 |
| | 6.6 | | The classes of John Park | 157 |
| | 6.7 | | Other art classes | 158 |
| 7. | **PRINTMAKING IN ST IVES DURING THE ETCHING BOOM** | | | |
| | 7.1 | | Introduction | 159 |
| | 7.2 | | Alfred Hartley | 159 |
| | 7.3 | | The etchings of Sydney Long | 165 |
| | 7.4 | | The 1919 visit of Donald Shaw MacLaughlan | 167 |
| | 7.5 | | Other specialist printmakers in the colony | 168 |
| | 7.6 | | The St Ives Print Society | 172 |
| 8. | **VISITORS OF NOTE IN THE TWENTIES** | | | |
| | 8.1 | | Introduction | 177 |
| | 8.2 | | The visit of Effie Charlton Fortune in 1922-3 | 177 |
| | 8.3 | | The 1923 visit of Wilson Henry Irvine | 180 |
| | 8.4 | | Return visits by former colonists | 185 |
| | 8.5 | | Some temporary residents | 188 |
| 9. | **THE NOVELTY OF THE NAIVE VISION** | | | |
| | 9.1 | | A meeting hailed as "one of the great milestones in 20th Century British Art" | 197 |
| | 9.2 | | The first visit of Christopher Wood in 1926 | 197 |
| | 9.3 | | Ben and Winifred Nicholson | 203 |
| | 9.4 | | The 1928 visit and the discovery of Alfred Wallis | 205 |
| | 9.5 | | Alfred Wallis' true background | 211 |
| | 9.6 | | Ben Nicholson's promotion of Wallis | 212 |
| | 9.7 | | Breakdown | 215 |
| | 9.8 | | Afterglow | 217 |
| 10. | **THE DAWN OF THE CRAFT TRADITION IN THE COLONY** | | | |
| | 10.1 | | Introduction | 219 |
| | 10.2 | | Frances Horne and the St Ives Handicraft Guild | 220 |
| | 10.3 | | The Leach Pottery - Introduction | 222 |
| | | 10.3.1 | Bernard Leach's background in the Far East | 222 |
| | | 10.3.2 | Shoji Hamada's background | 226 |
| | | 10.3.3 | The establishment of the Leach Pottery by Leach & Hamada | 227 |
| | | 10.3.4 | George Dunn | 228 |
| | | 10.3.5 | Edgar Skinner | 230 |
| | | 10.3.6 | Shoji Hamada in St Ives | 231 |
| | | 10.3.7 | Refining an underlying philosophy | 233 |

# CONTENTS

|  |  | 10.3.8 | Educating the locals | 235 |
|---|---|---|---|---|
|  |  | 10.3.9 | Bernard Leach's early Cornish pots | 236 |
|  |  | 10.3.10 | Early patrons | 239 |
|  |  | 10.3.11 | First exhibitions | 241 |
|  |  | 10.3.12 | Hamada's return to Japan | 242 |
|  |  | 10.3.13 | The first students - Michael Cardew & K. Pleydell-Bouverie | 243 |
|  |  | 10.3.14 | Tsuranosuke Matsubayashi | 246 |
|  |  | 10.3.15 | Robert Morton Nance | 248 |
|  |  | 10.3.16 | Pottery demonstrations for the locals | 250 |
|  |  | 10.3.17 | Further exhibition in Japan | 251 |
|  |  | 10.3.18 | Norah Braden | 251 |
|  |  | 10.3.19 | Leach's efforts to form a creative community | 252 |
|  |  | 10.3.20 | Changes in approach | 254 |
|  |  | 10.3.21 | Leach and his fellow artists | 256 |
|  |  | 10.3.22 | Eloquent visionary versus shambolic businessman | 258 |
|  | 10.4 |  | Other handicraft makers in the colony | 261 |
|  |  | 10.4.1 | The art needlework of Doris Barry and Lucy and Vera Bodilly | 261 |
|  |  | 10.4.2 | The hand-loom weaving of Florence Welch, Irene Turner and Luned Hamilton-Jenkin | 264 |
|  |  | 10.4.3 | The craftwork of Ruth Davenport | 265 |
|  |  | 10.4.4 | The millinery of Marcella Smith | 265 |
|  |  | 10.4.5 | The painted lampshades of Kathleen Bradshaw | 266 |
|  |  | 10.4.6 | The painted tableaux of Marjorie Ballance | 266 |
|  | 10.5 |  | The heyday of Cryséde hand block-printed textiles | 267 |
|  |  | 10.5.1 | "The most complete independent achievement of our time" | 267 |
|  |  | 10.5.2 | Alec Walker and the establishment of Cryséde in Newlyn | 268 |
|  |  | 10.5.3 | The Independent Gallery exhibition of 1925 | 268 |
|  |  | 10.5.4 | The appointment of Tom Heron | 269 |
|  |  | 10.5.5 | The transfer to the Island Factory, St Ives | 270 |
|  |  | 10.5.6 | The formation of Cryséde Limited | 270 |
|  |  | 10.5.7 | Alec Walker's designs | 271 |
|  |  | 10.5.8 | Cryséde fabrics | 275 |
|  |  | 10.5.9 | The hand block-printing process | 276 |
|  |  | 10.5.10 | A wonderful place to work | 278 |
|  |  | 10.5.11 | Expansion | 279 |
|  |  | 10.5.12 | Breakdown | 280 |
|  |  | 10.5.13 | Craft or Industry | 282 |
| 11. | SEEKING A NEW IDENTITY |  |  |  |
|  | 11.1 | Introduction |  | 283 |
|  | 11.2 | London, Paris and Pittsburgh |  | 283 |
|  | 11.3 | Exhibitions outside Cornwall |  | 284 |
|  | 11.4 | The formation of the St Ives Society of Artists |  | 287 |
| 12. | BLUEPRINT FOR THE FUTURE |  |  | 291 |

APPENDICES

| A | Borlase Smart War Drawings | Table A | At the Imperial War Museum | 293 |
|---|---|---|---|---|
|  |  | Table B | At Plymouth City Art Gallery | 293 |
| B | Artists Exhibiting Locally | Table A | 1914 - 1920 | 294 |
|  |  | Table B | 1921 - 1927 | 296 |

ACKNOWLEDGEMENTS 298

SELECTED BIBLIOGRAPHY 299

INDEX 300

Front Cover Illustration : George Turland Goosey  *Boats in St Ives Harbour*  (Private Collection)
Back Cover Illustration : Terrick Williams  *White Boats, St Ives*  (1924)  (Private Collection)

# AUTHOR'S NOTE

Readers of one or more of my other books on early St Ives art will know that when, in 2003, I decided to turn my attention to the pre-1930 history of the colony, I envisaged being able to record it in a single volume. However, the quite exceptional range of artists, of varying nationalities, who have derived inspiration from this small Cornish sea port, has meant that this is the fourth, and last, book in what has become an extensive series.

In my previous books, I have tended to find that I am dealing with artists who have not been the subject of any detailed research previously. In this period, though, there are a number of artists, such as Ben and Winifred Nicholson, Christopher Wood, Alfred Wallis, Bernard Leach and Frances Hodgkins, who have been written about extensively by leading art historians.[1] I wondered, therefore, whether I could offer anything new on these subjects. However, all these artists' stays in St Ives have been considered previously *in vacuo*, and any study of the output of other artists working in St Ives at the time thought unnecessary, in the light of the constant refrain by modernist art historians that their aesthetic was outdated and of no consequence. Such modernist painters have also often been presented as intellectually superior to these "arch-reactionaries", and yet no attempt has been made to understand the intellectual backdrop to the colony, inspired by figures such as Greville Matheson, Edgar Skinner, Robert Morton Nance and Will Arnold-Forster. I hope, by dealing in this one book, not only with traditional and modern paintings, but also with handicraft, that a far more rounded view of the colony emerges, for, despite the horrors of the War and the financial constraints of the 1920s, this period saw an astonishing variety of work being produced in the colony, much of it of considerable interest. The mastery of light, tone and colour, coupled with the technical skill required to capture fleeting effects or quick movement, developed by artists, such as Charles Simpson, Borlase Smart and John Park, after numerous hours working on the spot, warrant as much respect as novel approaches to the use of colour or to the texture of painted surfaces, or the adoption of a naive viewpoint. The inter-play between handicraft, newly introduced into the colony, and fine art brings a further fascinating dimension, particularly as Alec Walker based his textile designs for Crysède on his modernist paintings of the local landscape and some of Bernard Leach's best pot decorations had pictorial elements.

This will be my last book on St Ives art. Eight books, five of which have been major surveys, in the last decade has taken its toll in a number of respects, and the constant failure to secure any funding has been intensely frustrating. However, I can only hope that, at some stage, the extraordinary importance of the art colony in St Ives, on both national and international stages, will become more widely appreciated, and that the results of the full-time research that I have done in the last decade will prove valuable. Yet again, this book demonstrates the need for St Ives to have a public Art Gallery willing to display St Ives representational art on a year-round basis, for the brief flicker of hope that Tate St Ives might change its attitude, by virtue of its involvement in the 2008 *Dawn of a Colony* exhibition, has been quickly extinguished. Notwithstanding the difficulties faced, a concerted campaign with this objective is long overdue.

There will always be new information coming to light and I intend to lodge with a select group of organisations - namely, Penlee House Gallery & Museum, Penzance, St Ives Archive Study Centre, St Ives and the Cornish Studies Library, Redruth - additions and corrections to all my titles, which I will update from time to time. In due course, it is also my intention to produce a comprehensive list of artists, who have worked in St Ives, with brief details of the source material available for each one, which I doubt will be economic to publish, but which I will provide to the afore-mentioned organisations. Obviously, these can be obtained direct from myself as well.

I have not previously adopted the standard practice of making dedications of my books but, as this is the last one, I must dedicate it to my wife, Sherry, who has been unfailingly supportive during all the highs and lows of the last decade.

Finally, once again, I must stress that as a one-man researcher, writer, editor, designer, publisher and publicist, I need YOUR help. If you do enjoy the book, please spread the word.

# ABBREVIATIONS

| | | | |
|---|---|---|---|
| RA | Royal Academy | ROI | Royal Institute of Oil Painters |
| RBA | Royal Society of British Artists | RSA | Royal Scottish Academy |
| RBC | Royal British Colonial Society of Artists | RWA | Royal West of England Academy |
| RCA | Royal Cambrian Academy | SMA | Society of Marine Artists |
| RCPS | Royal Cornwall Polytechnic Society, Falmouth | STISA | St Ives Society of Artists |
| RE | Royal Society of Painter-Etchers and Engravers | SWA | Society of Women Artists |
| RI | Royal Institute of Painters in Watercolours | WIAC | Women's International Art Club |

---

1 Even representational artists, such as Charles Simpson and John Park, have been the subject of biographies.

## SEA CHANGE

The years 1914-1930 brought about a complete sea change in the St Ives art colony. From whatever viewpoint one adopts - artistic, social, economic, political, cultural, demographic, physical - there was significant change. Unsurprisingly, the colony struggled to adapt speedily to all these new factors, and the period is one of transition during which it sought to find a new identity for itself. Nevertheless, St Ives, as always, retained the ability to attract and inspire a wide range of talented artists, so that, despite any underlying malaise, works of art of considerable interest, variety and significance were created.

In the early years of the century, the colony at St Ives had established a worldwide reputation for both the practice and the teaching of landscape and marine painting. This had resulted in the permanent residents of the colony, many of whom had established significant reputations on both the national and international stages, constantly being complemented by young aspiring artists and keen students not only from this country but also from abroad. Art in St Ives, therefore, had never stagnated, but had always reacted to new influences and fostered distinctive personal visions. In the years immediately preceding the War, the colony had gained a significant reputation in America, because numerous American artists of distinction had found inspiration in the town, and friendships made had led to the British artists being hung regularly, and with significant success, at the prestigious Carnegie International Exhibitions at Pittsburgh. This reputation is amply demonstrated by the fact that, in the summer of 1914, there were no fewer than fifty American artists, including several parties of students, working in the town. The Edwardian years had been good to artists and there had been a strong demand from Museums established and funded from the fruits of the Industrial Revolution, and from wealthy owners of large homes, for the huge canvases that were still considered essential for Royal Academy exhibits. The outbreak of War, however, brought the excesses of the era to a shuddering halt.

In truth, though, the colony had, by 1914, become a pale shadow of its former self, for many of the artists who had made the most significant contributions to its considerable reputation in its first thirty years, such as Julius Olsson, Arnesby Brown and Algernon Talmage, had moved on. In fact, Richard Hayley Lever, the young Australian artist, who had settled in the town for more than a decade after marrying a local girl, was moved in 1912 to call St Ives "the land of the dead".[2] This meant that the marine painter Moffat Lindner, the landscape artists John Noble Barlow, Arthur Meade and Fred Milner, the genre painter William Fortescue and the etcher Alfred Hartley were now the leading senior members of the colony. They were all respected figures but, although they continued to have reasonably regular success at the Royal Academy, they were not at the forefront of British art, as many St Ives artists had been in the past, and their paintings were no longer considered sufficiently novel or interesting to be illustrated as Pictures of the Year.

The War obviously had a dramatic effect on the colony. Sales dried up almost immediately, leading a number of artists to experience considerable financial hardship. Some, including, very commendably, several foreign nationals, felt obliged to enlist, even though they were over-age, whilst those that remained in the town sought "to do their bit". This could be time-consuming and enervating, and the terrible news coming from the front line made it difficult for some artists to feel any inspiration to paint at all. Others probably felt guilty at indulging themselves in such an activity, given the loss and hardship being suffered all around. A ban on outdoor sketching was, for many, the last straw. However, even in this very difficult period, there were still some artists, such as the New Zealander, Frances Hodgkins, the Dutchman Dirk Smorenberg, and the aspiring artists Louis Sargent and Claude Barry, who produced interesting work - work too modern for the Royal Academy but noticed at the International Society and other more liberal exhibition venues. The town also played host, during the War years, to two esteemed Belgian refugee artists - the renowned watercolourist, Louis Reckelbus, who introduced the colour of the Fauves into the colony, and Emile Fabry, a highly regarded painter of monumental symbolist works and a Professor at the Brussels Academy, whose enormous, recently re-discovered, mural, *War and Peace*, must rank as one of the most extraordinary achievements in the history of the colony. Accordingly, despite all the disruptions and difficulties, St Ives witnessed during the War years a considerable variety of new styles, and it is clear that a number of artists in the town derived inspiration from these novel approaches.

Despite its relative isolation from the hostilities, the colony also viewed some important first hand graphic depictions of the horrors of War, most notably in the fine series of sketches done on the Western Front by Robert Borlase Smart, forty-six of which are now in public collections (see Appendix A). Also on view

---
2  Letter from R Hayley Lever to W E Schofield dated 12/2/1912 - Schofield Archives, Godolphin House.

Fig. 1.1  Henry Snell    *St Ives*    (Freemans Auctioneers, Philadelphia)

were some of George Bradshaw's paintings from his time as a distinguished submarine commander, whilst William Parkyn developed a speciality as a painter of Naval vessels.

The resumption of peace, not surprisingly, brought fresh hope, and there were certainly, initially, good grounds for optimism. Frances Hodgkins was making significant progress and was being acclaimed in some quarters as "the first woman painter in England". Her classes were also attracting to St Ives some pioneering Antipodean artists, such as her compatriots, Edith Collier and Beatrice Wood, and the Australians, Bessie Gibson and Vida Lahey. It was also hoped that the School of Painting established by Charles and Ruth Simpson, who had arrived from Lamorna in 1916, would draw down to the colony aspiring artists in the same way as the Schools run by Julius Olsson, Algernon Talmage and Louis Grier had done in the pre-War period. Indeed, in November 1919, Hodgkins declared a renewed enthusiasm for the town. "It is so light & blue & bright & the herring season at its height & everyone doing well and making money." [3]

Unfortunately, though, the spirit of optimism did not last long and, for various reasons, most of the leading artists had left St Ives by the early 1920s. St Ives was not the only art enclave that suffered at this time, and many of the colonies that had flourished throughout Europe in the period 1880-1910 ceased to exist, as the attention of artists and writers turned away from quaint rural hideaways to modern city utopian dreams. The widespread pre-War enthusiam for landscape and marine painting out of doors had also largely dissipated. Accordingly, St Ives had to come to terms with the fact that it could no longer entice artists of renown to settle in the town. It was too removed physically and artistically from the centre of the art world.

Whilst retaining a number of its quaint charms, the local townscape also changed. The early 1920s saw the completion of Wharf Road, which ran around the edge of the harbour. Accordingly, many of the artists' studios, instead of fronting directly on to the beach, now had a busy road just outside, and it did not take landlords long to realise that these premises would be better exploited as cafés or souvenir shops rather than as bedraggled studios for hard-up artists. The advent of the motor car and the charabanc also demanded changes, and more and better accommodation was required for the increasing tourist hordes. Christopher Wood's girlfriend, Frosca Munster, would not have been the only visitor to complain

---

3  Ed. L Gill, *Letters of Frances Hodgkins*, Auckland, 1993 at p.344.

about the lack of a bath. There were also health concerns about the state of the old fishermen's cottages and plans for slum clearance. The sights in the harbour had changed as well. Gone were the brown sails of the fishing fleet, as, not before time, the St Ives boats became motorised. Whilst this gave them much needed extra flexibility, it could not solve the problem of vanishing fish stocks, and the fishing industry continued its inexorable decline. Accordingly, the town relied increasingly on tourism.

Whilst long-term residents might have grumbled about the changes, the town still had the ability to inspire visitors. One, writing in 1921, exclaimed, "St Ives is a painter's paradise. It is so unfailingly picturesque that there is scarcely a foot of the older part of the town that does not provide a 'subject'. Artists are as plentiful as blackberries, and there are few hours of the day during the summer months in which one does not stumble across half-a-dozen or so men and women at their easels capturing effects of light and shade in ancient archways or quaint streets." [4] Another, for whom the town was "a veritable gem of beauty, and inexhaustible in its attractions to artists", felt that what was particularly special was "the art atmosphere of St Ives". "The presence of other artists, who have made a success of their work, sustains and encourages the young aspirant. Many a morning as you wander through the narrow alleys of Down-along, you may meet a figure, dressed almost as casually as the fisherfolk, hastening along, a canvas tucked under her arm. You turn to your companion and whisper, 'that is the brilliant M. whose pictures hang in the Academy' - or that plainly-dressed elderly woman, who goes in to make her purchases at the butchers, with a crowd of less-gifted housewives, you recognise as one of the foremost water-colour artists of the day." [5] In truth, though, the likelihood of seeing distinguished artists with regularity was now much reduced.

There was also a significant change in the demographics of the colony. Many of the remaining artists from the colony's pre-War heyday were now elderly, with less energy and enthusiasm, and with little desire to embark on changes in style. However, it is unfair to infer that they were all arch-reactionaries, who stifled any new development, as is demonstrated, for instance, by the considerable support that Moffat Lindner gave to Frances Hodgkins. There was also a noticeable increase in the proportion of female artists in the colony. This was partly, of course, because of the huge death toll during the War, but it also reflected the surging numbers of women who had been attending art school since the turn of the century, as art became a more acceptable career for females. Many of these women artists took the view that, in light of the prevailing prejudice against women in the field of painting, they had more chance of making a mark in handicraft. Accordingly, for the first time, the decorative arts began to play a major role in the colony, particularly as Frances Horne, the founder of the St Ives Handicraft Guild, managed to persuade Bernard Leach, on his return from Japan in 1920, to establish his new pottery in St Ives.

Fig. 1.2  Terrick Williams  *White Boats, St Ives*  (1924)  (Private Collection)

---

4 *St Ives Times*, 20/5/1921.
5 D P Sedding, *St Ives Times*, 14/1/1921.

Fig. 1.3   Paul Dougherty     *Cornish Coast near Zennor*                                (Lloyd family)

Amongst the many things that the War changed was the old social hierarchy, and the landed gentry, who had been patrons of artists previously, now struggled, as a vastly reduced workforce demanded higher wages. For much of the 1920s, economic conditions were dire, as Britain, and many other countries, coped with the debt and the disruptions to trade caused by the War, and the decade ended with the most serious financial crisis of the twentieth century. Art became a luxury that few could afford, and artists accused the leisured classes, that still did have funds, of ignoring their historic role as champions of the Arts and, instead, indulging themselves in vacuous pursuits, such as motor cars, yachts, horse racing, gambling, golf and bridge.[6] Accordingly, the size of paintings needed to change, so that they could be afforded by the middle classes and hung in smaller homes. The 'big picture', which took a sizeable proportion of the year to paint, but which, if sold, defrayed a whole year's expenditure, became a rare commodity. Sales at large prices were now much more difficult to achieve; in fact, any sale was not easy, but there was still some interest in cheaper items such as watercolours and etchings. Not unnaturally, this market also encouraged the production of 'pot-boilers'.

The difficulty of securing sales sapped morale and self confidence, and the impact that this had on the resident artists' treatment of visiting artists is graphically demonstrated by the experiences of the American, Wilson Henry Irvine, who spent several months in the town in 1923. Despite local artists constantly passing him at work, "rubber-necking" to get a glimpse of his subject, his style and his methods, not one had the courtesy to speak to him for *six weeks*! In the pre-War years, he would have had an immediate invitation to the Arts Club and he would have been encouraged to tell all his American artist friends of the beauties of St Ives. Now, he was just perceived as a rather too talented competitor in a distressed market.[7]

In such economic conditions, artists, like many others, came to the conclusion that the cost of a servant was no longer justifiable, and so the management of the household changed. This was recognised by the potter, Michael Cardew, who argued that women taking over kitchen duties would want more "more homely and sympathetic and civilised" pots and pudding bowls.[8] The ability to maintain both a home and a large studio now proved beyond the resources of many artists. Studios became smaller, and single female artists, in particular, often opted for a studio-cum-living room in their home, rather than incur the rental and heating bills of separate premises.

---

6 See David Tovey, *St Ives (1860-1930) - The Artists and the Community - A Social History,* Tewkesbury, 2009 at p.354.
7 See further David Tovey, *St Ives (1860-1930) - The Artists and the Community - A Social History,* Tewkesbury, 2009 at p.366-7.
8 M A Cardew, *New Pots for Old*, *St Ives Times*, 22/1/1926.

There were also noticeable changes at the St Ives Arts Club, for the town, in the 1920s, become a popular retirement venue, not only for artists, but for writers, actors and others with an interest in the Fine Arts. This led to an increased interest in the town in literature and drama, and to the Arts Club having a more extensive programme of plays, entertainments and lectures than ever before. Indeed, artists even began to be in the minority in such productions, but the spirit of unity and the feeling of achievement that these productions inspired were to prove essential, when the artists decided that they needed to create a new identity for the colony. Key figures, who play a part in this story, include Greville Matheson, the former head of publicity for the Union Castle shipping line, who was a literature buff, with a collection of ten thousand books, who took over the role of sub-editor of the *St Ives Times*, resulting in it having an extraordinarily high intellectual content. Henry Jenner and Robert Morton Nance inspired a revival of interest in the Cornish language and Cornish folklore, whilst Will Arnold-Forster, who had worked with the League of Nations, and his wife, Ka, were outspoken advocates of socialist policies, with Will being the first Labour candidate to stand in St Ives and Ka becoming the first female magistrate. However, this influx of outsiders had an effect on the relationship between the artists and the locals. Whereas, before the War, the artists had mixed happily with the local dignitaries, they were now drawn more towards the intellectual circles of the new arrivals. Accordingly, the Arts Club became seen as a more exclusive enclave, and the artists ceased to put on shows for the locals.

During the 1920s, the impact on social relationships of the extent of an individual's involvement in the War effort needs to be borne in mind. However horrendous the War had been, it had played a large role in many people's lives, and there were a series of talks by members at the Arts Club recounting their experiences. In addition to Captain Smart and Lieutenant-Commander Bradshaw D.S.O., as they were regularly addressed, another artist with a distinguished service record was Engineer-Captain Francis Roskruge D.S.O, O.B.E., whilst non-artist members of the Club included several leading military and Government figures, such as General Herbert Blumberg, Commander in Chief and Governor of certain Greek Islands, Colonel James Findlay, Commander of the 8th Scottish Regiment, and Sir Herbert Thirkell White, who had been Governor of Burma. Was it merely their organisational skills that resulted in Smart, Bradshaw and Roskruge all being important long-term officers of STISA? Was it merely coincidence that those who had avoided enlisting, such as Louis Sargent and the pacifist Claude Francis Barry, left town shortly after the War? And what did ex-servicemen make of Charles Simpson, who, despite not participating in the fighting due to a hearing problem, continued to dress in old army uniform with the buttons cut off? Unsurprisingly, there are likely to have been some tensions on these issues.

Fig. 1.4  Will Potter    *Cornish Coast near St Ives*    (Private Collection)

Fig. 1.5  Henry Snell   *Along the Waterfront, St Ives*
(Harlowe-Powell Auction Gallery, Charlotteville)

Amongst the resident artists at the beginning of the 1920s, it was Charles Simpson, who dominated the scene in a way no single artist had ever done before and, during the eight years that he was based in St Ives, he produced an astonishing variety of exceptional paintings. Simpson is unique in Cornish art history, as he is the only artist to have been involved to a significant degree with all three of its principal art colonies at Newlyn, Lamorna and St Ives, but his St Ives works, without doubt, represent the highpoint of his career. Nevertheless, there were in the town a number of other artists, who were beginning to make names for themselves, including former Olsson students, Borlase Smart, John Park and Mary McCrossan. These artists have frequently been accused of practising the now out of fashion genres of landscape and marine painting in much the same way as their Victorian predecessors, but, in truth, their work was very different, being much looser and employing what Smart described as "a quickened sense of colour". Indeed, they can be considered to be notable figures in the movement that has been christened 'British Impressionism'. However, the departure of Charles and Ruth Simpson and Borlase Smart in the middle of the decade was a significant blow, which raised serious concerns as to the colony's future.

As always, the resident community of artists was complemented by numerous visiting painters, who stayed for varying lengths of time. Old friends, such as Julius Olsson and Terrick Williams, made repeated return visits, whilst some highly regarded work was produced by such distinguished artists as William Lionel Wyllie, Lucy Kemp-Welch and Dorothea Sharp. Although the level of foreign visitors to the colony did not match the pre-War years, new research has revealed some exceptional work done during the 1920s by artists from abroad. The New Zealander, Francis McCracken, had a painting of the St Ives fishing fleet bought by Auckland Art Gallery in 1920 (Fig. 8.14), whilst the Australian, Charles Bryant, who had studied under Olsson in the immediate pre-War period, returned in 1922 for an extended visit, which resulted in three works being acquired by the Art Gallery of New South Wales, Sydney (see Figs. 1.6 and 8.8). Of the American visitors, Wilson Henry Irvine decided to work in a new style during his time in the colony, producing some fine pictures of the harbour and the coast around Zennor, whilst Euphemia Charlton Fortune fell completely under the spell of the town. "This place would make a sick cat paint", she exclaimed, and her painting *Summer Morning, St Ives* (Monterey Peninsula

Museum - Fig. 8.1) created a sensation at the Paris Salon in 1924.⁹ The Dutchman, Hendrik Jan Wolter, also produced one of the seminal works of his career, *Misty October Morning, St Ives* (Fig. 8.15), during his visit to the colony.

The 1920s proved the heyday of the etching market and the printmaking skills of Alfred Hartley not only won international acclaim, but also drew several distinguished figures down to the town, including the futurist war artist, Christopher Nevinson, the Canadian, Donald Shaw MacLaughlan and the Australian Sydney Long. Several other residents, such as Borlase Smart, Dorothy Cooke and Francis Roskruge, also displayed considerable talent as printmakers, with the work of 'Dossie' Cooke being particularly innovative. However, St Ives also held attractions for some of the most advanced artists of the day and, during his initial visit in 1926, Christopher Wood, whose family had ancient links with the town, developed, for the first time, his own distinctive naive style, which led him in avant garde circles to be hailed as "England's first painter". His return trip in 1928, with Ben and Winifred Nicholson, not only resulted in further more mature work, but also in the discovery of the extraordinary naive paintings of Alfred Wallis, who, after some time at sea, had run the local marine stores. Here was the ultimate primitive, demonstrating instinctive, untutored creativity - the very characteristics that Wood and Nicholson were championing in their quest to dethrone the sophisticated, highly finished, academic easel painting. Whilst St Ives in the 1920s is so often portrayed as a reactionary backwater, it is interesting that prominent members of the most advanced Society of the time, the Seven & Five Society, included Hodgkins, Wood, the Nicholsons, Cedric Morris and Jessica Dismorr, all of whom had found inspiration in the town.

The 1920s also proved to be a decade in which the perceived inferiority of handicraft to painting was challenged, with handicraft makers championing their right to be seen as creative artists. Studio potters, in particular, emphasized the range of skills required to produce a finely proportioned, well-decorated pot, and the art critic Herbert Read argued that pottery was "plastic art in its most abstract form".¹⁰ The presence in the colony after 1920 of Bernard Leach brought this issue into sharp focus, but Leach was no ordinary potter, having acquired an oriental aesthetic and philosophical outlook after spending more

Fig. 1.6  Charles Bryant   *The Wharf, St Ives*   (Art Gallery of New South Wales, Sydney)

---

9  Letter to E A Grubb dated 29/1/1922 - Fortune papers, Monterey Peninsula Museum.
10 Bernard Rackham, Herbert Read, *English Pottery*, London, 1924 at p.4.

# SEA CHANGE : FINE AND DECORATIVE ART IN ST IVES 1914-1930

Fig. 1.7  Alec Walker     *The road across the moors to Zennor*     (Polly Walker)

than a decade in Japan and China. Accordingly, he brought a totally different dynamic into the colony, one tinged with rather an exotic aura, particularly as he was accompanied for more than five years by one or more Japanese assistants. The presence of Leach and other handicraft makers in the colony led to novel arrangements at Lanham's Galleries, where one room became devoted principally to exhibitions of craft work, which even included two displays of Marcella Smith's raffia hats. Nevertheless, the inclusion of a number of Leach's pots in the exhibition organised by the St Ives artists in Cheltenham in 1925 was still quite a radical decision. However, it was not repeated, either because Leach began to move away from 'art pots' to concentrate on more utilitarian ware, or because his objectives became rather out of step with his painter colleagues. Nevertheless, some of his pot and tile decorations, using simplified depictions of oriental landscapes and objects, provide an interesting contrast to the work of both representational artists and modernists, whilst other decorations, relying on colour and shape or on the incidental effects of the firing process on natural materials, have an abstract quality to them.

Of equal interest are the designs that Alec Walker did for Cryséde, which moved its hand block-printing textile business to St Ives in 1926, for these were based on his own modernist paintings of the local landscape. Accordingly, the manner in which he selected, simplified and assembled motifs from these paintings for his designs makes a fascinating comparison to the untutored approach of Alfred Wallis and the more self-conscious work of Christopher Wood and Ben Nicholson. He was also one of the first artists to concentrate on the patterns in Cornish landscape. His incorporation into some designs of shapes imitating brush marks was most original, whilst his creation of designs with an abstract feel, whilst featuring recognisable motifs, was again novel and inspired. Finally, his use of vibrant colour dovetailed in with the interest in heightened colour prevalent in the colony, rather more than the sparse aesthetic of Leach.

This interesting juxtaposition of fine and decorative art, and the wide range of styles that both resident and visiting artists employed during this period, could not hide the fact that, in the late 1920s, the colony was in serious trouble. In 1927, two aspiring artists, George Bradshaw and Herbert Truman, appalled at the state of apathy that had engulfed the community, put forward proposals for the formation of a new Society, to be known as the St Ives Society of Artists. Membership invitations were extended not only to those artists, such as the Royal Academicians Adrian Stokes, Arnesby Brown and Julius Olsson, who had made their name initially in St Ives, but to other prominent artists working in Cornwall, such as Stanhope Forbes and Samuel John Lamorna Birch. The involvement of these artists transformed the quality of exhibitions in the colony. However, the position at the end of the decade was still most uncertain, and the majority of artists, if questioned in 1930 as to their hopes for the future, would have been very downbeat, as the Great Depression took hold. Yet, it can now be seen that the blueprint not only for the colony's revival but also for its success for the rest of the century, had been established. The sea changes had been absorbed, the period of transition was over and, during the 1930s, the St Ives Society of Artists would bring St Ives art to a wider public than ever before.

# WAR

## 2.1 The American invasion of 1914

I discussed, in some detail, in my book *Pioneers of St Ives Art at Home and Abroad (1889-1914)*, the extraordinary confluence of American artists upon St Ives during the summer of 1914. This led Fred Milner, who estimated the number to be at least fifty, to feel that the Harbour Front ought to be renamed Broadway.[11] Accordingly, I will merely provide a summary here, for the presence of so many artists from just one country at one time does give a clear indication of the status that the colony had gained on the international stage at this juncture.

A number of the Americans were long-term residents. Lowell Dyer (1856-1939), for instance, had arrived in 1888 and stayed for the rest of his life, whilst Henry Turner Keasbey (1882-1953), from Philadelphia, had been resident since 1904. Although not making much of a success of his art, he had made a significant financial commitment to the town by acquiring, in 1910, a long lease of property fronting Porthmeor Beach, which he had converted into the Island Studios. Arthur J. Beaumont (1877-1956), a marine painter from Staten Island, had also been in town for the past couple of years, having been a regular visitor from 1902, whilst New Yorker, William J. Potter (1883-1964), who specialized in seascapes (see Fig. 1.4), had been around since September 1911.

Two other Americans, who had settled in the town recently, were the children's book illustrator, Frank Ver Beck (1858-1933) and his multi-talented second wife, Hanna Rion. They had arrived in the summer of 1913, and had clearly fallen in love with the town, for a local correspondent commented, "I have seldom met with any [Americans] more appreciative of its natural beauty." [12] They were also accompanied by Hanna's daughter from her first marriage, Theresa Abell, who was keen to study art in the colony. Others newly settled in the town included Nina Weir-Lewis (1858-1937), and her talented daughter, Helen Stuart Weir (d.1969), who had also arrived in 1913, and Frances Lloyd (1855-1921), the daughter of the American portrait and history painter, William Henry Powell, who had been invited by her son, Will Lloyd, to join him and his wife, Primrose, at 'St Eia' on Porthminster Hill.

Milner records in his letters the presence of his old friend, George Gardner Symons (1863-1930), in June. Symons, having married a St Ives girl, Sarah Trewhella, during his first visit to the colony in 1898-9, was a regular return visitor, whilst the local paper recorded in July the arrival of Paul Dougherty (1877-1947) (see Fig. 1.3), who had been making yearly visits to the colony since 1908, during which time he had become close friends with Will Lloyd. Another American to pay a return visit that summer was Guy Carleton Wiggins (1883-1962), who had accompanied his father, John, to St Ives in 1895-7 during his teens. His return trip to St Ives in 1914 proved particularly memorable, as it was whilst staying at 'Chy-an'Drea' that he met his wife, Dorothy Stuart Johnson, an English girl who was also visiting the town.

The bulk of the American visitors during the summer, however, were made up of students. One party seems to have been led by Richard Emil Miller, an instructor at Colarossi's, who tended to take groups of his female students off on summer sketching sessions. Certainly, his arrival was expected to be imminent in an article in *The Western Echo* on 18th July 1914. Another group of American students that arrived in July were the pupils of Henry Bayley Snell (1858-1943), an English-born artist, who had emigrated to the United States at the age of seventeen and had married, in 1888, fellow artist, Florence Francis (1850-1946), also originally from England. They were quite regular visitors to Cornwall, and had come to St Ives a number of times since 1910. An eminent landscape and marine painter, Henry won several leading awards and was elected on to the selection jury at the National Academy of Design on numerous occasions. In the past two years, a number of St Ives subjects by him have come up at auction (see Figs. 1.1 and 1.5), and he seems to have been particularly attracted to the harbour at low tide, when men were working on their boats and mooring chains and ropes provided decorative patterns over the sand. He was also an instructor at the Philadelphia School of Design for Women, where he taught from 1899 to 1943, and the party that he brought to St Ives in the summer of 1914 were female students from this College. Numbering over twenty, they stayed for some six weeks at Trenwith Hotel. Milner considered some of the students that he saw around the town "very weird objects". "There are a lot of women, not things of beauty by any means, either very fat or very thin." [13] Among them was Felicie

---

11 Letter to Mrs Brumfit dated 5/7/1914, Tate Gallery Archives ('TGA') 9511.14
12 'Bleistift', *Art and Artists*, *St Ives Times*, 7/11/1913.
13 Letter to Mrs Brumfit dated 5/7/1914, TGA 9511.14.

Waldo Mixter Howell (1897-1968), who herself became a teacher at the New York School of Fine and Applied Art. Marcella Smith (1887-1963), an old student of Snell, who was then working in Paris, seems to have joined the party for a while. With the town packed and the skies blue, locals and visitors revelled in a glorious summer, unaware that the like would not be seen again.

## 2.2 The outbreak of hostilities

The impact of War was immediate. On 28th July 1914, Fred Milner, who was desperate to get away from the tourist masses to go sketching in the Cotswolds, commented, "The place is absolutely crowded. I believe Chy-an-Drea are refusing dozens every day. I shall be so pleased to get out of it and be absolutely quiet at work." [14] Sixteen days later, with his summer sketching plans scotched by the declaration of war, and the American students having fled home, he reported, "Here the harbour seems very deserted as nearly all the men were in the naval reserves and have gone to their ships. I find it very difficult to do any work, as one's mind is full of the serious outlook." [15] At first, everyone hoped that the conflict would be over quite quickly, but, by the New Year, it became clear that it might be a long haul. Of course, no-one even began to suspect how horrendous the death toll would be, and, in the initial burst of enthusiasm, a number of members of the artist community joined up. Commendably, these included the New Zealanders Herbert Fitzherbert and Herbert Babbage and, later, the American Elmer Schofield. The colony, however, was swelled by artists displaced from Paris, who included the Americans William Chadwick, Marcella Smith and Charles and Helen Judson, the New Zealander, Frances Hodgkins, and the Paris-based English artist, Arthur Lyons.[16]

By March 1915, it was clear that every able-bodied man could help in some respect, and eighteen members of the Arts Club joined the newly established St Ives Volunteer Training Corps. Fred Milner related how this involved a considerable amount of training. "Our drill is the ordinary infantry drill, rifle drill and shooting. We drill Monday, Tuesday, Wednesday and Friday and shoot Thursday and Saturday afternoon and evenings." [17] In addition, a number of artists threw themselves into fund-raising activities for a whole array of causes. Against such a backdrop, it was difficult to find the time, energy or enthusiasm for painting, particularly as the art market was dead. Milner's letters of the period are full of comments such as "Everything seems depressing", "There seems nothing to work for", "What is the use?".[18]

Fig. 2.1    Fred Milner    *West Pier, St Ives*    (Court Gallery, Somerset)

---

14 Letter to Mrs Brumfit dated 28/7/1914 - TGA 9511.16.

15 Letter to Mrs Brumfit dated 13/8/1914 - TGA 9511.17.

16 Lyons had a studio on The Quay and took part in Show Day 1915, when his work *Au Cinema* was highly regarded. He painted a picture to raise funds for the families rendered homeless by the fire that destroyed the Salvation Army building in March 1915, but left the colony that summer.

17 Letter to Mrs Brumfit, dated 16/6/1915 - TGA 9511.30.

18 Letters to Mrs Brumfit dated 1914-5 - TGA 9511.20, 21, 24.

## 2.3 Outdoor sketching restrictions

The mood of the artists darkened considerably when outdoor sketching restrictions were imposed in February 1915. Initially, they had hoped that Cornwall's situation would make the War seem rather distant, and so early reports of German submarines sinking local ships was a big shock. Then it was contended that spies were active in the county and that a close friend of the artists, Count Frank-Joseph Larisch, who had sublet the 'Blue Bell Studio' in St Andrew's Street from the artist-photographer John Douglas, and had joined in the artists' social life on and off since 1910, had actually been operating as a secret agent.[19] Frances Hodgkins passed on the tittle-tattle to her mother on 4th February 1915. "St Ives people are feeling very sick because they were so nice to a young German Count who took a Studio here last year. After war was declared Studio was raided - charts of every cove, road, track, rock, tides and currents were found and copious diaries. The Count himself escaped." [20] In fact, Count Larisch, who was actually an Austrian and a professional oceanographer, had been working on an atlas, which was close to publication. He had departed from St Ives in August 1914 immediately after War was declared, rightfully fearing internment, and had left the country with members of the Austrian Embassy that month, declaring his distress at being forced to leave "my dear old England" and opining that the German Emperor "seems stark mad".[21] Nevertheless, his hasty departure from St Ives had been construed by the locals as implying guilt. Subsequently, the state of paranoia engendered by the mass media about "the enemy within" led John Douglas, on 1st February 1915, when asked by the landlady of the 'Blue Bell Studio' to move Larisch's trunk, to use his "confidential porters", when arranging for it to be delivered to Will Lloyd's studio at 'St Eia', in order to avoid running "the risk of fresh 'rumours' for the *St Ives Times* "That so-and-so has come back to the land by means of a submarine at Zennor Cove etc etc".[22] It seems from Hodgkins' letter, three days later, that the "confidential porters" had thought the move of the trunk deeply suspicious and had spilt the beans, thus causing the rumour about Larisch being a spy to be rife again - the very thing that Douglas, who had been entrusted with his atlas pictures, had hoped to avoid.

Fig. 2.2 Count Larisch (Sydney Carr)

Another incident confirming that artists, particularly foreign ones, were now suspicious personages occurred in January 1915 in Newlyn, when Rolf Jonsson, a Swedish artist, who had married a local girl, Annie Payne, and who had been a student at the Forbes School for four out of the last seven years, was arrested and imprisoned for allegedly signalling to the enemy, using different coloured lights. In fact, it transpired in court that all he had been doing was walking at night, with the aid of his electric pocket lamp, from one room in his home to another, each having different coloured curtains![23] Unsurprisingly, with paranoia about spies at such levels, sketching restrictions were imposed in February 1915. A letter from Fred Milner indicates their scope. "The restrictions with regard to sketching are very strict - one cannot sketch anywhere without a permit and no sketching on the coast or within sight of the coast but only about the Harbour and immediate neighbourhood." [24] Even in such out of the way places as Zennor, artists staying with Mrs Griggs record idyllic holidays being spoilt by coastwatchers who "collared" their sketches or "seemed to take a delight in thinking we were German spies".[25]

---

19 Count Larisch was not Georg Larisch, the husband of the infamous Marie Larisch, as indicated in my Social History, but their eldest son, Franz-Joseph Ludwig Georg Maria Larisch (1878-1937). He was a particularly good friend of the Lloyds, the Douglases and the Carrs. Will Lloyd's son, Walter, recalls an anecdote told by his father, that, one evening, as they were discussing poetry over dinner, someone commented how wonderful it must have been to hear Homer's *The Iliad* in the original Greek. Larisch then began to speak the opening lines and, pausing only to obtain confirmation that he should continue, recited, from memory, the whole of the epic poem throughout the night, finishing at mid-day!

20 Letter dated 4/2/1915 - Ed. L Gill, ibid, at p.303.

21 See letter dated 7/8/1914 and two other letters that month from Count Larisch to Will Lloyd - Lloyd family archive. In his letter of 7th August, he comments, "I had finished the entire atlas and everything after months of pretty hard work and I was looking forward to reaping the reward of it all and also enjoy a nice summer rest. And now comes this. Somehow I can't seem to realise yet, it came so suddenly, & so terrible and seems so utterly useless." As his bank account was frozen, Will Lloyd lent the Count £30 to enable him to subsist, pending his departure. A letter from the Count to Lloyd dated 27/9/1919 acknowledges the loan. In this, he comments, "I often think of the good old times in St Ives, when we were together. Do you remember when we used to go 'mad'? But I shall (see) you again some day that's sure."

22 Letter from John Douglas to William Lloyd, dated 1/2/1915 (Lloyd family archive).

23 See *St Ives Weekly Summary*, 4/3/1915. It was just this sort of prejudiced paranoia that led to D.H.Lawrence and his German wife, Frieda, being hounded out of Zennor in 1917. Jonsson later exhibited in St Ives on Show Day in 1928 and 1929.

24 Letter to Mrs Brumfit dated 14/3/1915, TGA 9511.25.

25 Mrs Griggs' Visitors' Book May-September 1915.

Frances Hodgkins, who had been joined by some students keen on landscape and marine work, tried to buck the system but, in late July, told her mother. "The shock of the week was being turned off a nice little rocky retreat we had found for ourselves far from the madding crowd - and we hoped the Constable's eye....No such luck. He found us out and out we had to go - sketching is strictly prohibited within sight of the coast which means it is practically prohibited everywhere." [26] Three weeks later, she was still trying to get around the problem. "It is so tantalizing to be within sight of so many beautiful things to paint, rocks, pools, skies, paddling children & bits of coast - I tried my best blandishments on the Sergeant from time to time promising not an inch of coast line to be included but he is adamant & threatens to confiscate my painting gear if I don't look out. He says the Cornish artists "worry him awful" they are so "teasy". I told him it was very worrying to the poor artists to be so treated." [27] Laura Knight, who was in St Ives painting that month, recorded similar difficulties with the Sergeant, when she was painting some children playing in the harbour. As soon as she put a dab or two of paint to represent the sea horizon, she was interrogated as to their meaning.[28]

In September 1915, the position became even worse after an alleged abuse of a sketching permit.[29] "Since last writing," Hodgkins tells her mother, "a new edict forbidding all sketching in Cornwall has been issued which came like a thunder bolt, scattering my pupils & placing me in the novel position of wondering what I would do next. A fine of £40 if one is caught with an easel or a camera - some conscientious coast watchers even confiscate strangers' field glasses and spectacles, but these are the rabid ones. We have protested and made all the fuss we dare." [30] Quite clearly, though, the position was now impossible and a strong letter was published in the local paper from Moffat Lindner, Millie Dow and Julius Olsson, who happened to be staying with Lindner at the time. This made the point that the vast majority of winter visitors to the town were artists and these would now go elsewhere, causing loss all round, and suggested that the Mayor should assume responsibility for the issue of permits, as most artists, whether residents or regular visitors, would be known to him.[31] Eventually, it was agreed that a limited number of permits, for three months at a time, could be obtained from the Penzance Divisional Coast Watching Officer.[32] However, it was difficult for the artists to feel at ease, particularly when everyone was so much on edge. Sometimes, they found that they could not even relax in their studios. In the midst of a letter to her mother, Hodgkins writes, "A diversion here - Coast watcher, in khaki, six ft. tall with a couple of dogs and a revolver, just looked in to say I have too much light in my window." [33]

## 2.4  Casualties

Soon the artists, and their friends in the town, started to receive news of the death of close relations and friends. Moffat Lindner, for instance, lost his nephew, Leonard, at the Battle of Jutland, whilst Frances Hodgkins was deeply sorrowed by the death of Jack Rich, the son of one of her major patrons, whom she had shown off in St Ives prior to his departure for the Front. Whilst she had enjoyed, on that final visit, "great larks flying round the country in the depth of winter in an open car with a dashing young subaltern", she had had little doubt about the eventual outcome. "He looked little more than a child & yet there he is with the power of life & death over 50 stalwart men." [34] However, it was the death of fellow artist, Herbert Babbage, that was most deeply felt. He had enlisted as a private in the 4th Duke of Cornwall Light Infantry for home defence duties, and his unit was posted to Wales to guard railway facilities used for the distribution of coal. He still found some time for painting and his friends in St Ives - John Douglas, Lowell Dyer, Alfred Hartley, Moffat Lindner and Frank Ver Beck - organised an exhibition of his watercolours in St Ives in December 1915, to which he was able to make a fleeting visit.[35] He also exhibited *The Viaduct,* painted in the Edwardsville/Quaker's Yard, near Treharris, at the Royal Academy in 1916. However, he died in Cardiff Hospital in October 1916, following what was described in his obituary in the local paper as a short illness and an operation, but one account of his death indicates that it was caused by exposure whilst on sentry duty.[36] A close friend, possibly Edith Skinner, published anonymously a poem in his memory in the local paper, highlighting his love of Cornwall.[37]

---

26 Letter dated 22/7/1915 - Ed. L Gill, ibid, at p.307.

27 Letter dated 16/8/1915 - Ed. L Gill, ibid, at p.308.

28 Laura Knight, *Oil Paint and Grease Paint*, London, 1936 at p.205.

29 See *St Ives Times* 1/10/1915 - *The Restriction on Sketching.*

30 Letter from Frances Hodgkins to her mother, 16/9/1915, see L.Gill, *Letters of Frances Hodgkins*, Auckland, 1993 at p.310.

31 *St Ives Times,* 1/10/1915.

32 See Advertisement 'Sketching and Photography', placed by G Warrender, Commander-in-chief, Plymouth, and Competent Naval Authority, in *St Ives Times*, 14/7/1916.

33 Letter to her mother dated 10/1/1916 - Ed. L Gill, ibid, at p.313.

34 Letter to her mother dated 28/1/1915 - Ed. L.Gill, ibid, at p.302-3.

35 *St Ives Weekly Summary,* 16/12/1915.

36 Obituary - *St Ives Times*, 27/10/1916 - see also Una Platts, *Nineteenth Century New Zealand Artists*, 1980.

37 See *St Ives Times*, 27/10/1916.

Fig. 2.3 Herbert Babbage in uniform
(Margaret Edgar)

*The Spring will come and carpet wind-swept Clodgy,*
*With those dear flowers, you always found so fair,*
*Rich golden gorse, sea-pink, the sweet pale primrose,*
*Deep orange lichen on the grim rocks bare,*
*And I shall grieve because you may not see them,*
*Not know that they are there,*
*In God's own Heaven, there blossom flowers more rare.*

*When the lark rises in the dews of morning,*
*And tries at Heaven's gates, his song to sing,*
*I shall remember how you loved to hear him,*
*And watch his fluttering wing,*
*And I shall grieve to think that nevermore,*
*May you hear any-thing,*
*In God's own Heaven the angels sing.*

*When the sea foams in wild majestic grandeur,*
*Covering dark rocks with snowy wind-lashed spray,*
*Or, gently murmuring, washes with soft caresses,*
*The golden-sanded bay,*
*My heart will ache because you may not see*
*The glory of the day,*
*In God's own Heaven, there is a Golden Way.*

*My friend, who with no thought of ought but duty,*
*Left all you loved to answer England's call,*
*Giving up ease and liberty and comfort,*
*To fight against odds, your back set to the wall,*
*When I remember all you have suffered,*
*My tears will fall*
*In God's own Heaven sits one who gave his life for all!*

Babbage is one of four names on a bronze plaque, designed by Borlase Smart and produced by Edmund Fuller, which was erected in the Arts Club in memory of members who lost their lives in the War. The other artist member recorded on the plaque was Harold Milford Norsworthy, who died in France in 1917. He was a former student of Louis Grier, but he had had little connection with the colony in recent years.[38]

## 2.5   Borlase Smart's War - 'Vimy Ridge to the Somme'

Borlase Smart's depictions of the shattered townscapes and bleak landscape of war-torn France now give us some small semblance of an idea of the true horrors of the War. However difficult life was in St Ives, the locals were very aware from newspapers and from first-hand accounts from men on leave in the town that the situation at the Front was appalling. Progress seemed minimal, conditions were atrocious and losses were horrendous.

Born in Kingsbridge, Devon, Robert Borlase Smart (1881-1947), who was to prove one of the most important figures in the history of the colony, had studied art initially in Plymouth, before taking an Art Class Teacher's Certificate at South Kensington in 1901. From 1903-1913, he was art critic for the *Western Morning News*, and he contributed a number of sketches, principally of naval craft, to *Navy and Military Record*. He enlisted in the Territorial Force in January 1915 and, by June, had become a Sergeant. He then joined the Artists' Rifles Officer Training Corps and was made a Second Lieutenant at the end of July. After the Artists' Rifles were subsumed into the 24th Division of the London Regiment that autumn, he was seconded to the Machine Gun Corps. In January 1916, he was promoted to Temporary Lieutenant, and he served on the Western Front between June and September 1916, arriving immediately before the Somme Offensive and witnessing its after effects. However, rather than go with his Division of the London Regiment to Salonica in November, Smart stayed on at the Machine Gun Corps' Training Centre at Grantham. Indeed, he produced a Christmas Card for the Corps that year.

---

38 Norsworthy's time at St Ives and Bushey is discussed in detail in David Tovey, *St Ives (1860-1930) - The Artists and the Community - A Social History*, Tewkesbury, 2009. Since then, I have also discovered that he was a friend of Bernard Leach, when they were studying together under Frank Brangwyn.

Fig. 2.4  Borlase Smart    *The Somme Offensive as seen from the Madagascar Dump, Arras Road*
(Imperial War Museum/Borlase Smart papers)

Fig. 2.5  Borlase Smart    *Near Vimy*    (Imperial War Museum/Borlase Smart papers)

Fig. 2.6  Borlase Smart  *Big Gun Emplacement Screened from Aerial Observation*
(Borlase Smart papers)

Given both his teaching and art qualifications, Smart found his niche as an instructor at Grantham, specializing in "instruction diagrams for cavalry, infantry and machine gun training" and in camouflage.[39] He was well-regarded, for his application to join the Indian Army, in August 1917, was rejected, as he could not be spared. His son, Brian, recalls his father mentioning that one of his projects was the design of wooden structures, which were laid flat on the ground, but which, when pulled upright, looked like fighting men. These were used to make the Germans believe that a night attack was being launched at this spot, whereas the true point of attack was very different. A postcard amongst his papers appears to demonstrate how the ploy worked. Brian also recalls that his father had some involvement with the development of modications to the Lewis machine-gun.

Smart was also involved in using art to help with the recuperation of soldiers. One member of the Machine Gun Corps, who was on light duties after being hit on the Somme, recalled, "I served for a while with an unusual section of the Corps, 'The Studio' at Grantham. I did quite a lot of illustrations for text books. Handley Read was in charge...The 2i/c was Borlase Smart." [40] Edward Harry Handley Read (b.1870) was a portrait and landscape painter and a black and white illustrator. He was some eleven years older than Smart and had been elected an RBA in 1895, a society with whom, over a long career, he exhibited 123 works. Working together, the pair seem to have found a useful role for their artistic skills. Another artist at the Camp, who became a lifelong friend of Smart and an important figure in the colony at St Ives, was Leonard Fuller, who ran the bombing school.[41] He recalled, after first meeting Smart at lunch in the Instructors' Mess, "The three characteristics which soon revealed themselves were his boundless enthusiasm, his forthrightness and his helpfulness. These three things governed his life." [42]

Having been turned down for the Indian Army, Smart, in the autumn of 1917, married nineteen year old, Irene Godson, at Godstone in Surrey. She was the sister of a friend who had been killed in action, and they had met because Smart, in typical fashion, had felt it his duty to visit the parents of all his colleagues who had made the ultimate sacrifice.[43]

---

39 From Smart's application to join the Indian Army in August 1917. I am indebted to Graham Sacker of the Machine Gun Corps Old Comrades Association for information about Smart's War.

40 *Boy David* magazine, 2/1967, kindly supplied by Judith Lappin, Machine Gun Corps Old Comrades Association.

41 Smart eventually persuaded Fuller to move down to St Ives in 1938 and set up the St Ives Painting School, which still exists.

42 Leonard Fuller, Foreword to the catalogue of the Borlase Smart Memorial Exhibition at the Penwith Gallery, St Ives 1949.

43 Irene's brother, George Godson, aged 20, who was with 2/24 Battalion London Regiment, to which Smart's Machine Gun Corps unit was attached whilst in France, was killed on 24/8/1916. Despite his age, Brian Smart believes that Godson was his father's platoon sergeant.

Smart's limited time at the Front calls into question the first hand authenticity of a number of his sketches, particularly those relating to operations in 1917-8.[44] Nevertheless, during his 1916 assignment, he will have witnessed the atrocious conditions and the destructive impact of shell-fire upon both the landscape and the villages, and so he could imbue his drawings with a realistic flavour, even if he was, in truth, working from photographs and from accounts of wounded survivors based back at Grantham. A sketchbook (9"x 11") containing a number of pencil and charcoal sketches, clearly done whilst on active service, has survived, but the size and quality of finish of the works now in public collections indicate that they were done in the studio. The majority are in the region of 18"x 24"and show very detailed drawing in charcoal and the application of numerous different coloured washes.

Smart called the exhibition at Harris and Sons, Plymouth, where the drawings were first exhibited in July 1917, *Sketches from the Western Front - Vimy Ridge to the Somme*. Ten works were acquired from this for what was then called the Plymouth War Museum (now Plymouth City Art Gallery) (see Appendix A - Table B). The exhibition was then remounted at the Fine Art Society in London. It now contained thirty-eight works and was well received, with the recently founded Imperial War Museum acquiring seven of them. As these are numbered 4 to 10 in the Museum's Inventory (see Appendix A - Table A), they were some of the very first purchases made. Smart held another exhibition of 'Battle Pictures' at Harris and Sons in June 1918, and a further four works were acquired by the Plymouth Gallery (see Appendix A - Table B). Smart clearly hoped that his works would prove of interest to the Press, as he had photographs taken of them. One, *The Road from Aubigny to Arras* (FAS No 11), is marked as approved for publication in 1918, with the reason for the interest in this scene being suggested by Smart's note on the back that the King and the Prince of Wales watched this bombardment of the German lines from the towers of the Abbey of St Eloi.[45]

Smart's success was noted in St Ives, as he had been working in the colony in 1912-3, taking tuition from Julius Olsson, and, having settled in the town in 1919, a further set of drawings was exhibited locally at Lanham's Galleries that May. In 1929, Smart donated twenty-one other works to the Imperial War Museum, and it has subsequently acquired a further four, so that it now holds thirty-two works in total, whilst Plymouth City Art Gallery retain the fourteen acquired in 1917-18.

Fig. 2.7    Borlase Smart    *The Ruins of the Sugar Refinery, Vimy*
(Imperial War Museum/Borlase Smart papers)

---

44 In his application to join the Indian Army, he listed his 1916 stint as his sole front line experience.
45 Borlase Smart papers.

Many of the drawings concentrate on the sad sight of architectural gems reduced to ruins by shellfire, and still surrounded by debris. Sometimes Smart depicts the bombardment still in progress, or the fires still raging. Whilst well-known chateaux, forts, churches, town squares and the famous Cloth Hall at Ypres tend to capture his eye, he also depicts the ruins of a humble bar (Fig. 2.15) and of a sugar refinery (Fig. 2.7). Other drawings show roads churned up into muddy quagmires or made impassable by shells. One sketch is simply entitled *Mud*, for it became one of the worst obstacles to the campaign. Most trees depicted have also been shattered by shell fire, and their broken trunks produce bleak patterns across the landscape. Figures rarely feature and so the human toll is normally avoided, although there are regular depictions of grave markers. Smart also gives us glimpses of trench life (Fig. 2.10) and of a dug-out (Figs. 2.8 & 2.9), whilst a pencil sketch reveals the joy of a bathe and a change of clothes at Etrun. Notwithstanding the widespread desolation, his artistic eye has managed to impart into these scenes a measure of lyricism.

The crossing of Smart's Division to France in June 1916 was not completed until the 29th. Therefore, it was probably not ready to take an active role at the outset of the Battle of the Somme, which started on 1st July - a day on which the British suffered nearly 60,000 casualties. However, one of Smart's first drawings is likely to have been *The Somme Offensive, as seen from the Madagascar Dump, Arras Road* (Fig. 2.4). This is an evocative scene, with a deeply rutted muddy road along which men and equipment will have recently passed, lined by battered trees, leading to the battlefield over which shells explode with regularity. As the Government had not yet commissioned artists to depict the War, representations of the Battle of the Somme are rare. A number of the drawings feature places taken during the Somme offensive. In *Ovillers*, Smart depicts, from another rutted road, through broken trees, the jagged outlines of the ruined buildings of the hilltop village, the sky still glowing from the flames. This was attacked on the first day of the offensive. In *Fricourt*, a village which was taken on the second day, Smart, from the cover of a wood, shows shells still landing on the houses and smoke rising from fires. In *Beaumont Havel*, another settlement just behind German lines, where the 1st Newfoundland Regiment was wiped out in one day, every single tree surrounding the village has been shattered, leaving a mass of stunted pinnacles, stretching away into the distance.

Fig. 2.8 - 2.10  Borlase Smart

Top left :  *A Dug-Out*

Top right :  *Old French Dug-Out, near Vimy*

Bottom left :  *The Germans Fired a Mine the Afternoon we took over, South of Vimy*

(Imperial War Museum/Borlase Smart papers)

# SEA CHANGE : FINE AND DECORATIVE ART IN ST IVES 1914-1930

During his time at the Front, Smart seems to have been based on Vimy Ridge. A sketch of the village of Thelus across an area of no-man's land, inscribed *Thelus, Vimy Ridge, Forward German HQ, Opposite 60th London Div.* indicates the front line there. Another sketch entitled *The Germans fired a mine the afternoon we took over, S.of Vimy* (Fig. 2.10) indicates that his unit was given a welcome. This shows a few figures in a trench taking cover as a mine exploded throwing soil high into the air. Apparently, there had been little action in the area for some months and the Germans had used the time to build underground tunnels leading towards or under the Allied positions, which they then mined. Whilst no harm was done on this occasion, Smart depicts in the trench two grave markers. The area had previously been occupied by the French, when they had made an unsuccessful offensive in 1915, and Smart depicted a communication trench, a big gun emplacement and an old dug-out that they had used (Fig. 2.9). He also drew the skull of a French soldier, to which his helmet was still attached.

Borlase Smart

p. 22    Figs. 2.11 and 2.12

Top :              *Grandmother*

Bottom :       *Portrait of a W.A.A.C.*

p.23     Figs. 2.13 - 2.17

Top :              *All that was left of Péronne*

Middle left :   *Ruins of the Fort Péronne*

Middle right : *Ruins at Béthune*

Bottom left :  *Arras in Flames*

Bottom right : *Arras under Shell Fire*

(All Imperial War Museum/Borlase Smart papers)

# WAR

Fig. 2.18  Borlase Smart    *Tanks in Action*
Smart used this image for his invitation to an exhibition of 'Battle Pictures' at Harris and Sons, Plymouth in 1918.         (Borlase Smart papers)

*With the Machine Gun Corps near Vimy Ridge* shows his unit in action in the area, whilst the powerful sketch, *Grandmother* (Fig. 2.11), depicts a heavy howitzer being loaded. Using terminology clearly employed in the Corps, another drawing of a howitzer is called *Grandmother prepares to distribute her cough lozenges*! His own camouflage expertise is presumably featured in *Big Gun Emplacement Screened from Aerial Observation* (Fig. 2.6). Several titles indicate personally experienced brushes with the Germans, such as *Hindering Our Transport; A Road near Arras Traversed by German Fire* and *Morning Hymn of Hate - A Little Liveliness North of Arras*.

Smart also depicted one of the sights that soldiers at the Front all remembered - the 'Leaning Virgin' of Albert (Fig. 2.19), for the town was just three miles from the front lines. This was the name given to the statue of Mary and the infant Jesus, designed by sculptor Albert Roze, on top of the Basilica of Notre-Dame de Brebières in Albert, after it was hit by a shell on 15th January 1915, and put into a precarious horizontal position. The Germans said that whoever made the statue fall would lose the war, and a number of legends surrounding the 'Leaning Virgin' developed among German, French, and British soldiers. In the end, after the Germans had recaptured the town in March 1918, the British, to prevent the Germans from using the church tower as an observation post, directed their bombardment against the Basilica, destroying the statue. Both the Basilica and statue have since been rebuilt.

Tanks were first used at the Battle of the Somme in September 1916, and so, just before his departure, Smart will have witnessed both the advantages and disadvantages of these early models. Whilst they struck fear into the Germans and were useful for overcoming barbed wire, they were very slow, prone to mechanical breakdown and easily put out of action. A dramatic sketch, *Tanks in Action* (Fig. 2.18), shows the psychological impact that they could have on defenders, but, in fact, it was their inability to traverse such craters that often proved their undoing, as captured in another sketch *A Derelict Tank Caught on the Edge of a Shell Hole ; Near Bouleaux Wood*. They also could not cross soft ground, and so most of Smart's sketches of tanks depict them out of action, their effectiveness short-lived.

Fig. 2.19  Borlase Smart
    *Albert*   (Smart papers)

It was in April 1917 that British forces fought the Battle of Arras, during which the town of Arras was taken, at the same time as all four Canadian divisions fought together for the first time, when they successfully stormed Vimy Ridge, an event of considerable significance for Canadians, as it was felt to signify the birth of a nation. The painting commissioned by the Canadians to record this historic encounter was executed by the portrait painter, Richard Jack (1866-1952), recently made an ARA and a regular visitor to St Ives during the War, where his singing voice was much admired.[46] Whilst Smart does not appear to have been involved in these contests, he knew the area where they were fought, and could refer to some graphic descriptions of the destruction caused by the new seventeen inch guns that had been able to rip open the German dugouts. For instance, the Canadian journalist, F.A.McKenzie, described the scene a month later, "Vimy Ridge itself was an awesome witness to the results of war. Every yard of the old German lines was torn up by shell-fire...one mere mass of tangled wires, shivered timbers, and ploughed-up earth.....The villages are so destroyed that one recalls the prophecy about "not one stone standing upon another." The very trees are blackened, leafless, and branchless with the long fighting. Trenches and wire entanglements, old dug-outs and temporary shelters tell where Fritz was.....I have travelled through miles of this country without seeing a sign of life save a wild cat struggling amid the wire entanglements or a solitary crow hovering overhead." [47]

The evocative *Near Vimy* (Fig. 2.5) and *Ruins of the Sugar Refinery, Vimy* (Fig. 2.7) capture the total devastation. A similar scene Smart merely entitled *Chaos*. However, these and sketches such as *Arras in Flames* (Fig, 2.16), *Arras under Shell Fire* (Fig. 2.17), *All that was left of Péronne* (Fig. 2.13) and *Ruins of the Fort Péronne* (Fig. 2.14), may well be based on photographs. Nevertheless, they have a convincing air about them. The same presumably applies to later works showing the ruins at Ypres. Smart's drawing, in charcoal only, of the ruins of the Cloth Hall at Ypres (Fig. 2.20) was particularly well regarded, and was especially invited to be exhibited at the Royal Scottish Academy in 1922. The fate of this building became emblematic of the destruction of War; dating from 1200, the Cloth Hall had been one of the largest industrial buildings of the medieval ages, but was now an utter ruin. However, Smart has depicted, in the foreground, a small tree that has survived the carnage and can be seen as representing new life and, accordingly, new hope. Initially, the task of rebuilding the Cloth Hall to its original design seemed too great, but work was started in 1933 and eventually completed in 1962.

At the end of the War, Smart was offered the chance to join the Indian Army as a Major, but he had set his heart on returning to St Ives to pursue his artistic career. On resigning his commission in March 1919, he was granted the rank of Captain.[48]

Fig. 2.20 Borlase Smart     *Ruins of the Cloth Hall, Ypres*
(Imperial War Museum/Borlase Smart papers)

---

46 Richard Jack may have studied briefly in the colony, as he is recorded on more than one occasion in the Arts Club in the autumn of 1896.
47 F.A.McKenzie, *What I learned on the Western Front*, The War Illustrated, 23/6/1917.
48 At the end of April 1917, Smart was promoted to Acting Captain. This was apparently by mistake, due to a mix-up on his file. However, when the mistake was eventually discovered, he was allowed to retain the rank of Acting Captain and the increase in pay until he resigned.

## 2.6 George Bradshaw's paintings of submarine warfare

Albeit boasting a family lineage that could be traced back via Kings of Scotland to Charlemagne, George Fagan Bradshaw (1887-1960) was born in Belfast and endured an unhappy childhood, as his father, an estate manager, was an alcoholic. At the age of fourteen, he joined the Naval training ship, *H.M.S. Britannia*, at Dartmouth, and, at the completion of his training in 1909, he enrolled in the fledgling submarine service, purely because it paid more, as he wanted to help his mother and siblings. During his leisure hours, he enjoyed sketching, and he took the opportunity, whilst based in Malta in 1912-3, to take lessons from Edward Caruana Dingli, a local artist of some renown. On the outbreak of War, Bradshaw had been in command of his first submarine - C-7 - since February that year. With limited armament and underwater capabilities, it could only perform home defence duties. However, in August 1916, he was given command of a new boat - G-13, which was faster, had a much greater range and was significantly better armed. His friends rated his chances of survival as pretty slim, as, due to the large death toll, the submarine service was now known as 'the Suicide Club', whilst boats numbered -13 were notoriously unlucky. In early 1917, Bradshaw, who was then based in the River Tees, was detailed to patrol the waters between Scotland and Norway on the look out for U-boats and, on 10th March, he managed to torpedo UC-43 near Muckle Flugga Light, an action for which he was awarded a D.S.O.. Bradshaw also contended that he had sunk a much bigger scalp - no less than the large mercantile submarine the *Bremen*, the sister ship of the famous *Deutschland*, which, in July 1917, managed to cross the Atlantic. However, Bradshaw, to his intense annoyance, could not get official confirmation of his achievement, and the fate of the *Bremen* is recorded as unknown.

Whilst, at one juncture, being hailed as "an exceptional officer of the highest ability", Bradshaw's days in the Navy ended in 1921 with a messy Court Martial, after the loss of his second submarine. In November 1918 - just a few days after the end of hostilities - the submarine that he commanded at the time - G-11 - ran aground near Howick, and two men were drowned. Whilst the blame was placed on faulty equipment, not on Bradshaw, the loss of two of his crew at such a time was hard to take. The second loss, which occurred when his new submarine K-15 sank, through a design fault, whilst in dock, could hardly have been Bradshaw's fault, particularly as he was not present, but nevertheless the powers that be insisted on a Court Martial. Whilst acquitted, the authorities, having no doubt been privy to some choice words from Bradshaw, decided that he should not again be placed in charge of a submarine. Whilst furious at the indignity of his exit from the Navy, he later admitted that his nerves had been shot through.[49]

During his time in the Service, Bradshaw developed a good reputation amongst his fellow officers as an artist, and he received commissions to paint a number of their submarines. The Royal Navy Submarine Museum at Gosport now own a large number of these works, depicting submarines of each of the C-, D-, E-, J- and L- classes. Several of these were made into postcards. By far the most assured work is a large oil, *On Patrol 1914-1918* (Fig. 2.22). Another interesting oil is *U-boat sinking barque by gunfire* (Fig. 2.21), an event Bradshaw will surely have witnessed through his periscope. After settling in St Ives, Bradshaw occasionally returned to wartime subjects, which he exhibited on Show Day and elsewhere. Indeed, his exhibits on his very first Show Day in 1922 included *A Broadside from a Super-Dreadnought*. Even as late as 1937, his Royal Academy exhibit of the year, *Surface Patrol*, featured a submarine.

## 2.7 Dazzle-Painting - The St Ives connection

The frequent loss of ships to submarines during the War led to discussions as to whether the application of paint in certain colours or designs might assist in rendering ships less visible. Various proposals were put forward, but the one eventually accepted was that of Norman Wilkinson, one of the most illustrious alumni of the Schools of Painting run by Julius Olsson and Louis Grier. As a result of many years' observation of the effect of light and colour on ships at sea, and extensive experiments during the earlier years of the War, Wilkinson recommended the use of extreme contrasts of colour and shapes, which would so distort the appearance of the vessel as to symmetry and bulk that it would deceive an attacker as to her size and course. He also recommended that no standard pattern be adopted, but that the size and length and bulk of each vessel to be painted needed to be considered before a colour arrangement was designed. The scheme, which became known as 'dazzle-painting', was felt to have been very successful, when it was put into effect in 1917-8, and Wilkinson got his old tutor, Julius Olsson, involved in the design process. One of the best depictions of dazzle-painted ships is, appropriately, by another alumnus of Olsson's School, the Australian Charles Bryant, a regular visitor to the colony before, during and after the War. *Dazzle-Painted Leave Ships, Boulogne* (Fig. 2.23) was painted by Bryant in 1917, a year in which he exhibited at Lanham's Galleries.

---

49 Bradshaw's Naval career is dealt with at length in my biography, *George Fagan Bradshaw - Submariner and Marine Artist - and the St Ives Society of Artists*, Tewkesbury, 2000.

Fig. 2.21  George Bradshaw     *U-boat sinking barque by gunfire*
(Royal Navy Submarine Museum, Gosport)

Fig. 2.22  George Bradshaw     *On Patrol 1914-1918*
(Royal Navy Submarine Museum, Gosport)

Fig. 2.23  Charles Bryant  *Dazzle-Painted Leave Ships, Boulogne*        (Imperial War Museum)

However, Wilkinson found it difficult to get any financial recognition of his input and, having given evidence in support of his claim in 1922, it was not until 1925 that the *St Ives Times* recorded that he had been paid £2,000 for his efforts.[50]

## 2.8    The Naval paintings of William Parkyn

One of the only artists to exhibit war-related scenes in St Ives during the course of the War was the marine artist, William Samuel Parkyn (1875-1949), who had studied in St Ives under Louis Grier from 1900 and settled in the town in 1907.[51]  The son of an Army Colonel, Parkyn was born in Lee in Kent and was educated privately, before studying art at Blackheath and Rochester.  In 1913, he married Margaret Day, the daughter of the Rector of Sandwich, and moved from 'Reculvers House', Hawke's Point into a property on Ventnor Terrace, St Ives, which he called 'Richboro'.[52]  After 1909, he worked from one of the Malakoff Studios, which he called 'Trevose Studio'.  Principally a marine painter, he depicted a range of boats but, even before the First World War, he had a particular interest in naval vessels. Initially, he worked in watercolour but, by 1914, he had started to produce oil paintings and, thereafter, seas played a more prominent part in his themes.  Works from this era that were reproduced as prints include *The Lone Patrol* and *Hun Hunters*, whilst *Heavy Weather* and the watercolour, *The Trooper's Escort*, showing torpedo craft protecting a crowded troopship, were hung at the Royal Academy in 1916. Parkyn was also a regular exhibitor at the RWA, where he was elected an Associate.  Again, wartime scenes, such as *Picked Up - A French Destroyer to the Rescue* (1917), were prevalent initially.  He clearly had some success with these works and, in 1919, his battleship picture, *Steam, Steel and Spray*, was purchased on the opening day of the RI exhibition.[53]  Furthermore, his picture of a hospital ship is in the Royal Collection and is hung at Sandringham. Although employed as a deputy coast-watcher, his subjects were not local and were probably produced from photographs.  He also offered to paint and present to St Ives Town Council a picture of any battleship or cruiser that they selected, and their choice was *HMS Albion*, in which many St Ives men served.   However, it is difficult to pass comment on the quality of these paintings, as very few have appeared on the market.

---

50 *St Ives Times*, 16/1/1925.

51 When Parkyn first came down to Cornwall, he lived in Newquay and he exhibited a number of Newquay scenes at the RCPS in 1896 and 1897.  After studying under Louis Grier in 1900 (see his brief Curriculum Vitae in Tate Gallery Archives 724.252), he is noted as a visitor again in July and August 1903.  He joined the Arts Club in December 1907 and he first exhibited on Show Day in 1908.

52 See Rate Books & Kelly's Directory for 1914 & 1919.  By 1919, he had moved to 14 Barnoon Terrace.

53 See *St Ives Times*, 21/3/1919.

In September 1919, Parkyn held a one-man show of his work at Lanham's Galleries. By this juncture, he had started to concentrate on marine watercolours, often featuring sand-dunes, and these became very popular. Shortly afterwards, Parkyn moved to the Lizard, where he lived for the rest of his life, later becoming a member of STISA and SMA. A collection of his works hangs in the Queen's Hotel, Penzance.

## 2.9 Other depictions of the War

As artists that remained resident in St Ives during the War did not witness any hostilities, they tended to prefer to concentrate on more attractive subjects. However, Charles Simpson did exhibit at the Royal Academy in 1916 *The Serbian Retreat into Albania*. The cause of the Serbians was one that was taken up with vigour by Gussie Lindner, with numerous events being held in the town to raise funds for the wounded and the orphans, but Simpson's painting seems to have been the result of a commission to produce illustrations for a book on the experiences of a Lieutenant Beavor in the Balkans, which never came to fruition.[54]

Figure painters, such as Frances Hodgkins and Charles and Ruth Simpson, were often faced with the sad task of producing posthumous portraits of those killed in the War. With merely a photo of the deceased, normally in uniform, and a note of the colour of his hair and eyes, it was unsatisfactory and depressing work. Ruth Simpson produced them for five guineas, letting her students fill in the background.[55] However, a much more impressive work was *A Company Commander* (Fig. 2.24 - Imperial War Museum), which she exhibited at Lanham's Galleries in 1920. Borlase Smart commented, "Mrs Simpson's life size portrait of *A Company Commander* is really excellent. There is actually a feeling as if he were painted in the trenches. There is an atmosphere of trench soil about him, and the clasped revolver suggests the alertness of mind, and the faculty of responsive and automatic action. The 'tin helmet' is the finishing touch to a work full of much character." [56] In the same Lanham's exhibition, there was not only one of Smart's war drawings, but *A shell wrecked house in France* by the New Zealander, Herbert Fitzherbert, who won a Military Cross during the War. However, Fitzherbert, a stalwart of the colony in the pre-War period, is better known for his caricatures, and settled after the conflict in Exmouth.

Arthur Hayward, who became the colony's leading portrait painter, served as a Captain in the Royal Field Artillery and appears to have done some sketching during his service on the front line, but it was not until 1929 that he exhibited *Leaning Virgin, Albert* (see Fig. 2.19), which depicted puffs of shrapnel above the prone statue on the church tower as searchlights picked up German aircraft. It was considered a dramatic work of considerable historical interest.

## 2.10 War poetry

There were three resident poetesses in St Ives during the War - Edith Skinner, Joan Barrett and Mary Du Deney. Their works were reproduced with some regularity in the local paper, but have little lasting merit. Frances Hodgkins recorded one studio party in 1915 where "a lady with a face like St Augustine's Mother recited some bad poetry in a sobbing voice & upturned eye - about the War", which an injured submariner present said "made him sick & wouldn't help recruiting".[57] This was probably Mary Du Deney, as Hodgkins became friendly with Edith Skinner, examples of whose work are quoted elsewhere, whilst Joan Barrett secured some national recognition in 1917 with a poem *The Women Who Save the Bread*, highlighting the important role of women during the food shortages. Of greater interest and merit, however, are the poems written at the Front by Will Lloyd. The son of the artist, Frances Lloyd (see further Chapter 3.5), Will had studied art under Louis Grier in 1904 and taken over Julius Olsson's home 'St Eia' in 1909. However, having inherited a large estate, Cowesby Hall, in North Yorkshire, Will did not pursue his interest in art and was known in the colony primarily for his musical prowess and for his love of literature. Having written a memoir of Vincenzo Bellini in 1908, his first book of poems, *The Return from the Masque and other poems*, was published in 1911.

The War affected Lloyd deeply. He joined 7th Battalion (Leeds Rifles), Prince of Wales Own West Yorkshire Regiment, in October 1914 as 2nd Lieutenant, and, in April 1915, was promoted to Staff Captain, attached to the General Staff. Shortly after this, he was awarded the Military Cross, reputedly for turning round a group of retreating soldiers and successfully defending a position. From April 1915,

---

54 See John Branfield, *Charles Simpson*, Bristol, 2005 at p.50. Simpson's painting is illustrated in David Tovey, *St Ives (1860-1930) - The Artists and the Community - A Social History*, Tewkesbury, 2009 at p.360.
55 See John Branfield, *Charles Simpson*, Bristol, 2005 at p.57.
56 *St Ives Times*, 14/5/1920.
57 Letter to her mother dated 14/1/1915. Ed. L.Gill, *The Letters of Frances Hodgkins*, Auckland, 1993 at p.301.

Fig. 2.24  Ruth Simpson  *A Company Commander*
(Imperial War Museum)

he served continuously to the end of the War in France and Flanders.  Having shared his experiences with members of the working classes and witnessed personally the appalling casualties in engagements such as the Battle of the Lys and Passchendaele, he found his role as an English squire after the War utterly distasteful and sold Cowesby Hall for a song.  In a book of poems published in 1928, several, such as *Lines written during the Battle of the Lys, In Memoriam E.T., Passchendaele, Summer* and *A Grave on the Vimy Ridge*, were written during the War.  The latter, dated February 1918, about an agricultural labourer from North Yorkshire, is not only the best, but gives an inkling of his mindset.

*Here lies a man from Malton, a tiller of the field;*
*There was much within his nature that seldom was revealed -*
*Pride, tenderness, affection, 'neath a rugged face concealed.*

*He could plough as straight a furrow as you'd find upon the wold;*
*There was no one in the village who could tend the lambing fold*
*More skilfully than he could, who now lies here so cold.*

*He'd not complain, for others were unhappy too, and he*
*Was told by those who took him that he fought for liberty,*
*That every son of England must fight that she be free.*

*He wondered at this freedom as some hidden mystic thing;*
*He longed to see his wife again, to hear the blackbirds sing;*
*And he wondered when the war would end till he gave up wondering.*

*Then death he dreaded found him driven blindly to this place*
*With courage born of terror.  Shattered body!  Bloody face!*
*Through its martyrs, O, so slowly! learns the tortured human race.*[58]

---

58 *A Grave on the Vimy Ridge*, from William Lloyd, *Poems*, London, 1928 at p.20.

# FRESH FACES DURING DARK DAYS

## 3.1 Displaced artists

Whilst the War led many painters to leave the colony, either to enlist or to return home, it also resulted in a number of artists, who had been working in Continental Europe, to seek sanctuary in the town in the hope that the hostilities might be brief, or that they could continue to work in a safe artistic environment as events unfolded. These included the Americans William Chadwick, Charles and Helen Judson, Marcella Smith, Frank Ver Beck and his wife, Hanna Rion, the New Zealander Frances Hodgkins, the Dutchman Dirk Smorenberg and the Belgians Emile Fabry and Louis Reckelbus. The relative security of the town, the poor financial backdrop and the difficulties and dangers involved in travel led a number of these artists to base themselves in the colony throughout the hostilities. Employing a wide variety of styles, some quite modern, they introduced new ideas, approaches and techniques, which proved influential. Accordingly, the output of the colony during the War, albeit considerably reduced, was broadened, with some innovative work of considerable interest and merit being produced.

## 3.2 The experimental figure paintings of Frances Hodgkins

One of the most important new arrivals was the New Zealander, Frances Hodgkins (1869-1947), who had been working and teaching in Paris. Indeed, her art classes there had acquired quite a following, attracting, on occasion, over forty pupils. Whilst she had many qualities, she admitted that physical courage was not one of them, and she told her mother, in October 1914, that she was going to St Ives "where I can live cheap & quiet for the winter, & come the worst it is a prudent spot to be in well out of the way of Zeppelins etc." [59] Her choice of St Ives, rather than Penzance, where she had stayed before in 1902, was clearly influenced by her friendship with Moffat Lindner. "He is a queer silent brusque old thing, sparing of words," she commented, "but with the kindest of hearts to anyone he takes a fancy to", and she was to be considerably indebted to him as the War dragged on and on, and her finances, always precarious, frequently became non-existent.[60]

The outstanding New Zealand artist of her generation, Hodgkins was born in Dunedin, where her father was a lawyer and keen amateur artist. After considerable success during her studies in Dunedin, she left for England in February 1901 and enrolled at the London Polytechnic, where her drawing teacher was former Bushey student, Ernest Borough Johnson. Between 1901 and 1903, Hodgkins went on a series of painting trips with Newlyn artist, Norman Garstin, in France, Belgium and the Netherlands and it was whilst she was in Caudebec, in 1901, that she first met Lindner. Garstin welcomed her as a friend and fellow artist and refused to accept fees. Whilst staying in Penzance in 1902, she popped over several times to St Ives, which she called "a paradise of beauty", to see fellow Kiwi artist, Margaret Stoddart. She also attended Show Day. "It was great fun going round - the Studios were hidden in the queerest places - down dark subterranean passages, up chicken ladders, in old boat houses, up sail lofts - anywhere where they could get a whitewashed wall & a top light." [61] She returned to New Zealand at the end of 1903, but she could not settle, and came back to England in February 1906. She resumed her friendship with Norman Garstin and also spent time in Dordrecht with Lindner in 1907. In July 1908, she told fellow Kiwi artist, Dorothy Richmond, "That kind dry old stick Moffat has been a real trump to me & is going to introduce me to some of the right sort when I go to Town." [62] In October that year, she went to stay with the Lindners in Dorset for four days, and reported to her mother, "Dear old Moffaty bought one of my pictures, a small one, but the compliment was bigger than the cheque and my heart swelled within when he said he wanted one. He is so transparently honest in his likes and dislikes that I knew he wouldn't buy one unless he really liked them." [63] In 1908, she shared first prize in the Australasian section of women's art at the Franco-British Exhibition before moving to Paris. Here, she studied oil painting briefly under Pierre Marcel-Béronneau, having previously worked solely in watercolour. Nevertheless, she continued to paint mainly in watercolour and showed at the Salon in 1909. She paid a brief visit to St Ives in August 1909, when she stayed at Hendra's Hotel in Carbis Bay, but, in 1910-11, she was again based in Paris, acquiring a considerable reputation for her watercolour classes.

---

59 Letter from Frances Hodgkins to her mother, 23/10/1914, see L.Gill, *Letters of Frances Hodgkins*, Auckland, 1993 at p.298.
60 Letter dated 10/10/1908 - Ed L Gill, ibid at p.237-8.
61 Letter dated 27/3/1902 - Ed. L Gill, ibid, at p.123.
62 Letter dated 2/7/1908 from Pension Nulaander, Rijsoord - Ed L Gill, ibid at p.231.
63 Letter dated 10/10/1908 - Ed L Gill, ibid at p.237-8.

Fig. 3.1   Frances Hodgkins
*Loveday and Ann : Two Women with a basket of flowers*
(Tate, London, 2010)

Although she had now decided that her future lay in Europe, she returned to exhibit in Australia and New Zealand for a year from November 1912. She was back in France, though, when war broke out. She arrived in St Ives in November 1914, and Lindner arranged for her to take one of the Porthmeor Studios.[64] She told her mother, "It is [a] huge barn that will do nicely for a Class, not pretty but useful. It gives on a yellow sandy beach & at high tide the waves beat against the walls & sometimes the window; for this commodious loft - studio - pigsty - barn, I pay £10 sterling a year - & no supplements as in Paris where you first tip the concierge, postman, policeman and dustman before installing *yourself*."[65] Hodgkins developed a bit of a love-hate relationship with the studio. In good weather, she appreciated its uniqueness and told her mother, "I will go a long way before I find another Studio like the one I have now."[66] However, during the winter, it was a cold, noisy, draughty place, particularly after financial pressures forced her in June 1915 to use it for her living quarters as well. Indeed, she found the constant noise of the sea a trial, particularly at high tides, when the shingles were hurled about. She also experienced, in November 1915, the worst storm to hit the town for forty years. "The Studio rocked like a baby's cradle & at dawn looked like a drunkard's home. The sky light blew in & of course floods of rain. About 4 o'c, a fisherman came round & begged me to shelter in their house but I stuck it out..... Tiles rained down in the courtyard & windows and chimneys crashed and banged. One man's Studio close by was blown clean down & half out to sea."[67]

Of all the artists working in St Ives during the War years, Frances Hodgkins has become the best known, for she went on to carve out for herself a distinctive place in the evolution of British modernism. However, due to the outdoor sketching ban and the economic circumstances of the time, she found herself forced during her time in St Ives to concentrate on portraiture and figure paintings. These varied from formal conversation pieces to intimate depictions of the mother and child relationship. She later described the period in St Ives as her "experimental years", and she moved away from the Impressionist-influenced style that she had developed in France. Indeed, her style often changed from work to work, her striving after a more modernist form of expression not always winning universal approval. Importantly, however,

64 Hodgkins' letters indicate that she occupied No 7, but I am not certain whether this equates with Studio No 7 today. See David Tovey, *St Ives (1860-1930) - The Artists and the Community - A Social History*, Tewkesbury, 2009 at p.139.
65 Letter dated 19/11/1914 - Ed L Gill, ibid at p.299.
66 Letter dated 17/2/1915 - Ed. L Gill, ibid, at p.303.
67 Letter dated 16/11/1915 - Ed. L Gill, ibid, at p.312. The studio blown down was probably Lynn Pitt's 'White Studio' on Porthmeor Cliff.

although continuing to work in watercolour, she took up oils again in the autumn of 1915, at the instigation of Moffat Lindner, and some of her best work was in this medium, albeit that, initially, she tended to apply the paint thinly in a similar way to watercolour and tended to mix her colours in much the same manner as well.[68] Forced to abandon her previous peripatetic lifestyle, she was also able to adopt larger formats. Accordingly, whilst beset by difficulties, as all artists were during the War, her St Ives years were an important part of her development as an artist.[69]

The first difficulty to overcome, having settled into her studio, was to find the will to work. After further news of disasters and fatalities at the front, Hodgkins commented to her mother, "You can imagine it is not easy to paint in the circumstances. And yet I am - I drive myself to it but the feeling of insecurity weighs one down with depression and dark doubts."[70] The news from the front got no better and soon friends and relatives were receiving the dreaded tidings of the loss of loved ones. Hodgkins, though, had her own battle just to survive, as her pupils drifted away due to the sketching restrictions, and so had to clasp at any opportunity to earn a crust. Her single-minded devotion to her art appears to have restricted her circle of friends. The Lindners proved stalwart supporters. She also admitted that Arthur Meade would help her out, if she was really up against it, whilst Edgar and Edith Skinner and Nina Weir-Lewis became valued acquaintances as well. Hodgkins, though, is not recorded as taking part in any of the fund-raising activities for the numerous relief causes espoused in the town or as donating any work for such causes.

Fig. 3.2  Francis Hodgkins    *Mr and Mrs Moffat Lindner and Hope*
(Dunedin Public Art Gallery)

---

68 The first reference in her letters to working in oils is on 29/9/1915, when she says that she has a 'night-piece' in oils on the go. There is no obvious 'night-piece' in her surviving work, unless she is referring to *Belgian Refugees*.
69 This summary draws on Pamela Gerrish-Nunn, *A Wartime Haven - Frances Hodgkins in St Ives* - Notes for a lecture given at the St Ives Arts Club during the September Festival 2008. I am indebted to Pamela in numerous respects as regards Hodgkins.
70 Letter dated 17/2/1915 - Ed. L Gill, *The Letters of Frances Hodgkins*, Auckland, 1993 at p.303.

Fig. 3.3 Publicity photograph for Hodgkins'
1920 Hampstead Gallery solo exhibition

Hodgkins' work was first seen publicly in St Ives on Show Day in 1915, and she was successful that year at the Royal Academy for the first time in ten years. However, it was the following year that the modernity of her work, with its "broad decorative style and relentless use of colours to express idea", attracted the most attention. Works shown included *Gipsies*, a study of children, which was again accepted at the Royal Academy, and her portrait of the American illustrator, Frank Ver Beck (location unknown), which was described by Edgar Skinner as "a brilliant bit of painting, bold in colour with subtle drawing, especially noticeable in the nervous rendering of the right hand holding a cigarette".[71] An early work in oils is *Loveday and Ann : Two Women with a basket of flowers*, which was exhibited at the National Portrait Society exhibition in 1916 and is now owned by the Tate Gallery. This depicted two daughters of a local fisherman, sitting in an Interior, either side of a window. Loveday seems a little uneasy with the modelling process, but Ann beams with a radiant smile. Elizabeth Eastmond, the foremost Hodgkins scholar, has commented. "Stylistically, there was now more in common with the Post-Impressionists and such Intimists as Bonnard and Vuillard, while Hodgkins conveys her increasingly individual painterly approach by engagingly free brushwork and a subtle witty response to the different personalities of the figures. She links them in a formal and symbolic sense in terms of their relationship and femininity by the dominant motif and vivid colours of the foreground basket of flowers." [72]

One of the subjects that Hodgkins tackled on several occasions during her first couple of years in the colony were the Belgian refugee families in the town. As a result of Gussie Lindner's proactive approach, St Ives was the first town in Cornwall to welcome a group of refugees from that country and, from the ninety-nine refugees initially received, sixty-two remained at the end of 1915. Many artists were weekly subscribers to the Belgian Relief Fund and were regular collectors of goods and money for them. Hodgkins helped by using a number of the mothers and their children as models, but, very surprisingly, she makes no mention of these pictures in her letters, so there is no record of the families featured.[73] The most significant of these paintings is a large oil, *Belgian Refugees*, which is believed to have been exhibited for the first time as *Unshatterable* at the International Society's Autumn Exhibition in 1916.

---

71 *The Western Echo*, 11/3/1916.

72 Quoted in Pamela Gerrish-Nunn, *A Wartime Haven - Frances Hodgkins in St Ives* - Notes for a lecture given at the St Ives Arts Club during the September Festival 2008.

73 She also makes no mention of Louis Reckelbus, the Belgian artist, whose colourful watercolours might have interested her.

Fig. 3.4   Frances Hodgkins         *Refugee Children*
            (Auckland Art Gallery Toi o Tamaki,
            on loan from the Thanksgiving Foundation)

Fig. 3.5   Frances Hodgkins         *Belgian Refugees*                    (Christchurch Art Gallery)

As Ken Hall of Christchurch Art Gallery comments, "The [initial] choice of title would suggest a greater sense of resilience than is actually conveyed by this family group. Here only the baby is oblivious to trouble, while the nursing mother seems devoid of expression, and the older children tense with anxiety or fear. Behind this group, a gap in the swirling grey suggests the fact of the missing father, and this steam and smoke speaks of displacement, the atmospheric backdrop of a train station or the symbolic clouds of war. Within the wall of monochrome, intense colour is reserved for mother and child." [74] A rather happier mood is captured in the watercolour, *Refugee Children* (Fig. 3.4), also dating from 1916, in which the varied expressions of the three youngsters, posed as if facing a camera, include a beaming smile. Here, the refugee status is suggested by the odd assortment of clothing that the youngsters wear - no doubt cast-offs from assorted well-wishers.

During her time in St Ives, the support of Moffat Lindner, financially and emotionally, was crucial for Hodgkins. When she was seriously ill in April 1916, he paid for her to have the best treatment. He invited her up to 'Chy-an-Porth' for meals regularly, and introduced her to his contacts. Despite being a traditionalist in many respects, he appreciated Hodgkins' vision and colour sense, and constantly encouraged her, telling her that her work had improved beyond measure and that she would make a big name for herself.[75] As already mentioned, it was at his instigation that Hodgkins made her first serious attempt to master oil painting and, by way of further encouragement, he was the initial purchaser of one of her first efforts, *Loveday and Ann*. When times got really tough, he gave her commissions to paint members of his family.[76] The most well-known of these is a conversation piece now owned by Dunedin Public Art Gallery. In a letter to her mother dated in early 1916, Hodgkins comments, "Mr Lindner and his little girl Hope are posing for me against his great Studio window - open, with the wind tossing her brown hair, the sea beyond. They wear such jolly tweed clothes, he snuff coat, check waistcoat and orange tie with black spots - & his jolly pink face & white curls - very dapper. Hope in grey tweed, berry red buttons & bright blue Tam, white stockings. This is a 4ft x 3ft canvas in oils - and so far shapes well." [77] The finished work, however, is very different. Firstly, it is not executed in oils on canvas, but in tempera on linen on hardboard, but this again is an unusual medium for her, showing her keenness to experiment at this juncture. Secondly, it is far bigger - 78.75" x 39.5" - and, thirdly, Moffat and Hope, in a very different outfit, are posed against the outside of a closed and curtained window, rather than against an open window in Lindner's studio (probably Studio 8). New Zealand art historians have tended to assume that the painting was eventually executed at Lindner's home, but the fenestration of 'Chy-an-Porth' is far grander than this. Whilst there are still windows of the design in the painting in the Porthmeor Studios complex, it is not easy to place the exact position where Hodgkins got the Lindners to pose. Her inclusion of a side-on view of Gussie Lindner has always puzzled art historians, as it is undoubtedly awkward. Hope, though, explained that her mother came along to talk to her father, as Hodgkins was working on the picture and, on the spur of the moment, was added into the composition.

Hodgkins continued to exhibit at a variety of different venues in London. Whilst her work was not accepted again at the Royal Academy after 1916, she was always welcomed and well hung at the International Society and, in 1917, she had seven works hung together to good effect at the Grosvenor Gallery. Two works shown at the National Portrait Society in 1916 led Frank Rutter of the *Sunday Times* to praise her as "one of our most skilful and individual aquarellists". This might not have been perceived by Hodgkins as a great compliment, given that one work was in oils and the other in tempera, for it demonstrated that she was still using these media in the manner of a watercolour painter. However, early in 1917, Louis Sargent brought to her studio an unnamed authority who wanted to salute "the first woman painter in England". Hodgkins, who thought Laura Knight deserved this accolade, found this rather amusing, given that "the best woman painter etc the day before yesterday could not pay her washing bill & had to wash her own clothes".[78] However, any good notices were appreciated, as praise for her work was not universal in St Ives. Whilst Lindner and the Skinners applauded her novel approach, others, whilst admiring her wonderful handling of watercolour, quite understandably found her work rather wild and incomprehensible. She herself confided in her mother, "I find I am too modern for people down here & I am conscious of the cold eye of distrust & disapproval by the older members of St Ives."[79] However, this comment was made very early in her stay and, gradually, she won more people round. Indeed, in 1917, when times were particularly tough, she made a significant impression on Mr and Mrs Raymond Hellyer, who were to prove her best and most important local patrons. Here again, Moffat

---

74 Ken Hall, *Belgian Refugees by Frances Hodgkins*, The Press, 28/2/2007. Also Christchurch Art Gallery website.

75 For instance, in a letter to her nephew, Will Field, on 30/3/1918, she comments, "Told yesterday Mr. Lindner stakes his reputation that my future *is* certain." - Ed. L.Gill, ibid, at p.329.

76 In October 1917, at another low point, Lindner gave Hodgkins a commission to paint his niece for 5gns, but it had to be done in three days.

77 Letter dated 10/1/1916 - Ed. L Gill, ibid, at p.312-3.

78 Letter dated 22/2/1917 - Ed. L Gill, ibid, at p.319.

79 Letter dated 17/2/1915 - Ed. L Gill, ibid, at p.303.

Fig. 3.6   Frances Hodgkins            *The Family after Dinner*
(Jonathan Grant Galleries, Auckland)

Lindner is likely to have made the introduction, for Mrs Hellyer is recorded as buying an oil and two watercolours off him that year (and a further watercolour in 1919).

Her first reference to the Hellyers was in a letter to her mother dated 17th July 1917, when she said, "Luckily things are looking up with me.  Have just finished a very successful portrait of Mrs Hellyer wh. everyone likes, especially the husband who has just been down for the week end & now insists on my painting him as well as a large group of children - wh. will mean £100 in my pocket if I pull it off.  Have already a cheque for 25 gns.  So I am off on Friday to stay with them for a week or 10 days at their cottage down the Coast, where they are now.  They are pleasant keen people, nicely well off, just come into a fortune & know how to spend it..."  Their holiday home was at Port Isaac and, during the week that Hodgkins spent there, a close friendship developed.  She spent the first three days doing the family group.  "Luckily it was fine so I was able to do a big portrait group of them in the garden in the hammock, round the tea table, sunshiny effect, which came off happily & they were awfully pleased." [80]  They then had a day travelling around North Cornwall together, before she tackled the portrait of Mr Hellyer, which she did not finish, but brought back, with some difficulty, on a crowded train to her studio in St Ives.  Despite the pressures of the commissions, she told her nephew that she had had "a ripping good time & loved the rest & change".[81]  As a thank you, she appears to have given Mrs Hellyer a very loosely painted work called *Children Playing* (Fig. 3.7).

She kept in touch, getting a pair of silk stockings from Mrs Hellyer that Christmas, and spending another week with the family in April 1918.  There is the possibilty that, during this week, she might have done a delightful, loosely-painted interior, called *The Family after Dinner* (Fig. 3.6).  It is thought to date from her St Ives period, but is not felt by Lindner's grandson, Nik Halliday, to be a depiction of either the Lindners or the interior of their home, 'Chy-an-Porth'.  If it is indeed a St Ives work, then the Hellyer family seems a decent bet, albeit, in truth, there is very little information upon which to gauge whether it might be them, except that the man looks considerably older than any of the women depicted.  This might tally with Hodgkins' next entry concerning the Hellyers, on her return to St Ives in November 1918, for she records,  "The first week end Mrs Hellyer bore me off to their lovely new house at Carbis Bay ['Headlands House', the boarding house recently sold by the artist, Moulton Foweraker].  She is now a widow, beautiful & not yet 40 fascinating - and such a house to fascinate in!  Much reduced in wealth by her husband's sudden death so there will be no more pictures by Frances Hodgkins bought alas."[82]

80 Letter dated 7/8/1917 - Ed. L Gill, ibid, at p.324.
81 Letter to Geoffrey Field, 30/7/1917 - Ed. L.Gill. ibid, at p.323.
82 Letter dated 18/11/1919 - Ed. L Gill, ibid, at p.344.

# SEA CHANGE : FINE AND DECORATIVE ART IN ST IVES 1914-1930

In October 1917, Hodgkins finally gave up on her Porthmeor Studio and moved to the Wharf Studio, which seems to have been in the building that had been the White Hart Hotel.[83] She confided to a friend, "I moved in here last week & am so much more comfy & warm in this smaller Studio, facing the East & out of the bleak winds from the sea. It is such a rest not to have the waves nagging at one night and day. I can breakfast with the sun on me & have all the mysteries of the harbour unfolded to me, & keep an eye on the British navy at the same time." [84] However, it too had its drawbacks and the following January, she was complaining, "This is a draughty old loft & the roof flaps about in the wind." [85]

Throughout her time in St Ives, Hodgkins regularly produced mother and child depictions. This was, of course, a classic subject, which had proved perennially popular, and it was one to which female artists, in particular, were drawn. As Pamela Gerrish-Nunn has pointed out, Hodgkins will have been familiar, from her time in Paris, with the *maternités* of Morisot, Cassatt, Simon and Carriere.[86] However, in her own case, the concentration on such subjects was largely due to the circumstances of the times. Firstly, there was, of course, the paucity of other suitable models in wartime. Secondly, she found that such subjects sold well, as did paintings of babies on their own. In one letter, she exclaimed, "Yesterday I sold a 12gn baby. Item: Paint more babies! In fact keep the cradle full." [87] Furthermore, at a time when the demographic balance of the country had been decimated by the slaughter of hundreds of thousands of young men, there was an intense appreciation of the significance of new life, carefully nurtured; indeed, it was felt that the future of British society was at stake. Finally, another consequence of the huge death toll that gave grounds for great concern was the vast number of orphans that needed to be cared for - a cause that the Lindners supported with regular fund-raising events for Dr Barnado's. Accordingly, when a whole wall was reserved for her work at the International Society in October 1918, Hodgkins decided to put on a special display of mother and child watercolours. Given very little notice, she painted most of them during her summer class at Porlock that year, using five local mothers and their offspring - "Dear women all of them with husbands fighting & one a prisoner who had never seen his beautiful baby." [88]

Fig. 3.7 Frances Hodgkins     *Children Playing*
Inscribed 'To Mrs Hellyer from Frances Hodgkins 1917'
(Jonathan Grant Galleries, Auckland)

---

83 A postcard in Edith Collier's papers is addressed to her in 1915 at Wharf Studios, White Hart House, St Ives.
84 Letter to Isabel Field dated 23/10/1917 - Ed. L Gill, ibid, at p.328.
85 Letter to her mother dated 7/1/1918 - Ed. L.Gill, ibid, at p.328.
86 In Pamela Gerrish-Nunn, *A Wartime Haven - Frances Hodgkins in St Ives* - Notes for a lecture given at the St Ives Arts Club during the September Festival 2008.
87 Letter to Will Field dated 30/3/1918 - Ed. L.Gill, ibid, at p.329.
88 Letter to her mother dated 18/9/1918 - Ed. L Gill, ibid, at p.332.

Fig. 3.8  Frances Hodgkins     *Belgian Mother and Child*
(Serjeant Art Gallery, Wanganui)

The display contained twenty-two works, and no fewer than eleven of these featured one of two children, Peter and Lilian, asleep, an unusual departure from the normal way in which children were depicted. Even some London critics, though, found it hard to take babies with orange faces and mothers with green countenances. Not many of the works have been located, but one child study was acquired by a pupil, Vida Lahey, and later bequeathed to Queensland Art Gallery, whilst another was in the collection of one of her favourite pupils, Beatrice Wood.

What is generally recognised as the most important work from Hodgkins' time in St Ives is a conversation piece, completed in 1918, called *The Edwardians*. This is a large oil depicting Edgar Skinner, his wife, Edith, and their maid, Elsa, in their property, 'Salubrious House', in Salubrious Place, St Ives. It is by no means her most advanced work, but it displays good draughtsmanship, whilst also giving free rein to her vivid colour sense and delightful decorative touch. It also demonstrates her greater mastery of oil painting, as she is now utilising the density and texture of the medium. Edgar Skinner was a retired Bank Manager, who had lived for some time in Italy. He was multi-lingual and had a considerable interest in literature, music and art. He and his wife had been members of the St Ives Arts Club for some six months from December 1907, before deciding to settle in the town c.1910. He dabbled in watercolour, had a studio created in his home, and exhibited occasionally on Show Days (and at the RWA in 1913), whilst Edith was a poetess, whose work was published regularly in the local paper. They immersed themselves fully in St Ives society. Edgar assumed the role of Borough Accountant for a few years during the War, after the Town Clerk had made a mess of the finances. He took charge of the allotments that the artists, at Lindner's instigation, created during the food shortages of 1917, and was elected first President of the St Ives Literary Society in 1919. He also gave a lecture to the Arts Club on Van Gogh and assumed, during the War years, an occasional role as art critic, with his reviews making it clear that he was, from the outset, a great admirer of Hodgkins' art. "The greater part of Miss Hodgkins' work has a poignant charm which is overpowering and irresistible", he commented in 1915. "The richness of her colour, with her courage and originality of outlook and truth of values, combine to produce a result both stimulating and mentally suggestive." [89] Edith also was a great admirer and penned a poem, *Friendship's Garland*, in tribute to her as a Christmas present in 1917, which may possibly have led on to the painting.

---

89 *Western Echo*, 20/3/1915.

*Who's this tripping down the street I see?*
*Most dainty, gallant, merry, sparkling, true,*
*All captivating garbed with broidery new;*
*Sporting with witty speech and pleasantrie;*
*Daring all other women's rivalry.*
*Oh this is she who lives laborious days,*
*Who toilsome works, heedless of blame or praise.*
*Here, Womanhood to Art has bowed the knee,*
*And body, soul, and spirit all are bent*
*On making permanent the vision sent:*
*This painter grudges not to life the cost,*
*So Art achieve, the world may be well lost.*
*This is her portrait, just my thought's surmise*
*Touching the splendour of a soul's emprise.*[90]

Whilst confirming Hodgkins' dedication to her work, the poem also reveals that, whereas her letters to her family during the War years tend to be weighed down with worries and complaints, she did reveal her true warmth and sparkling personality to her chosen friends.

The painting shows the Skinners formally attired and just about to leave their home for an engagement - Edgar already having his top hat and overcoat on -, as the maid clears away, on a silver tray, the decanter and glasses that they have used to fortify themselves. Given her friendship with the couple, Hodgkins is unlikely to have intended any criticism of their lifestyle. Presumably after Edith Skinner's death, the painting came to be owned by Lucy Carrington Wertheim, Hodgkins' principal dealer friend, who donated it to Auckland Art Gallery in 1969.

Fig. 3.9   Frances Hodgkins   *The Edwardians*
(Auckland Art Gallery Toi o Tamaki, gift of Lucy Carrington Wertheim, 1969)

---

90 Quoted in E.H.McCormick, *Portrait of Frances Hodgkins*, Auckland, 1981 at p.91.

Fig. 3.10  Frances Hodgkins    *Portrait of Arthur Lett Haines*
(image courtesy Auckland Art Gallery Toi o Tamaki)

After the War ended, Hodgkins tried on three occasions to establish herself in London, but was always driven back to St Ives, as she was not a fan of city life.  Being away led to a greater appreciation of the benefits of St Ives, and she exclaimed on her return in November 1919, "St Ives feels very different coming back to it on a short visit - I can easily spend 3 months & be well employed with models etc and stray sitters amongst my friends.  It is so light & blue & bright & the herring season at its height & everyone doing well and making money.  The old Studio has changed landlords & wonderful to relate it is to be done up, inside and out, and made snug and watertight for me - it seems too good to be true."[91]  This was not entirely a philanthropic gesture by her new landlord, as the Government Inspector had decreed that, unless it was restored, it would be pulled down.  It is unclear whether Hodgkins ever enjoyed the benefit of the refurbishment, as she does not use the 'Wharf Studio' address again and, in fact, one letter dated in June 1920 is headed 'Porthmeor Studio'.[92]

Having settled back in St Ives, Hodgkins let her Kensington studio to two aspiring artists, Cedric Morris and Arthur Lett-Haines (always known as Lett Haines), who had recently fallen in love and who were to live together for the rest of their joint lives.  Hodgkins had become friends with Morris during 1917, when he spent time in Zennor, studying plants and insects and painting watercolours.  It appears that he also spent some time in Newlyn this year, for  the earliest surviving work by him is a portrait, in gouache, of Hodgkins sitting in an armchair in a small sitting room, which is inscribed by her 'Newlyn 1917?' (Tate Gallery).  When they took over Hodgkins' studio as their London base, Morris and Haines were already living in Newlyn, where they converted a row of old cottages overlooking the harbour into what Hodgkins termed "a Futuristic abode", which they called 'The Bowgie'.[93] They made quite a splash there, with their lively parties and eccentric ways, and Hodgkins became good friends with them, sparking a series of portraits of each other.  By far the best of these is Hodgkins' portrait of Lett (Fig. 3.10).

---

91 Letter dated 18/11/1919 - Ed. L Gill, ibid, at p.312-3.
92 As I do not recall any other reference to the Wharf Studio, the property, after its refurbishment, may well have been used for other more profitable purposes.
93 Letter to her mother dated 15/5/1920 - Ed. L Gill, ibid, at p.347.

Hodgkins' portraits at the International Society's exhibition in 1919 again prompted Frank Rutter to proclaim her as "one of the most richly gifted and personal painters of either sex that we have today" and, on the basis of her success there, she was offered a solo show - her first in London for ten years - at the Hampstead Gallery in February 1920. This received notices praising the unusual "virility" of her work, for a female artist, but resulted in a meagre profit of fifteen pounds. In St Ives, she contributed to shows at Lanham's and had four works in the 1920 RCPS show. She also had her work *Seaside Lodgings* hung at Pittsburgh in 1920, the only time that she exhibited there. However, despite now being able to sketch outside, Hodgkins does not appear to have been tempted to capture the local landscape and coastal scenery that she had been pining for during her early days in the colony and, in October 1920, she told her mother, "The die is cast. My old Studio is let & the furniture sold.....I decided to give it up & burn my boats definitely turning my back on St Ives - a wise move I think - it is no great catch being down here." [94] She decided that it was time to travel again and spent the next year in France. During the 1920s, her style changed and she allowed her very personal imaginative outlook freer rein. As a result, she began to be associated with some of the most avant-garde artists in England, such as Ben and Winifred Nicholson and Christopher Wood, who were also to find inspiration from St Ives. Cornwall, however, remained in her blood and she returned several times.

### 3.3   The symbolist works of Emile Fabry

Amongst the Belgian refugees, who sought refuge in St Ives, were two highly acclaimed Belgian artists - Emile Fabry and Louis Reckelbus. Over fifty Belgian artists had fled to Britain on the invasion of their country by Germany at the outset of the War, and, with the aid of philanthropists, these artists combined together to hold various exhibitions of Belgian art around the country. They were aided by the fact that an exhibition of Belgian art was being held in Scotland when War broke out, so that this could form the basis of the later wartime shows. Whilst the principal purpose of these exhibitions was to promote fund-raising for Belgian charities, a side effect was that Belgian art gained greater exposure in this country than it had ever enjoyed before. Accordingly, the presence of two such distinguished personages in St Ives aroused great interest.

Fig. 3.11  Emile Fabry     *Portrait of Johanna* (St Ives 1917)
(courtesy Jacqueline Guisset)

---

94 Letter dated 26/10/1920 - Ed. L Gill, ibid, at p.349.

Fig. 3.12  Emile Fabry     *Self Portrait* (1919)          (courtesy Jacqueline Guisset)

Emile Barthelemy Fabry (1865-1966) had been a Professor at the Brussels Academy since 1901 and was considered one of the leading Belgian painters of monumental art. Born in Verviers, he studied under J. Portaels at Brussels Academy of Fine Arts between 1885-7 and, impressed by Puvis de Chavannes' mural decorations, he went to work in a studio specializing in architectural painting. He was a member of Cercle Pour l'Art, a society of artists, founded in 1892, which was interested in the literary painting of ideas and feelings, somewhat akin to Romanticism. Fabry himself became well-known for his symbolist compositions, inspired by literary subjects, music and mythology. His idiosyncratic imagery gave him a special place among Brussels' Symbolists. His pictorial vocabulary, which comprised large scale figures, with an intensity of expression, but with other details often eliminated, was defined early on, and is instantly recognizable throughout his work. His early pieces tended to revolve around a singular theme, the portrayal of suffering and grief, and his figures often appeared anxious or trancelike, the deformation of faces lending these images a hallucinatory effect. Fabry himself described the period before 1900 as "the period of my nightmare", acknowledging the influences of Wagner, Maeterlinck, and Edgar Allan Poe. In the late 1890s, he began to work with the Art Nouveau architects Victor Horta and Paul Hankar. At this point, his work became more serene and increasingly monumental. He designed the interior of the sculptor Philippe Wolfers's villa, built by Hankar, and also the interior of Horta's Hotel Aubecq. In 1914, he was in the middle of a significant commission to produce decorative panels, illustrating musical themes, for the grand staircase of the Theatre de la Monnaie in Brussels.

Fig. 3.13  Emile Fabry     *The Stages of Life and its Achievements*     (from *Belgian Art in Exile*)
This work was exhibited on Show Day in 1916.

Fig. 3.14  Emile Fabry     *The Call of the Sea*     (Sotheby's)
This work, dated 1915, may be *The Exiles*.

On being displaced on the outbreak of War, Fabry lived briefly in Hereford and Cardiff, before joining Reckelbus in St Ives. His distinctive style made a considerable impression on the occasions that his work was on public display, and his subject matter was frequently inspired by the fate of his homeland, as titles such as *Poet Leave Thy Lyre Take Thy Sword and March*, *The Exiles* and *Nature, War and the Ideal* attest. They showed figures, often reduced to harmonious forms, decoratively arranged, moving through dreamland. *The Exiles* was stated to depict figures looking towards home with an intensity of longing and, therefore, may be the work, dated 1915, given the name *The Call of the Sea*, when sold in 2005 at Sotheby's (Fig. 3.14).[95] One of the major works that he exhibited on Show Day in 1916, which is very typical of his style, was *The Stages of Life and its Accomplishments* (Fig. 3.13), which was illustrated in the book, *Belgian Art in Exile*, published to raise funds for Belgian charities. By this juncture, Fabry was employing pointillism in his work, although not in such a considered manner as Seurat. In order to avoid the problems of reflective glare off his large pieces, he often mixed oil and distemper in the same works. The cold tonalities of his earlier work also changed during the War years, as his palette became dominated by the russet-red and orange colours associated with fire and War. Accordingly, there were a number of novel aspects about his technique that would have interested artists with a progressive outlook in St Ives.

Since 1903, Fabry had been a drawing master at the Royal Academy of Fine Arts, Brussels, and his work demonstrates his mastery of the anatomy and musculature of the human body. He seems to have taken pride in his own body, and used photographs of his muscular torso as the basis for several figures in his works. He also completed, in St Ives in 1918, an extraordinary, rather menacing monochrome portrait of his own head and naked upper body, with fists clenched (Fig. 3.15). The following year, though, he produced a rather more appealing self-portrait, in panama hat and *pince-nez* (Fig. 3.12). As a background, he painted three vertical stripes, the colours of which are taken from his shirt and tie. It is a masterful work.

Fig. 3.15  Emile Fabry    *Self Portrait* (1918)    (courtesy Jacqueline Guisset)

---

95 Sotheby's Olympia, 9th March 2005 (Lot 151).

# SEA CHANGE : FINE AND DECORATIVE ART IN ST IVES 1914-1930

Figs. 3.16 - 3.23   Emile Fabry
               Red chalk and charcoal portrait sketches

Page 46

Left :   Top :     *Woman* (c.1917)

         Middle : *Theresa Abell*  (inscribed St Ives) (c.1917)

         Bottom : *Frances Horne*  (inscribed St Ives 1918)

Right :  Top :     *Young Woman* (dated 1915)

Page 47

Left :   Top :     *Young Woman* (inscribed St Ives 1915)

Right :  Top :     *Young Man*

         Middle :  *Helen Rice* (c.1915)

         Bottom :  *Edgar Skinner*

(all courtesy of Jacqueline Guisset)

On Show Day in 1916, the reviewer commented, "M.Fabry expressed himself in splendid draughtsmanship and decorative style......Local scenes as dealt with under his treatment are a revelation; remarkably original and very beautiful." [96] Unfortunately, none of these local scenes have been discovered, but a work called *The Sphinx*, dated 1/19/1917, does appear to feature the fishing fleet off a rocky coast.[97] What have survived, however, are a number of very fine drawings of heads, done in red chalk or charcoal, several of which are inscribed 'St Ives'. Unfortunately, the identities of the majority of the models are unknown, but they include Theresa Abell (Fig. 3.17), the daughter of the American artist, author and musician, Hanna Rion Ver Beck, who was the first member of the artistic community to marry into an old established St Ives family, the Trewhellas, Frances Horne (Fig. 3.18), the founder of the St Ives Handicraft Guild and the person responsible for bringing Bernard Leach to St Ives, and Edgar Skinner (Fig. 3.23), who, during Fabry's time in St Ives, was acting as Borough Accountant. One of the finest portraits in red chalk, which is inscribed St Ives, is recorded as of a girl called Johanna, possibly one of Fabry's fellow refugees (Fig. 3.11). An excellent example of his work in charcoal is his sketch of a Miss Helen Rice (Fig. 3.22). Another portrait exhibited on Show Day in 1916 was said to be of his hostess. However, most of these works remained in the possession of the Fabry family, suggesting that his asking price, seemingly fifteen guineas, was considered too high.[98]

Fabry was accompanied in St Ives by his wife, Virginie, whom he had married in 1897, and his daughter, Suzanne, who was born in 1904, and he used photographs of them, clothed and nude, for his works as well. The local paper records Suzannne as passing her music exams whilst in the town and also of taking part in a number of entertainments put on by the artists.

---

96 *St Ives Times*, 17/3/1916.
97 In April 1917, the local paper also noted that he had designed the poster for the Lifeboat Concert.
98 Fifteen guineas was the price paid for the drawing acquired on behalf of the National Museum of Wales.

Fig. 3.24  Emile Fabry    *War and Peace*        (Galerie Patrick Lancz, Brussels)

Fig. 3.25  Emile Fabry  Design for his mural *War and Peace*
in the Entrance Hall of University College Cardiff
(courtesy Jacqueline Guisset)

Fig. 3.26 Emile Fabry *War*
(National Museum of Wales, Cardiff)

Fig. 3.27 Emile Fabry
*Woman with violin*
(National Museum of Wales, Cardiff)

Fabry's initial stay in Cardiff resulted in some important contacts. Through the initiative of the Davies ladies of Llandinam, who funded the entire enterprise, Dr Polderman, a Belgian Professor at University College, Cardiff, had gone out to Belgium in September 1914 to invite some ninety-one refugees "of the better class" to come to Wales. Fabry is likely to have been one of these, and the group included several other distinguished artists, including Emile Claus, Belgian's best known painter. Having settled them at various venues around Wales, Dr Polderman then urged that their presence should be utilised to remedy what he considered was the "deplorably backward condition" of the study of painting and sculpture in Wales.[99] Aided by the Davies family and Bernard Leach's father-in-law, Dr William Evans Hoyle, the first director (1909-1924) of the newly established National Museum of Wales, the Belgian section of the War Relief Exhibition, held at Burlington House in February 1915, was brought down to Cardiff. From this, Fabry's work, *War* (Fig. 3.26), a crayon sketch which showed a dead soldier, with a rifle, being received into the arms of a visionary figure, was bought by the Davies sisters themselves and later donated to the Museum. Fabry's work also impressed Dr Hoyle and, in September 1918, he encouraged a local collector, R.Cory, to purchase and donate to the Museum, an example of Fabry's portrait drawings from a batch that Fabry had sent him. Cory chose one of a woman holding a violin, which is dated 1917 and inscribed 'St Ives' (Fig. 3.27). The most likely model is Harriet Solly, another Belgian refugee based in St Ives, who was a fine musician and whose contacts with other Belgian musicians resulted in the standard of musical performances in St Ives during the War years being higher than ever before.

Finally, Dr Polderman arranged for Fabry to receive a commission from Lord Plymouth to produce a major work for the entrance hall of University College, Cardiff. Entitled *War and Peace*, this decorative panel, which was shaped to go over an archway and measured over 13ft x 22ft, was the highlight of Show Day in 1919, when it was exhibited not in Fabry's studio, possibly one of the Island Studios, but in the Drill Hall. It had taken Fabry two years to complete. As usual, the message was conveyed through a series of figures striking dramatic poses, with symbols of peace on the right hand side of the arch and those of War to the left. An attractive female nude, representing beauty, is the principal symbol of Peace and her open posture is contrasted with the back view of a man flexing his muscles, the symbol of War. The man is also placed lower than the female to signify the ascendancy of Peace. A favourite motif, the poet and his lyre, representing literature, music and the Arts, and another figure representing science and learning are also included as symbols of peace. Beneath War, a naked woman seeks to escape from the raised sword of a muscular soldier, having more concern for the safety of her child than herself, whilst flying across a lurid sky, a rider on horseback with flaming torch, carries war and rapine to the end of the world.[100] Again, a pointillist style is used for the application of the paint. The mural was to bear two inscriptions, one dedicating it to the work of King Albert and the heroic defenders of Liege, and the other recording that the gift was in acknowledgement of the generous hospitality afforded the Belgians whilst in England. However, for some reason, the commission was never installed at the College and the work of art remained, rolled up, in the possession of Fabry's descendants, until bought by a Belgian collector in 1987. However, it was only shown in public again, mounted in its full glory, at the 2008 Belgian Antique Dealers Fair by Galerie Patrick Lancz.

---

99 In *The Welsh Outlook*, November 1914, quoted in *The Davies Family and Belgian Refugee Artists & Musicians in Wales*, *The National Library of Wales Journal*, Vol XXII (1981-2) at p. 227. This article is the source for much of this paragraph.
100 See *St Ives Times* 10/3/1916.

In March 1919, Fabry was selected by the Belgian Government to be one of the artists to decorate its monument to commemorate Victory, and he returned that year to his homeland. St Ives had never before witnessed symbolist art of this type or scale, and it is difficult to judge his impact. His desire to use paintings to express emotions might have had some resonances with artists keen to explore the use of colour to this effect, but, in general, one feels that his work will have been viewed with curiosity rather than positive appreciation. However, it clearly struck a chord with one artist, Frances Lloyd, who went on to produce her own symbolist works as a triumphant swansong. Other artists, such as Betty Thompson, took advantage of the presence of an esteemed teacher to take lessons, whilst Fabry's use of pointillism may have been Claude Barry's inspiration for his own experiments with this style. Fabry's memories of England must have been sullied by the rejection of his masterpiece but, writing from Belgium in 1925, he commented that St Ives "still dwells in my heart like sunshine full of light" and that he recalled it "as the ideal shelter where life is calm and peaceful like some blest shore on which break all the troubles and tumults of existence, only as white waves to die away." [101] Back in his homeland, Fabry joined the L'Art Monumental group, taught architectural painting at the Brussels Academy between 1933-1936 and won commissions for a number of major decorative schemes. He lived to the ripe old age of 101. However, his style did not keep pace with modern trends and he has now become a somewhat neglected figure, albeit an excellent biography has recently been published by Jacqueline Guisset.[102]

### 3.4  The colourful and decorative watercolours of Louis Reckelbus

The work of Fabry's Belgian colleague, Louis Joseph Reckelbus (1865-1958), could not have been more different. A highly regarded watercolourist, he produced, during his time in St Ives, a series of very decorative and colourful watercolour studies of the town, as well as exhibiting some bright and vigorous landscapes of his native land. These works were inspired by the intensity of colour of the Fauves, and so introduced into St Ives novel colour values, which clearly had an impact, particularly as such strong colour was not normally associated with this medium.

Born in Bruges, Reckelbus attended art school in his home town, but he was largely self-taught. He exhibited regularly at the triennial Belgian Salons from 1890 and with the Royal Belgian Watercolour Society, of which he was a member. He occasionally showed with Cercle Pour l'Art and exhibited internationally in London, Paris, Berlin, Rome, Venice and Barcelona, where he won a gold medal. He specialized in urban sights and picturesque and romantic views of Bruges, but also painted landscapes, marine subjects, interiors and still life. He worked principally in watercolour, strengthened by a body medium to convey warm and beautiful light effects. Edgar Skinner, reviewing his Show Day exhibits in 1916, commented, "Here we find the joy of life and the open-air. M.Reckelbus revels in sunshine and summer, blue skiffs and fleecy clouds and sunlit buildings." [103] One of the works on view was *Flemish Village* (Fig. 3.30), which was included in the book, *Belgian Art in Exile*. Local scenes evidencing his vivid colour sense and decorative design occasionally appear in the auction rooms. A typical example is *St Ives Fishing Boats off Godrevy* (Fig. 3.28), which shows the bright red sails of a pair of local boats reflected in the waters of the Bay. The big sky, with fleecy clouds, is executed in Reckelbus' unique manner, where he appears to use a cloth to remove sections of paint to reveal the colour of the underlying board or the brown paper on which he invariably worked.

During his time in St Ives, Reckelbus appears to have been more involved with the local community, than Fabry, probably due to a better command of English. He became a member of the Belgian Refugees Fund Committee, and donated work to local fund-raising events. He became particularly friendly with the photographer and musician, Herbert Lanyon, who allowed him to use his studio, 'Attic Studio', in his home, 'The Red House' in the Bellyars. In thanks, Reckelbus gave him the watercolour, *Cottage Front, St Ives - Autumn* (Fig. 3.29).

Reckelbus also proved an inspiration to Frances Lloyd, who was fired with a new enthusiasm for painting (see Chapter 3.5), and the Lloyd family collection contain a number of his works, including a fine example of his still life painting (Fig. 3.33) and two depictions of an old mill (see Fig. 3.31). His art was clearly in tune with the developing interest in St Ives in the use of heightened colour, as seen, for instance, in the work of Louis Sargent and Robert Langley Hutton. Frustratingly, there are few sources from which to gauge his own contribution to this trend, but, in my view, it could well have been significant. Certainly, a fan which contained drawings by Reckelbus, Sargent and Arthur Burgess, as well as being signed by them and Sarah Bernhardt amongst others, is intriguing.[104]

---

101 *St Ives Times*, 18/12/1925.

102 Jacqueline Guisset, *Emile Fabry 1865-1966*, Brussels, 2000. For images and much else in this section, I am totally indebted to Jacqueline.

103 *The Western Echo*, 11/3/1916.

104 See Christies Auction dated 21/9/1999 Lot 52.

Fig. 3.28  Louis Reckelbus  *St Ives Fishing Boats off Godrevy*  (Private Collection)
A sketch by Frances Lloyd of a similar scene sees her trying to replicate Reckelbus' sky.

Fig. 3.29  Louis Reckelbus
*Cottage Front, St Ives - Autumn*
(Private Collection)

Fig. 3.31  Louis Reckelbus  *Old Mill*
(Lloyd family)

Fig. 3.30  Louis Reckelbus
*Flemish Village*  (*Belgian Art in Exile*)

On his return to Belgium, Reckelbus kept in contact with events in St Ives by taking the local paper. Writing in 1925, he commented, "Now - once again at my own fireside - I often think of my exile, which I always associate with a little unspoiled Paradise, full of nature's loveliness, inhabited by a noble and generous people to whom no form of suffering appeals in vain." [105] He does not appear to have pursued his own art with any great vigour subsequently and, having become the Curator of Bruges Museum in 1930, he devoted himself principally to this position. However, a work dating from 1934, *The Fountain of the Little Fawn*, which is very typical of his style, is owned by Cheltenham Art Gallery.

## 3.5 The swansong of Frances Lloyd

Frances or Fanny Lloyd (1855-1921) was the daughter of the prominent American portrait and history painter, William Henry Powell. Whilst studying under Lucien Doucet in Paris in 1883, she had married an elderly retired English naval officer, Walter Lloyd, who was a fellow student, but, whilst they were living in Italy, he had died of cholera in 1889, leaving her with a young son, William. She decided to bring him up in England, often staying with her husband's siblings, one of whom lived in the family mansion, 'Cowesby Hall' in the North Yorkshire Moors. Others, though, lived in Wadebridge and, in the 1890s, Fanny discovered Zennor, where she often did some painting. She exhibited at the RCPS exhibition in Falmouth in 1900 and in St Ives with her son on Show Day in 1904, when Will had taken some painting lessons in the colony. Her exhibits, on that occasion, included *The Reverie* (Fig. 3.34), which was well-regarded, in particular, for its colouring and drawing. "In the face, one seems to trace the influence of a maiden's first love, touching everything with a roseate hue, and causing her to dream on the happiness of the tomorrow." [106] However, Frances had not really dedicated herself to her art.

Having inherited 'Cowesby Hall' from his uncle, Will Lloyd, and his bride, Primrose, who were both more inclined to music than art, took over, in 1909, Julius Olsson's former home, 'St Eia', on Porthminster Hill. On learning that Fanny, back in England after a five year spell in America, was not really looking after herself properly, William invited her down to stay in St Ives. When this did not work out, Fanny moved to 'Bridge Cottage' at Zennor, where she spent most of the War years. Having had some Belgian connections in the past, she took a great deal of interest in the work of the two Belgian artists in St Ives. She took lessons off Louis Reckelbus, who transformed her sense of colour values, whilst it appears that the symbolist work of Emile Fabry inspired her to produce compositions reflecting her own spiritual thoughts.

Fig. 3.32   Frances Lloyd   *Light and Sound* (Lloyd family)

---

105 *St Ives Times*, 18/12/1925.
106 *In St Ives Studios*, Unidentified newspaper cutting in Lloyd family archive reviewing Show Day 1904.

FRESH FACES DURING DARK DAYS

Fig. 3.33   Louis Reckelbus
            *Still Life*
            (Lloyd family)

Fig. 3.34   Frances Lloyd
            *The Reverie*
            (Lloyd family)

Fig. 3.35  Frances Lloyd   *The Planetary Spirit*   (Lloyd family)

The death of her first child, Eugenie, at the age of two, had had a significant impact on Frances, as she firmly believed that she had seen his spirit leave his body and be embraced by angels. Her exhibits in the early years of her career were nearly all religious scenes, but she gradually developed a more mystical outlook. During her spell in America shortly before the War, she became a member of the New York Theosophical Society, who welcomed "all seekers after Wisdom" and whose objects were "(1) to form the nucleus of a Universal Brotherhood without distinction of race, creed, caste or sex; (2) to study and make known the ancient Religions, Philosophies, and Sciences; and (3) to investigate the Laws of Nature and develop the Divine powers latent in man." [107] During 1909, she addressed the Society on two occasions. In January, she spoke on 'Religion', during which she passed the comment, "The Bible is full of hidden wisdom – it is occult Theosophy, veiled in symbolic language." She continued, "There have been ancient Revelations, and there will be new ones, until we learn the whole scheme of the life of the Cosmos, and the laws that are working in it and the forces that uphold it. The world must become morally as well as mentally strong – it must be spiritualised before it can receive the full light. The spiritual nature of Man has its centre in the Heart." In June that year, she addressed the Society again - this time on the teachings, philosophies and ethics of Lao-Tze (c.604-c.521 BC), a famous Chinese sage, who was the founder of Taoist religion, whom she called "a 'Lord of Wisdom', a prophet for and a precursor of the Theosophists".[108]

It appears to have been Louis Reckelbus, who re-ignited Frances' interest in art and whose advice led her to master tempera as a medium, in a manner which particularly suited her artistic temperament. Her work is first referred to in Borlase Smart's review of a show at Lanham's Galleries in July 1919, in which he described her painting *Votive Offerings* as "a remarkably able bit of painting powerfully expressed and very rich in colour." [109] In essence, a still life, the inanimate objects selected "represented attributes of homage to a deity, and a spirit of elevation pervaded the painting and the whole scheme".[110] In 1920, however, Frances' work was considered one of the highlights of Show Day, when she exhibited, in Olsson's old studio at 'St Eia', what Smart considered a remarkable series of distinctive allegorical subjects. Particularly impressive was the large work, *Light and Sound* (Fig. 3.32), which showed "light emanating from a Divine Symbol and striking the wires of a musical instrument held by an angel, causing music to burst forth, and the happiness of an angel on the right of the picture finds expression in song when that celestial being is bathed in its glory. In like manner, the wonders of colour respond to the rays from a big crystal in the immediate foreground. This work is not the usual type of allegorical representation so often seen. It is more of an effort to express inspired thoughts along the lines of a sympathetic medium." [111]

---

107 As stated on Theosophical Society, Syllabus of Discussions, 1909 (Lloyd family archive).
108 Extracts from speeches from Lloyd family archive, courtesy Bill Lloyd.
109 *St Ives Times*, 4/7/1919.
110 Borlase Smart, *The Art of Mrs F.Lloyd*, *St Ives Times*, 18/2/1921.
111 *St Ives Times*, 5/3/1920.

Another symbolist work was *The Planetary Spirit* (Fig. 3.35), but this was in monochrome. "Here we have a celestial being, strong in conception and suggestive of the mighty power capable of modelling a world from nebulous matter. A mass of nebulae is seen in suspension on the left of the picture, and the celestial spirit is turned in profile gazing at the possibilitiies of its future existence." [112] An article in *Country Life* from November 1906 on the "Great Nebula in Andromeda", described as "really the immense spirit of a yet unborn universe", seems to have been the inspiration for this work.[113]

Sadly, by Show Day the following year, she had died, but three of her works, including her final painting, *The All Pervading Light,* were shown in 'St Eia' in her memory. Painted in a similar colour scheme to *Light and Sound*, it depicted a mother, with her arm around a sleeping child, bathed in a golden light, whose rays fall, in particular, into the outstretched palm of the child. This spiritual glory protects the pair from a serpent, shown slivering over a globe in the background. Smart was saddened that she had found herself so late in life, her talent having lain dormant for many years through want of a sympathetic medium.

## 3.6  The brief but productive visit of Dirk Smorenberg

The visit to St Ives in 1915-6 of the Dutch artist, Dirk Smorenberg (1883-1960), has not been given any attention before, but a recent biography of the artist reveals not only that his visit led to a change of style, which resulted in the production of some very different decorative work, but also that he completed in St Ives the first of his water-lily paintings, the subject for which he became best known.[114]

Smorenberg, who was born in Alkmaar, was the son of a stonemason and displayed talent at painting at school. However, between 1898 and 1906, he served in the Dutch Navy, painting in his spare time. In 1906, he started to concentrate on his art in Amsterdam and impressed Professor Allens of the Academy there, who arranged some financial support for him. He exhibited his work for the first time in Amsterdam in 1907 and soon found that his paintings sold well. He travelled widely, spending the summer of 1910 in England and then holding an exhibition of twenty-four works in New York that October. In 1913, he married the portrait painter, Luiza Kamermer (alias Tula di Vista) and held a solo exhibition in Rotterdam. In 1914, the couple had their first child in Bativia, Indonesia, where he held an exhibition, but, on the outbreak of War, returned to England rather than Holland. The first reference to him in a St Ives context was in February 1915, when he was signed in to the Arts Club by Frank Ver Beck, and he became a member the following month. Although not participating in Show Day, he had a work hung at the Royal Academy and, later in the year, two at Liverpool. Initially, he lodged at 14 Ayr Terrace, but, in September 1915, he applied for the tenancy of a run-down cottage at Hellesvean near St John's-in-the-Fields at £8 per annum, evidencing an intention to stay some time. However, his application was not exactly helped by the reference given by his Amsterdam bankers, who wrote, "The fact that Mr S is letting a cottage of such a low rent shows already that his financial position is not a very strong one." [115] However, no sooner had he taken the cottage than the total ban on outdoor sketching impacted on his plans to a significant degree, for he was an artist who enjoyed painting the Cornish coastal scenery.

Before his arrival in St Ives, Smorenberg was known for his luminous canvases, with the paint applied thickly and loosely and brushstrokes readily apparent. In St Ives, though, he changed his style completely and used a very precise technique, with outlined, flat and decorative forms, whilst pastel shades replaced strong colours. Two surviving works show coastal rock faces, decoratively treated, framing long distance stylised views of the fishing fleet off the coast (see Fig. 3.37), whilst a further one depicts very stylised waves breaking on a rocky coast (Fig. 3.36). A sunset scene shows the fleet offshore, with a purple sky reflected in the sea, broken up by vivid orange and green light. If Smorenberg did develop this new style in St Ives, it is difficult to think of a local artist, who might have inspired him, other than, perhaps, Louis Reckelbus.

Smorenberg's biography records that he stayed in St Ives until July 1916, but there is little reference to him in the normal local sources. However, it appears that, due to the sketching ban, he negotiated the use of a country property of an artist who had London connections. No name is given, but, if such benefactor was a St Ives artist, Moffat Lindner again springs to mind. Here, Smorenberg became fascinated with ponds and water-lilies and a painting of water-lilies dated 1915 is his first known depiction of this subject. An undated panel, *Pond with Swans*, also has a Lanham's Gallery label on its back.

---

112 *St Ives Times*, 5/3/1920.

113 *A Spectral Universe*, Country Life, 3/11/1906.

114 See Emke Raassen-Kruimel and Jan de Ruijter, *Dirk Smorenberg - In de ban van de natuur*, Laren, 2005. As this publication is in Dutch, I am totally indebted to Els Strandberg for a translation of its salient sections.

115 Letter from Kas Vereeniging to Glanville and Hamilton dated 16/9/1915 - Mornington Estate Papers, County Records Office, Truro, GHW/12/3/6/1/182/36.

# SEA CHANGE : FINE AND DECORATIVE ART IN ST IVES 1914-1930

Fig. 3.36 Dirk Smorenberg    *Sea*    (courtesy Singer Laren)

Fig. 3.37 Dirk Smorenberg    *Coastal Impression near St Ives*    (courtesy Singer Laren)

On his return to Holland, he specialized in very decorative depictions of water-lily ponds and continued to have regular exhibitions until the late 1930s. The 2005 exhibition of his work at Singer Laren, with accompanying biography, has re-awakened interest in his career.

## 3.7  Claude Francis Barry and Louis Sargent

Both Claude Francis Barry (1883-1970) and Louis Sargent (1881-1965) had been involved with the colony since 1908, and so it is difficult to label them as "fresh faces", but they were both considered during the War to be rising stars, with unusual, distinctive styles that were attracting attention in London circles. As I dealt with their early careers at some length in *Pioneers of St Ives Art at Home and Abroad (1889-1914)*, I will merely concentrate here on the work that they produced in the years after 1914 until their respective departures from the colony in the early 1920s.

Barry was a pacificist and spent the early part of the War near his family's home in Windsor. The six months that he was forced to spend digging potatoes, he recalled as the worst time of his life. In 1917, however, he settled in St Ives again, taking over, from the mentally ill Dorothy Robinson, the large property, 'Belliers Croft', which she and her husband, Harry, had built at the turn of the century. He rented initially one of the Porthmeor Studios, but moved shortly thereafter to a studio in Porthmeor Square, which he named 'St Leonard's Studio' and in which he held exhibitions with his wife, Doris, in the summer of each of the years 1918, 1919 and 1920. During this period, he produced work of great variety, but he imbued all with his own poetic vision. Borlase Smart commented, "He feels the mystery of twilight, the romance in a moonrise, or the happiness of a spring day." [116]

Whilst based in Windsor, Barry was particularly attracted by the local woods. "Trees", he proclaimed, "are the glory of landscape", and in his treatise on painting, he told students to beware of thinking of them as green, for they were "very often blue, and can be crimson, orange-yellow, grey or black; anyhow almost anything except green".[117] The large painting (46" x 67"), *A Glade in Windsor Park* (Fig. 3.40), is a fine example of his woodland scenes of this period, whilst his painting, *The Merry Woods of Windsor*, was highly complimented when it was hung at the Paris Salon in 1919. Other well-regarded woodland subjects were *Monarchs of Windsor Forest* (Show Day 1920) and *Autumn Glory* (RBA 1920). These works demonstrate that Barry had become a realist landscape painter of consummate skill. However, realising that the more progressive artists were utilising alternative techniques, Barry began to experiment with different styles and different subject matter. His new-found interest in both pointillism and symbolist subjects might suggest the possible influence of Emile Fabry, although it is hard to be certain, as very few of Barry's paintings in this style have come to light, despite the acclaim that they received at the time.

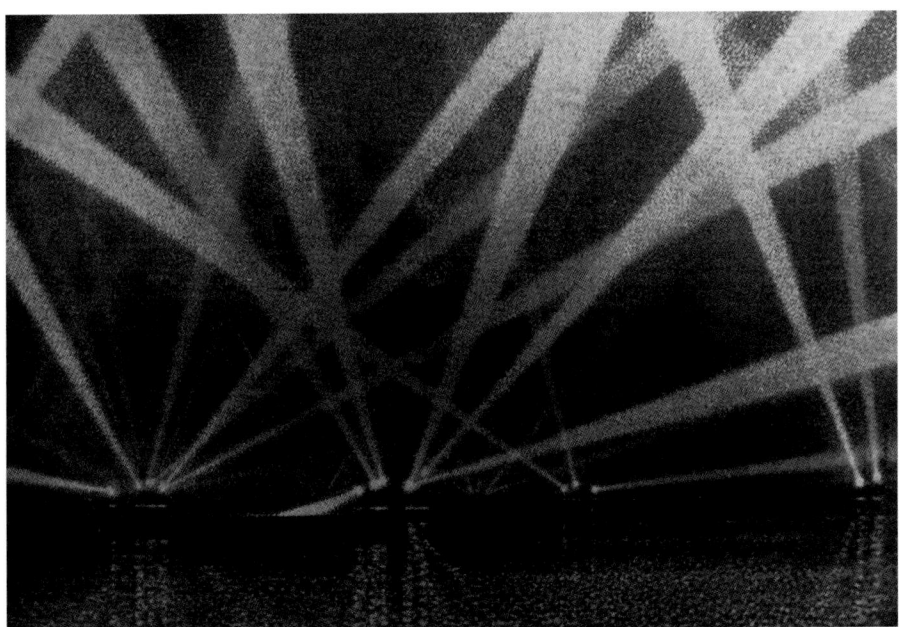

Fig. 3.38  Claude Francis Barry      *The Grand Fleet* on *Peace Night*
(*Naval and Military Record*)

---

116  *St Ives Times*, 28/5/1920
117  Quoted in Katie Campbell, *Moon Behind Clouds - An Introduction to the life and work of Sir Claude Francis Barry*, Jersey, 1999, at p.209.

Fig. 3.39  Claude Francis Barry    *Springtime in Lombardy*    (David Capps)

The first mention of Barry's work, after his return to St Ives, was a note that his Royal Academy exhibit of 1917, *The Serenity of the Night*, had been rendered poetic by "the division of tones", the manner in which the pointillist technique was often referred to at the time. However, no indication is given as to its subject or of any symbolism. However, his next major work, *The Twilight of the World*, did have symbolic intent, and when it was exhibited at the Cornish Artists exhibition in Plymouth in November 1917, it was hailed "as a landscape that stands in a class by itself, and is bound to arrest attention and to give rise to sharp controversy".[118]    It is believed that the scene featured many grave markers. Certainly, this was the case with a work that he exhibited at Lanham's that December, entitled *The Glory that is France*, intended to be a withering commentary on the futility of War. It was a theme to which Barry returned later in works such as *We Shall Remember Them*, depicting the crosses at Monte Cassino.

Fig. 3.40  Claude Francis Barry    *A Glade in Windsor Park*    (David Capps)

---

118 *St Ives Times*, 9/11/1917.

Fig. 3.41  Claude Barry   *Peace Night in Trafalgar Square*   (David Capps)

Barry's pointillist style made a particular impression when he turned his hand to seachlight paintings - the works for which he eventually became best known. Feeling that Peace Night at the end of the War would make a good subject, he spent months in London waiting for peace to be declared and then his wife and himself spent the evening making notes to work up into big pictures. *Peace Night in Trafalgar Square* (Fig. 3.41) showed joyous crowds "madly jazzing under the shadow of Nelson's monument", with the scene illuminated by a magnificent firework display, whereas *The Grand Fleet on Peace Night* (Fig. 3.38), an illustration of which was reproduced in *Naval and Military Record* in March 1920, showed the Fleet outlined by criss-crossing searchlights. Pointillist-painted searchlights also featured in his 1919 Royal Academy exhibit *London and War Time*, which received numerous favourable reviews for its combination of realism and decorative effect. "On this canvas, showing a dim vision of Westminster from the Surrey side of the river, the searchlight rays criss-cross each other, covering the heavens with a curious pattern of geometrical figures; yellow spots of light on the bridge cast twinkling reflections in waters already alive beneath the moonlight. The impression is clever and well sustained." [119] In 1920, he used this technique in a Cornish nocturne, *The Hills of Home*, which, for boldness of conception and originality of outlook, was considered to be the leading work in the RBA exhibition that year and was hung in the place of honour. "In the weird light of a young moon, the country stretches away - the whole seen through a 'snow-storm' of variously coloured dots." [120] This was novel work of great interest. However, in 1921, Barry deserted his family and moved to the Continent and he did not take this style of work forward until his return to St Ives in 1939.[121]

119 Quoted in *St Ives Times*, 16/5/1919.
120 *St Ives Times*, 30/4/1920.
121 Barry was also a fine croquet player, winning the open championship challenge cup at Roehampton in 1919 and, for the croquet player, the ultimate honour, the Menton Croquet Championship in 1922, 1923 and 1929.

Fig. 3.42  Louis Sargent   *Basaltic Shore - Trevail Cove, near St Ives, Cornwall*
(Private Collection)

Louis Sargent was another St Ives artist, who created a stir in London circles during the War. In an article in *The Studio* in 1919, Folliott Stokes hailed him as one of the true pioneers of the age, for his ability "to see and think outside the circle of custom and convention".[122] Yet this unique vision was based on the mastery of technical issues. "Throughout the whole period of his studentship, Sargent concentrated his energies on mastering the craftsmanship of his profession and acquiring the ability to produce faithful facsimiles of the subject before him, fully realising that until he had obtained this power he would be unable adequately to interpret the idealism which he felt all Nature's phenomena symbolize."[123]

Sargent, who suffered from nervous dyspepsia, a digestive disorder, had been advised by his doctor to take a two hour walk every day, and, during these walks, he derived inspiration from the Cornish coast. Like Barry, Louis Sargent developed an interest in nocturnes, but rather than use night as a symbol for wartime woes, he sought to evoke its mystery and poetry. Accordingly, his nocturnes were sprinkled with stars and purple waters and evoked the solitude and vastness of night. Sargent was also recognised as a distinctive portrait painter, and, by 1914, he had also turned his attention to a series of allegorical figures, which writer and critic, Charles Lewis Hind, described as an "array of vast anatomical nudes posing majestically by the sea". One of these works, *The Triton*, was hung at Pittsburgh in 1914, but none have appeared in the sale-rooms. Lewis Hind felt that their "aggressive decoration" was overdone.[124] Tellingly, Sargent did not pursue this type of subject, but returned to his Cornish coastal scenes, employing ever heightened colour. As one critic commented, "Mr Sargent is essentially a colourist : all his artistry is expressed in colour."[125] His progression can be seen by comparing his later works with *Basaltic Shore*, a depiction, dated 1914, of Trevail Cove, which is between St Ives and Zennor, for this is, for Sargent, quite restrained in its use of colour, with only the vivid blue used in the foreground rocks a little unusual.

Sargent occupied one of the Piazza Studios and a reviewer of Show Day in 1916 commented in relation to his work, "Unorthodox in his methods, when first he came into the county, his productions did not find favour with the more prosaic, but his ability was undeniable, till now he is recognised as taking a high place among British artists...It was he who apparently discovered the real beauty of the Cornish rocks, and, possessing a genius for colour, he invested them with a charm that was irresistible."[126]

---

122 A.G.Folliott Stokes, *The Paintings of Louis Sargent*, The Studio, 1919, Vol. 77 at p.129.
123 ibid, p.130.
124 *The Chronicle*, reproduced in *St Ives Weekly Summary*, 28/10/1915.
125 *St Ives Times*, 17/3/1916.
126 *St Ives Weekly Summary*, 16/3/1916.

Fig. 3.43  Louis Sargent
*Kynance Cove*
(Private Collection)

Fig. 3.44  Louis Sargent
*Coast neat St Ives*
(Private Collection)

Fig. 3.45  Louis Sargent
*Gull Rock, Kynance Cove*
(Private Collection)

Fig. 3.46 The couple in this photo in Andrew Lanyon's collection have never been identified, but the man might well be Louis Sargent, if one has regard to Fitz's caricature of him in *Everyone's Doing It*.

His wife, Kathleen (née Clayton), was a fruit and flower painter, who exhibited at Lanham's and enjoyed some success at the Royal Academy between 1918 and 1929.

Too advanced for the Royal Academy, Sargent tended to show his works at the International Society, of which he was a member, but, in 1916, he had a highly regarded group of works hung at the Goupil Gallery, a number of which also featured on Show Day. *The Lizard from Kynance* was described as "a marvellous riot of brilliant pigments" and other highly acclaimed works were *Clodgy Rocks* and *Serpentine Cove*.[127] Sargent was an irregular exhibitor in the colony, as he divided his time between London and St Ives, but he contributed to various exhibitions at Lanham's Galleries and to the Cornish artists show at Plymouth in 1917. Borlase Smart was a keen fan of his work and was undoubtedly influenced by him. "Mr Sargent feels the colour of the surfaces he paints."[128] "He appears to be the only artist who realizes the individuality of the Cornish coast and its characteristic colouring. Such colour as Mr Sargent shows really does exist if one only looks for it. Each picture is a harmony of beautiful colour passages."[129] Folliott Stokes also highlighted his colour sense. "Few men in landscape have used colour so boldly or with such consummate knowledge and disregard of convention."[130] In particular, Stokes mentioned Sargent's use of cool colours in the foreground and warm colours in the background, against all accepted wisdom. "Unfortunately the public fail to realize the immense gulf that separates the work of the man who eliminates detail because it is superfluous to his theme, and simplifies his colour scheme to obtain the most perfect harmony, from the work of him who eliminates detail because he cannot draw it, and simplify colours because he is unable to render its subtle gradations."[131] By 1921, Sargent was being described as "the most distinguished painter of coast scenery who is associated with St Ives", with a small painting of Perranporth being hailed as "a fine exercise in massive form and glowing colour".[132]

After the War, Sargent discovered another subject that inspired him - the Alpine scenery of Switzerland, a country that he probably visited in order to link up with his lifelong friend, Frank Budgen, who had moved there at the outset of the War. Folliott Stokes was particularly taken with Sargent's painting, which he called *The Breithorn*, albeit when it was sold at Christies, London in 2003, it was said to be inscribed *Evening View from Wengen* (Fig. 3.48).[133] "In this picture, by his elimination of non-essential details, by his recognition of the structural rhythm of the mountain, by his massive incidents of light and shade, and by the dignified voluptuousness of his colour-scheme, Sargent has...realized a chord of harmony in Alpine scenery which has not been revealed before in painting. It is not a literal rendering, but an ideal; not a guide-book picture of a Swiss scene... but something infinitely truer, insomuch as it reveals the spiritual significance and sublimity of one of those vast sanctuaries of silence which, for want of a better word, we call mountains; and which, in their godlike isolation, seem to our human vision to be endowed with some of the attributes of eternity itself."[134] Folliott Stokes' article was also illustrated with Sargent's depiction of *The Jungfrau* (Fig. 3.47), whilst another major work from this visit was *The Gothard Mountains from Mont Bré*, priced at £100, when exhibited at the RWA in 1919.

---

127 *St Ives Times*, 17/3/1916.
128 *St Ives Times*, 25/6/1920.
129 Review of 1919 Lanham's Gallery exhibition in *Western Monring News*.
130 A.G.Folliott Stokes, *The Paintings of Louis Sargent*, The Studio, 1919, Vol. 77 at p.133.
131 ibid at p.129.
132 *St Ives Times*, 1/1921.
133 Sale dated 13/2/2003 Lot 144.
134 A.G.Folliott Stokes, *The Paintings of Louis Sargent*, The Studio, 1919, Vol. 77 at p.133.

Fig. 3.47  Louis Sargent      *The Jungfrau*      (*The Studio*)

It was through Budgen that Sargent was introduced in the autumn of 1920 to James Joyce, for Budgen had begun researching his book on the making of *Ulysses*. Joyce's letters to Budgen make a number of references to Sargent, albeit often mentioning his ill-health, and Sargent's portrait of Joyce is in the collection of the Harry Ransom Center, albeit it is not one of his more successful pieces. Although in his obituary in 1965, it was stated that St Ives had been his permanent home for more than half a century, Sargent disappears from the local art scene after 1921 for the whole inter-war period and it seems that, in the 1920s and 1930s, for reasons largely connected with his health, he spent a great deal of time in the south of France, only returning to St Ives in 1939 on the outbreak of War.[135]

Fig. 3.48  Louis Sargent    *The Breithorn - Evening View from Wengen*
(Private Collection/ Photo © Christie's Images/ The Bridgeman Art Library)

---

135  See James Joyce's letters to Frank Budgen of 18/2/1921, 28/8/1933, 25/4/1934 and 18/12/1934.  Ed. R Ellmann, *Letters of James Joyce*, Vol 3, London, 1966.

Fig. 3.49 Robert Langley Hutton  *St Ives Harbour*      (Collection of Gerald & Susan Mayne)
This work was originally acquired by Herbert Lanyon.

## 3.8   Robert Langley Hutton - "a universal favourite"

Robert Langley Hutton (1883-1919) was described as "a universal favourite" on the occasion of his untimely death at the age of 36. Hutton's parents were Scottish, but he had been born in India, where his father was plying his trade as a broker. He himself is recorded as a merchant's clerk in 1901 but, after his health had broken down in Burma, he came down to St Ives to paint, although he was largely self-taught. He seems to have first visited St Ives with his family in August 1908, when they stayed at 10 Sea View Terrace, and then he returned on his own in September. He eventually settled in 5, Porthminster Terrace, where he was looked after by his sisters, Lizzie and Dorothy, who themselves took an active role in the community. He joined the Arts Club in December 1909 and made many friends there, becoming Secretary in 1913, but his poor health obliged him to resign. Although he did not start exhibiting until Show Day in 1913, by the following year, the reviewer was commenting, "Among the younger generation of St Ives artists, there are none who give greater promise than Mr Hutton".[136] London subjects indicate that he returned home to his family from time to time, whilst a painting of a Breton market indicates a trip to Brittany, but it is his colourful depictions of St Ives and its harbour for which he is best known. The intensity of colour utilised in a work, such as *St Ives Harbour* (Fig. 3.49), suggests the influence of Reckelbus and/or Sargent. On other occasions, it was the "pearly tones" of his work that delighted critics, who found his work "full of life and expression".[137] The winter of 1917 produced an unusual sight - heavy snow in St Ives - a subject that a number of artists tackled.[138] Hutton produced several snow scenes, which he exhibited at the RWA in 1918, and these included *Snow in the Harbour* (Fig. 3.51).

In August 1919, Hutton held an exhibition of his work at Arthur White's 'Attic Studio' in St Andrew's Street, but he died that October. His obituary recorded, "His work was a delight to the artist, owing to his charming sense of colour, whether his motive was in subtle greys or the full range of colour. If he had lived, there is no doubt that he would have risen to a high place in the ranks of landscape painters."[139] His popularity can be gauged from the extraordinary number of artists who attended his funeral. His sisters stayed on in St Ives, and Lizzie Hutton (d.1963) married leading citizen, Robert Sawle Read, in June 1920, before becoming one of the town's first female magistrates.

---

136 *St Ives Times*, 27/3/1914.
137 *St Ives Times*, 25/7/1919.
138 Also hung at the RWA in 1918 were Marcella Smith's *Snow in St Ives* and Alfred Hartley's etching *St Ives under Snow*.
139 *St Ives Times*, 17/10/1919.

Fig. 3.50  Marcella Smith
   *The Old Lighthouse, St Ives*
   (Newlyn School Gallery, Penzance)

Fig. 3.51  Robert Langley Hutton
   *Snow in the Harbour*
   (Collection of Gerald & Susan Mayne)

Fig. 3.52  Marcella Smith
   *The Quayside, St Ives*
   (Private Collection)

## 3.9 Marcella Smith and Helen Stuart Weir

Marcella Smith (1887-1963) and Helen Stuart Weir (d.1969) both lived in England for the rest of their long lives, becoming stalwarts and leading officers of the Society of Women Artists, and so it comes as a surprise to find them referred to in St Ives during the War years as two American girls, particularly as Smith had been born in England, but they both had spent a considerable part of their early lives in America. They may also have shared a studio together initially, as Frances Hodgkins mentions taking a visitor "to call on two pretty Americans in their Studio who turned up the gramophone for us & were cordial".[140] Although both became well-known for their still life subjects, they had other very different interests at this juncture.

Helen Stuart Weir, who was born in New York, arrived in St Ives with her mother, Nina Mary Weir-Lewis (1858-1937), in 1913. Nina was an artist as well and, although she indicated in the 1929 edition of *Who's Who in Art* that she was married and the mother of four sons and two daughters, there is no reference to any husband or other children in a St Ives context. She remained in the colony until her death in 1937, initially studying under Frances Hodgkins and then working from Rose Lodge Studio. She described herself as "an oil and watercolour painter of landscapes, still life and figures" and not only had work hung by a number of London Societies, including ROI, RI and SWA, but also had several paintings reproduced. Her work, though, elicited little comment and is rare.

Given that her mother studied under Hodgkins, Helen, who had trained initially in America and Germany, may have done so as well, although Hodgkins makes no specific reference to her. Fred Milner, though, mentions that he was giving etching lessons to two American girls, and signed Marcella Smith into the Arts Club in November 1914. Accordingly, Helen may have preferred to study under him. However, her initial success came as a sculptor for, in 1919, her bronze of a doe and fawn, called *The Caress*, was shown at the Royal Academy and she won a medal for her sculpture in Budapest. Nevertheless, she was also producing still life paintings, one of her first successes being hung at the RWA in 1917. From 1919, she was a regular exhibitor of such works at the Royal Academy - that in 1919 was hailed as being "of exceptional merit...brilliant in its notes of scarlet and emerald", whilst Borlase Smart considered her 1920 contribution, featuring a big brass vessel, glass globe and china vase filled with marigolds, to be a triumph of still life art.[141] She was particularly fascinated by the play of light on contrasting surfaces, and her arrangements were always very decorative. She listed her principal works during the 1920s as *Cargo of Flowers* and *Rainbow Hues*. In 1922, she held a joint show with her mother at Lanham's Galleries and, in 1927, had a one-man show at the Goupil Gallery in London, entitled *Flowers and Still Life - Brittany and the Basque Country*, which included twenty coloured drawings, including two of St Ives, twenty-three oils and *The Caress*. She was made an Associate of the SWA in 1921, a member of the ROI in 1924 and the RBA in 1929 (Associate 1926). In the 1930s, she was Acting President of the SWA for a number of years. Despite being based in London for most of her career, she retained Rose Lodge Studio and was a regular visitor to St Ives. Both her mother and herself became members of STISA.

Fig. 3.53 Nina Weir-Lewis and Helen Stuart Weir in Rose Lodge Studio
(Lanyon family archive)

---

140 Letter to her mother dated 28/1/1915 - Ed.L.Gill, *The Letters of Frances Hodgkins*, Auckland, 1993, at p.301.
141 *St Ives Times*, 16/5/1919 & 14/5/1920.

Fig. 3.54  Marcella Smith     *The Pool in the Wood*
(Lawrences Auctioneers, Crewkerne)

One of a pair of identical twins, Marcella Smith (1887-1963) was the daughter of a clergyman and had actually been born in East Moseley, Surrey, but her family moved to America when she was two, living first in Baltimore and then in Washington. She studied at the Philadelphia School of Design for Women under Henry Snell and then attended Colarossi's in Paris, where she was taught by Eugène Delecluse. The presence of a Miss Smith amongst Snell's students staying at the Trenwith Hotel in August 1914 may signify that she first came to St Ives to link up with her former tutor, and then decided to return later that year when she was forced to leave Paris. She made a significant impression right from the outset and Edgar Skinner commented in his review of Show Day in 1915, "Miss Smith possesses a rare feeling for colour and great originality of outlook, which are likely to produce, in the course of time, work of real and lasting merit." [142] She had her first success at the Royal Academy in 1916 with *St Ives Harbour*, which was described as "a bright, atmospheric canvas" (possibly Fig. 3.55), whilst her exhibit the following year, *A Western Harbour*, was a scene along the foreshore in St Ives, "painted in a most cheerful atmosphere of light and colour and displaying animation".[143] At this point, she gave her address as 'Chilton', St Ives, although she later moved in with her eccentric aunts, Ada and Gertrude Smith, who had opened a convalescent home at 7 Sea View Terrace. By 1918, she was considered to be one of the rising stars of the colony, and her painting at the Royal Academy that year, *The Pool in the Wood*, was highly regarded by the critics, surprised that "such a subject could have been so vigorously and broadly treated by a woman".[144] *The Gentlewoman* felt that Smith had the potential to remedy the lamentable lack of a great female landscape painter, commenting, "This has romance and grandiosity; it is bravely handled in technique; it has something of the secret power, majesty and mystery of nature - some of the primeval spirit; and it is full, as a satisfying landscape must be, of decorative charm." [145]

In August 1918, Smith held an exhibition in her Porthmeor Studio (No 3), which was hailed in the local paper as "a brilliant and clever display of paintings". Sixty-four works were on display, several of which were of large dimensions - a testament to her industry. "It would be interesting to speculate on the line of development that Miss Marcella Smith's talent would have taken had the war not driven her from Paris to take up her residence in St Ives. But it seems fairly certain that, sooner or later, the subtle feeling for the open air - the freedom and grandeur of great skies and wide expanses - would have asserted itself. The masculine vigour of Miss Smith's technique lends itself to a rendering of largeness, which is tempered by a feminine instinctiveness for charm. Although distinctly modern, she does not set out to *épater les bourgeois* and her subtle insight into the values of diffused light and the decorative quality of a high key are among the predominating characteristics that should be noted." [146]

---

142 *Western Echo*, 20/3/1915.
143 Review of her 1918 exhibition in *Western Morning News*, reproduced in *St Ives Times* 16/8/1918.
144 ibid.
145 Quoted in *St Ives Times*, 14/6/1918.
146 *St Ives Times*, 2/8/1918.

Fig. 3.55  Marcella Smith *St Ives Harbour*  (Newlyn School Gallery, Penzance)

Fig. 3.56  Helen Stuart Weir   *White Gigs in St Ives Harbour*  (Richard Read)
This most unusual work by Weir was given to Dorothy Read, the wife of
Robert Sawle Read's son, Richard, as an impromptu birthday present.

Quite a large percentage of the works were local townscapes or views of the harbour; there were also some further paintings of sylvan glades and studies of spring blossom, and a well-regarded painting *Evening in the Cotswolds*. A flower piece, *Rhodedendrons*, was described as a "brilliant little colour note".[147]

Smith's work continued to get good, but not effusive reviews, and occasionally criticism was made of the clumsiness of her drawing, particularly relating to figures (see, for example, *The Old Lighthouse, St Ives* - Fig. 3.50).[148] However, in April 1920, in a joint show with Francis Raymond, she exhibited a further twenty-seven oils in her studio, which impressed Borlase Smart immensely, not only due to the works themselves, but also due to the manner in which they were hung. "Miss Smith's pictures are very deliberate, and her technique is suggestive of freedom of purpose and a full brush. Thus the canvases have all the freshness of feeling as if they were executed, so to speak, in 'one sitting'. The calculation of tonal values in the pictures of St Ives shows much power of perceptions, and there is fine composition in the landscape series. There is a very happy medium struck in the way the expressive brush touches convey so much form and yet leave so much to the imagination. The spontaneity of transcription and the essential grasp of Nature's facts is especially to be noticed in the harmony in grey, under the title *Grey Day. St Ives*. Here we have the quality of tone one associates with a rainy day in the old harbour. The plaster of the houses is toned by the atmospheric conditions, and reflects the grey sky. The perspective of the harbour front is accentuated in the mist. The artist is especially successful in her paintings of morning sunlight. The feeling of glowing light is full of reality, and the buildings are deftly suggestive..... One of the best landscapes is *A Cornish Cottage, Ponsanooth*. It is beautifully suggested in cool tones and, as a colour scheme, is an excellent canvas." [149] The exhibition also included some paintings of Hampton Court, a work *September in Sussex* and some studies of clouds above Porthmeor Beach. She then held a further exhibition of her work, jointly with Percy Ballance, at the Grey Studio on the Foreshore in October.

By this juncture, Smith felt sufficiently confident of her abilities to advertise that she was giving lessons in oil painting during the summer months of 1920 at 3, Porthmeor Studios, and, in January 1921, she was appointed as supervisor of the Arts Club drawing sessions. She was elected to the RBA in 1920 and became a member of the SWA in 1922. She had two further successes at the Royal Academy with St Ives scenes - *A Blue Day* in 1921 and *Silver Morning, St Ives* in 1922 - and was invited to produce a work for Queen Mary's Doll's House. However, in 1921, she moved to London to live with Dorothea Sharp, who was to be her life-long companion. She retained her Porthmeor Studio for a decade, but their visits to the colony were irregular. Furthermore, either in frustration at her inability to sell her work, or disenchanted by comparisons with the work of Sharp, she gave up painting in her previous style entirely. After a brief excursion into making raffia hats (see Chapter 10.4.4 below), she concentrated, almost exclusively, on flower paintings in watercolour. In 1929, she was in charge of the SWA exhibition, when Queen Mary paid an unexpected visit. As she showed Her Majesty around, the Queen spotted a painting of marigolds and enquired who the artist was. When Smith admitted that she was, the Queen bought it on the spot.[150] Smith went on to become a leading figure in the SWA for many decades and published a book on flower painting in watercolour. However, her still life work is totally out of favour at the moment and it seems a great shame that she did not pursue her original style of broadly handled oil painting further, for her early work showed distinct promise.

## 3.10  Some other American visitors during wartime

William Chadwick (1879-1962), who went on to become closely associated with the colony at Old Lyme, Connecticut, was one of the artists caught in Europe by the War, who decided to stay in St Ives for a while, in case prospects improved. Chadwick had, in fact, been born in Dewsbury, Yorkshire, where his father was a textile manufacturer, but, in 1882, when Chadwick was just three years old, his father had taken the extraordinary decision to move all his factory equipment and more than seventy employees out to Holyoke in America. William studied at the Art Students League between 1898 and 1903, and began exhibiting at the National Academy of Design in 1907. He made several visits to Europe, and it was in September 1914 that he and his wife took a house in St Ives. He was first signed into the Arts Club by Fred Milner in November and joined that month. He seems to have stayed until the spring of 1915, probably leaving when the sketching ban was imposed. He is known to have executed a number of fine paintings of St Ives harbour (see Fig. 3.57), several of which were included in an exhibition, *William Chadwick - An American Impressionist*, held at R.H.Love Galleries Inc in 1978.

---

147 *St Ives Times*, 2/8/1918.
148 See Review of Lanham's Exhibition by Borlase Smart - Second Article - *St Ives Times*, 4/7/1919.
149 *St Ives Times*, 16/4/1920.
150 *St Ives Times*, 22/2/1929.

# SEA CHANGE : FINE AND DECORATIVE ART IN ST IVES 1914-1930

Fig. 3.57  William Chadwick     *St Ives Harbor*     (Eldred's, East Dennis)

Fig. 3.58  Ruth Simpson    *Portrait of Frank Ver Beck*
(Royal Cornwall Museum, Truro)

A similar length of stay was enjoyed by the American impressionist landscape painter, Charles Chapel Judson (1864-1946) and his wife Helen, the daughter of Carmel artist, Sydney Yard. Born in Detroit, Michigan, Judson was raised and educated in Kansas City, but, at this juncture, was living in San Francisco, where he had been head of the art department at University College, Berkeley since 1902. Judson and his wife are signed into the Arts Club in November 1914 and found a house at 3 Albert Place. In March 1915, they subscribed to the Belgian Relief Fund, but then decided to leave, returning to the colony after Judson's retirement in 1924.

Frank Ver Beck and Hanna Rion stayed in the town throughout the War years and became popular members of the community. Herbert Lanyon, in particular, became a close friend, and Hanna Rion's skills as a concert pianist were much appreciated at his soirées. Frank sat for portraits by Frances Hodgkins and Ruth Simpson (Fig. 3.58), and did caricatures of John Noble Barlow and Folliott Stokes (Fig. 3.59). Hailed locally as "the originator of the teddy bear", he published, during his time in St Ives, a number of new children's books, including *The Little Bear Lost - A Short Little Tale from Bruintown* and *Timothy Turtle's Great Day*. He also produced some illustrations for a projected book called *Tanky Tunk - The Little Cat Who Journeyed to St Ives*.[151] He held occasional exhibitions of the original illustrations from these books not only on Show Day but also in his studio, known as 'The Den'.[152] He also arranged for his bears to be produced for sale in various forms, such as a doorstop, and invented something that he called a 'War baby', which was stocked in leading London stores. His wife also did some painting and writing, but devoted most of the War years to promoting 'twilight sleep', a mixture of drugs aimed at easing the pain of childbirth.[153] Her beautiful daughter, Theresa Abell (see Fig. 3.17), studied art, sat as a model at Arts Club sketching sessions, and acted in some vaudeville productions in London, before marrying local boy, Bernard Trewhella, who had lost an arm in the War, in 1918.[154] However, the Ver Beck family's involvement with St Ives came to a sad end, for Frank deserted Hanna and ran off with a lady from the Arts Club in 1918, Hanna, having re-married, died young, aged only 49, in 1924, and Theresa died in childbirth in 1927.

Fig. 3.59  Frank Ver Beck  *Caricatures of Folliott Stokes and John Noble Barlow*
(Priscilla Fursdon)

---

151 Further details of Ver Beck's books and stay are set out in David Tovey, *St Ives (1860-1930) - The Artists and the Community - A Social History,* Tewkesbury, 2009 at pp.272-4.
152 See *St Ives Times*, 8/8/1919.
153 See further David Tovey, *St Ives (1860-1930) - The Artists and the Community*, as above at pp.339-40.
154 See further David Tovey, *St Ives (1860-1930) - The Artists and the Community*, as above, p.308 for Mabel Douglas' portrait of Theresa and pp.351-2.

Fig. 3.60  William Spittle  *Breaking Waves, St Ives*  (Private Collection)

## 3.11  Other visitors during the War years

A new arrival in the colony shortly before the War was William Maxwell Spittle RBA RSBA (1858-1917), the son of a Birmingham button manufacturer. He had spent most of his career based in his home town working as a figure painter, but, in 1913, he decided to settle in Carbis Bay and turn to marine painting. He rented 6 Piazza Studios and exhibited on Show Day in 1914 and 1916, when his coastal scenes and paintings of colourful rock pools were highly regarded. He got involved in the local community and organised one evening of *tableaux vivants*, which received high praise. Accordingly, his death in 1917, aged only 59, was a shock. He is buried at St Uny, Lelant.

During August 1915, Laura and Harold Knight, then based in Lamorna, came to work in St Ives for a while, and Laura decided to paint children playing in the Harbour. Lizzie Whitehouse, who largely abandoned her painting during the War to concentrate on her work for the St Ives War Hospital Supply Depot, did a small sketch of Knight painting at the Harbour's edge (Fig. 3.61). However, Knight's presence worried the local Sergeant on two counts. When she put some dots of paint on her picture to represent the horizon, he quizzed her as to their purpose and, when she told him, commented, "How am I to know they don't mean something?"[155] Accordingly, Knight admitted that she was forced to confine her studies to boys swimming, looking straight down on them. However, Frances Hodgkins recorded that this was not the only difficulty that the Sergeant had, for Knight had some thirteen boys in the picture, all nude, "with all St Ives looking on, the horrified & the un-together & even the Sergeant himself not knowing whether to interfere in the interests of public morality or not."[156] The mother of one of the boys, Frankie, told Hodgkins, "lor miss to see 'er paint the parting in the boy's 'ed & down his back would frighten yer". Next day, the same woman told Knight that, if she didn't instantly put bathing drawers on all the boys in the picture, she would go for the Sergeant. "Mrs Knight realising the situation & anxious to avoid trouble gave 2/- to the biggest youth & told him to clear off & buy pants but whether she altered her picture or not is doubtful."[157]

The portrait painter, Frederick Samuel Beaumont (b.1861), settled in the town in 1916 for several years, having been living previously in Wimborne in Dorset, where he won commissions from leading families not only for portraits but also for house interiors. He had been signed into the Arts Club in February 1912 by Alfred Hartley, but he decided to base himself in the town in 1916, taking 9 Richmond Terrace from July that year and renting one of the Porthmeor Studios. He exhibited at Lanham's Galleries and, in 1918, was elected on to the Hanging Committee. However, his only known St Ives works are a

---

155 Laura Knight, *Oil Paint and Grease Paint*, London, 1936 at p.205.
156 Letter dated 8/1915 - Ed.L Gill, ibid, at p.309.
157 ibid.

Fig. 3.61  Lizzie Whitehouse     *Laura Knight painting in St Ives*
(Whitehouse Family/Penlee House Gallery & Museum)

Fig. 3.62  Garstin Cox     *A Morning with the Pilchard Fishers, St Ives*     (John Noott Gallery)

Locally-born artist, Garstin Cox (1892-1933), had a studio in St Andrew's Street, St Ives from 1910 to 1916 and, although this fine work is not mentioned in any local reviews, it is likely to date from this period, as the pilchard fishery had collapsed completely by the 1920s. The majority of the fleet were also fitted with motors during the War years. Cox's progress was keenly followed in St Ives, even after his move to the Lizard. His 1919 Royal Academy exhibit was bought by Johannesburg Art Gallery.

Fig. 3.63  Frank Watson Wood    *A Grey Day, St Ives*    (1917)
(The Great Western Auction Ltd, Glasgow)

The presence in the colony of well-known marine painter, Frank Watson Wood (1862-1953), is only revealed by this dated work.

Fig. 3.64  Frederick Beaumont
*The Artist's Daughter, Helen*
(Lawrences Auctioneers, Crewkerne)

portrait sketch of Edgar Skinner (Fig. 10.12) dated 1918, and a portrait in oils (Fig. 3.64) of his daughter, Helen, who may have been studying art in the town, as a Miss H.Beaumont did exhibit at Liverpool in 1916.  They moved away shortly after the end of the War, because Beaumont won a commission to decorate the entrance hall of the P. and O. Steamship Company's office in Cockspur, a task that took him two years.[158]  He later joined STISA.

Tom Mostyn, then based in Torquay, whose daughter, Marjorie, was to be a long-term resident of the colony, paid a number of visits during the War.  He is recorded as present at the dinner at the Queen's Hotel put on by the artists in September 1915 to pay tribute to the decision of the American artist, Elmer Schofield, to enlist.  He also was present at Noble Barlow's funeral in 1917.  A work, *St Ives Through the Trees* (Fig. 3.65), is likely to date from this time.

Other artists, who exhibited locally during the War years, are listed in Appendix B Table A.  Dated paintings also indicate the presence of Cuthbert Crossley (1883-1960 - later STISA), Wilfred Knox (1884-1966), Herbert John Finn (b.1860) and W.H.Pearson in 1915, Harry Frier (c.1849-1919) in 1916, Frank Watson Wood (1862-1953) and William Edward Croxford, a former resident, in 1917 and Edith E. Morris, Frank Lewis and the Newlyner, Henry Meynell Rheam (1859-1920), in 1919.

Fig. 3.65  Tom Mostyn    *St Ives Through the Trees*
(Private Collection)

---

158 See *St Ives Times*, 13/5/1921.

# THE OLD GUARD

## 4.1 Introduction

A significant new feature of the artistic community during this period was the presence of numerous elderly artists. The colony had been established by a group of young, up-and-coming painters, filled with enthusiasm and ambition, and had been supplemented by students from the next generation. Now these early artists had reached the end of their careers, and had less energy and enthusiasm, whilst there were also those, who had "discovered that the fame dreams of youth would never be realised, and were content to admire, where they formerly worshipped".[159] St Ives also was now being recognised as an attractive retirement location for artists. These elderly painters tended to continue to work in the style that had first brought them renown, and to have little interest in new ideas or techniques. For a young student in the early 1920s, such as Averil Mackenzie-Grieve, the colony could be disappointing. "The coterie of painters in St Ives had reached a low ebb. The young Bohemians who had settled years before in the fascinating little port, using the net lofts above the quays and shores as studios, had grown old and academic, content to turn out competent paintings year after year, each in his own genre. A bare half-dozen could rely on what one might call sure seats in the Royal Academy and other established galleries in London."[160] Whilst these artists were clearly no longer at the forefront of artistic developments, it is not necessarily fair to dismiss their work out of hand or to categorise them as arch-reactionaries, who stifled the development of younger artists in the colony.

## 4.2 Moffat Lindner

During the War years, Moffat Lindner (1852-1949), who was blessed with substantial private means, devoted his attention primarily to fund-raising for a variety of causes and to helping those less fortunate than himself. Apart from his natural philanthropic nature, Lindner was keenly aware that his father was German and wanted to demonstrate his commitment to Britain's cause. As President of the Arts Club in each of the years 1911-1917, except for 1913 when Arthur Meade took over for the year, he was clearly regarded as the figurehead of the colony during these difficult times.

In December 1925, Lindner gave a talk at the Arts Club, looking back over his career, and this proved so popular that he was asked to repeat it on at least two other occasions. His notes for the talk have survived and make fascinating reading. In particular, he indicated that he was not in favour of *plein air* sketching as he felt that, with the constant changeability of sky and water effects, such work could never be "real, true and perfect". Instead, he made quick notes on the spot, using brush and colour, rather than pencil or charcoal, and noting the different tones and colours. "Then I just sit there until the effect is gone, letting it soak into my mind and making mental notes...I can remember effects like these years afterwards if I refer to my notes."[161] Accordingly, sketches made previously of the River Maas at Dordrecht, the estuary at Etaples, the waterways of Amsterdam and the canals of Venice were drawn upon many times by Lindner in his later years. A new subject was Riga, where Gussie Lindner's sister, Isabel, was living with her secret agent husband, 'Toby' Farina.[162] Whilst Lindner did occasionally paint St Ives and other Cornish subjects, they are surprisingly rare. He repeated his very Whistlerian vision of St Ives at night under the light of the moon a number of times, but works such as *A Wild Night, St Ives* (first exhibited at the ROI in 1921) and *Sleeping Waters, St Ives Bay* (Paris 1929) are by no means his best and proved difficult to sell.

Lindner continued to paint both in oils and watercolour and was equally adept in each media. Whatever he painted, he sought out its "essence or truth" and rejected detail. Accordingly, he developed a loose, fluid impressionistic style. His watercolours were particularly distinctive for thier "brilliant directness of handling, ..dainty charm of colour and..luminous freshness of tone quality".[163] In a talk to STISA on

---

159 Adapted from A.G.Folliott-Stokes, *A Moorland Princess*, London, 1904 at p.131.

160 Averil Mackenzie-Grieve, *Time and Chance*, London, 1970 at p.37.

161 Lecture Notes - Lindner family archive.

162 Toby Farina is probably the same person as Raffael Farina, the son of Baroness Farina and the half-brother of the artist, Stuart Hobkirk. Certainly, Nik Halliday, Lindner's grandson, understood that Toby had studied at the Camborne School of Mines, whilst that School only has a record of a R.Farina, who was there in 1897-8. After the War, he took a job with the Secret Service and was posted to Riga. Family folklore indicates that he handled the infamous Zinovief letter, purporting to reveal Soviet plans to infiltrate the Labour Party, which, when leaked to the *Daily Mail*, brought down the Labour Government of the day. For further details of Baroness Farina, see David Tovey, *St Ives (1860-1930). - The Artists and the Community - A Social History*, Tewkesbury, 2009.

163 *The Studio*, Vol 60, 1913, p.141.

watercolour painting, he observed that the charm of the medium was in "its transparency, its purity and its luminosity...A good watercolour has the air of being done easily and rapidly but is the result of much concentration, observation and training of the memory".[164]

Lindner painstakingly kept ledgers of the work that he exhibited and sold.[165] The exhibition ledger reveals the sheer volume of work that he continued to produce, even into his seventies, and the range of Galleries and Societies who invited him to exhibit, whilst the sales ledger (see Table A) signifies how successful he was, not only in sales to private individuals, but also to public Art Galleries at home and abroad. Indeed, these ledgers reveal that, far from being past it, here was an artist of worldwide renown at the height of his popularity.

Lindner's reputation was clearly significantly enhanced by the success of his exhibition at the Fine Art Society in 1913, entitled *Waterways of Venice and Holland*. This, on its own, produced sale receipts of £231-11s. During the War, Lindner still managed to send over twenty works to various exhibitions around the country each year, and, in 1914, had work included in exhibitions in Winnipeg and Cape Town. During the period 1914-18, when most artists were struggling to sell anything, he sold four oils and no fewer than forty-three watercolours. His biggest success was *In Dutch Waters* (Fig. 4.2), which was illustrated as a Picture of the Year in 1915, and was sold for £150 to Albert Ernest Kitson, 2nd Baron Airdale. A notable local patron was Mrs Hellyer (see pages 38-9 above), who acquired the oil *The Giudecca, Venice* (£20) and the watercolours *Evening Glow, Venice* and *The Salute, Venice* (£40 the pair) in 1917, and a further watercolour, *Dutch Boats* (£12-12) in 1919.

Fig. 4.1   Moffat Lindner   *Sunset, Dordrecht*                               (Ferens Art Gallery, Hull)

---

164 Notes of Talk - Lindner family archive.
165 Other Cornish titles, with the location and date of their first showing, include *Moonrise, St Ives Bay* (Bristol 1916), *Roseworthy Valley, Kynance Cove* and *Cornish Cliffs, Kynance* (all RWS 1918), *Church Cove, Cornwall* (RWS 1919), *St Ives Fishing Fleet - Moonrise* (Pittsburgh 1921), *The Coast of Cornwall* (RWS - Japan 1921), *Sunset, St Ives* (RWS 1921), *Lion Rock, Kynance* (Newcastle 1921), *The Moonlit Bay, St Ives* (Newcastle 1922), *Moonlight, St Ives Harbour* (Newcastle 1923) and *French Crabbers off St Ives* (RWS 1930).

Fig. 4.2  Moffat Lindner    *In Dutch Waters*

TABLE A                SALES FIGURES FROM MOFFAT LINDNER'S SALES LEDGER

| YEAR | OIL SALES No | Proceeds | W/C SALES No | Proceeds | TOTAL SALES | YEAR | OIL SALES No | Proceeds | W/C SALES No | Proceeds | TOTAL SALES |
|---|---|---|---|---|---|---|---|---|---|---|---|
| 1919 | 5 | £190-12s | 29 | £260-12s | £451-4s | 1925 | 2 | £55 | 13 | £110 | £165 |
| 1920 | - | - | 15 | £126-17s | £126-17s | 1926 | 2 | £110 | 13 | £172-2s | £282-2s |
| 1921 | - | - | 12 | £109-7s | £109-7s | 1927 | 6 | £175 | 9 | £93-7s | £268-7s |
| 1922 | 2 | £40 | 30 | £303-15s | £343-15s | 1928 | 2 | £92 | 12 | £123-11s | £215-11s |
| 1923 | 1 | £50 | 17 | £213-1s | £263-1s | 1929 | 3 | £155-10s | 6 | £40-19 | £195-19s |
| 1924 | 2 | £115 | 16 | £173-18 | £288-18s | 1930 | 1 | £75 | 8 | £110-18 | £185-18s |

Having struggled to get his work hung at the Royal Academy prior to 1906, Lindner was now a regular contributor and, during this period, repeatedly had two or three works hung each year.  He did not, though, have another work illustrated as a Picture of the Year.  He also resumed exhibiting at the Carnegie International Exhibition in Pittsburgh, where he had enjoyed success before the War, having five works hung there in the years 1920-2, before the change of Curator there led to a new direction.  After the War, Lindner more than doubled his output, often sending over fifty works to a wide variety of exhibitions each year.  For instance, in 1919, he sent three works to the Royal Academy, twelve to the RWS exhibitions, four to the Ridley Art Club, three to each of the RBC, the ROI, the Fine Art Society, Hull, Liverpool, and Cardiff, and two to each of Aberdeen, Huddersfield and Bristol.  Other regular exhibition venues were Nottingham, Derby, Doncaster, Oldham, Stoke-on-Trent, Ipswich, Southport, the Grafton Galleries, Hampstead Art Gallery, Falmouth, Newlyn and, of course, Lanham's in St Ives.  The Laing Art Gallery at Newcastle-upon-Tyne, having accepted seven of his works in 1921, put on, the following year, a dedicated show of twenty-two works, of which six were oils.  He was also invited to exhibit at a number of exhibitions abroad.  In 1921, he took part in the Japanese exhibition organised by the RWS and sold from it for £22-10s an important work, *The Coast of Cornwall*.  In 1923, he sold all three of the watercolours that he submitted to the Milan International Exhibition, and sent further work there in 1925.  That year, he also sent works to shows in Dunedin, where he sold both exhibits, Sydney and Jamaica, and, in 1927, to Adelaide, where again he made a sale.  Towards the end of the decade, he liaised with the New Zealand dealer, Murray Fuller, and sent six works out there in 1928, nine in 1929 and three in 1930, and Fuller was able to secure several sales.  In 1928 and 1929, he decided to submit work again to the Paris Salon, whilst, in 1930, he exhibited works in Colombo, Ceylon and Buenos Aires, and, in 1932, in Bombay and Jamaica.  Accordingly, Lindner's paintings were seen and appreciated by a worldwide audience.

# SEA CHANGE : FINE AND DECORATIVE ART IN ST IVES 1914-1930

Fig. 4.3  Moffat Lindner  *Golden Afternoon, Dordrecht*
(Doncaster Museum Service, Doncaster Metropolitan Borough Council)

Fig. 4.4  Moffat Lindner  *The Storm Cloud, Etaples*  (Grundy Art Gallery, Blackpool)

Sales also improved markedly in the years immediately after the War. 1919 proved the best year, for he sold five oil paintings for the total sum of £190-12s, including one of his Royal Academy exhibits, *Sunset, Dordrecht* (Fig. 4.1), to the Ferens Art Gallery, Hull for £100, and no fewer than twenty-nine watercolours for the total sum of £260-12s. When exhibited on Show Day that year, Hull's painting was felt to show "his keen observation of sky and cloud effects".[166] Lindner had another good year in 1922, when he sold thirty watercolours and two oils to bring in £343-15s. Then, despite demand dropping off from individuals in England due to the economic conditions, he found his work in demand from Art Galleries. In 1924, he sold *Golden Afternoon, Dordrecht* (Fig. 4.3) to Doncaster Art Gallery for £35. This painting had originally been shown at the Royal Academy in 1921, and a reviewer of the exhibition commented, "Lagoon subjects continue to claim Mr Moffat Lindner. His *Golden Afternoon, Dordrecht* shows the Dutch town dimly through the misty atmosphere, and the murky sun setting above. In the foreground of smooth, oily water a touch of strong colour is provided by a couple of barges huddled together. The feeling is, as usual, Turner-esque, but it carries an individual message."[167] Doncaster appear to have acquired the painting at a knock-down price, as it had been exhibited at Pittsburgh and a number of Galleries around the country with a price of £60.[168] Like Hull's work, this now needs a clean, as does Cheltenham Art Gallery's *Golden Autumn* (ROI 1920, Pittsburgh 1921, Newcastle 1922), which was acquired for the discounted price of £25 from the exhibition that the St Ives artists held there in 1925 - an exhibition which Lindner had played a leading role in organising, as he had a brother who lived in the town.[169] Accordingly, one of the few publicly owned works by Lindner from this period that still retains some of its original freshness of colour is *The Storm Cloud, Etaples* (Fig. 4.4), one of his 1929 Royal Academy exhibits, which was acquired that year by the Grundy Art Gallery, Blackpool for £73-10. It was highly regarded when it was exhibited on Show Day that year. "*The Storm Cloud, Etaples* by Moffat Lindner is undoubtedly one of the outstanding works of the Colony this year. In fact, we may say that it is the finest painting Mr Lindner has shown for many years. At first, one may feel the picture is painted in a very high key of colour, but this is of course suggested by the brilliant lighting and hilation [sic] produced by the sunlight playing on the huge and dominant thundercloud at the top of the picture, and reflected in certain dexterous touches in the low lying planes of the estuary in the foreground. Supporting this brilliantly painted sky, various fishing craft lie at anchor, and these are powerfully painted with very rich broken colour passages. The work is of the inspired order and radiates the real light of nature."[170]

Fig. 4.5  Moffat Lindner   *Venice*                                                                                    (Private Collection)

---

166 *St Ives Times*, 14/3/1919.
167 Review by F.J.Maclean in *The Western Morning News*, reproduced in *St Ives Times*, 16/5/1921.
168 Huddersfield 1921, Newcastle & Pittsburgh 1922, Cardiff, Hull & Aberdeen 1923.
169 In 1925, Lindner also sold a watercolour, *Approach to Venice*, to Northampton Art Gallery.
170 *St Ives Times*, 22/3/1929.

In 1930, the representative of the Trustees of the Mackelvie Collection, on a visit to Cornwall, bought for Auckland Art Gallery one of Lindner's finest oils, *On the Giudecca, Venice* (Fig. 4.7), for £75, as well as a watercolour *River Maas at Sundown* for £25. Lindner exhibited works entitled *The Giudecca* or *On the Giudecca* regularly throughout the 1920s, but descriptions of his 1922 Academy exhibit seem to tally with the Auckland painting.[171] Frank Maclean, Henry Moore's biographer, felt that the painting revealed "a welcome broadening in technique; the chromatic water is painted more boldly, more clearly, more decisively than in any work of his I can remember." [172]

Lindner also seems to have been very well connected, for a number of his purchasers were titled or were high-ranking officers in the forces. For instance, in the oil paintings sale ledger, Sir Edward Mountain is recorded as buying *The Gorgeous Bloom of Evening, Amsterdam* for £50 in 1923; Lady MacRobert as acquiring *Etaples Fishing Boats going to Sea* for £80 in 1924 and Lord Plunket as the purchaser of *Fishing Boats, Etaples* for £50 in 1926, whilst purchasers of watercolours included Sir Benjamin Dolman, Sir Alfred Dobbin and Lady Asheton Smith. The Read, Bodilly, Dow, Grier, Farina, Knapping, Jenner, Rule and Fowler families were amongst local purchasers.

As a result of his success, his outstanding range of contacts and his wealth, Lindner was, without doubt, the pre-eminent figure in the colony during this period. Indeed, Richard Heyworth, in his speech at the opening of the Cheltenham Exhibition in 1925, commented that, when he had been painting in St Ives shortly before the War, "Mr Lindner was then recognised 'King of St Ives', and he had never been dethroned." [173] Accordingly, when plans for the formation of a new Society were being hatched in 1926, Lindner's support was essential, and he was the only option as President. Lindner, though, used the power and influence that he had to good effect. He was not prepared just to be a figurehead, but devoted significant time to ensuring that the new Society was a success, and was pleased to offer advice and encouragement. His purchase of the freehold of the Porthmeor Studios in 1929 was a significant financial outlay at a time of considerable economic uncertainty, which resulted in this historic group of studios being saved from development, and he proved to be a benevolent landlord, not only making available studios to STISA for their exhibition gallery at reduced rentals, but encouraging the use of the studios by some of the more dynamic of the colony's residents. He also was not reactionary in his views on art, as demonstrated by his support of Frances Hodgkins. This was re-affirmed by Terrick Williams, in his address at the opening of STISA's 1930 exhibition, when he complimented Lindner on being broadminded "with a ready eye in noticing the excellence in all types of work, including the advanced".[174] Accordingly, Lindner's contribution to the colony during this period was wholly beneficial and unrivalled.

Fig. 4.6 Moffat Lindner    *Shipping on the Giudecca*    (Private Collection)

---

171 See *Western Morning News* 16/3/1922 & *St Ives Times*, 5/5/1922.
172 *St Ives Times*, 5/5/1922.
173 *Gloucestershire Echo*, reproduced in *St Ives Times*, 10/4/1925.
174 *St Ives Times*, 18/4/1930.

Fig. 4.7  Moffat Lindner   *On the Giudecca*
(Mackelvie Trust Collection, Auckland Art Gallery, Toi o Tamaki)

Fig. 4.8  Moffat Lindner   *St Mark's Basin*   (RA 1915)           (Private Collection)

In a letter to the purchaser of this work, Lindner wrote, "I chose the moment when some large ships were drying their sails in the afternoon glow of the sun off the island of San Giorgio Maggiore, Venice.  The atmosphere is soft and warm after rain.  I know Venice well and have painted it under all kinds of effects.  I trust much to memory in painting, as the finest effects only last a few moments & it is well to impress them on the mind."

Fig. 4.9  Fred Milner in Piazza Studio No 2 with a seascape,
probably *A Dangerous Corner*     (Milner family archive)

### 4.3    Fred Milner

The letters of the landscape painter, Fred Milner (c.1860-1939), a colony stalwart, to the New Zealand singer, Mrs Brumfit, whose stage name was Ethel Goode, give a useful insight into the problems faced by artists during the War years, in much the same way as the correspondence of Frances Hodgkins. They also vividly demonstrate the importance still placed by established artists on getting their work hung at the Royal Academy, and the despair engendered by rejection. Whilst the earliest surviving letter is dated in September 1913 and the latest in December 1932, evidencing a long friendship, the vast majority of the extant correspondence is from the years 1913-1916. Milner seems to have been a great fan of Ethel's voice, and she clearly had shown, at some juncture, an interest in his paintings. However, there is no specific reference to her ever having been a purchaser of anything other than the odd etching, albeit Milner was always hopeful. However, she did come down to St Ives and visit him in his studio in 1931, prompting a besotted Milner to comment, "I feel you much more in the studio than at 'Chy-an-Drea' and shall remember the pleasant times we had there." [175]

The death of Milner's mentor and close friend, Sir Alfred East, in 1913, had an immediate impact on his chances at the Royal Academy, for East had been a champion of his work when on the Hanging Committee. Accordingly, in 1914, Milner had two of his submissions rejected outright, and the other accepted but not hung. Milner described it as "a very great disappointment. I feel very sad and discouraged....I have not had such a thing occur for years." [176] One reason why Milner was especially downcast was that he clearly hoped that Ethel Brumfit might have been tempted into a purchase, for, in his next letter, he wrote, "Some of the rejections this year are extraordinary to put it mildly. I am not the only one to suffer. As I said, I am very disappointed as I should have liked to have had one of the pictures you specially liked hung." [177]

A couple of weeks later, Milner's self-esteem was rapidly replenished when he heard that his work *Picquigny on the Somme* had been accepted at the Carnegie International Exhibition at Pittsburgh. This, he confided to Ethel, was "one of the very finest exhibitions in the world & one of the hardest to get in to. I do not think the majority of pictures at the RA would have a very remote chance of being hung....So Lady Ethel you need not yet be ashamed of your friend." [178] In a subsequent letter, he then related gleefully, as confirmation of his views, that a Royal Academician, who had been a member of the Hanging Committee that year, had had both his works "chucked" by Pittsburgh.[179]

Milner spent the summer of 1914 working on endless sea studies, as he wanted to complete a large marine of waves pounding on the rocks at Clodgy. He called the work *A Dangerous Corner* and it featured a wild sea, in a strong light, dashing and swirling around the rocks (see Fig. 4.9). During June, he also linked up with an old American artist friend, George Gardner Symons, with whom he shared his

---

175 Letter to Mrs Brumfit dated 11/9/1931 - Tate Gallery Archives ('TGA') 9511.37.
176 Letter to Mrs Brumfit dated 16/4/1914 - TGA 9511.8.
177 Letter to Mrs Brumfit dated 18/4/1914 - TGA 9511.9.
178 Letter to Mrs Brumfit dated 24/4/1914 - TGA 9511.10.
179 Letter to Mrs Brumfit dated 5/7/1914 - TGA 9511.14. Milner's own record at Pittsburgh was patchy. He had works hung there in 1905, 1907, 1908 and 1914, but had a second work rejected in 1907 and was 'chucked' in 1913 and 1920.

studio and went out sketching. Buoyed by his success at Pittsburgh and by Symons' enthusiasm for his work, Milner decided, after the outbreak of War, to try his luck at the 1915 exhibition at the National Academy of Design in New York, for Symons was on the Jury. He told Ethel Brumfit, "I am afraid the arts in England for a time at any rate will be under a cloud, so one must look abroad." [180] He decided, though, that, to get inspired to paint again, he needed to leave St Ives. "My north country blood after a time feels too much the soft air of the west & makes me feel very slack." [181] Indeed, he indicated that he had become so depressed in St Ives that he dreaded each day.[182] Accordingly, he returned to a favourite haunt in the Cotswolds, 'The Old Mill' at Upper Swell. This was an area that he knew well, as he had lived in Cheltenham for most of the 1890s and continued to exhibit with the local art society. There he painted *September in the Cotswolds*, showing the headwaters of the Thames, with the banks of a pool in the foreground fringed with rushes, whilst behind rose a hill dotted with trees. It was a peaceful, still scene and was considered one of his finest works. It is not known whether he did attempt to send it to New York, as he was worried about finishing it in time, but it was not hung there in any event. It was accepted, however, by the Royal Academy in 1915. When shown in the exhibition put on by the St Ives artists in Cheltenham in 1925, the local paper felt that it ought to be bought for the town's public gallery, but this did not happen and its current whereabouts are unknown.[183]

Milner's second success at the Royal Academy in 1915 was *The Valley* (Fig. 4.11), and this was illustrated as a Picture of the Year. It was painted in the Vale of Lanherne, near Newquay, and was again a tranquil scene, with trees by the side of a river, in a deep valley, lit up in the late afternoon sun. However, Milner was still not satisfied, as *A Dangerous Corner* and a work called *The Pool* had been "chucked". The latter work had been rejected the year before as well, and Milner commented, "My best picture *The Pool* is out again. I will send it till they do have it, because I know it is one of my best." [184] He had exhibited this originally on Show Day in 1913, when it had been hailed as his finest work yet. "It is a pastoral from the Cotswolds, painted with a wonderful transparency and a fine sense of colour harmonies." [185]

Fig. 4.10  Fred Milner  *The Hayle Estuary*  (Woolley and Wallis)

---

180 Letter to Mrs Brumfit dated 27/9/1914 - TGA 9511.19.
181 Letter to Mrs Brumfit dated 31/8/1914 - TGA 9511.18.
182 Letter to Mrs Brumfit dated 10/1914 - TGA 9511.20.
183 Cheltenham Art Gallery do have three works by Milner, but all are mediocre.
184 Undated letter to Mrs Brumfit, but clearly sent during April 1915 - TGA 9511.26.
185 *St Ives Times*, 28/3/1913.

Fig. 4.11  Fred Milner  *The Valley*  (Sunderland Museum and Art Gallery)

Fig. 4.12  Fred Milner  *In the Heart of the Cotswolds*  (Sunderland Museum and Art Gallery)

# THE OLD GUARD

Back in St Ives, Milner was already finding it difficult to motivate himself to work, when the sketching ban was imposed in February 1915. Drill work for the St Ives Volunteer Training Corps provided some diversion, but, that June, he commented, "I am sorry to say I cannot settle down to work. I want to get out to nature - here we are so limited at present. The regulations are so stringent. One gets after a time stale with studio work and want fresh inspiration." [186] Eventually, in August, he decided to return to the Cotswolds, but, as 'The Old Mill' had been sold, he was forced to stay in Stow-on-the-Wold. Nevertheless, he still returned to Upper Swell to paint, and recounted his daily routine to Ethel Brumfit. "I am down at Swell all day...I go immediately after breakfast, taking my lunch (all my painting materials are in the empty cottage which used to be my sitting room) & I do not get back until dark for dinner - nearly eleven hours in the open air. In the middle of the day, after my sandwiches and water (no beer or anything to be got), I lay down for an hour and have a rest. After work in the evening, I have a try at the trout, but have not had very good sport." [187] Some six weeks later, the result was "one big picture - would normally be two - but what's the use. Rest quite small", but at least he felt that they were "an advance on what I have done before". [188] He showed two Cotswolds scenes on Show Day in 1916, *St Luke's Summer*, which featured a well rendered simmering haze, and *Early Autumn*. The latter was described as "a bright, vibrating sunny landscape...; a glorious warm, sunlit sky and the earth beaming with joy under its golden kiss. It is a real song of life." [189] However, to his chagrin, neither was accepted by the Academy in 1916, and all his works were rejected from the 1917 show, leading him to comment, "I believe it is said to be one of the worst known & many well known painters treated very badly." [190]

After this, surviving correspondence with Ethel Brumfit is rare, although letters in 1924 and 1931 again find Milner raging against his fate at the hands of the Academy Hanging Committee. In 1924, he commented rather amusingly, "From an Art point of view, [I] do not care a 'hang'. On the other hand, the RA is one's big picture sale room of the year, & from a commercial point of view, one hopes for good to come out of it."[191] Having sold one of his previous year's exhibits, a view of Arundel Castle, entitled *Between Showers, Arundel*, to an American dealer, he had been hopeful of enticing him to make a further purchase. However, between 1918 and 1930, Milner did have ten works hung at the Academy, but only one of these, *The Deserted Mine* (RA 1926), was a Cornish scene. This depicted the old mine building near Knill's Monument, with a glimpse of Hayle Estuary and Towans in the background, and had won high praise from Sir Claude Phillips in *The Daily Telegraph*, when it had been shown at the Guildhall Art Gallery in 1921. "The most original landscape in the exhibition and, in many respects, the best picture is Fred Milner's spacious solemn scene of desolation, *The Old Mine*." [192] This paucity of local subjects is somewhat surprising, but Milner appears to have followed a pattern of going off in the autumn to complete, or make sketches for, his major pieces in other parts of the country. He continued to return to the Cotswolds (e.g. *A Peaceful Vale* - RA 1923), whilst other popular locations were the River Lambourne in Berkshire and the South Downs (and the towns of Rye and Lewes). However, Milner's precarious financial position, which saw him often indicating to Ethel Brumfit that he did not have enough money for the fare to London, meant that, prior to these trips, he would have to ensure that both his home, 'Zareba' on Porthminster Hill, and his vast studio, Piazza Studio No 2, were sublet during his absence.

Milner's style does not appear to have changed greatly over the years. His work was still being described as Victorian in feel in the 1930s. Quite often his landscapes seem rather dull, for he has not really conveyed to the spectator the particular thrill which caused him to raise his brush in the first place. Hills, fields and other features can often be depicted with long, uninteresting brush strokes. It tends to be in his smaller works, perhaps sketches done direct from nature, that one finds looser, broken brushwork that does reveal a true artistic touch. His marine studies can be particularly attractive, and a depiction of some gigs at low tide on Porth Kidney sands, by the side of the Hayle Estuary (Fig. 4.10), attracted considerable interest, when it appeared at auction recently.[193] The scene is merely waterlogged sand reflecting tints from the sky, but it is depicted with some bravura brushwork. Despite being conservative in his own work, Milner seems to have been well liked by the whole colony. In an Appreciation written after his death, Borlase Smart summarised Milner's characteristics as "An intense loyalty and faithfulness of purpose, hard work in the open air and in the studio, a distinguished style of painting, a charm of friendly intercourse with other artists and interest in their work, and a broad principle of encouragement to younger painters." [194] These do not appear to be the characteristics of an arch-reactionary.

---

186 Letter to Mrs Brumfit, dated 4/6/1915 - TGA 9511.31.
187 Letter to Mrs Brumfit, dated 13/9/1915 - TGA 9511.34.
188 Letter to Mrs Brumfit, dated 24/10/1915 - TGA 9511.35.
189 *St Ives Times*, 17/3/1916.
190 Letter to Mrs Brumfit, dated 7/5/1917 - Court Gallery archive.
191 See Letter to Mrs Brumfit dated 20/4/1924 - Court Gallery archive.
192 *St Ives Times*, 24/6/1921.
193 Woolley and Wallis auction dated 24/3/2010 Lot 425.
194 *St Ives Times*, 10/1939.

## 4.4 Arthur Meade

Arthur Meade (1852-1942), who lived at 'Godrevy' on Porthminster Hill and was, accordingly, Fred Milner's next-door neighbour, was also a stalwart of the landscape section in St Ives, having settled in the town in 1892. Like Milner, though, he produced the occasional marine. His studio was in Back Road West, probably what is now known as 11, Porthmeor Studios.

Because his wife, Mabel, came from Dorchester, Meade had always spent part of each year in Dorset and, as a result, often submitted Wessex scenes to the Royal Academy. Being an advocate of open air painting, it seems that the sketching ban forced him during the War years to base himself in Dorset for his principal exhibition pieces. However, he did not desert St Ives completely, and exhibited, as always, on Show Day. Indeed, he showed some local marine work, possibly done before the War, and *Perilous Seas*, depicting a storm approaching Gurnard's Head, was not only rated his best seascape yet, but also "one of the finest marine studies ever exhibited locally...It is a big work, massively conceived and carried through with a strength that gives it an air of magnificent grandeur." [195] However, it never found favour with the Hanging Committee at the Royal Academy, although another seascape *The Cornish Coast* was hung in 1918. Meade had three works hung that year, and two in 1919, of which the major work was *The Winding Road*, which showed a rutted track curving through a heather-clad moorland landscape.

Until 1920, Meade had enjoyed astonishing success at the Royal Academy, regularly having two or three, and sometimes five, works hung a year. However, between 1920 and his death in 1942, he only had six works hung, the last of which was in 1929. This was a six-footer entitled *The Wreck* (Fig. 4.14) and featured Meade's favourite subject, Porth Kidney sands at the mouth of the Hayle Estuary, upon which pools of water collected at low tide, sporting reflections of the very different weather patterns that swept across St Ives Bay. On this occasion, there had been a violent storm which had caused a barquentine to run aground on the sands. Meade depicts the storm disappearing off to the right over Godrevy, whilst, on the left, the sun breaks through. The pools of water in the foreground pick up the varying overhead conditions. Despite the date at which it was hung at the Royal Academy, there is a good chance that the painting was executed at the beginning of the decade, for a work entitled *After the Storm*, exhibited first on Show Day in 1921, sounds remarkably similar. The painting was bought by Rochdale Art Gallery in 1929, and was Meade's last major success.

Meade seems to have continued to paint with enthusiasm during the 1920s, always having a range of work on offer on Show Day. However, like Milner, he does not appear to have changed his approach or loosened his brushwork, and reviews of his work in the 1930s still refer to his Victorian Academic style.

Fig. 4.13  William Cave Day    *Low Tide, St Ives*
(St Ives Arts Club, photo Marie Keeling)

---

[195] *St Ives Weekly Summary*, 16/3/1916.

Fig. 4.14  Arthur Meade   *The Wreck* (also known as *After the Storm*)     (Touchstones Rochdale)

He also repeated tried and tested subjects. Nevertheless, the local paper noted in 1930 that he had sold three of his four exhibits at the ROI, and so he still had a following. He also remained a well-liked member of the colony, and it is interesting that Frances Hodgkins commented that she could rely on Meade to help her out if she ever got into financial difficulty.

## 4.5    Farewells

Another key figure in the landscape section prior to the War, John Noble Barlow (1861-1917), had moved to Penzance, albeit retaining a studio in St Ives, and he seems to have had less trouble with sketching restrictions in the Lamorna Valley. His landscapes were some of the highlights of Show Day in 1915 and 1916, and his painting, *Autumn Morning*, in 1915 was considered one of the most joyous and luminous paintings that he had ever produced. Therefore, his untimely death in 1917, just as he was planning to return to live in St Ives, was a shock. His widow, Elizabeth, held a memorial exhibition in his Porthmeor Studio in April 1917, and Plymouth City Art Gallery acquired the very fine *Marazion Marshes* and *A Devonshire Valley - The Dewerstone*. She also held further shows of his work in the Tregenna Hill Studio in March 1919, and in 7 Piazza Studios in May 1920. In his review of the 1919 display, Borlase Smart commented, "The outstanding attraction of Mr Barlow's work is undoubtedly his rendering of large open spaces and fine cloud effects. A subtle open air feeling pervades all his canvases; whether in sunshine or storm, wind-swept or wrapped in mist, his landscapes present themselves with convincing reality to the spectator." [196]

Barlow's death was shortly followed by those of the Scot, Thomas Millie Dow, whose family lived at 'Talland House', in July 1919, and of the 'founder' of the Arts Club, Louis Grier, in October 1920. However, both artists had not completed any new work for some time. The return of another former stalwart, the figure painter, Allan Deacon, also ended in tragedy. In January 1920, Deacon was welcomed back to St Ives, when he returned on a visit, with his old friend, William Titcomb. He decided to stay and, on Show Day that year, he exhibited at his old Virgin Street Studio a selection of new and old work, including *The Mirror*, which depicted a girl in a blue and gold dressing gown sitting in front of a mirror "braiding her masses of Titian coloured hair".[197] However, in 1921, the studio was destroyed in a serious fire, which resulted in the loss of the life of Fireman W.P.Uren. The damage to the building itself was so great that it had to be demolished and Deacon, who was away at the time, lost a large number of his works. He did not return and his death in Innsbruck was noted in July 1928 in the local paper.[198]

---

196 *St Ives Times*, 21/3/1919.
197 *St Ives Times*, 5/3/1920.
198 *St Ives Times*, 10/8/1928.

Fig. 4.15 William Fortescue
*By Hammer and Hand all Art doth Stand (The Forge)*
(Penlee House Gallery & Museum, Penzance,
on loan from Newlyn Art Gallery)
This work was included in the artist's Memorial Exhibition

Another senior artist in the colony, William Fortescue, a figure painter, who specialized in genre scenes, did not exhibit any major works on Show Day during the War, but *George and Brownie and I*, featuring his son and himself with their donkey, was one of two works hung at the Royal Academy in 1915. The other was *The Shoeing Forge*, a work which saw Fortescue return to the untidy lair of his local blacksmith at Trelyon, which had also featured in *The Village Smithy* (RA 1905). This is likely to be the work owned by Newlyn Art Gallery now called *By Hammer and Hand all Art doth Stand* (Fig. 4.15).

After the War, Fortescue seems to have suffered failing health. His last success at the Royal Academy was a painting of bees in 1919, and his last recorded exhibit outside Cornwall was *Gleaning* (possibly Fig. 4.17) in 1921. Nevertheless, *Cutting Bracken*, which was painted near Giew Mine, was well thought of on Show Day in 1920, the feeling of motion in the figure of the old man being excellently rendered. However, Fortescue died in March 1924, "after a long and painful illness", and his funeral was held at Zennor. In May that year, a memorial exhibition was held at Lanham's Gallery for two weeks, and this then moved to Plymouth City Art Gallery, where sixty works were hung, of which twenty-two were watercolours and two pastels. *Sunny September in Cornwall* (RA 1913 - £50), which depicted cattle standing in a patch of gorse on the summit of a cliff, with a wide expanse of sea, was considered the most striking work in the show, whilst *Intruders* (RA 1911 - £35), showing a hen and her chicks on a foraging expedition into a dairy, where a maid was busy with the churns, was felt to be a charming subject, well painted.[199] The exhibition also included some of the paintings of Iceland that he had done following a visit in 1913, as well as several examples of his depictions of what he termed "bits of old St Ives", both in oils and watercolour (see Fig. 4.16). There were also a number of paintings of Trelyon Downs, the area that surrounded his home, 'Trelyon Cottage', from which there were fine views over St Ives Bay.

199 *St Ives Times*, 16/5/1924.

# THE OLD GUARD

The 'Old Guard' was complemented by the arrival, in 1919, of former Bushey student, William Cave Day (1862-1924), who had first come down to St Ives during his student days in the late 1880s and early 1890s. Indeed, he exhibited *Gossips in St Ives, Cornwall* at Southport in 1893. However, he had spent the majority of his career in his native Yorkshire, based in Harrogate, and had become a member of the RBA in 1904, a Society with whom he exhibited 120 paintings. He had also exhibited at the Royal Academy, at Liverpool and Manchester. Having decided to retire to St Ives, his wife, Kathleen, who also had artistic inclinations, and himself acquired 'Hilbree', Godrevy Terrace, an impressive property, with its own studio with a northern light, which commanded extensive sea views. He also took 1, Island Studios. He exhibited on each of the Show Days from 1920 to 1924, with *Landing Fish for Auction, St Ives* being hung at the Royal Academy in 1922. When exhibited in St Ives that year, it had been described by Borlase Smart as "full of silvery light and delicate tonalities happily expressed".[200] Cave Day also took part in the exhibition held by the Cornish artists in Plymouth that year and exhibited numerous Cornish works at the RBA. However, he died in 1924. In July that year, a memorial exhibition of his work was held in Lanham's Galleries, leading Borlase Smart to comment, "The spirit of the open is reflected in every one of the choice examples on view." [201]

In February 1925, a collection of over eighty works was put together for a memorial show at Plymouth City Art Gallery. The reviewer was impressed, "Plymouth exhibitions have not been favoured with samples from his studio until now, which is to be regretted, because rarely has work of a better quality reached Plymouth from the St Ives and Newlyn schools of painting. While adopting the same broad principles of brushwork and lavish colour as his brother artists of the St Ives school of painting, Cave Day exercised very considerable restraint and extreme skill." [202] There were four major oils in the show, demonstrating the variety in his output - *Woodland Song* (£200), which had been painted near Branscombe, *The Fish Sale, St Ives* (£150), a scene on the slipway, which had won praise for his depiction of movement in the crowd, when exhibited on Show Day in 1922, *Au Revoir* (£100), a three-quarter-length study of a lady, which had been hailed as a charming subject, when exhibited on Show Day in 1921, and the fanciful *The Captive* (£100), featuring a fiddler in red and gambolling lambs (Show Day 1923). However, the reviewer was particularly taken by *Reared with Care* (£20), which depicted an old man with a long white beard and rough workaday clothes, feeding a little wren in a Cornish cottage interior. "The disposition of light and shade is masterful, and the modelling as near perfection as possible." [203] Although Cave Day's work does not appear to have been acquired by any public collections, he is represented by a pleasant small work at the St Ives Arts Club (Fig. 4.13). His widow, Kathleen, remained in the town until her death in 1953. She was a popular figure at the Arts Club, and became a member of STISA, whilst their son, George Cave Day, also became a stalwart of the Arts Club, being elected President in 1948.

Figs. 4.16 & 4.17 William Fortescue

Left :   *In front of the Sloop Inn*

Right :   *The Gleaner*

(both Newlyn School Gallery, Penzance)

---

200 *Western Morning News*, 16/3/1922.
201 *St Ives Times*, 18/7/1924.
202 *St Ives Times*, 6/2/1925.
203 ibid.

Fig. 4.18 Frances Tysoe Smith  *St Ives Harbour*  (Private Collection)

Edmund Fuller, one of the leading marine painters in the colony in the pre-War period, produced very few new paintings, his last exhibit at the Royal Academy being *Sea-Breezes* in 1916. During the War, he did munitions work in another part of the country and, on his return, devoted his time to a history of Union Castle Line ships during wartime, a commission that Greville Matheson, that shipping company's former publicity officer presumably entrusted to him. However, this does not appear to have come to fruition. He also designed Matheson's new library at 'Boskerris Vean', Carbis Bay and amused himself producing bookplates for Matheson and other friends. Following the death of his wife, Emma, in 1923, and his sister, Clara, in 1925, Fuller decided to leave St Ives for Portishead, where he was based until his death in 1940. One final boost was the sale in March 1925 to Plymouth City Art Gallery of his large painting, *A Last Hope* (RA 1911).

Another loss that the colony suffered was the death of Frances Tysoe Smith in 1927. She was a landscape and flower painter, who first exhibited her work in 1891 and who had been involved with the colony intermittently since 1907. However, from 1920, she had become a regular participant in Show Day, albeit using a variety of studios. She died of pneumonia in January 1927, whilst on a visit to relations in Llandrindod Wells, and, accordingly, her one success at the Royal Academy that year was posthumous.

## 4.6     Other elderly painters

Other elderly artists included Alfred Hartley, whose considerable success as a printmaker is discussed in Chapter 7.2, John Bromley and Arthur White, who both continued to produce watercolours of the harbour and other local scenes, Lowell Dyer, who occasionally exhibited some of his paintings of angels, and Jack Titcomb, who always showed more aptitude for organising social activities. Nora Hartley, Alfred's wife, was only an occasional exhibitor at the Royal Academy, but her works *Sister Susie*, featuring a woman knitting, and *A Fisherman's Child* were hung there in 1916 and 1917 respectively, the latter work later being exhibited at the Paris Salon. The miniature portraitist, Mabel Douglas, had regular success at the Royal Academy during the decade to 1920 and her wartime portraits included Lilian Lanyon (1916) and Doris Barry (1917). Her husband, John, best known for his photographs, seems to have devoted himself more towards his art in the 1920s, and, in fact, was the first artist to sell a work from STISA's new Porthmeor Gallery in 1928. He, though, was well aware of the decline in standards in the colony, telling the visiting American, Wilson Henry Irvine, that he should have come twenty years previously, when the colony boasted the best artists in both Britain and America.

# LEADING LIGHTS IN THE TWENTIES

## 5.1 All Change

Whilst the presence in the colony, during the War years, of a number of displaced artists had resulted in the production of much interesting and innovative work, the end of the War, unsurprisingly, led to a mass exodus, as a number of artists had stayed on in the town purely because of the hostilities. The foreign artists were some of the first to leave. The Belgian refugees, Emile Fabry and Louis Reckelbus, naturally returned home in 1919; Frank Ver Beck and Hanna Rion split up, with Frank going back to America and Hanna going to Bermuda, whilst Frances Hodgkins felt, in 1920, that she must move on. The loss of such a vibrant talent as Hodgkins was compounded by the departure of most of the young English artists, who had been enlivening the colony. Having deserted his wife and young family in 1921, Claude Francis Barry worked, principally as a printmaker, in various parts of Continental Europe during the whole of the inter-War period, whilst Louis Sargent, who also ceased to be involved in the local scene after 1921, spent much of his time in Southern France for health reasons. Meanwhile, Marcella Smith moved up to London to live with Dorothea Sharp.

There were, however, some new arrivals. Charles and Ruth Simpson had moved across from Lamorna to St Ives in 1916, and set up a painting school in 1920, which aimed to attract young new talent. Borlase Smart, after his discharge from the Army in 1919, settled in the town and immediately made an impression not only with his art, but with his energy and enthusiasm. Having worked as an art critic before, he also published numerous reviews of local exhibitions, in an attempt to fire the enthusiasm of both artists and local patrons. One of Olsson's most highly rated students, John Park, also settled in the colony in 1923, and immediately enjoyed national and international success. All these artists tended to favour landscape and marine subjects, sketched *en plein air,* and so were following in the footsteps of the great landscape and marine painters of the pre-War years, to a certain degree, but their work, particularly in its use of heightened colour and more broken brushwork, is distinguishable. There were various other reasonably talented artists in the colony as well, and a surprising number had some success not only at the Royal Academy, but also at the Paris Salons, Those who were hung in Paris included Arthur Hayward, the siblings Percy and Marjorie Ballance, George Bradshaw, George Turland Goosey, Francis Raymond Spenlove, Alexander Akerbladh, Ernest and Esther Borough Johnson, Reginald and Hettie Tangye Reynolds, Nora Hartley, Mary McCrossan, Helen Stuart Weir, Mary Williams, Vera Bodilly, Ellen Fradgley, Leslie Hervey, and Annie Falkner. However, few went on to forge significant reputations that have endured. Although St Ives could certainly not claim to be at the forefront of British art during this period, there were some very fine paintings produced, which have proved of enduring popularity. Whilst most of the resident artists had little interest in either the move towards abstraction or the novel fascination with the naive, working unheralded in their midst was the primitive painter, Alfred Wallis, who was to prove an extraordinary inspiration to the whole British modernist movement, after his discovery by Ben Nicholson and Christopher Wood in 1928 (see Chapter 9).

## 5.2 Charles Simpson

In no other period of the history of the St Ives Art Colony can it be said that one artist completely dominated the local scene but, in the years 1916 to 1924, Charles Walter Simpson (1885-1971) was far and away the most pre-eminent artist in the colony, and his departure in 1924 left a void that was difficult to fill.

Born in Camberley in Surrey, Simpson was the son of an Army Major General, who became Colonel of the Lincolnshire Regiment, but his own desire to follow his father into the Army was thwarted by a fall from the family pony, which affected his hearing. As his father was also called Charles, he was known in his own family as Walter, but, in the art world, he presented himself as Charles Simpson. His interest in art, and, in particular, the depiction of animals, came from frequent visits to his grandparents' house, Pickhurst Manor, in Kent. Indeed, as a result of the frequent moves associated with Army life, Pickhurst Manor seemed to Charles 'home'. Largely self taught as an artist, he spent a brief session in 1904 at the School at Bushey, just after it had been taken over by the distinguished animal painter, Lucy Kemp-Welch, and first came down to St Ives in the autumn of 1905, as he was a great admirer of the work of John Arnesby Brown. He also took lessons from John Noble Barlow. He then began to fraternise with the artists in Newlyn and, in 1913, married Ruth Alison, a student from the Forbes School.

During his time in St Ives, Simpson produced a succession of very fine canvases showing great variety in styles and subject matter. After a period during which artists had started to drift back to studio work, Simpson was a firm believer in *plein air* painting, and he was regularly seen transporting, in his motorcycle side-car, huge canvases around West Penwith, and then attacking them on the moors and cliffs, "even in the roughest and dirtiest weather".[204] Borlase Smart, another fervent believer in open-air painting, commented, in respect of Simpson's first show at Lanham's Galleries in September 1919, "It reflects great credit on an artist who can paint his subjects on the spot and finish them so, without the almost inevitable 'touching up' in the studio, which is the bane of many an otherwise good artist's work. Mr Simpson RI, RBA, is such a one, a *plein air* painter, who never lets a single inspiration run to seed. From first to last his touch is at one with his subject, and is fresh, full of pure colour and searching after tone."[205] His handling of the problems of light was very personal, and he seemed particularly interested in the exceedingly difficult task of painting *contra jour*. One critic felt that his works reflected "a deeper-seated sense of beauty, and exultation is positively wrought into the texture of the paint with which he sets on record some evanescent magical glamour of sun and air that only the quick eye of the artist could catch".[206] An intelligent and well educated man, Simpson also wrote well about his very varied interests, often using musical analogies when discussing his paintings and revealing a keen interest in Japanese art.

An indefatigible worker, Simpson produced an extraordinary number of paintings, and was equally adept in oils, gouache, tempera and watercolour. He was also prepared to experiment, using gold leaf in one sunset picture.[207] Whilst his major works were oils on canvas of significant proportions, he made great use of tempera, as it suited him best when he wanted to work quickly; and he was renowned for painting at high speed - "like quicksilver". Borlase Smart described his work as "big in style and full of fresh interpretation".[208] His subject matter was more varied than any other major Cornish artist, evidencing an astonishing array of skills and superb technique, and yet it may well be this factor, which has led to him not getting the recognition that he deserves, for his work is impossible to categorise. He is, at one and the same time, one of Britain's leading bird painters, a fine depicter of farm animals, an equestrian artist, who also covers racing, hunting and rodeo scenes, an accomplished landscape painter, with or without animals, a marine artist, a figure painter, and a magnificent historian of numerous aspects of the fishing seasons.[209] An exhibition of his work in Plymouth in 1920 was hailed as "one of the most striking collections of modern work ever shown in a provincial gallery".[210] In summary, he is one of the true greats of Cornish art.

---

204 *St Ives Times*, 16/4/1920.
205 *St Ives Times*, 5/9/1919.
206 *Striking Pictures at Leicester Art Galleries, St Ives Times* 2/6/1922.
207 ibid.
208 *St Ives Times*, 23/5/1919.
209 He also produced several decorative screens, showing Japanese influence, featuring ducks and seagulls - see *St Ives Times*, 17/3/1922.
210 *Western Daily Mercury*, August 1920.

Figs. 5.1 - 5.4

Charles Simpson    Wild Bird Series

Page 92    *Puffins*

Page 93

Top :      *Herring Gulls Nesting*

Middle :   *Gannet rising after a dive*

Bottom :   *Moorhen*

           (All Private Collection)

## 5.2.1 Charles Simpson's Wild Bird Series

After the birth of their daughter, Leonora, in 1914, the Simpsons settled at 'Little Gonwin', a small farm of seven acres, near Carbis Bay. This was a short walk from the entrance to the Hayle Estuary and the Lelant salt marshes, which were a haven for birds, and Simpson, a keen naturalist, spent many hours watching and painting the wide variety of birds that could be seen there. When War broke out, Simpson made repeated attempts to enlist, but was always rejected due to his ear injury. After a fire at 'Little Gonwin', he moved across to Lamorna briefly, where he was forced to sell two hundred paintings from his studio for a mere £100. In 1916, though, he decided that St Ives held better prospects, and Ruth, Leonora and he settled at 'Loyalty Cottage', The Meadow.

During his time at 'Little Gonwin' and on his return to St Ives, Simpson continued work on a massive project - his Wild Bird Series - which he had begun with the painting of a Great Black-backed Gull in 1910. Taking advantage of the spring migration over the north-west coast of Cornwall, he was able to note the habits and flight patterns of the many thousands of birds that passed overhead on an hourly basis. With his field glasses always to hand, he was constantly observing the traits of the different species, and he did this not only on the cliffs and moors, but also from his studio, from which he could see gulls in the harbour and birds flying across the Bay. A visitor to his studio also recorded that, in one corner, there was "a kind of bird mortuary, where hang all kinds of stuffed birds. These are used to learn the formation and colouring of their feathers." [211] Accordingly, by way of example, Simpson's anatomical knowledge of the gannet (see Fig. 5.3) led him to conclude, "The smoothness of the feathering accounts for the brilliant white of their plumage, whiter in degree than any other bird, and the way it reflects the prismatic colour of the sun's rays and the blues and greens of the water." [212] However, Simpson was rarely interested in painting all the intricate detail of birds' feathers, for, as he commented, "The plumage of a bird cannot be seen in detail in certain lights, its colour is as much subject to modification according to the conditions under which it is seen as that of any other object made visible by light. The fault of many draughtsmen of birds is that they put in detail from knowledge, afraid to leave a feather out, with the eye of the ornithologist upon them...The painter must have the naturalist's knowledge, but he must have an equal facility for forgetting it. The sun will make this easy for him." [213] He also was of the view that "No laboured detail can give the light poise and swift energy of a flying bird." Instead, "the secret of suggesting flight lies in the contrast between sharp definition and the beauty of detail lost." [214] In this way, Simpson was able to capture birds' movement in a far more convincing way than most bird painters. He also used flight patterns to provide a rhythm that he could incorporate into a decorative composition.

Fig. 5.5   Charles Simpson   *Long-Tailed Duck*   (Wild Bird series)

---

211 Vera Hemmens, *A Cornish Chelsea, The Daily Graphic*, reproduced in *St Ives Times*, 8/1923.
212 Charles Simpson, *Wild Birds in Art*, *St Ives Times*, 5/11/1920 & *Animal and Bird Painting*, London, 1939, at p.117.
213 Charles Simpson, *Animal and Bird Painting*, London, 1939, at p.103.
214 Charles Simpson, *Wild Birds in Art*, *St Ives Times*, 12/11/1920.

Fig. 5.6  Charles Simpson     *Gulls over a Breakwater*     (Private Collection)

Invariably executed on the spot, his Wild Bird works are fresh and vigorous and, whether using oils or gouache or a combination of both, boldly painted. Eventually comprising some eighty paintings, capturing both the birds normally seen on the moors and cliffs of West Penwith, and some spring migrants, this series was exhibited in 1920 both at the Laing Art Gallery, Newcastle, and at Plymouth City Art Gallery.[215] Unsurprisingly, not all the works in the series are flawless, but it a great shame that the poorer ones, which constantly reappear at auctions, have reduced interest in the series as a whole, for works such as *Moorhen, Long-Tailed Duck, Herring Gulls Nesting, Gannet Rising After A Dive, Puffins* (Figs. 5.1 - 5.5) and many more are superb examples of bird painting. They are also diverse and attractive subjects, for Simpson depicted the birds in perfect relation to their natural surroundings. He commented, "Wild birds should be painted as an impressionist treats a landscape, painted in their surroundings of space and light." [216] Accordingly, his ducks and moorhen hide in reed beds or swim on marshy pools, glinting in the sunlight, his predators patrol wind-swept moorland, whilst his sea-birds fly over turbulent waters, sit on colourful sea-weed strewn rocks or perch on precarious ledges on steep-sided cliffs. When a selection was shown at the Mayflower Tercentenary Exhibition in Plymouth, a critic singled out *Mallards - Twilight* as "one of the best things Mr Simpson has ever produced. Here again there is a strange note of elegy. A decorative conception of a supremely high order is united to the simple dignified sentiment".[217] Simpson clearly hoped that the paintings would be used for a book, but this never came to pass.

### 5.2.2  Charles Simpson's seagulls

During his time in Newlyn, Simpson developed a particular interest in depicting the vast numbers of seagulls that were an ever present feature of a fishing port. He managed to persuade his friend, Charles Vulliamy, who was studying half-heartedly at the Forbes School, whilst exploring the local antiquities, to bring "a bucket full of sloshy dog-fish offal, pink and oily with bluish membranes, down to the harbour; to keep those awful birds wheeling in the air or scuffling on the water while Simpson painted them". However, Vulliamy was impressed by the results. "Simpson portrayed these gulls in yelling multitudes, as large as life. He painted them with tremendous ability, so that you were deafened and excited as you looked at the pictures." [218]

---

215 He published a pamphlet to go with the exhibitions, in which he not only talked knowledgeably of habits, habitat, flight patterns and anatomy, but also spoke of his admiration for the manner in which Japanese artists captured the vitality of birds, in contrast to Western artists, who too often portrayed them dead, as objects of still life.

216 Charles Simpson, *Animal and Bird Painting*, London, 1939, at p.105.

217 *Western Daily Mercury*, reproduced in *St Ives Times*, 20/8/1920.

218 C.E.Vulliamy, *Calico Pie*, London, 1940 at p.121.

Fig. 5.7   Charles Simpson         *The Sand Pool - Low Tide, St Ives*
(Newlyn School Gallery, Penzance)

With the seagull population of St Ives being equally vast, Simpson continued to be attracted to capturing the play of light over the noisy, quarrelsome throng, as they followed the fleet or fought over fish scraps. He commented that, amongst a concourse of hoverings birds in harbour, "every resource of their structure for balance, control of speed and direction is manifest in the evolutions of their flight". Accordingly, they could "be painted with every possible variation of wing spread and poise, all so harmonious in design and contributing so perfectly to the general action that no incidental turn or twist of a wing, no fan-like spread of a tail is out of place." [219] In working out a composition, Simpson felt that, "Seagulls wheeling and circling overhead present a series of curves which can be made the basis of a design built up of circular forms, having both two-dimensional and three-dimensional value, the latter in their suggestion of the recession of planes; but with hovering gulls, the fan shape predominates, and the angles sharply opposed must form the design, sometimes after the manner of a Futurist painting." [220]

Simpson also depicted herring gulls foraging at the tide line, as in *The Breakwater* (RA 1921, Paris 1925), or in the pools of water left by the receding tide (see Fig. 5.7). The contrast between the white undersides of their wings and the black and grey of their upper surface also afforded design possibilities. "Beautiful design can be obtained from the merging of the grey tone with the colour of the water, brilliant whites and the black, white-spotted tips of the primaries being sharply defined, whilst the dove-grey forms an undertone that softens and blurs the outlines. In sunlight against blue water the shadow of one wing cast on another gives a double value to this grey, tones darker and lighter than the water below, but always it plays its part as a subdued harmony moving with subtle progressions among accents of brilliant contrast." [221]

Simpson also painted gulls in their nests, commenting, "A canvas can be taken down the cliffside and the nesting gulls painted as easily as ducks might be sketched in the farmyard. Not only gulls but most seabirds can be studied at close quarters, once the easel is set up and there is no sudden movement to disturb them." [222] In addition to several works featuring seabirds in their precipitously-situated nests in the Wild Bird series, Simpson also completed a major oil painting, *Seagulls Nesting* (RA 1923, Paris 1924) (Fig. 5.8). This contained "daring stabs of pure colour", and was clearly a favourite of the artist, as he asked, in his book on Animal Painting, whether any landscape setting could be finer than this

219 Charles Simpson, *Animal and Bird Painting*, London, 1939, at p.114.
220 ibid, at p.114/5.
221 ibid, at p.116.
222 ibid, at p.106.

spring scene on the cliffs between Hell's Mouth and Godrevy, "where the white campion grows on a slope of Cornish cliff, where sea pinks and bluebells and heather mingle as far as the last precipitous ledge of rock, but twenty feet above the sea, gulls hover and swoop above half-hidden nests. The smooth blue of the sea is given kaleidoscopic change and glitter by sudden flashes of white, by black-banded, dove-grey wings, by heads thrust forward in the balance of a momentary poise, by the metier-like sweep of a descending flight and the wing-spread of an upward rise - scores of gulls like great white butterflies, hovering, uncertain, tentative, almost alighting, then whirling away." He went on to describe clusters of blotched brown eggs lying in shallow nests hollowed out of the reddish soil, the green tangle of the campions and the fronds of young ferns, and bluebells drooping off the very edge of the cliffs. "And all the scene is over-shot with blue, reflected from a sky that pulsates and quivers, leading the eye to constantly ascending heights where vision becomes confused and colour lost in space. Broad shadows from the promontories of the cliff tumble over this prismatic carpet of bluebell and heather, shining rock and rusty soil, like avalanches of darkness; but the shadows glow with a sombre blue, and flash with white as a gull rises from them into the sunlight." [223] Rarely does one find an artist being able to encapsulate in words so vividly the artistic inspiration that gave rise to a work of art - words revealing not only his naturalist's knowledge, but also his artistic eye and his love of nature's beauties. Unfortunately, the painting has not been located and a black and white image cannot do it justice.

Fig. 5.8  Charles Simpson    *Seagulls Nesting*

Another major work was *Black-blacked Gulls* (RA 1922, Wembley 1924), showing two of these large, vicious predators rising off storm-driven waves out in the Bay. Simpson commented, "The wings of a full grown 'black-back' often measure over four feet from tip to tip if extended. The head is long, and the bright yellow bill with a red spot on the lower mandible, gives a rich note of colour....It's wild cry heard on a lonely shore has a desolate and melancholy sound." [224] However, although he painted them in a number of different situations, he felt that, as here, "they are seen at their best for colour against the dull, leaden greens of a stormy sea." [225]

Fig. 5.9  Charles Simpson    *Black-backed Gulls*

---

223 Charles Simpson, *Animal and Bird Painting*, London, 1939, at p.105.
224 Charles Simpson, *Wild Birds in Art*, St Ives Times, 5/11/1920.
225 Charles Simpson, *Animal and Bird Painting*, London, 1939, at p.116.

### 5.2.3 Charles Simpson's ducks

In addition to seagulls, Simpson also made a special study of ducks. Charles Vulliamy, who considered Simpson a trifle lacking in sentiment, for eating his beautiful models frequently and with enthusiasm, was, nevertheless, also an avid admirer of Simpson's paintings of ducks, commenting that he depicted them "as no one ever painted them before" and "with a high, an unsurpassable degree of skill." [226] In the years immediately before Simpson settled in St Ives, ducks had featured regularly in his Royal Academy exhibits and, indeed, his only work hung there in 1917, *A Breeze on the Water*, was of ducks on the Lamorna Stream. Perhaps thinking that he was in danger of becoming classified as simply a painter of ducks, Simpson, during his early years in St Ives, rarely returned to this theme, but his two most successful paintings in his last years in St Ives were depictions of duck rising in alarm off the Lelant salt marshes, silhouetted against the rays of a low sun.

Simpson developed a friendship with Tom Pomeroy, the ferryman at Lelant, who had been hailed as a "native naturalist" by W.H.Hudson in his book *The Land's End - A Naturalist's Impressions in West Cornwall* (1908), and he spent many hours, sheltering out of sight under one of the railway bridges, observing flocks of duck. He commented, "When watching birds on a clear winter morning by some estuary where the mud flats glitter and shine like molten metal, it is difficult to make out the birds at all, beyond their blue silhouettes on the water and their shadowy forms, motionless or animated, dotted along the reaches of mud and sand." However, at Lelant, shelving clay banks ran out into the water, and on these spits of land, reflected in the pools surrounding them, parties of duck, particularly mallard, grouped together. "One or two stand in shallow water, preening themselves, others are swimming leisurely among the submerged weeds. The low sun casts the shadow of a drake on the ripples at its feet, a film of purple just touching the clay bank....The speculum feathers of both drakes and ducks glow with their blue and metallic black, barred with white; the olive-brown, drab and silver of their plumage tone with the ochreous reds of the clay. Wavy threads of light reflected from the moving water pulsate over birds and bank alike, as the sun plays upon the curves of the ripples. It is remarkable how these lines impart a liquid quality to every object they cover, the reflected ripples succeeding one another like the shimmer on watered silk." [227]

Fig. 5.10　Charles Simpson　　*The Flight of Wild Duck*　　(Private Collection)
(photo courtesy of John Branfield/Douglas Chome-Wilson)

---

226 C.E.Vulliamy, *Calico Pie*, London, 1940 at p.120-1.
227 Charles Simpson, *Animal and Bird Painting*, London, 1939, at p.103-4.

Fig. 5.11  Charles Simpson      *Duck Shooting : The Punt Gunner*
(Russell-Cotes Art Gallery, Bournemouth)

It was principally mallards that Simpson depicted in his huge canvases *The Flight of Wild Duck* (RA 1922) (Fig. 5.10) and *Duck Shooting : The Punt Gunner* (Paris 1924, RA 1925) (Fig. 5.11). He commented, "Mallards are very tame in a locality they are not molested", showing no fear of cattle who came to drink nearby or of their herdsmen. "They often rise at once, however, on the approach of a stranger. When disturbed by wildfowlers and shot at from land, or from the treacherous punt with its heavy long-barrelled gun mounted on the bows, they become very wild and shy. There is little resemblance about them to tame ducks as they leave the water with a rush and scud of foam, necks outstretched, and wings beating the air with short rapid strokes. The mallard is not as graceful as many wild birds, but it gives a fine impression of strength and freedom in full flight." [228]

It was this strength and freedom in flight that Simpson desired to convey in these two works, but he has given himself an even more difficult task, for he elected to depict the scenes at sunset with the duck seen *contra jour*. In *The Flight of Wild Duck*, there is a strong sense of composition, with the 'flight' running in an oval shape through the picture, before losing itself in the sedges and the curlews at rest in the foreground. No two ducks are seen in the same posture or the same light. Only one, to the far right of the canvas, has the full plumage of the male mallard clearly visible. Some are mere silhouettes without colour, others are surrounded by a glow of reflected light off the water, whilst the presence of those slower off the mark, and still in shadow, is only revealed by the odd glint of light on part of their bodies. Apart from being wonderfully well observed, with the movement of the duck captured perfectly, the painting is a superb decoration. It won a silver medal at the Paris Salon in 1923, when it was hailed as "une émouvante symphonie naturiste" by the *Revue du Vrai et de Beau*, and was sold at the 1924 Wembley Exhibition.[229]

*Duck Shooting : The Punt Gunner* was a similar sunset scene, with the sunlight even more dazzling. The mallard have been disturbed by the firing of the large punt gun, but the sportsman, in his punt, is almost as invisible to the spectator, as he was to the duck, being hidden amongst the rushes of the boldly painted marshland. A puff of smoke from the firing of the gun is all that reveals his position, whilst his success is shown by the highest duck plunging towards the ground. Aiming at a much more decorative effect than in *The Flight of Wild Duck*, Simpson has included more often the distinctive

---

228 Charles Simpson, *Wild Birds in Art*, St Ives Times, 12/11/1920.
229 Quoted in John Branfield, *Charles Simpson - Painter of Animals & Birds, Coastline and Moorland*, Bristol, 2005 at p.65.

colouring of the mallards' heads and speculum feathers. The painting was also well received in Paris, winning a gold medal at the exhibition of sporting pictures held in conjunction with the Olympic Games in 1924.[230] It is a huge picture (78" x 89"), in a fine frame (89" x 100"), and, sadly, will not fit into Penlee House Gallery and Museum, Penzance. His 1926 Royal Academy exhibit, *Sunrise - The Birds flutter in their marshes*, was a similar subject, albeit capturing the scene at sunrise rather than sunset.[231]

This rare combination of acute observation of birds in the wild, first-hand anatomical knowledge, keen interest in the effects of direct and reflected light on colour and tone, awareness of decorative impulses, considerable technical skill and the ability to work at high speed made Simpson a very individual painter of birds. He was later described by his friend, Guy Paget, as one of Britain's foremost bird painters, an accolade that is not misplaced, and yet his work in this field is much neglected. Whether or not one has an interest in ornithology, these paintings are art of the highest order.

### 5.2.4 Charles Simpson's landscapes and marines

Simpson was also a master of landscape painting, whether or not including animals, and his first major award was a gold medal and diploma for a large moorland study at the Panama-Pacific International Exhibition at San Francisco in 1915. This had been painted on Clodgy Moor, close to Newlyn, which had proved a fertile source of subjects. However, when his landscape *Trink Hill* (RA 1920, Paris 1924) was first exhibited in St Ives in 1920, the local reviewer commented, "One cannot help regretting that a painter with so vital an outlook and such amazing technical resource does not devote more of his time to serious landscape." Feeling that a landscape should be judged "not by the realisation of likeness", but by its "emotional and decorative value", he considered *Trink Hill* a great picture, "distinguished not only by rare skill in the handling of surfaces but by that dignity of conception which reveals the artist".[232] The painting showed cows grazing on boulder-strewn moorland on a November afternoon, just before the sun dropped down behind the hill, which is in the Zennor district. Accordingly, the low rays of the sun intensified all the light and shade of the undulating ground, the boulders and the cattle. To make his task even more difficult, Simpson chose to depict the scene looking into the sun, and a beautiful lurid glow permeated the whole picture. As he insisted on completing the huge work on the spot, it took him two years to finish, for the exposed position rarely resulted in favourable conditions. Several critics felt that it was his best work yet.

In discussing his painting *Trink Hill*, Simpson passed the comment that Cornish moorland scenery was "nearly as fine as that of Dartmoor", for, following his parents' retirement to Tavistock, Simpson had explored the local moorland scenery around there and found copious subjects.[233] Indeed, his major exhibition in Plymouth in August and September 1920, at the time of the *Mayflower* tercentenary celebrations, had a section entitled *The Freedom of Dartmoor*, and he did not shirk from showing the most grim and rugged aspects of the moor, as well as its more attractive summer hues.

Fig. 5.12 Charles Simpson     *Trink Hill*

---

230 Simpson was awarded two diplomas at this exhibition as well - *St Ives Times*, 8/1924.
231 The painting, measuring 57" x 69", was Lot 21 at Sotheby's London on 3/12/2003, albeit the title was not known. Both it and *The Flight of Wild Duck* were priced at £300 at Simpson's 1924 Exhibition in Plymouth, whereas *Duck Shooting* was £500.
232 *St Ives Times*, 16/4/1920.
233 *St Ives Times*, 5/3/1920.

Fig. 5.13  Charles Simpson   *Otter Hunting*   (Shipley Art Gallery, Gateshead)

Fig. 5.14  Charles Simpson   *Otter Hunting - The Kill*   (Derby Museums and Art Gallery)

All these works were executed in tempera and a critic commented, "He paints very broadly and masterly, ignoring detail, and aiming, almost wholly, at creating a suggestion of breath and aerial effects, and at indicating the hard and rugged character of the soil and undergrowth. With a very few well-selected colours, Mr Simpson paints straight away and leaves his painting immediately the need for expression is satisfied. His skies are spacious with boldly drawn clouds rolling on from tor to tor, and his distances are vast and unrelieved by detail." [234] Many of the landscapes, however, contained animals, and the harshness of the lives of the wild ponies was emphasized, as they huddled together for warmth or searched for food through the frozen snow. The Mappin Art Gallery, Sheffield, whose collection is now in storage, own one of the principal works in the exhibition, *Sunset on Dartmoor*.

The sporting aspects of the moors were also depicted, with red-coated huntsmen riding on horseback and hounds flushing out otters. A keen huntsman himself, Simpson was later to receive a number of commissions to depict hunts and huntsmen, but perhaps the most interesting of his sporting paintings of this period are his depictions of otter hunting, a sport that now seems abhorrent, albeit not banned until 1978, but which had its heyday in the years immediately before the First World War, when there were some twenty-four packs of otter hounds around the country. Simpson was particularly good at portraying hounds, and two works (Figs. 5.13 and 5.14) capture the distinctive otter hounds leaping off a tree-lined bank into a river, before honing in on the kill. These are brilliant portrayals of movement. A two-page reproduction of the oil painting, *Otter Hunting - the Kill* (ROI 1923), now owned by Derby Museum and Art Gallery, appeared in *Illustrated Sporting & Dramatic News*, in April 1923.[235]

Marine backdrops featured in many of Simpson's works, but he also produced some pure marine work. *On the Fringe of a North Easter* (RA 1922) was a large canvas painted on Porthmeor Beach, depicting a rough sea and breaking waves, with a line of flying gulls. Borlase Smart commented, "There is fine movement in the curving lines of foam and in the banking of the birds as they move against the wind."[236] The following year, he exhibited at the Royal Academy another huge marine, *Five Points*, depicting, in heavy impasto, the much-painted run of headlands as seen from Clodgy. This was considered "full of action", with "the lash of the waves against the rocks excellently caught".[237] He also exhibited a series of marine scenes at the ROI in 1924, which included *The Old Ruins*, *Surf*, and *Near Hell's Mouth*.

Fig. 5.15 Charles Simpson     *Dartmoor*     (Lander Gallery, Truro)

---

234 *Daily Mercury*, reproduced in *St Ives Times* 3/9/1920.
235 A watercolour, *Otter Hunt*, is owned by South Shields Museum and Art Gallery.
236 *Western Morning News*, 16/3/1922.
237 Extract from *Western Morning News*, reproduced in *St Ives Times*, 11/5/1923.

Fig. 5.16  Charles Simpson     *On the Beach*     (RA 1918)
(Christchurch Art Gallery Te Puna o Waiwhetu)

### 5.2.5  Charles Simpson's figure paintings

Notwithstanding Simpson's supreme skill as a bird and animal painter, it has been his figure paintings that have attracted the most interest in the salerooms recently. These often featured members of his family or his students, and quite a number were done on the beach. Either Simpson got bored whilst his family enjoyed hot summer days on the sands, or his wife and child were cheap models for *plein air* sketching sessions for his Painting School! One of his paintings of Ruth, sitting on the beach, hugging her knees (Fig. 5.16), which was exhibited at the Royal Academy in 1918, is now owned by Christchurch Art Gallery in New Zealand, being one of a number of paintings bought off Simpson in 1919 during a visit to his studio by the Christchurch builder and art enthusiast, James Jamieson.[238] However, Ruth is not dressed in beach-ware, but is elegantly attired wearing a red and white striped skirt, white jacket and wide-brimmed white hat. Another painting, *The Sand Castle*, shows her wearing the same jacket and hat, as she sits on the beach next to Leonora, who has plumped herself down on top of the sand castle that she has just made. The work, though, is much sketchier, with more attention paid to the pair's head-gear, than their faces, which are turned away.

Unsurprisingly, as his daughter grew up, Simpson used her as a model in a number of works, two of which were hung at the Royal Academy. *Leonora and the Pet Goat* (RA 1920) is a delightful painting, showing his daughter sitting in a paddock, feeding hay to the family's pet goat. A London critic commented, "The execution is rough and ill-defined, but the effect is complete and appealing." [239] However, seeing the child dressed completely in blue, he assumed that it was a boy! The painting was bought by the Grundy Art Gallery, Blackpool. *The Pergola* (RA 1924) shows a more grown-up Leonora, now dressed all in white, with a straw sunhat, holding a doll, in the shade of a garden pergola. The play of light on the background foliage and into the shaded area where she is standing provides the key interest in the work. Indeed, Simpson has observed that the effect of this is to tint her white dress green. The painting was used as the front cover illustration of the *Woman's Pictorial* on 27th September 1924.

Other paintings captured holidaymakers on Porthminster Beach. *The Tent* (RA 1918) featured the lissome forms of half-nude youths disporting themselves on the sands, whilst *The Evening Sun* showed a group of happy children making a sandcastle. Another work, called *By the Sea*, showed two girls

---

238 Twenty-eight paintings from Jamieson's collection eventually became part of the permanent collection of the Robert McDougall Art Gallery in Christchurch, renamed in 2003 Christchurch Art Gallery Te Puna o Waiwhetu.
239 Reproduced in *St Ives Times*, 27/10/1922.

SEA CHANGE : FINE AND DECORATIVE ART IN ST IVES 1914-1930

Fig. 5.17   Charles Simpson        *The Pergola*
(Royal Cornwall Museum, Truro)

Fig. 5.18  Charles Simpson        *Leonora and the Pet Goat*
(Grundy Art Gallery, Blackpool)

in high heels on the sand.[240]   A large seven foot painting, which was the principal work at his show at Lanham's Galleries in 1919, was called *The End of the Holidays*, and depicted a pensive young man and a pretty girl walking arm-in-arm along rocks at the edge of the sea after a swim.  Borlase Smart commented, "Not the least inspiring feature is the expressive rendering of the breakers which form the background to the group.  The strength and movement of the tide is very real and yet the line of design is subservient to the movement of the figures." [241]  A very different work in the same show, which Smart called "very spirited and quite inspired", was *Snowballing*, which depicted a scene in the harbour on a wintry day as two groups of boys, strung out in a line, advanced towards each other hurling snowballs.[242]

Simpson also completed a large self-portrait and a portrait of his wife.  The self portrait shows him standing in Shore Studio, holding in his right hand, his palette, with an array of brushes ready for use. Dressed in a grey suit, with waist coat, yellow shirt and blue tie, he makes little attempt to make himself look handsome, and the customary cigarette droops from his mouth.  In the background, is depicted a sofa, over which hangs a large mirror, which reflects the scene in the harbour, disconcertingly back to front.  His portrait of Ruth is more aesthetically pleasing.  She is shown in the large-rimmed black hat, with black and white ribbon, which she had been wearing when Simpson first set eyes on her.  This colour scheme is matched by her black jacket, with white edges to the lapels, and a frilly white blouse. A vermillion scarf, tied at the neck, is the only strong, alternative colour note.  Whilst her face is painted with care, the rest of the work is done in Simpson's usual broad manner.

Fig. 5.19  Charles Simpson   *Portrait of the Artist's Wife, Ruth*
(John Branfield)

---

240 See *St Ives Times*, 23/5/1919.
241 *St Ives Times*, 5/9/1919.
242 ibid.

Fig. 5.20  Charles Simpson  *The Line Fishing Season*
(Plymouth City Art Gallery)

### 5.2.6  Charles Simpson's depictions of the fishing seasons

When the artists first settled in St Ives in the 1880s, the local fishermen had enjoyed the benefit of three distinct fishing seasons - the mackerel season in the early part of the year, the pilchard season in the autumn and the herring season towards the end of the year.  Pilchards had been the principal livelihood for many in the town for much of the nineteenth century, but now they were seen no more.  The mackerel season had also become less dependable, and failed completely in 1923.  This left the herring season, itself unpredictable, as the key time for the dwindling numbers of fishing boats operating from St Ives.  However, there were other fish to be caught at different times, and, based in Shore Studio on The Wharf, Simpson could not fail to witness the varied unfolding dramas in the harbour as one fishing season followed another.

In 1920, at the instigation of Martin Cock of James Lanham Limited, the Newlyn Art Gallery put on its first exhibition for six years.  Simpson sent a work painted during his Newlyn days, *The Mackerel Season* (RA 1914), which a reviewer of the exhibition described as "possibly the best picture of sea-gulls that anyone has ever painted".[243]  Gulls were regular participants in Simpson's depictions of the fishing seasons, as they were an ever present feature of a fishing port.  Whilst they could be a nuisance, the fishermen learnt to appreciate them.  One commented, "They snap up all leavings of the fish off the shore, and keep us a nice clean beach." [244]

In 1919, Simpson exhibited at the Royal Academy one of his best known works, *The Line Fishing Season* (Plymouth City Art Gallery), showing gulls squabbling over rays laid out on the harbour beach.  Again, the principal focus is on the gulls.  A single man is shown gutting a ray, and normally this waste would be tossed for the gulls.  However, in the absence of any other humans to shoo them away, Simpson has depicted the gulls tucking into the fish themselves.  Pony and carts wait in the background to take the catch away.

Also in 1919, Simpson showed at Lanham's Gallery *Dawn, Herring Season*, which was described as depicting a couple of old fishermen landing part of their catch in the harbour in the early morning.  This would appear to be the work now known as *Landing Herrings* (Fig. 5.21), which is again owned by Christchurch Art Gallery, New Zealand.  A pony and cart are drawn up beside the boat, as the two fishermen sort their catch into baskets, which are then loaded into the cart.  The Gallery's records reveal

---

243 *Cornish Artists - Exhibition at Newlyn*, St Ives Times, 27/8/1920.
244 *St Ives Weekly Summary*, 10/6/1905.

that the above-mentioned James Jamieson, having purchased a number of works from Simpson's studio, including *On the Beach* (Fig. 5.16), managed to persuade the artist to give this painting to the Canterbury Society of Arts.[245]

The herring season became increasingly unpredictable, but, in November 1923, there was a glut of herring, with half a million fish being caught in three days.[246] The scenes played out in front of his studio window inspired Simpson to produce a record of all aspects of the fishery - from the moment that the boats, which fished at night in the Bay, started to head back to port, their paraffin oil lamps glistening on the waters, to the time when the last cart load of fish had trundled off over the cobbles. Working in his usual swift manner, he was able to exhibit at Lanham's Galleries in mid-December that year no less than twenty-two studies. A reviewer described it as "a sort of cinema story of the fisherman and his fish, set in the infinitely picturesque surroundings of the quaintest town in the British Isles." [247]

The first sketch in the series was *The Empty Quay,* and this was followed, by way of contrast, with *A Crowd on the Quay*, as the imminent arrival of the boats was anticipated. Sketches entitled *Packers waiting for the Boats*, *Girls awaiting the Gurries*, *Landing Baskets*, *Packers in Oilskins*, *Packers at Work* and *Loading the Carts* indicate other aspects of the scene, as the fleet arrived, the packers got to work, and the ponies and carts were taken down on to the sands, drawn alongside and loaded up. Gulls, of course, were not slow to spot opportunities for an easy meal, and are regular participants in the sketches. One entitled *Loading Herrings on St Ives Quay* (Fig. 5.23) contains a number of interesting features, for it depicts the novel sight of a lorry being utilised. This mode of transport is sharply contrasted with a gentleman, who has arrived with a friend on horseback, whilst a fisherman and a fishwife make off with their respective small quotas. The principal work, a large canvas in oils, *From My Studio Window during the Herring Season* (RA 1924 - Laing Art Gallery, Newcastle) (Fig. 5.22), depicted a busy scene on The Wharf as men and women packed barrels and loaded pony-drawn carts. One man with a basket, who is in some shade thrown by a horse, is depicted in some detail but all the other figures are mere outlines silhouetted, with warm colour round the edges, as the low early morning sun penetrated the mist. It is a very daring and novel approach and reflects again Simpson's fascination with the effect of objects seen against the light. Other works from the series in public collections are *Packers on the Quay* (Harrogate), and *On The Quay* (Dunedin, New Zealand) (Fig. 5.25). The series provides an invaluable historical record of an industry that, despite the odd good years during the 1920s, had collapsed by the 1940s.

Fig. 5.21 Charles Simpson     *Landing Herrings*
(Christchurch Art Gallery Te Puna o Waiwhetu)

---

245 See Minutes of Canterbury Society of Arts, dated 19/1/1920 and the *Christchurch Press*, 21 January 1921. The Canterbury Society of Arts collection was in large part given to the Robert McDougall Art Gallery, the public gallery of the city of Christchurch, when it opened in 1932, and this became the Christchurch Art Gallery Te Puna o Waiwhetu in 2003 - Information kindly supplied by Tim Jones, Christchurch Art Gallery.
246 *St Ives Times*, 9/11/1923.
247 *St Ives Times*, 4/1/1924.

SEA CHANGE : FINE AND DECORATIVE ART IN ST IVES 1914-1930

Figs. 5.22 - 5.24

Charles Simpson
The Herring Fishing Season series

Top : *The Herring Fishing Season : From My Studio Window* (Laing Art Gallery, Newcastle-upon-Tyne)

Middle : *Loading Herrings on St Ives Quay*

Bottom : *Herring Packers*

Fig. 5.25  Charles Simpson  *The Herring Fishing Season : On the Quay*
(Dunedin Public Art Gallery)

Fig. 5.26  Charles Simpson  *The Herring Fishing Season*
(David Messum Fine Art Ltd)

## 5.2.7 Charles Simpson and 'El Rodeo'

In areas such as Texas and New Mexico, the Rodeo had originated as a competition for riding wild horses and roping steers. Tex Austin, however, saw its entertainment potential and, in 1924, he brought his Rodeo show, which had previously toured America, to Wembley. It was called 'The Great International Contest', for the cowboys and cowgirls in the party were competing against each other, and amateur riders were encouraged to see how they fared. The event proved a sensation, attracting a vast amount of publicity and huge crowds. Simpson, being a horseman himself, was fascinated by the skills on display, and managed to get permission to sketch in the actual arena itself throughout the whole three weeks that the event ran, working from early morning through to midnight. He found the experience exhilarating, as he tried to capture the bucking and rearing of the animals, and the poise of the riders, as they desperately tried to stay mounted. There were scenes of bronk riding, with and without a saddle, steer roping (Fig. 5.29), trick riding, relay racing and bulldogging, which involved wrestling with steers (Fig. 5.28). He soon learnt to tie his drawing and painting materials to his waist with string, as, on occasion, he had to scramble up the wire fence to avoid some stampeding steer or wild bronk.[248] He also went behind the scenes to places such as the Stable Tent to view horses, such as Deerfoot, which had already kicked two men to death, and he made friends with some of the cowboys and cowgirls, who wore colourful costumes and had equally colourful names, such as Nowata Slim, Buck Lucas or Skeeter Bill Robbins. A number sat for quick portrait sketches, and he also captured them as they prepared for performances. In this period of intense activity, he managed to produce no fewer than one hundred and twenty-five sketches, which were exhibited at the Arlington Gallery in August 1924, to great acclaim. As a result, they featured in a quickly produced book, *El Rodeo*, published by John Lane that December. In this, Simpson wrote that the Rodeo had left "an impression of something quite above and beyond the thrill of its contents, the pageantry of its scenes, or the fine sense of open air and freedom that its ensemble conveyed - it has left an impression of something classic, belonging to all time".[249]

Given the speed at which Simpson worked, it is not surprising that many of the sketches, particularly those in pencil and crayon, are little more than rough notes. However, several sketches do give a flavour of the exoticism of the occasion, and indicate how the various skills were performed. *The Times* commented, "For general pictorial merit, *Finish of the Relay Race : Tad Barnes and Vera McGinnis* (Fig. 5.27), *A Mishap - Steer Wrestling* and *Steer Wrestling - A Rapid Impression* (Fig. 5.28) might be selected from among the larger paintings in gouache." [250] A more highly finished example is *Steer Roping : Leaving the Chute* (Fig. 5.29), which does not feature in the book and was executed later.

Fig. 5.27  Charles Simpson            *Finish of the Relay Race : Tad Barnes and Vera McGinnis*

---

248 When this happened, the cowboys commented that "he made as good time as a bull buffalo before a prairie fire"! Charles Simpson, *El Rodeo*, London, 1924 at p. 19.
249 Charles Simpson, *El Rodeo*, London, 1924 at p. 29-30.
250 Reproduced in *St Ives Times*, 1/8/1924.

Fig. 5.28  Charles Simpson     *Steer Wrestling - A Rapid Impression*     (from *El Rodeo*)

Simpson's Rodeo sketches made a big impact in America, for Americans were astonished that an entertainment, that they considered crude and boisterous, should have received such rapturous notices in England and be the subject of acclaimed art.  The sketches also changed Simpson's life, for they led to a commission from John Lane for a book on the Leicestershire hunts.  This prompted the family's departure from St Ives, although 'Loyalty Cottage' proved difficult to sell, and, for the next decade, Simpson became primarily an equestrian artist and author, based in London.  Whilst Simpson enjoyed fraternising with leading figures in Society, during his equestrian period, and clearly had some success when his works were shown at the Fine Art Society, it is noticeable that it was only when he reverted to Cornish scenes in 1936 that he was hung again at the Royal Academy, for he rarely bothered to work up his hunt sketches into a major canvas.  His departure from St Ives, after a final major exhibition of his work at Plymouth City Art Gallery in November 1924, was a bitter blow to the colony.[251]

Fig. 5.29  Charles Simpson     *Steer Roping : Leaving the Chute*
(Russell-Cotes Art Gallery, Bournemouth)

---

251 In addition to 108 Rodeo works, this contained 44 other works, including two priced at £500, two at £300 and three at £200.

Fig. 5.30 Ruth Simpson  *Maroon and Gold*
(Penlee House Gallery & Museum, Penzance)

## 5.3 The portraits of Ruth Simpson

The portraits of Ruth Simpson did not merely receive attention because her work tended to be included in exhibitions devoted to the work of her husband; they provoked favourable comment in their own right, and she was considered an excellent and innovative portraitist - the best in the colony. Indeed, in a review of her exhibits at the Mayflower Exhibition in Plymouth in 1920, the critic felt that she "bids fair to become the best-known portrait painter in the West Country".[252] However, whilst her work is now owned by the Imperial War Museum and various Art Galleries in Cornwall, it received very little national recognition at the time. She had three works hung at the International Society, but was never successful at the Royal Academy.

With there being no Show Days in 1917 and 1918, and very few art reviews during 1918, the first reference to Ruth's portraits in St Ives is in the critique of the joint show that the Simpsons held at Lanham's Galleries in September 1919. Ruth exhibited six works. These included her portrait of Frank Ver Beck (Fig. 3.58), about which Borlase Smart commented, "Apart from being a very successful portrait, it has great qualities of painting and is simple in transcription and convincing in handling."[253] Smart was also taken with "the passages of lovely colour" in *The Lustre Jar*, which showed a girl, "clad in raiments of almost Eastern brilliance", holding such a jar, with one side of her face lit with pale daylight, whilst the other side grew ruddy in the artificial light.[254] He also liked the "dignified work", *Lady in Black*, a portrait of her mother, which had been hung at the International Society, but was very taken with the powerful portrait study, *Maroon and Gold* (Fig. 5.30), which showed a lady in a maroon dress shown against a simple background of glowing cadmium. This work, concluded another critic, "shows how a portrait can be also made a real picture".[255] The identity of the model has not been recorded, although it is thought that she resembles Sophie Bodinnar, a friend from Newlyn.

---

252 Reproduced in *St Ives Times*, 20/8/1920.
253 *St Ives Times*, 5/9/1919.
254 See also *St Ives Times*, 18/6/1920.
255 *St Ives Times*, 27/8/1920.

A similarly designed portrait, *Orange and Green*, was of the artist herself. Unfortunately, one critic failed to appreciate this, and described the sitter as "a charming, slightly malicious lady"! However, he felt that the work was "painted with a freedom and freshness of technique, which positively exhilarates".[256] She employed a similar daring colour scheme in her portrait of Ella Naper (Fig. 5.31), an artist friend from Lamorna - this time using a red background to set off her blue check dress. This was shown at the Mayflower Exhibition in Plymouth in 1920 and was considered one of the most striking, if not the best, of her eighteen exhibits. "It is happily placed, facile in treatment, and really personal."[257]

I have already made reference in Chapter 2 to her large portrait, *A Company Commander* (Fig. 2.24 - Imperial War Museum), first exhibited in St Ives in 1920, which was rated "a convincing and brilliant performance" by the critic of the *Daily Mercury*.[258] He also liked her portrait of the visiting American artist, Rollo Peters (see Fig. 6.13). "Whether you like Mr Peters or not, there he is, assertively himself, vitally portrayed and very distinctive in character."[259] Borlase Smart also rated the work, considering that there was "a quiet restfulness in the pose and a softness in the modelling of the youthful features".[260] This comment about "youthful features" by Smart makes it unlikely that the sitter was Charles Rollo Peters (1862-1928), an artist whose mastery of nocturnes led him to be called 'the Poet of the Night', for he would have been in his late fifties. Furthermore, other critics refer to Rollo Peters as a "theatre artist" and the author of "the New Art". Presumably, therefore, the sitter was Charles Rollo Peters' son or other close relation, about whom little is known. No help is given by the normal St Ives sources, for there is no reference to a Rollo Peters at all.

Fig. 5.31 Ruth Simpson   *Portrait of Ella Naper*
(Private Collection : photo courtesy of Penlee House Gallery & Museum)

---

256 *Daily Mercury*, 14/5/1920 reproduced in *St Ives Times* 28/5/1920.
257 *Daily Mercury*, 8/1920, reproduced in *St Ives Times*, 20/8/1920. The critic was not so impressed with her portrait of Edmund Naper, which he considered "too conscientious and too formal".
258 *Daily Mercury*, 14/5/1920 reproduced in *St Ives Times* 28/5/1920.
259 *Daily Mercury*, 14/5/1920 reproduced in *St Ives Times* 28/5/1920.
260 *St Ives Times*, 14/5/1920.

Other known portraits are of her students, Winifred Humphrey, and George Bradshaw. She depicted the latter in his Naval uniform and therefore had the problem of rendering quietly the recurring spots of gold in the uniform. The painting of the head and hands was considered to be some of her very best work, but the painting does not appear to have survived. Other portraits were entitled *The Kimono, The Amber Necklace, The Chinese Cloak* and *The Yellow Jumper*, the latter being said to have an "atmosphere of self-reliant modernity".[261] She also exhibited on Show Day 1923 a portrait of the novelist, Crosbie Garstin, son of Newlyn artist, Norman Garstin. However, as soon as Charles decided to move to London, which she did not like and where she had no studio, she soon lost her motivation to paint and gave up altogether. Even when she managed to return to Cornwall, following illness in 1930, she did not feel inspired to paint again. This is a great loss, as she had produced some innovative work of high quality.

## 5.4 Robert Borlase Smart

Immediately upon his discharge from the Army, Borlase Smart settled in St Ives and even took part in Show Day in 1919, when he had on display *Munitions 1918*, a painting of blast furnaces near to Grantham seen across a river, which was hung that year at the Royal Academy.[262] His arrival was a real boost to the colony, as his energy and enthusiasm was infectious. As already seen, he immediately took on the role of art critic, a somewhat delicate task given the ease with which fellow artists could be offended, but he took care to highlight positives rather than negatives, and so encouraged artists to work hard and strive for ever better results. His influence was not only felt in the colony itself, for he developed a considerable interest in the well-being of the town and, within a year, had been elected on to the Town Council. Always keen to experiment, he worked in different media and tackled different genre and, before leaving the town briefly in 1925, produced an astonishing variety of work of considerable interest and merit. His advice to fellow artists was, "Nature is ever varied. Don't repeat yourself therefore in your subjects and in your general work....Give your public an element of surprise, like nature gives you out of doors. Don't let them get accustomed to your art." [263]

### 5.4.1 Borlase Smart's depictions of Old St Ives and Old Plymouth

Smart had a deep appreciation of history. As seen, his War drawings, which were exhibited in a one-man show at Lanham's Galleries in May 1919, often highlighted buildings of considerable architectural interest that had been decimated in the fighting, and the first paintings that Smart did on his return to the colony were a series of charcoal and wash drawings of Old St Ives, for he was aware that many old buildings in the town were at risk. The speed at which he worked can be demonstrated by the fact that he held a one-man show of these works, described as the 'first series', at Lanham's Galleries in July 1919. The best of these were considered to be *The Rampers*, which featured the gaunt piles of the old wooden breakwater, *Smeaton's Pier* and *The Old Fish Cellar*, which depicted "the dilapidated interior of a quaint and ancient dwelling containing numerous barrels, ropes, sails and appliances of a fishing craft".[264] Other works in this series included *Bethesda Hill, Old Houses in The Wharf, Old House, Chy-an-Chy* (Fig. 5.33), *Carnglaze Street, In Pudding Bag Lane, The Oldest House in St Ives, Reconstruction of The Wharf, Morning in the Harbour*, which depicted a fish sale, and *A View from Pednolver Rocks* (Fig. 5.32), showing some old timber buildings in the foreground.

Although there is no mention of a further exhibition featuring another series of such scenes, Smart clearly did produce further charcoal and wash drawings of old segments of the town. The St Ives Town Collection includes his depictions of Royal Square (see Fig. 5.35) and the site of the Primitive Methodists School, whilst his sketchbook features original drawings for a scene in Bunkers Hill (Fig. 5.34). In 1920, Frank Emanuel used five of Smart's drawings to illustrate his article on St Ives for the *Architectural Review*. These were *Down-Along, St Ives*, showing old houses on The Wharf, *Norway Lane, Hick's Court, St Andrew's Street* and *The Harbour Shore*, featuring the upper section of Mariners' Church in the centre, Emanuel, a regular visitor to the town from the early 1890s and an esteemed art teacher, commented, "To the connoisseur, his masterly drawings, done with bold outlines of charcoal, duly set and completed with washes of frank water-colours, are bound to appeal. The sureness of their drawing and the directness and rapid completenes of their handling are bound to tell." [265]

---

261 *St Ives Times*, 17/3/1922.

262 A watercolour version of *Munitions* is owned by Plymouth City Art Gallery. Smart followed this work up with further industrial scenes - *The Nitrate Works, Plymouth, The Chemical Works, Cattedown* (Plymouth City Art Gallery) and *The Steel Works, Lincoln* - but these paintings had limited commercial appeal.

263 *St Ives Times*, 2/6/1933.

264 *St Ives Times*, 25/7/1919.

265 *Architectural Review*, July 1920.

Figs. 5.32 to 5.35  Borlase Smart

Top :    *A View from Pednolver Rocks*
         (Private Collection)

Middle : *Old House, Chy-an-Chy*
         (Private Collection)

Bottom:

Left :   *Bunkers Hill*

Right :  *Royal Square*

(both from sketchbook, courtesy Brian Smart)

Fig. 5.36 Borlase Smart painting *The Pilot's Boathouse*
(Smart family papers courtesy St Ives Trust Archive Study Centre)

Smart also did a series of charcoal and wash drawings of Old Plymouth, which he exhibited in August 1920 in a joint show with Charles and Ruth Simpson at Messrs Harris and Sons, Plymouth at the time of the Mayflower Tercentenary.[266] The show was clearly aimed at the Americans, who would be visiting Plymouth for this important anniversary, and so included many places that would have been familiar to the Pilgrim Fathers. Accordingly, he depicted various scenes in the area of the Barbican, including the old house, which was said to have been the last 'meeting-house' of the emigrants. However, Smart was also very concerned at the attitude of the town authorities to the quainter parts of the town and sought to record these before they were swept away. Some had already gone, and he used a sketch that he had made at the age of sixteen to recreate the look of Old Town Street as he had known it as a child. *Sutton Pier* and *High Street* were two works acquired for the permanent collection of Plymouth City Art Gallery.

Smart was a superb architectural draughtsman and this skill, coupled with a striking colour vision, make his charcoal and wash sketches of old buildings of considerable artistic merit. In his later depictions of places of architectural interest in the town, such as *The Pilot's Boathouse* (Leamington Art Gallery), Smart tended to work purely in oils, not necessarily to better effect. Smart's fears about the future for the ancient parts of St Ives and Plymouth proved well-founded and his architectural studies now also have exceptional historical interest. Indeed, even at the time of his death in 1947, the importance of these records of lost buildings was widely acknowledged.

### 5.4.2 Borlase Smart's depictions of "England's Wooden Walls"

In July 1922, Borlase Smart held an exhibition at Messrs. Ackermann's Fine Art Galleries, New Bond Street, entitled *England's Wooden Walls*, which comprised thirteen "watercolour drawings illustrating the passing of the Old Wooden Sailing Battleship". The inspiration for this was the realisation that many of the old wooden fighting ships, many of which had been converted into training establishments or depot ships for the accommodation of officers and men, had reached the end of their useful life, with little realistic prospect of being saved. Quite a number of these had been familiar sights in the harbours of Devon and Cornwall, and, as Francis Roskruge recorded in his Foreword to the catalogue, Smart felt that he would like to record for posterity the appearance of these fine old vessels in the last stages of their Service career. Ships featured included *The Britannia* at Dartmouth, Nelson's old flagship *The Foudroyant* at Falmouth, the training ship *Mount Edgecumbe* at Saltash, *The Impregnable* and *The Indus* at Devonport, as well, of course, as *The Victory*.

---

266 Of the forty-five works in the show, more than half were said to relate to Plymouth - *Western Daily Mercury,* reproduced in *St Ives Times*, 3/9/1920. Scenes in Modbury, Newton Ferrers and Dartmouth were also included.

Fig. 5.37 Borlase Smart  *Reconstructing the Implacable*  (drawing version)
(Private Collection)

The watercolours were well received and considered to be executed with remarkable skill and observation. "While preserving the actual appearance of the ships with almost photographic detail, Capt. Smart has added that touch of imagination and beauty to every one of them which is the hallmark of real art." [267]

It appears that the exhibition may not have been a commercial success, as Smart re-exhibited a significant number of the works in a similarly titled exhibition at Messrs Harris and Sons, Plymouth in February 1926. This was prompted by further drawings recently done by Smart of *The Implacable*, a 3,223 ton vessel that had been built by the French in the 1790s before being captured at the Battle of Cape Ortegal in 1805. Having been used as a training establishment for boys at Devonport between 1860 and 1904, it was noted in the 1922 catalogue that it had recently been lent to the philanthropist, Wheatley Cobb, for preservation at Falmouth. In fact, the reconstruction of the old wooden ship took place in Devonport, beginning in 1925, and Smart was granted special permission to study her, whilst she was in dry dock. The resultant charcoal and wash drawing, *Reconstructing the Old Implacable*, (Fig. 5.37) which has an unusual orange sky/background, was exhibited at the Plymouth exhibition, whilst an oil painting of the same scene was hung that year at the Royal Academy. It is a powerful image. Seen out of the water, the huge vessel dwarfs the men who work on her, and fills the entire picture space. The distinctive characteristics of the battleship and the cranes, chains, props and pulleys used for the reconstruction are all recorded in detail. The painting that Smart exhibited at the Paris Salon in 1930, *The Old 'Duguay Trouin'*, is probably the same work, as this was the ship's original French name. Smart did an etched version of the scene as well - one of his most highly regarded etchings - and this, in particular, recalls the atmosphere of Frank Brangwyn's classic lithograph *Breaking Up the Caledonia*.

When the reconstruction work was close to finalisation in 1930, an appeal was launched for the preservation of the vessel in its former role as a holiday training ship for boys, and Smart gave to the appeal fund the plate of the etching of the scene, and offered to donate to the fund fifty per cent of the proceeds of the sale to the Royal Naval Museum at Greenwich of the oil version. However, it appears that the Museum, whilst keen to have the painting, was not able to raise the asking price of £100, for the work is not now in its collection.[268] *The Implacable* survived until 1949, when she was scuttled off the Isle of Wight, when it was decided that the continued costs of maintaining her were not justifiable.[269] However, her figure head and stern galleries can be seen at Greenwich.

---

267 *Western Morning News*, reproduced in *St Ives Times*, 7/1922.
268 *The Times*, 20/1/1931, reproduced in *St Ives Times*, 23/1/1931.
269 The French Government, to whom she was offered in 1947, also declined to save her.

### 5.4.3 Borlase Smart's early marine paintings

Despite all these watercolour drawings, Smart's principal aim, inspired by his time as a student of Julius Olsson prior to the War, was to become a marine painter in oils. One of the first works that he exhibited in this genre was *Clear Shining After Rain* (St Ives Town Collection), a work that he had completed before the War and which clearly reveals Olsson's influence. However, as already seen, Smart was also impressed by the high-toned renderings of the Cornish coast being produced at that time by Louis Sargent, and his own work was often highly keyed. Like Charles Simpson, Smart was also an avid advocate of *plein air* painting, describing Nature as "the supreme teacher and critic".[270] Accordingly, he explored at length the coastline to the west of St Ives up to Zennor, working out what vistas offered good subjects not only at different times of the day or year, but at different states of tide. This often entailed steep climbs with his painting equipment. His sense of history also made him track down vistas painted by Arnesby Brown, Adrian Stokes and other early colonists of note.[271] However, whilst the fashion in the pre-War years had been for flat or gently curving outlines, Smart also liked the grandeur of rugged cliff-faces. Hence the area around Zennor proved of enduring fascination. He commented, "The variety of interest between Trevail and up to and including Wicca Pool is astounding. From the high ground of the cliffs, the hills of Buttermilk, Trevalgan, Eagle's Nest, Zennor and Carn Galva make a glorious background. Here again their definition and connecting outline with the big cliffs becomes more apparent as one proceeds, until the climax is reached at Carn Galva, where this 'nearly a mountain' rises from the bold outlines of Bosigran castle. Between the cliffs and the hills, the nestling farms and lines of hedges make up a fine foreground, especially beautiful in the afternoon and evening side light." [272]

Like a number of St Ives marine painters of the pre-War era, Smart found, during the 1920s, that his work was more appreciated in Paris than it was at the Royal Academy. In 1921, he had his first success at the Paris Salon with *La liberté des mers* and, the following year, won a Mention Honorable for his work *Evening on the Cornish Coast*. This was renamed *Sunset at Clodgy*, when it was sold in October 1922 at the Private View of the Autumn Exhibition of the Walker Art Gallery, Liverpool to the Sunderland Philharmonic Society for presentation to their musical director, Dr Wilburn.[273] Smart also had his first success at the Royal Academy that year with a marine. This was the fresh and breezy *Morning Light, St Ives* (Fig. 5.38), which depicted waves pounding on to rocks at Clodgy, now owned by the Royal Cornwall Museum, Truro, who also have his Academy success of the following year, *Cornish Cliffs*, (Fig. 5.39 - Paris 1924), featuring a well-composed section of the rocky coastline at Zennor. On the right can be seen rocks of blue elvin or ironstone, which, in Smart's own words, "contrast delightfully with the intense green of the slopes".[274] Plymouth City Art Gallery also have one of his paintings of Carn Galva, but this needs restoration.

Whilst Smart did not have another marine hung at the Academy until 1929, he continued to be successful in Paris. *Jewels in a Cornish Setting* (Paris 1923) was described as a daring and successful rock piece, when it was first shown in St Ives in October 1922. No sky was featured and the painting contrasted broken rocks, piled up in red masses, against a dark, calm sea, shot through the middle with a vivid slash of rich green.[275] In 1926, he showed in Paris *The Fringe of the Atlantic*, a boldly painted work depicting a turbulent sea, with masses of colour. This had been criticised when first exhibited in St Ives on Show Day in 1925, as it was felt that Smart had been a little over-exuberant, with the waves giving the impression of being of paint rather than water, and it had not been hung at the Academy. This was a fault suffered by a number of Smart's works from the 1930s. Other marines shown in Paris included *Cloudland and Sea* (1926), *Ebb Tide on the Bar* (1927) and *Moonlight on the Reef* (1928).

With Olsson as President of the ROI, Smart managed to get a number of his marine paintings hung there and was made a member in 1922, having been elected to the RBA in 1919, where he also enjoyed some success. *September Morning, St Ives*, with its " 'flying' sky, rugged rocks full of power" and "real living mass of blue-green water", was another typical example of Smart's vigorous work and was shown at the RBA in 1922, whilst *Autumn, Penwith Cliffs*, which was dark and sombre in sepias and greens, with rugged cliffs rising majestically from an emerald sea, was rated his finest achievement to date when hung at the ROI in 1923.[276]

---

270 *St Ives Times*, 2/6/1933.
271 See Borlase Smart, Art Notes - *Unknown Sketching Grounds*, *St Ives Times*, 11/8/1933.
272 ibid.
273 *St Ives Times*, 6/10/1922. In its report on the 1923 Salon (8/6/1923), the *St Ives Times* indicated that this work also won a Mention Honorable, but the official listing by Beatrice Crespon-Halotier does not record this.
274 Borlase Smart, Art Notes - *Unknown Sketching Grounds near St Ives - Wicca and Zennor*, *St Ives Times*, 8/1933.
275 *St Ives Times*, 20/10/1922.
276 *St Ives Times*, 10/11/1922.

Fig. 5.38  Borlase Smart  *Morning Light, St Ives*  (Royal Cornwall Museum, Truro)

Fig. 5.39  Borlase Smart  *Cornish Cliffs*  (Royal Cornwall Museum, Truro)

Fig. 5.40  Borlase Smart     *Venetian Palace*     (Private Collection)

Fig. 5.41  Borlase Smart     *Venetian Boats*     (Private Collection)

### 5.4.4 Borlase Smart and the inspiration of Venice

In early 1924, Borlase Smart took his wife, Irene, on a delayed honeymoon to Venice. They intended the trip to last two weeks, but ended up staying several months.[277] Like many artists before and since, Smart was immediately taken with the unique atmosphere of this city on water and its architecture. However, instead of seeking to depict its extraordinary array of building styles in his normal charcoal and wash studies, he chose to experiment, working in a variety of media. In particular, probably due to the growing strength of the print market, Smart decided to take up etching. This meant that, instead of having a single original depiction to sell, he could run off several dozen prints, each one of which was able to be sold for a good percentage of the price of a watercolour drawing. Due to his talent as an architectural draughtsman, Smart was a very capable etcher and his prints are considered further in Chapter 7. However, due to his interesting colour sense, one does regret that he did not do any charcoal and wash studies of Venetian buildings. However, he did do some studies of boats (see Fig. 5.41), in which he started to use both pastel and watercolour to bring to life his charcoal sketches. For his major paintings, however, he worked in oils.

Smart's Venetian oils are characterised by an interest in reflected light. The narrow canals often reflected clearly the multi-coloured facades of the Venetian palaces, the waters only being disturbed by the gentle bow-wave of a gondola. Fig. 5.40 is a particularly fine example, featuring the hotel where Ruskin stayed, and Brian Smart believes that the figure depicted on the right is his mother. Surprisingly, none of his Venetian works were accepted by the Royal Academy, but *Moonlight on the Grand Canal* was hung in Paris. This was a large work, with an unusual composition, featuring a gondola gliding through tranquil waters reflecting not only the moon but an array of city lights. Another sizeable painting, *Traghetto della Casson, Grand Canal, Venice* (50" x 40") was specially invited to the Canadian National Exhibition in Toronto in 1927.

### 5.4.5 Borlase Smart's departure and return

Borlase Smart later commented about St Ives, "Everything is here for the artist. Perfection in every aspect of nature. A congenial climate. Magnificent colour and light. Good studios and an artistic and social atmosphere." [278] However, for family reasons, he felt compelled to move to Salcombe in 1925. His decision to call his new home 'Porthmeor' indicates where his heart still lay. His departure, so soon after the loss of Charles and Ruth Simpson, was a bitter blow to the colony, not just because of his art, but because of his enthusiasm and encouragement of others. Accordingly, his subsequent return in 1928 was warmly welcomed. Concentrating now on boldly painted seascapes, often of waves breaking on the reefs at Clodgy, Smart began to have regular success at the Academy and developed a considerable reputation. In 1934, he published the seminal book on the subject, *The Technique of Seascape Painting*, which sold particularly well in America. Despite this, there is an argument that the financial security which came with the death of his wife's parents in the early 1930s, coupled with his passionate commitment to the success of the St Ives Society of Artists, led to his own art stagnating to a certain degree, lacking the variety and dynamism that characterised his work of the 1920s. Certainly, his great friend, Leonard Fuller, commented in his Foreword to the catalogue of Smart's Memorial Exhibition, "One feels that had he allowed himself the time for his own work that he devoted to the service of others, he would have reached great heights. But the colony would have been so very much poorer for the lack of his unselfishness."

## 5.5 John Park

Another former Olsson student, who decided to settle back in St Ives after the War, was John Anthony Park (1878-1962), who was already known to Borlase Smart, as they had been based together in Plymouth for a while before the War. Indeed, Smart had often reviewed Park's paintings for the *Western Morning News*. The son of a Preston house decorator, Park had first studied in St Ives in 1898, before returning for a more concentrated period of tuition in 1904-5, during which Olsson considered him one of his star pupils. Park had then taken Olsson's advice and studied further in Paris, at the Atelier Colarossi, where his master was Eugène Delecluse. His time there was enlivened by the first exhibitions of the Fauves, who sought to give colour an emotional value of its own, and these clearly made an impression, for Park became well-known for his sumptuous colour. After Paris, Park led a somewhat nomadic existence, working sporadically from Westminster, Concarneau, Plymouth, Brixham, Polperro and Gorran Haven, but returning to St Ives with some frequency, as he rented a rat-infested studio, next to the 'Attic Studio' of Herbert Lanyon, in the Bridge Studios complex in St Andrew's Street, next to the graveyard.

---

277 Smart started exhibiting Venetian subjects in St Ives in June 1924.
278 *St Ives Times*, 2/6/1933.

# SEA CHANGE : FINE AND DECORATIVE ART IN ST IVES 1914-1930

On being conscripted in 1916, Park served as a Private in the East Surrey Regiment in the signalling and communications division, experiencing the misery of the trenches and considerable fighting at Arras, Ypres and Cambrai. However, a series of illnesses, which included rheumatic fever and bronchitis, resulted in him being discharged as medically unfit in March 1918. In December 1919, he married Annie Margaret Tyrrell (always known as Peggy), the daughter of John Tyrrell, a retired and widowed schoolmaster and amateur artist, who had invited Park to lunch, served by his daughter, after they had met one day on Porthmeor Beach in the early days of the War. Peggy was thirteen years his junior, but had the business acumen and organisational ability that Park lacked. They lived initially in Brixham, but came down regularly to St Ives to see Peggy's father, who lived at 3 Bowling Green, and Park took a studio in the town, 4 Island Studios. However, they settled in the colony on a more permanent footing in 1923, after Peggy's father's death.

During the 1920s, Park became one of the key figures in the colony, winning recognition internationally for his colour- and light-filled depictions of St Ives harbour. He was successful at the Royal Academy in 1921 with two local scenes. Henry Moore's biographer, Frank Maclean, was most impressed with both works. After discussing Marcella Smith's depiction of St Ives quayside, *A Blue Day*, which he considered "the frankest impressionism", but lacking tenderness, he commented, "Mr John A. Park's beach scene, *Silver Morn, St Ives* is much suaver. The expanse of shimmering sand, broken in places by pools left by the tide, is rounded off by the pierhead and lighthouse, and within this area, a quietly busy life is going on round and about the hulks of two stranded sailing ships and several smaller craft. The sky above is clouded, but not so much so as to obscure in any appreciable degree the morning light. The picture is full of the latter; soused in it, one might say." [279] Whilst Park is so often known for his brilliance of colour, he did have a particular fascination with grey days in the harbour, another example of which is Leamington Art Gallery's *Silvery Morn*.[280] On such days, sea and sky could be as one and, as the light reflected back and forth between water and cloud, its intensity could be blinding. However, his other exhibit at the Academy that year was more typical. Maclean continued, "Mr Park's second picture, *Sun and Tide, St Ives*, is a graphic impression of white boats riding at anchor on a bubbly sea in full sunlight; a vivid little tour de force." [281]

Fig. 5.42  John Park     *The Morning Tide, St Ives*
(Harris Museum and Art Gallery, Preston)

---

279 *Western Morning News* review, reproduced in *St Ives Times*, 16/5/1921.
280 Maclean's description makes it quite clear that Leamington's painting is not the 1921 RA exhibit.
281 *Western Morning News* review, reproduced in *St Ives Times*, 16/5/1921.

Fig. 5.43  John Park    *Morning in the Harbour, St Ives*    (Paisnel Gallery)

The following year, Park was successful at the Academy with two further St Ives scenes, described as "a notable pair".[282] When first exhibited on Show Day, they were called *Morning Light* and *Afternoon Light*, but, at the Academy, they were entitled *The Morning Tide, St Ives* and *When the Boats Are In*. Frank Maclean again provides us with descriptions. "Two harbour scenes, both of St Ives, come from Mr John A.Park.  The more daring is *The Morning Tide, St Ives*, showing a large smack, riding at her moorings in the middle distance, smaller craft in the foreground, the pier and lighthouse beyond.  The light is tremendous; the gently moving water palpitates with it in Mr Park's deft chromatic handling: the boats cast vibrant reflections.  In *When the Boats Are In*, the morning haze is more pronounced, and the brilliance less, but there is a little more human interest in the picture, centred round the boat drawn up on the sand." [283] Albeit seemingly mistaking the time of day in the latter work, this description is important, as it makes it clear that *The Morning Tide* is the work now owned by the Harris Museum, Preston, which is normally dated to 1924.  It also demonstrates that the Royal Academy listing, which refers in 1922 to a work *Morning Ride, St Ives* is incorrect.  Park exhibited *When the Boats Are In* at the Paris Salon the following year, where it won a Mention Honorable.  It was also his exhibit at the St Ives artists' exhibition at Cheltenham in 1925.

Park enjoyed further success in London in 1922 with his work *Summer Time*, shown at the ROI.  Again, it is probably Maclean, who waxes lyrical about it.  "*Summer Time* by John A. Park is the brightest picture in the gallery.  It is overflowing with light and gladness, the very spirit of summer; the placing of the boats and yachts in this picture is an inspiration.  It is quite a medium-sized canvas, yet Mr Park has succeeded in painting nearly a dozen boats of various kinds without crowding.  He leaves a wide expanse of wonderful sea, which scintillates in a million flashes of colour, a triumph of the artistic imagination.  It is a kind of thing that Shelley could do with a string of magic words." [284] It is interesting how Maclean recognises that Park's colour is not realistic, but designed to fire emotion, much in the same way as poetry.  Accordingly, the objective was similar to that of earlier marine artists in the colony; however, the means - heightened colour - was a development from the earlier artists' strict tonalism, but clearly owed a debt to Olsson's vividly coloured, romanticised seascapes of the immediate pre-War era, as well as the colour experiments of Louis Sargent, Louis Reckelbus and others.  Not surprisingly, with Olsson as President, Park was made a member of the ROI the following year.

282 *Western Morning News* review, reproduced in *St Ives Times*, 5/5/1922.
283 ibid.
284 *Western Morning News* review, reproduced in *St Ives Times*, 27/10/1922.

On Show Day in 1923, Park exhibited *A November Day* and *After the Storm, St Ives*, both considered to be fine examples of his work. However, the only painting accepted by the Academy was called *The Haven under the Hill*. No descriptions of the works survive to indicate whether a more romantic title had been given to *After the Storm, St Ives*. However, *The Haven under the Hill* later won a bronze medal at the Paris Salon in 1925.

Like Charles Simpson, Park was inspired by the successful herring season of late 1923 and did a series of depictions of it. He exhibited two of these on Show Day in 1924. The largest, *Drying Sails*, was described as "a clever study of water and multi-coloured sails and their reflections. It is a delightful harmony of colour, blue and brown predominating." [285] However, it was the other work, *Herring Time, St Ives*, which showed the fisherfolk busy on the Quay loading and packing fish, that was hung at the Academy. In Paris that year, he showed a work entitled *A Cornish Beach*, and this was hung also in Pittsburgh in 1925.

Following the Simpsons' departure, Park moved to 5 Piazza Studios, whose overhanging window was useful for the students that he was now teaching, and he exhibited there on Show Day in 1925. For once, his works, other than a painting of coal being unloaded from a ketch at low tide, were considered disappointing, and he was not hung at the Academy that year. However, that June, he had his first one-man London show, at the Camera Club in the Adelphi. This comprised over thirty works, some twenty of which were of Mediterranean ports, implying a good deal of travelling in the preceding year.[286] However, it was the Cornish sketches that attracted the most attention. "It is the singing quality of his drawing and colour harmonies which lifts his slightest picture above the common ruck and makes him the true artistic historian of the Cornish fisher folks." [287] This comment was inspired by further depictions of the herring season. "In the present collection, there is a beautiful suite of fishing pictures showing the fleet beaching the silver treasures in the dim dawnlit harbour of St Ives. The light in these little sketches is wonderfully rendered, elusive and semi-opaque, and hardly distinguishable from the darker masses of the waves."[288] Whilst a reasonable number of Simpson's series on the herring fishery have come to light, Park's series appears completely unknown.

Park, by now, had also turned his attention to depicting quaint corners of the streets of St Ives, and his depiction of the famous Sloop Inn was considered the stand-out work in the exhibition. "Among the shore pieces, *The Sloop Inn, St Ives*, with its light ochre walls and vivid green shutters, is outstanding. The blue jerseys of the fishermen lounging against the green and yellow walls in the bright sunshine make one realise that St Ives is the most Continental of all English seaside towns, both in its colour variety and what may best be described as the picturesque sprawl of its architectural outlines." [289] The exhibition proved a great success, with all but two works selling.[290]

Park's main picture of 1926 was a large oil *The End of the Season*. An unusual composition, with no sky, this depicted men at work cleaning their boats, whilst gulls hovered expectantly above. It was not only one of three works hung at the Royal Academy that year, but was also shown at the National Academy of Design, New York that December, his only exhibit there. Another well-regarded painting of the harbour, although quieter in key than some of his work, was *Morning in the Harbour, St Ives* (28" x 36") (Fig. 5.43), a view from the Wharf featuring the West Quay and, behind it, the houses of The Warren and Tregenna Woods, which was one of his Academy exhibits of 1927. However, towards the end of the 1920s, Park decided that he needed to branch out from his harbour subjects, popular as they were, and he embarked on a series of rural landscapes. His Royal Academy exhibit of 1928, *A Cornish Homestead*, featured Trenwith Manor House, with its outbuildings clustering around, with Rosewall Hill and Buttermilk Hill rising in the distance.[291] The following year, all three of his Show Day exhibits were landscapes. One featured the village of Relubbus, which captured "a sense of the joyous uplifting beauty of a quiet inland spot", whilst another was called *Bob Pollard's Farm*, a picturesque scene on the edge of moorland on the path to Carthew, which was hailed as a picture "full of brilliant colour" and "boldly painted".[292] The third work (Fig. 5.45), which featured cottages nestling below a hill on a spring day, was called *Vellonoweth near Crowlas*, but was re-titled *Rural Cornwall* for the Academy.

---

285 *St Ives Times*, 21/3/1924.

286 Harold Sawkins, in his article on Park in *The Artist* in September 1935 indicates that this show contained thirty-one paintings of Brixham and yet the contemporaneous review does not mention any Brixham paintings at all.

287 *Western Morning News* review, reproduced in *St Ives Times*, 19/6/1925.

288 ibid.

289 ibid.

290 Harold Sawkins, *John A. Park*, *The Artist*, September 1935 at p.24.

291 His other two Show Day exhibits that year featured the Medway at Rochester.

292 *St Ives Times*, 22/3/1929 & reproduction of *West Briton* review on 29/3/1929.

Fig. 5.44  John Park    *The Morning Ride*    (Private Collection)

Fig. 5.45  John Park    *Rural Cornwall - Vellonoweth near Crowlas*    (Private Collection)

# SEA CHANGE : FINE AND DECORATIVE ART IN ST IVES 1914-1930

Throughout 1929, his exhibits with STISA were also all landscapes, and work hung at the Academy in the early 1930s included *Merrifield's Farm* and his depiction of St John's-in-the-Fields, Halsetown, still at that time in a rural setting.

Park had always done portraits, as a remunerative sideline, and joked that he had invented, during his student days, "the hire-purchase system" of portrait painting, whereby he did portraits of less well-to-do locals for a shilling a week, which he collected himself. In 1930, however, he was flattered to be asked to be the first person to paint the portrait of his fellow townsman 'Trader Horn', then aged eighty. Aloysius Horn had been invited to St Ives by the writer, Charles Procter, who considered that the record of his adventurous life was "stranger than the most imaginative fiction. He has fraternised with cannibals, pigmies, savages of every kind and every colour, and has carried his life in his hand many a time and oft. He has been trader, peddler, prospector, pearler, elephant-hunter, explorer, soldier, sailor and almost everything else one can imagine. He is an author, artist, musician, poet, naturalist and comedian - a veritable Admirable Crichton." [293] Intending to visit for just a few days, Horn stayed a week and then returned again. A picturesque figure in his huge Stetson hat and leather coat, with a long silver beard and twinkling blue eyes, he made friends everywhere, particularly as he rejected "swagger hotels" and stayed in 'Downalong' amongst the fisherfolk. Procter commented, "I'll warrant there was some brave and strange yarns spun in the 'Lodges', not to mention the local hostelries, during his stay." [294] When he left, he told Procter, who often wrote under the alias, Marcus, "When I get to the Gate, Marcus, and Peter asks Trader Horn what he has seen, I'll start telling him.... And when I've told him, he'll ask, 'Have you seen St Ives?' I'll answer 'yes', and Peter'll say, 'Come inside, This is the next best thing'." [295]

Fig. 5.46  John Park     *Aloysius 'Trader' Horn*
(Harris Museum and Art Gallery, Preston)

---

293 *St Ives Times*, 10/1/1930.
294 ibid.
295 ibid.

Fig. 5.47  Arthur Hayward  *In A Sunlit Garden*
(Sotheby's)

In the early 1930s, Park continued with his mix of harbour scenes, townscapes, rural landscapes and the fruits of occasional trips away from Cornwall, but it was not an easy period financially. Accordingly, he was persuaded by Harold Sawkins, the Editor of *The Artist*, that, in the economic climate of the times, he needed to establish a London presence. His wife, Peggy, was rather more keen on the idea than Park himself, and, in 1933, they took a studio in Maida Vale next to Dorothea Sharp and Marcella Smith, who had become good friends. Whilst the move did result in Park tackling a wider range of subjects and making some important contacts, he was not unhappy to return to St Ives in 1940, and it is his colourful impressions of boats in St Ives harbour and his masterly portrayal of light upon the water's surface that have proved enduringly popular with collectors.

## 5.6  The figure paintings and portraiture of Arthur Hayward

A further important addition to the colony in the early 1920s was Arthur Hayward (b.1889), who was to become the leading portrait painter in the town for the next two decades. Born in Southport, Lancashire, Hayward had studied at Warrington School of Art and then under Stanhope Forbes in Newlyn. Having served as a Captain in the Royal Field Artillery, he returned to Paul, near Penzance, after the War, but decided to move across to St Ives in 1923, building a home in Carthew Quarry called 'Treveneth'. His work base initially was 4 Porthmeor Studios, and he was soon taking students.

Whilst later known for his attractive depictions of boats in the harbour, Hayward concentrated on portraiture and figure work during the 1920s. One of his most highly regarded paintings initially was *In A Sunlit Garden* (RA 1921) (Fig. 5.47), which was hung at the St Ives artists' show at Cheltenham in 1925 and at the Paris Salon in 1926, surprisingly his only exhibit there. It was later bought by the Mackelvie Trustees on behalf of Auckland Art Gallery in 1930.[296] However, he had limited success at the Royal Academy at this juncture, possibly as he did not always send there, but he was particularly pleased with his work *The Nursery Window* (RA 1927), featuring a mother, her child and its toy parrot, with the sun streaming through the window making patterns on the mother's dress, the child and the wall. Nevertheless, Hayward clearly began to develop a following as a portrait painter, for his sitters in the 1920s included Lady Jarvis and the Earl of Stratford, and, by 1929, he was being described as the colony's leading figure painter. It was, however, his self portraits with which he made his national reputation.

---

296 They also bought one of his depictions of the village of Paul, as did Warrington Art Gallery.

Fig. 5.48  Arthur Hayward     *A Cornish Painter*     (Phillips)

The first reference to a self portrait is in the review of Show Day in 1929.  This was called *Plein Air* and was described as an open-air effect with "harmony in the tones of the brilliant blue sky, the black hat and the yellow jumper".[297]  As no image is known, it is not possible to tell how similar this work was to *A Cornish Painter* (Fig. 5.48 - National Portrait Gallery), which was the first of Hayward's self portraits to be hung at the Royal Academy, in 1933.  It might possibly be the same work, re-named, but Hayward's next self portrait, *The Onion Man* (RA 1935), shows him wearing the same yellow jumper, the same scarf and black headwear, and so the colour scheme clearly appealed to him.

In 1930, Hayward also included an image of himself, with a guitar, in his work *Cornish Mendicants*, later re-named *Cornish Saints and Sinners* due to comments that some of the figures looked a little too prosperous for mendicants!  Charles Procter considered it "a quite remarkable achievement" that reminded him of the work of Laura Knight.  "The five figures in the picture are finely grouped and beautifully painted, and the colouring is excellent."[298]  However, it was not until 1933, when all three of his Academy exhibits (including *A Cornish Painter*) sold quickly, that Hayward came to national prominence.

### 5.7    The watercolours of Alfred Bailey

Fashion in art can be strange.  Today, the watercolours of Alfred Charles Bailey (b.1883), on the rare occasions that they appear at auction, arouse little or no interest, and yet, in the 1920s, no St Ives artist had more one-man shows in London, and his work was considered daring and innovative.  The son of Wilfred Bailey, a railway engineer who had made his money in America and Canada, Alfred was born in Brighton and had studied at his local School of Art, before coming down to St Ives in 1908 for further training under Louis Grier.  In 1910, he took a lease of premises in Porthmeor Road, which he converted into 'Atlantic Studio' and this was to be his working base for the next twenty-two years.  During the War, in c.1915, he decided to give up oil painting and went on to develop his own unique style of colourful watercolour painting, based broadly on the application of pointillist techniques used in oil painting to his chosen medium.  *The Times* commented, "Breaking up his colour into fragments, he combines these fragments in a manner which gives the appearance of shimmering light without sacrificing the composition which usually goes out when such minute analysis comes in." [299]

---

297 *St Ives Times*, 22/3 1929.
298 *St Ives Times*, 21/3/1930.
299 *The Times*, 12/6/1930.

From reviews in St Ives, one gains the impression that some of his fellow artists were not completely convinced by his work, and Wilson Henry Irvine records that the local fishermen considered him colour blind! Nevertheless, he had a succession of London shows, which gained favourable critical reviews. The first was in 1923 at the highly regarded Goupil Gallery, in Lower Regent Street, which had previously shown, for instance, the work of Cézanne and held exhibitions by the London Group. A reviewer commented that Bailey was "an artist with a distinctly original point of view and a healthy disregard for the hard and fast conventionalities of the old school. There are more than thirty Cornish pieces in the exhibition and they are more bright and colourful than anything we have seen for a long time. Mr Bailey is daring to the point of recklessness in some of his pieces, but always knows when to draw rein on his enthusiasm. He is courageous in his choice of subject-matter too." [300] The best work in the show was considered to be *From the Boathouse, Cadgwith*. "This is a brilliantly coloured drawing of Cadgwith Cove seen from the dark interior of a boatshed. The luminous void outside is almost blinding, but the whole thing is relieved by a rusty chain which hangs over the doorway, cutting the glare in the middle." Another well-regarded work was *The Empty Cottage*, the only interior in the show, which depicted the cottage formerly occupied by the novelist, Cyril Ranger-Gull, who had just died, where, in a room of brick-red walls, he had painted the door bright blue. Even in a hackneyed subject, such as *The Sloop Inn*, which Bailey had depicted several times, he had found something new. "He has lavished all the colours of his imagination on the rooftops and stranded boats, and brought out all the real glamour that is in the place." [301] One of the works in the show, *The Thames from the Tate Gallery* (Fig. 5.49), was reproduced in *Colour* with the comment, "This brilliant watercolour, full of dancing lights and colour, is a happy impression of the Thames Embankment in brilliant sunshine." [302]

In 1926, another highly regarded London dealership, the Redfern Gallery, held an exhibition of his work, which prompted praise in *The Studio* for "his recklessly clever landscapes, aimed at producing a gay and vivacious pattern rather than giving a credible transcription of nature." [303] He had another small show there in January 1928, which caused him to be hailed as "one of the most original of the younger school of painters...There is a remarkable vitality in these vague impressions of Cornish villages and an inspiring throb in the atmosphere which conveys much more of the true spirit of the Cornish landscape than a square mile of the almost photographic canvases which sometimes pass for art." [304]

Fig. 5.49  Alfred Bailey    *The Thames from the Tate Gallery*                    (*Colour*)

---

300 *Western Morning News*, reproduced in *St Ives Times*, 1/6/1923.
301 ibid.
302 *Colour*, September 1923 at p.8.
303 *The Studio*, Vol.91, 1926, p.123.
304 *Western Morning News*, reproduced in *St Ives Times* (with illustration) 8/1/1928.

# SEA CHANGE : FINE AND DECORATIVE ART IN ST IVES 1914-1930

Fig. 5.50   Donald Angier   *Old Timers, St Ives, Going Out*   (Private Collection)

Extensive foreign travel led to another exhibition of thirty works at the Goupil Gallery in January 1929, principally of Dutch and Italian scenes. This again attracted "more than ordinary attention", with all the works containing "unmistakeable marks of genius".[305] The following year he had a further show at a different venue, Twenty-One Gallery, in Mill Street, off Conduit Street, which even merited a review in *The Times*. Again, the subjects were mainly Italian, but some Cornish scenes were also included. He had also been experimenting, with his unique technique, in pastels. With his studio in poor repair, Bailey did not bother to renew the lease in 1932 and, although he remained a member of STISA until at least 1943, he does not appear to have returned to Cornwall to paint. Clearly, this is an artist, whose output needs re-evaluating, as and when more examples come on to the market.

## 5.8   Other male artists

Bailey is not the only St Ives artist of this era, whose reputation at the time is difficult to pass valid comment upon now. In the early 1920s, Percy des Carrieres Ballance (1899-1970) was hailed as one of the most promising young seascape painters in the colony, had several notable successes in Paris and had a well received one-man show in London. However, I have not come across a single seascape by him.

The child of a Birmingham surgeon, Percy and his sister, Marjorie, also an artist, moved down to Carbis Bay with their parents in 1919, and they both worked from 1 Piazza Studios. In October 1920, Percy joined Marcella Smith in an "exhibition of watercolour drawings and paintings of St Ives" at Grey Studio,

---

305 *Western Morning News*, reproduced in *St Ives Times*, 16/1/1929.

Foreshore, St Ives, and he continued, during the six years that he spent in the colony, to work both in oils and watercolour, displaying considerable versatility. However, it was his marine work, often pure seascapes, that attracted the most comment. In January 1921, he made a distinct impression in the first show of the year at Lanham's Galleries, his two works displaying "the rollicking gaiety of undaunted youth".[306] *Off Gurnard's Head* - a large picture of breaking waves and misty sunlight - is a first rate thing. It is a healthy revival of the St Ives tradition, painted with good humour and confidence. There is a sturdiness and vigour about the handling which is really delightful, the forms of the rocks and the water are cleverly realised by direct brushwork and the whole thing, even if unambitious, is a thoroughly sound accomplishment."[307] His other work, depicting moonlit breakers, again a traditional St Ives theme, was also well regarded.

His sketching trips tended to take him to Holland, particularly Dordrecht and Volendam, and, in September 1923, he had a one-man show at Lanham's Galleries, featuring watercolours of Holland and paintings of St Ives, and, in August 1924, he had a further show, both at Lanhams and in his studio, of watercolours and paintings of Holland, France and St Ives. In 1923, he had his first successes at both the Royal Academy and the Paris Salon but, like a number of St Ives marine artists, he enjoyed far greater success at the Salon than he had at the Academy. Between 1923 and 1926, he had eight works hung there, including *Dawn at Sea* (RA 1923, Paris 1924), which, when included in his one-man show at the Gieves Gallery in 1927, was hailed as "one of the best sea paintings that has come out of the West for a long time", and *Silver Sunset* (Paris 1925), which won a Mention Honorable.[308] Whilst the review of the Gieves Gallery show, which included some sixty works, still called Ballance a member of the St Ives art colony, he had moved away during 1925, having married Eleanor Bain of Illogan in April 1924. However, he became a member of STISA and returned from time to time, as his sister remained in the town for the rest of her life. It is a mystery why so little of his St Ives period work, either in oils or watercolours, has appeared at auction and so, again, judgement has to be suspended.

Fig. 5.51  Hurst Balmford        *St Ives from Clodgy*        (Private Collection)

---

306 *St Ives Times*, 28/1/1921.
307 ibid.
308 *Western Morning News*, reproduced in *St Ives Times*, 4/2/1927.

Fig. 5.52  Hurst Balmford  *Boats at St Ives*  (Private Collection)

Fig. 5.53  Hurst Balmford  *St Ives Harbour*  (David Lay, Penzance Auction House)

The position relating to Hurst Balmford (1871-1950) is almost the opposite - namely that his works do appear quite often at auction, revealing a not insignificant talent, and yet he seems to have enjoyed little critical acclaim during his life. The son of a Huddersfield builder, Balmford studied at the Royal College of Art and at Julian's in Paris. A letter to his landlord reveals that he had worked as an architect for some time, before becoming Head of Morecambe School of Art.[309] Accordingly, he appears not to have devoted himself to painting until quite late in life, and he only had his first success at the Royal Academy, with a painting of Polperro, in 1917. At the time of his second success, with *Boats at Anchor, St Ives* in 1924, he gave his exhibiting address as 'Meadow House', St Ives, but he appears, at all times, to have retained property in Blackpool, and so never became an integral figure in the colony. However, his presence became more regular after his purchase, in 1926, of the newly converted 'Beach Studio', on The Wharf, which now included accommodation. Later in the decade, he also took 5 Island Studios.

Balmford's most favourite subject was boats in the harbour, always interested in the play of light across the water (see Figs. 5.52 and 5.53). He employed quite soft, pastel colours in these works, making them distinctive. One of his largest paintings is *St Ives from Clodgy* (Fig. 5.51), an unusual vista of the town, in which the coastal path, flanked by yellow gorse, draws the eye of the spectator to the semi-circle of Porthmeor Beach, flanked by Man's Head and the Island. Balmford's only other success at the Royal Academy during the 1920s was *The Running Stream* (1926), but he sold two works, *Low Tide* and *Mousehole*, to the Mackelvie Trustees for Auckland Art Gallery in 1930. Although giving up his St Ives studio in 1933, he continued to return to Cornwall throughout the 1930s.

Two artists with strong American connections, who made distinctive contributions to the colony in the 1920s were W. Donald Angier (b. 1900) and George Turland Goosey (1877-1947). Donald Angier was born in West Newton, Massachusetts and was the son of George Angier, a wealthy manufacturer of medical chemicals and his Scottish wife, Emma. He was based in St Ives from 1925 to 1932, living in Carbis Bay and working from 'Meadow Studio'. When he held his first one-man show at Lanham's Gallery in 1927, the reviewer commented, "Mr Angier, who has had an adventurous life in many parts of the world, has only, we believe, begun to paint during the last few years." [310] Presumably, therefore, he took some tuition from Park or Hayward. An early work, such as *The Boatbuilder* (1925 - Fig. 5.54), depicting a man repairing boats on the edge of the Hayle Estuary, shows that he was already a fine draughtsman, but he developed his own unique style that was deliberately decorative, using pen, ink and gouache.

Fig. 5.54 Donald Angier     *The Boatbuilder*
(David Lay, Penzance Auction House)

---

309 Letter to Glanville and Hamilton dated 14/5/1931 - Mornington Estate Papers GHW/12/3/6/1/227/3.
310 *St Ives Times*, 22/4/1927. One suggestion I have heard is that he had been a racing driver.

Fig. 5.55  Donald Angier  *St Ives, Cornwall, The Harbour*  (Private Collection)

Angier is not listed at all in the *Dictionary of British Artists 1880-1940*, indicating that he had no success at the major exhibition societies, but a note in the local paper records that he was specifically invited to show ten works at an exhibition of British Modern Artists at the Whitechapel Art Gallery in January 1929, whilst labels on his work show that he exhibited at the Panton Club in Leicester Square.  Furthermore, when his work was included in an exhibition of the Thames Valley Arts Club in 1928, *The Surrey Comet* commented, "Some of the cleverest work to be seen is contained in the contributions of Mr W.D.Angier, who favours what may be termed the poster style for his landscapes and makes use of almost geometrically precise patterns of brilliant colour to achieve his excellently decorative effects." [311] *Old Timers, St Ives, Going Out* and *St Ives, Cornwall, The Harbour* (Figs. 5.50 and 5.55) are particularly fine examples, with delicious reflections captured by areas of flat colour, surrounded by bold lines. Painted on grey paper, as was his wont, the sky, in each case, is represented solely by cloud shapes outlined with a broad white line, with the odd small patch of blue.  Whilst his depictions of water show him at his best, he also did street scenes in St Ives and Mousehole and there are references to paintings of Polperro and the River Fowey at Lostwithiel.  He also did some work in oils, but these are not as effective.

Angier's novel style suited the burgeoning poster market, and it is no surprise to find that it was a design by him that was selected by STISA for its first sign outside the Porthmeor Gallery. However, in 1932, just as his style was likely to come more into vogue, Angier's parents seem eventually to have reined in his bohemian instincts, and he dutifully returned to America to become head of Angier Chemical Co, making numerous trips across to Britain in the course of his business.[312]  Sadly, he appears, on his return to America, to have given up painting completely, and so his distinctive work is little known.

---

311 Reproduced in *St Ives Times*, 18/5/1928.

312 See Melissa Hardie, *Artists in Newlyn and West Cornwall 1880-1940*, Bristol 2009, but note that Angier worked from 'Meadow Studio', St Ives not from Newlyn.

Fig. 5.56  George Turland Goosey     *Reflections, St Ives Harbour*
(W.H.Lane & Son, Penzance)

George Turland Goosey was born in Northampton and was the son of Nathaniel Turland, but had adopted the name Turland Goosey during his time as a successful architect in America.  There, he designed some of the early skyscrapers, "the famous Friars Club, the theatrical centre of America's capital" and no fewer than seven Roman Catholic Churches.  Having had some success already in New York with his etchings, Turland Goosey decided after the War to give up his architectural practice and settle in St Ives to learn how to paint in oils.  His work was first exhibited on Show Day in 1921.  In an article on the colony in 1923, entitled *A Cornish Chelsea*, Vera Hemmens recorded how he enjoyed his change of status; "He lives in a little studio perched on the rocks, where he paints and draws in black and white, so close to the sea that in the winter-time the foam dashes against the walls of his home...There he is, whiling the hours away, just doing the things that he likes best - and happy.  He and Rolf Bennett, the author, sit at the window, listening to the cries of the gulls and the music of the waves, smoking Dustman's Delight, a mixture of their own concoction." [313]

Fig. 5.57  George Turland Goosey     *Boats in St Ives Harbour*     (Private Collection)

---

313 *Daily Graphic*, reproduced in *St Ives Times*, August 1923.

The impressionist style that Turland Goosey developed would suggest that he may well have joined John Park's classes. Seemingly uninterested in wider recognition, he did not exhibit his work with any regularity, even in Cornwall, and rarely bothered at all outside the Duchy. Indeed, the only time that his oil paintings received fulsome praise was on Show Day in 1924, when he exhibited the fruits of a visit to Venice. A painting of old Adriatic boats, laden with wood, anchored against the wall of an ancient Venetian palace, was considered his best work to date. The boats were gorgeously coloured, whilst he had captured wonderfully well the texture and patina of the old walls. However, it is his colour-filled paintings of boats in St Ives harbour, with delicious reflections, that have ensured that he has a following amongst collectors of St Ives art. In the late 1920s, he appears to have reverted to his original name of George Turland and, on Show Day in 1930, he exhibited still lives "full of Oriental lacquer-like colouring and very decorative".[314] He remained in St Ives until the late 1930s, when, with War looming, he returned to America, ending his days in the Laguna Beach colony in California.

Born in London, Francis Algernon Spenlove-Spenlove (1897-1981) was the son of the well-known artist and art teacher, Frank Spenlove-Spenlove (1868-1933), but, in order to distinguish himself from his father, he exhibited under the name of Francis Raymond up to c.1923 and then as Francis Raymond Spenlove. His work was first mentioned in St Ives in 1917 and, in April 1920, he had an exhibition, along with Marcella Smith, at 3 Porthmeor Studios, in which he showed some thirty pen and ink drawings of St Ives. He had another exhibition of drawings of old St Ives at Lanham's in April 1925. However, it was as a portrait painter that he became best known, one of his most highly rated early attempts, in 1920, being a self-portrait in yellow waistcoat by candlelight. He did enjoy some brief success at the Paris Salon, his exhibits there including two paintings of his wife, 'Billie' - one in 1924, before their marriage in June 1925, and one in 1928.[315] Whilst his style was felt to be developing into something original and he was an early committee member of STISA, he did not pursue his artistic career with any vigour and eventually gave up painting to devote himself to market gardening.

Fig. 5.58 Francis Spenlove sketching his wife, 'Billie', on the rocks at Porthmeor Beach
(Marion Whybrow)

An important new arrival in the colony in the latter part of the decade was Hugh Gresty (1899-1958). The son of the founder of the furnishing firm, Waters and Kidd, Gresty was born in Nelson, Lancashire and initially studied at the local School of Art. Having served in the Army during the War, during which he was wounded at Ypres and suffered from being gassed, he won a scholarship to Goldsmith College. In 1926, shortly after his marriage, he settled in St Ives and made an immediate impact with his watercolours of ancient buildings sketched during his regular visits to Italy and Spain, in which he was able, despite the delicacy of the medium, to convey impressions of monumentality and calm dignity. Borlase Smart, when reviewing Show Day in 1929, commented, "This artist is quite an acquisition to the St Ives Art Colony and also shows three of the finest works this year. They reflect sound constructional ability and rich sense of colour, and a great searching after truth. Last, but not least in these *modern* days when so many so-called artists take the line of least resistance, they are full of the most beautiful and appealing sense of perfect drawing."[316] The works concerned were *The Baths of Caracalla, Rome* (RA 1929) (Cartwright Hall Art Gallery, Bradford) and two depictions of Alcantara Bridge, Toledo. The moonlit example of this is now owned by the Towneley Hall Art Gallery and Museum, Burnley, which

---

314 *St Ives Times*, 21/3/1930.
315 The note of his marriage refers to his wife as Miss Mai Douchier of London - *St Ives Times* 3/7/1925.
316 *St Ives Times*, 22/3/1929.

has a large collection of Gresty's works, including a further depiction of the Baths of Caracalla (Fig. 5.60).[317] One Spanish city that fascinated Gresty in particular was Avila, with its white-painted houses, with terracotta-tiled roofs, and, on Show Day in 1930, he exhibited *Spanish Caprice*, which depicted a busy street scene in that city, painted with meticulous accuracy and attention to detail. He also did a number of decorative depictions of the city's white painted battlements, merely entitled *Spanish City*. The first of these was exhibited in the 1930 Summer Exhibition of STISA and examples are owned by both the Walker Art Gallery, Liverpool and the Towneley (Fig. 5.59).

Figs. 5.59 and 5.60

Hugh Gresty

Top : *Avila*

Bottom : *The Baths of Caracalla, Rome*

(Towneley Hall Museum and Art Gallery, Burnley)

---

[317] *The Baths of Caracalla, Rome* is illustrated in colour (Plate 33) and *Alcantara Bridge, Toledo* is illustrated in black and white on p.102 of my book *Creating A Splash*, which contains a lengthy dictionary entry on Gresty.

Before seemingly falling out with Borlase Smart in the 1930s, Gresty was intimately involved in the early years of STISA, and remained in the town until his death, enjoying considerable success at the Royal Academy in the 1930s, where his decorative touch was appreciated as much as his faultless draughtsmanship. However, his concentration on foreign subjects has impacted upon his reputation in Cornwall.

## 5.9     Other female artists

From the early days of the colony, female artists, such as Marianne Stokes, Helene Schjerfbeck, Dorothy Robinson and Mia Brown, had done much to further the reputation of the colony, but, despite the number of women working in the colony in the 1920s, few made any appreciable impact as painters in London circles, and they have largely been ignored. Nevertheless, several had not insignificant success in Paris but, frustratingly, examples of their work are rarely seen, and so it is impossible to determine what qualities resulted in this divergence of reputation. Could it be possible that they were too modern for London tastes? Other female artists, as will be seen, enjoyed a measure of success as handicraft workers or as printmakers.

The figure painter, Mary Frances Agnes Williams, who first exhibited in St Ives on Show Day in 1920 and who worked initially from Norway House Studio and then from Enys Studio in Victoria Place, had done most of her art training in Paris and, accordingly, she sent her major works to the Paris Salon rather than to the Royal Academy. As a result, she seems little known in this country but, between 1920 and 1935, she had fourteen works hung in Paris. An unidentified local artist sat for two portraits - *The Mystic* (Paris 1924) and *The Enigma*. Could this have been Bernard Leach?

Fig. 5.61  Nell Cuneo     *March Sunshine*         (Private Collection)

Fig. 5.62  Mary McCrossan  *Sennen Cove*
(St Ives Arts Club, photo Marie Keeling)

Other female artists, who enjoyed great success in Paris, were Annie Falkner and her companion, Leslie Hervey, who rented 3 Piazza Studios for some twenty years prior to Annie's death in 1933. During the 1920s, Annie had no fewer than twenty-two works hung at various of the Paris Salons and, in the year she died, had actually been appointed on to the hanging committee of the Salon d'Automne, where she had been a member for many years. She was primarily a colourist, who specialized in decorative depictions of farm animals, such as *The Lunch Hour* (Southampton Art Gallery), and her obituary notice recorded that, although she had received a measure of recognition in this country, with paintings being acquired by the Contemporary Art Society and several other well-known agencies, "many works were bought and sold by dealers in Paris, where her pictures were highly appreciated".[318] Leslie Hervey, who painted townscapes and still life, again in a colourist style, also had seventeen works hung in Paris between 1921-26, and the pair would seem to have been based there for part of the decade.

Yet another female artist to have repeated success in Paris was Hettie Tangye Reynolds, a Redruth girl, who had married the London artist, Reginald Francis Reynolds in 1899. In 1916, they took a studio in St Ives and were regular visitors during the 1920s, particularly during the years 1921-3 and 1928-1932. She specialized in still lifes and, between 1924 and 1937, had twenty-five works hung at the Salon, with *Old World Blossoms* winning a silver medal in 1926. Her husband was also far more successful in Paris than the Academy, having sixteen works hung between 1926 and 1936, many of which were Cornish landscapes. In fact, in 1929, they held a joint exhibition at Walker's Galleries, New Bond Street, entitled *Beneath the Cornish Sun*.

A dynamic presence in the colony during this decade was Nell Marion Cuneo (1867-1953), the widow of the Italian American book illustrator, Cyrus Cuneo, who had died from blood poisoning in 1916, having been scratched by a monkey whilst wearing stage make-up. As an artist, she specialized in portraits and figure paintings. She was successful for the first time at the Royal Academy in 1912 and, having been elected as an SWA in 1917, remained a member until 1952. Following her husband's death, she moved to Dartmoor and then to Cornwall, living first in Halsetown and then in St Ives. She bought Down-along House, which she restored and which became the famous coffee shop, *The Copper Kettle*.

She also created for herself a studio on the top floor. She first featured on Show Day in 1922, and, in 1923, she exhibited three portraits of fellow St Ives artists - Pauline Hewitt, Dorothy Cooke and Edith Meta Alexander. Pauline Hewitt became a great friend and, along with George and Kathleen Bradshaw, acted in the plays that Nell wrote. Her figure paintings were often praised for their fine colour schemes and interesting arrangements, but she did not have any work hung at the Academy during the 1920s.

---

318 *St Ives Times*, 7/7/1933.

Fig. 5.63   Mary McCrossan   *The Harbour, St Ives* (1924)        (David Messum Fine Art Ltd)

Beatrice Pauline Hewitt (1873-1956) was to become, during the 1930s, one of the leading female artists in the colony, but, having taken a break from painting after her studies at the Slade to bring up her son, she was still developing her skills during the 1920s and only had her first success at the Academy in 1927. Nevertheless, in 1930, she sold her two exhibits there - *The Wedding* and *Maritime Alps* - very quickly. She tended to travel frequently to avoid becoming stale and *Herring Packing, St Ives* (RA 1928) was one of her few local scenes hung at Burlington House. She also did some portraiture. Another married female artist, who was to become an important figure in the 1930s, but who only had her first success at the Academy in 1927, was Alixe Jean Shearer Armstrong (1894-1983). At this juncture, she specialized in still life, a genre in which Helen Stuart Weir was making a reputation for herself both at the Academy and the SWA.

The most talented female artist involved with the colony during the 1920s was Mary McCrossan (1863-1934), who had studied under Olsson and Talmage between 1897-1899 and had made several return visits prior to the War. She came back for an extended stay in 1924-5, taking part in Show Day in 1925, when she exhibited at 4 Island Studios, recently vacated by John Park. Her principal work was *The Grand Canal, Venice*, which, when hung at the Academy, was applauded for the "air of festive gaiety" that she had managed to impart to this scene of life on the the blue waters of the canal rippling in the sunshine.[319] She also had four works included in the exhibition by the St Ives artists at Cheltenham that April, of which the principal work was an oil of St Ives Harbour (probably Fig. 5.63). Another painting in the show, a watercolour, *The Doge's Palace, Venice,* was shortly afterwards bought by Southport Art Gallery. She retained 4 Island Studios until 1927, the year that she was elected to the RBA - at the same time as Hugh Gresty. In 1928, she had a show at the Beaux Arts Gallery in London, from which her watercolour of Southampton Harbour was bought by the Contemporary Art Society, and she settled back in the colony permanently in 1929, when her works became a highly regarded feature of STISA exhibitions until her premature death in 1934. Other artists involved in the colony during the 1920s are listed in Appendix B Table B.

---

319 *St Ives Times*, 8/5/1925.

# TEACHERS AND PUPILS

## 6.1  Introduction

In the twenty-five year period prior to 1914, St Ives had gained a worldwide reputation as a centre for the teaching of landscape and marine painting. At one juncture, successful schools were being run by Julius Olsson and Algernon Talmage, Louis Grier, and John Noble Barlow. By 1914, however, only Noble Barlow was actively taking pupils, although now based in Penzance. Alfred Hartley had also started some printmaking classes in 1912. Keen to keep involved, despite his move to London in 1912, Olsson, in 1914, persuaded his former pupil, Will Ashton, to come across from Australia, with his wife and two young children, to resurrect his painting school, with himself and Talmage as visiting teachers, but, with the outbreak of War and the ban on sketching out of doors, Ashton stayed in London. Accordingly, for such students as there were in the colony during the War, the options were far fewer than they had been in previous years. However, some senior artists were prepared to work with a few pupils. We know, for instance, that the Americans, Marcella Smith and Helen Stuart Weir, and the marine painter Leslie Kent (later STISA) took some lessons from Fred Milner; that Betty Thompson (later STISA), a dwarf with severe curvature of the spine, who made a name for her Welsh slate quarry drawings, studied under Emile Fabry; that Fanny Lloyd had classes with Louis Reckelbus, and that the Australian, Sydney Long, and Christopher Nevinson were among those that consulted Alfred Hartley. However, there was one new arrival, Frances Hodgkins, who not only was financially dependent on the success of her painting classes, but also had developed, during her time in France, a devoted group of students, who were prepared to follow her wherever she settled.

## 6.2  The classes of Frances Hodgkins

A witty, intelligent and outspoken woman, Hodgkins made a good teacher and established long-lasting friendships with many of her pupils. She had secured, in 1910, a significant accolade by being the first woman to be appointed to the staff of the Colarossi Academie in Paris, where she held watercolour classes, and, in 1911, she started her own School of Water-Colour in Paris, which was very successful, often attracting over forty students. Accordingly, she had high hopes of being able to earn a living as an art tutor in St Ives. Indeed, her first comment about her new Porthmeor studio was "that it will do very nicely for a Class - not pretty but useful".[320]

By January 1915, she had got herself settled in and told her mother, "I start teaching next week with three pupils & more to come. But for the War I should now be in Paris with forty & three I expect. I have one local pupil - a nice woman who is going to be a great help to me in many ways - she has a glorious collection of old china & has given me carte blanche to borrow it when so disposed. She is having a tea party for me this week - 30 people - oh dear!" One of her first students was a Miss Henderson, with whom she walked the moors and attended a *tableaux vivants* evening put on by the artists, whilst the local woman was probably Nina Weir-Lewis, the mother of Helen Stuart Weir. In May, Hodgkins makes mention of two further pupils, Miss Winthrop, who lived in Exeter and with whom Hodgkins stayed on a number of occasions over the next six years, and Miss Eva Stafford, whose portrait she exhibited at the International Society that October.[321] However, the following month, with the restraints imposed by the sketching ban, she felt compelled to give up her rooms and sleep in her studio, telling her mother, "I feel it is a wise precaution to save as much as possible for pupils are dropping off & many who are expected are not coming."[322] Nevertheless, in July, she had a class of ten - "one just crossed from Paris & an old favourite - Bessie Gibson from Brisbane, come to England to say goodbye to a brother just off to the Dardanelles".[323] Elizabeth Dickson Gibson (1868-1961) had also worked with Hodgkins in Paris. Indeed, she had been based there since 1906. She was the daughter of a bank manager and, having studied at Brisbane under Godfrey Rivers between 1899-1905, had then left Australia for what was intended to be a three year trip to study in France. She ended up living in Montparnasse until 1939, and exhibited regularly at the Royal Academy and the Paris Salons. These works tended to be portraits or Whistlerian studies, but more highly regarded are her fresh and individualistic watercolours, where clearly Hodgkins had a marked impact. The group of students that summer also included fellow New Zealander, Edith Collier, who was to make such an impression on her return to the colony in 1920.

---

320 Letter from Frances Hodgkins to her mother, 19/11/1914, see L.Gill, *Letters of Frances Hodgkins*, Auckland, 1993 at p.299.
321 Letter from Frances Hodgkins to her mother, 15/5/1915, see L.Gill, ibid, at p.306.
322 Letter from Frances Hodgkins to her mother, 17/6/1915, see L.Gill, ibid, at p.306.
323 Letter from Frances Hodgkins to her mother, 22/7/1915, see L.Gill, ibid, at p.307.

Hodgkins hoped that she had managed to get round the sketching ban. "I discovered this nice little cove over an old mine - very private & secluded, walled in, & almost invisible to passers by....For 2 blessed weeks we posed our models there & crossed ourselves piously thinking how lucky we were. Then pounced the Sergeant himself & turned us out of our Eden. I am very low in my mind to know what to do. It is such a bore to have to work indoors when the sun shines....I am now searching for a garden where I can have my model groups - but even gardens are at a premium." [324]

In August, though, her spirits had been raised somewhat. "The weather is gorgeous and my girls have been painting imps up on the moors or in gardens or any mortal thing that turns up in the way of a willing model. I have been hard put to it keeping my Class together, converting landscape painters into figure dittos, pushed into it against their will, but liking it hugely once they start. Three girls went off today bubbling over with enthusiasm, one of them with a picture of mine under her arm wh. she bought for 10 guineas - a welcome windfall for me." [325]

A most interesting member of this class - Hodgkins certainly calls her one of her protogées, as well as a favourite model - was Irene Kitchen, a girl aged 23 who came from "a poor but honest family of a very sturdy Cornish stock".[326] This is the first reference that I can recall to a local from a poor family studying art. On hearing that the girl's brother, William, had just won the RSM in the Dardanelles, Hodgkins congratulated their mother on having a hero son, but was told, "So Lady 'Ayne says, but I make it out like this, miss, Willy 'ad to do it & he done it"! [327] Hodgkins indicated that Irene was the model for a Royal Academy exhibit, but it is not certain what work she was referring to.

September 1915 saw the total ban on sketching that outraged the whole of the artistic community. Its impact on Hodgkins' classes was immediate, and a large percentage of her pupils had little option but to leave. However, Hodgkins was determined to continue, as she could not afford to give up, and confided in her mother, "By keeping out of the eye of the Sergeant, who has promised not to run me in more often than he need, & sending my painting kit stealthily by night, I am able to work in Mrs Weir Lewis' garden round their lily pond, but it is nervy work & any moment may be stopped. A Concentration Camp and food allowance is what they should do with us seeing that they are depriving us of our daily bread and butter." [328] Clearly, Nina Weir-Lewis was a big support at this juncture, and Hodgkins commented, "Mrs Weir Lewis keeps on having lessons in a methodical and sensible way and pays me 4 guineas a month for helping her acquire a good imitation of the Hodgkins style." The arrival of one of her former protogées also perked her up. "An old pupil, with an unfortunate enemy name & appearance, but loyally British, who came down from Bristol to do a little work, I am helping along with lessons & assisting her to show her sketches, wh.are very able and attractive. She is hard hit & hardly knows where to turn." [329] This was Amy Eliza Krauss, who went on to become a successful potter, occasional painter and lifelong friend, and she exhibited a watercolour of St Ives at the RWA exhibition in 1918. She was also a guest at the Arts Club in 1921, after Hodgkins' departure.

Despite this unsatisfactory backdrop, Hodgkins, in a moment of optimism, rented the empty studio next door and rigged it up for Winter classes starting in October 1915. She told her mother, "I hope to fill it, with luck." [330] However, there is no further mention of these classes (or of the second studio), and, in February 1916, she commented, "It is some relief in one way, not to have pupils - it leaves so much more time & strength for work." [331] No doubt Lindner squared matters with the landlord as regards the second studio, and it was during this winter that he encouraged her to paint in oils in earnest, giving her a commission to ease her financial plight.

With a number of former pupils booking up for a summer class in 1916, Hodgkins realised that she needed to organise this outside Cornwall, due to the sketching ban. At the end of June, having done some exploring by bicycle in the Cotswolds, she settled on Chipping Campden as her base, and soon had a thriving class, which she ran until 10th September. However, she found the big party "rather a dull lot of human beings" and developed "great contempt for the pampered well fed English woman whose physical welfare is her only thought".[332]

---

324 Letter from Frances Hodgkins to her mother, 22/7/1915, see L.Gill, *Letters of Frances Hodgkins*, Auckland, 1993 at p.307.
325 Letter from Frances Hodgkins to her mother, 16/8/1915, see L.Gill, ibid, at p.308.
326 I am grateful to Janet Axten of St Ives Archive Study Centre for finding the Kitchen family in the 1901 Census. Irene was then 9, her brother, William, 8, and they were then living with their parents, William and Georgina, at Polmanter Farm, Halsetown.
327 Letter from Frances Hodgkins to her mother, 8/1915, see L.Gill, ibid, at p.309.
328 Letter from Frances Hodgkins to her mother, 16/9/1915, see L.Gill, ibid, at p.310.
329 Letter from Frances Hodgkins to her mother, 16/9/1915, see L.Gill, ibid, p.310.
330 Letter from Frances Hodgkins to her mother, 16/9/1915, see L.Gill, ibid, at p.310.
331 Letter from Frances Hodgkins to her mother, 10/2/1916, see L.Gill, ibid, at p.315.
332 Letter from Frances Hodgkins to her mother, 5/8/1916, see L.Gill, ibid, at p.317-8.

The following winter back in St Ives was a great trial and there were no pupils. In June 1917, she went to Burford clearly with a view to holding a similar class as the year before, but found it (and, possibly, the take up) disappointing. Accordingly, she was back in "beautiful" St Ives ten days later, commenting to a disappointed student "anywhere inland stifles one after this vast & splendid colour and air".[333] Two former pupils, who had worked with Hodgkins in France, Hannah Ritchie and Dorothy Jane Saunders, who had hoped to join the Burford class, got together with four other girls from Manchester to ask Hodgkins to give lessons there, but, having just got some commissions off the Hellyers, she turned the opportunity down. By mid-August, she was busy with a class of five pupils in St Ives, but told her mother, "It is not so trying as when there were only two, who were both fond of me but hated each other."[334]

Again, the winter period of 1917-8 was not easy, with severe food shortages, but she appears to have had at least two pupils. "They are my props and mainstay."[335] One of these may be Evelyn Chapman (1888-1961), an Australian artist, who was staying in the town with her husband at the time and who was signed into the Arts Club in February 1918 by Hodgkins' friend, Edgar Skinner. Evelyn had studied art in Sydney with Dattilo Rubbo and in Paris and London, and went on to do a series of paintings of the Somme battlefield in 1919-20. Although little known, eight of her works are owned by the Art Gallery of New South Wales, Sydney, amongst them an interesting and most colourful painting *Old Houses, St Ives* (Fig. 6.1), depicting what is now the entrance to the Penwith Gallery.

Fig. 6.1  Evelyn Chapman  *Old Houses, St Ives*
(Art Gallery of New South Wales, Sydney)

---

333 Letter from Frances Hodgkins to Hannah Ritchie dated 11/7/1917 - Ed. L Gill, ibid, at p.322.
334 Letter from Frances Hodgkins to her mother, 20/8/1917, see L.Gill, ibid, at p.324.
335 Letter from Frances Hodgkins to her mother, 7/1/1918, see L.Gill, ibid, at p.329.

Fig. 6.2   Frances Hodgkins     *Portrait of Beatrice Wood*
(Jonathan Grant Galleries, Auckland)

Things perked up in March 1918. "The other day 3 nice girls, all from NZ, blew into the Studio - Miss Denniston of Peel Forest - Barker - ditto & Beatrice Wood from ChCh, a bright fair headed girl with a fluffy dog in her arms. She wanted me to paint her a sketch of herself for her Dad - William Wood - which I did! She was awfully pleased & sent a cheque for 8 gns and has dunned her father for the balance of £12.12. She is a masterful young person - of the nice sort, & I would like to adopt her. Now *she* is endowed with a business sense, inherited no doubt from that big family of miller and merchant Woods I used to know as young men in my youth in ChCh." [336] The portrait, which was exhibited at the Grosvenor Gallery that year, is one of Hodgkins' best works from her St Ives period. Although executed in oils, the paint appears to have been applied thinly more in a watercolour style, whilst pastel tones are predominant. The face, though, with its green and pink contrasting colours is the most innovative section. Green might be novel for face colouring but does it really enhance the work? However, the Jack Russell in her arms, with the red of its collar being an important colour note, is a delight. Shown at the Canterbury Society of Arts in 1919, it was the first oil painting by Hodgkins seen in New Zealand. Whilst in St Ives, Beatrice Wood took a photo of Hodgkins sitting in her new studio, The Wharf Studio, upon which she has inscribed, "Rags I have on are the historic ones worn in NZ 1913". The War's financial pressures had precluded new clothes.

That year's summer class was held in Porlock, during which she commented, "I get very bored by pupils & fear I begin to show it - the temptation to tell them to go to the d......l is great. But they pay my hotel bill." [337] Nevertheless, she ultimately rated it quite a success, albeit brought to a premature end by the hoteliers going bankrupt. Back in St Ives in mid-September, she was joined by another ex-pupil from Parisian days, the Canadian sculptress, Katherine Wallis (1861-1957), who became known for her studies of children and animals. However, Katherine's time in St Ives was overshadowed by the death of her sister in the flu epidemic that raged that autumn. With the Armistice signed on 11th November, people could begin to look forward with hope and Hodgkins found her classes fuller that winter. She also started classes in Newlyn, as a result of the contacts that she had made there through Cedric Morris and Lett Haines.

---

336 Letter from Frances Hodgkins to Will Field, 30/3/1918, see L.Gill, *Letters of Frances Hodgkins*, Auckland, 1993 at p.330.
337 Letter from Frances Hodgkins to her mother, 25/8/1918, see L.Gill, ibid, at p.332.

Fig. 6.3  Frances Hodgkins     *Threshing in the Cotswolds*
(Dunedin Public Art Gallery)

Clearly prompted by Hannah Ritchie's trip there in 1917, during which she had sent sketches to Hodgkins for comment, the summer class in 1919 was held at Ludlow, which she found large and fatiguing.[338] "People always wonder how I can walk all the morning after my pupils & stand all the evening at my easel. I don't always feel very walkative or workified I can tell you - but one goes on & gets through somehow."[339] At the beginning of August, she moved on to Park Farm, Great Barrington, in the Cotswolds for just over a month, as Beatrice Wood had organised a party of six or seven girls there. It was a delightful place, with fine old barns and a great rick yard, where they were threshing corn. It is most likely, therefore, that the paintings of a traction engine done by both Hodgkins and Wood are of this farm. Hannah Ritchie and Jane Saunders, who were to be the subject of a double portrait by Hodgkins (1922-5) and were long-term friends, were also amongst the party.

Fig. 6.4  Beatrice Wood    *Traction Engine*
(Jonathan Grant Galleries, Auckland)

---

338 Hodgkins' letter to Hannah Ritchie dated August 1917, commenting on her sketches, is a unique record of her teaching methods.
339 Letter from Frances Hodgkins to her mother, 12/7/1919, see L.Gill, ibid, at p.342.

Fig. 6.5  Vida Lahey  *Selling the Catch, St Ives*  (Private Collection)

At this juncture vacillating between St Ives and London, Hodgkins was back in the colony in November 1919 and mentions the presence of a further ex-pupil, who had been part of her summer class at St Valéry in 1906 - Madeline Williams. She commented, "[She] grows more & more like a character out of Jane Austen every day...She is unique among my friends...but so true and gentle & unassuming - her only weakness is what school girls call a 'pash' for me - I love her for it." [340]

Any plans for a summer sketching class in 1920 were probably put off by the arrival in St Ives of Hodgkins' niece, Lydia, but, in any event, with the War over and the sketching ban lifted, there were plenty of artist visitors in St Ives interested in lessons. In early September, Hodgkins told her mother, "I have had a crowd of pupils and I prosper in a way that I have not done for years." [341] By early October, however, she was not unhappy that her class had been reduced to three, but she described two of them - Frances Vida Lahey (1882-1960) from Brisbane and Edith Marion Collier (1885-1964) from Wanganui, New Zealand - as "sterling good girls...Addicted to me and my works." [342] Edith Collier produced, during the couple of months that she spent with Hodgkins that autumn, such a significant body of work that I discuss it separately in the next section. Vida Lahey, who spent five weeks in the class, also completed a number of interesting works, several of which are illustrated in her biography produced by Queensland Art Gallery in 1989 to accompany an exhibition *Songs of Colour - The Art of Vida Lahey*, for she went on to become a highly influential figure in the Queensland art world, not only through her own artistic productions but also in her role as art educator and advocate. Having studied in Melbourne from 1905-9, Lahey had already had a work acquired for the Queensland National Art Gallery by the time that she sailed to England in 1916 to be closer to her brothers who were fighting in the War. Until the end of the War, she was engaged in war work in this country, but, during 1919 and 1920, she immersed herself in an extensive period of study, which included spells at Colarossi's and in the still life classes of former Olsson student, Ethel Carrick Fox, in Paris, whilst at the same time viewing art galleries and contemporary exhibitions. Fellow Queenslander, Bessie Gibson, whom she met in Paris, may have recommended Hodgkins to her, and she told a reporter in 1927, "It was Miss Hodgkins

---

340 Letter from Frances Hodgkins to her mother, 18/11/1919, see L.Gill, *Letters of Frances Hodgkins*, Auckland, 1993 at p.344.
341 Letter from Frances Hodgkins to her mother, 9/9/1920, ibid, at p.348.
342 Letter from Frances Hodgkins to her mother, 1/10/1920, see L.Gill, ibid, at p.349. The third girl may have been a Miss Cabdell, for a letter in Edith Collier's papers from an unknown correspondent (possibly Vida Lahey) runs, "How goes the painting? I am imagining you and Miss Cabdell hard at work on heads of fisher people and children, and do so wish I were doing them too." Quoted in Joanne Drayton, *Edith Collier - Her Life and Work 1885-1964*, Christchurch, 1999.

who first gave me an inkling into the aims of modern art."[343] Indeed, she came to regard her time with Hodgkins as valuable, stimulating and one of the most important of her European experiences. "A few weeks at Frances Hodgkins' sketching class...applied a quickening shock to my sensibilities. It was at this time that the ideas which developed into modern Art began to be diffused. I was very interested but too undeveloped to be really ready for its assimilation, and felt the need of proving my powers before attempting new flights with my fledgling wings."[344] Accordingly, she clearly was not completely comfortable with the new, somewhat mannered approach that Hodgkins encouraged her to take with the works that she did in St Ives, for instance of the local fish market and the town band, and, on her return to Brisbane in February 1921, she reverted to producing attractive, colourful paintings that owe more of a debt to the Impressionists, than to Hodgkins. The experience, though, was not wasted, and she came to believe that "At its greatest, art is the arrangement of areas and shapes in such a way as to stimulate our deepest and subtlest thoughts and emotions."[345] Furthermore, she became one of that rare breed - an artist, who was able to live off her art for the rest of her life.

Ever since the War ended, Hodgkins had been dreaming of returning to France. In June 1919, she told her mother, "Who knows by next July I may be back in France with all my girls & pals as in the good old days - Fills one with vim to think of it". By October 1920, though, she felt able to contemplate a future without the need for teaching. "I am longing for a large new region all to myself - I have sold so well this summer that I am full of hope it may continue and enable me to do without pupils in future." Later, that month, she gave up her studio in St Ives and left for France. Whilst her dreams of prosperity were not fulfilled, she had, in any event, had enough of St Ives.

## 6.3   Edith Collier's finest hour

In October 1920, Frances Hodgkins told her mother, "I have one very bright N. Zealander, Collier by name, who is coming on wonderfully - I'll make something of her I feel sure."[346] Edith Collier did indeed produce some interesting, innovative and important paintings in St Ives that year but, sadly, her career faltered on her return to New Zealand. Born in Wanganui, her father, Henry, was the son of a Manchester cloth manufacturer and had emigrated to New Zealand in 1877. He began as a music teacher but then made money in a music publishing business, investing the profits in land. He was, therefore, able to finance his eldest daughter's desire to train as a professional artist. Edith studied initially in Wanganui, but was encouraged to continue her training in England by her neighbour, Herbert Babbage. In 1913, therefore, she set sail for England and enrolled at St John's Wood School of Art, but she soon became rather disillusioned. "St John's is an old fashioned private school, very nice teachers, but it is really a bit out of date."[347] However, in 1914, she met the strong-minded, straight-talking Australian artist, Margaret Macpherson (later Preston), who was more modern and innovative in outlook, and, in 1915, she paid her first visit to St Ives, when she came to study under Hodgkins.[348] Edith continued to study intermittently under Macpherson until 1919, when many of her artist friends, including Macpherson, decided to return to their respective homelands. Edith, whose father had only anticipated that she would be away a year, was under constant pressure by this juncture to return to New Zealand, but she was determined to take her art further forward and she began exhibiting with SWA, WIAC and the International Society. She also started to concentrate on a more abstract approach to her figure work, inspired by exhibitions of work by Matisse and other modern French artists that she had visited in London. However, none of the styles that she tried really worked.

In 1920, she again attended Frances Hodgkins' Summer School in St Ives and it was during this visit that, almost instantaneously, she found her own distinctive style and approach; whilst influenced by Hodgkins, it was entirely original. During a relatively brief period of three months, Collier produced a significant body of oil, watercolour and gouache paintings, many of which are now owned or held on loan by the Sarjeant Art Gallery, Wanganui. The most distinctive works were her advanced portraits of local characters, with three depictions of a Cornish woman with Spanish blood being of particular merit. Sadly, the model's identity is not recorded. The major work, *A Cornish Woman of Spanish Descent* (Fig. 6.6), an oil on canvas, depicts her sitting on a chair in front of her kitchen table, upon which a variety of bowls, jugs and tins have been placed. Forms and shapes have been simplified, and this is even more evident in *The Spanish Woman* (Fig. 6.7), a close up of the same woman's face and upper body.

---

343 Gwendollyn Grant, *Daily Mail*, Brisbane, 14/5/1927.

344 Lilian MacArthur, *Vida Lahey - artist*, entry in the Society of Women Writers of N.S.W. literary competition, 1969, p.1.

345 In Manifesto of the Colour Club, Salisbury Chambers, George Street, Brisbane, 1940.

346 Letter from Frances Hodgkins to her mother, 1/10/1920, see L.Gill, *Letters of Frances Hodgkins*, Auckland, 1993 at p.348-9.

347 Letter from Edith Collier to her parents in 1915, reproduced in J.Drayton, *Edith Collier*, Canterbury, NZ, 1999 at p.33. She also commented that she had been particularly attracted by the syllabus' mention of Arnesby Brown as a landscape critic, and was disappointed when he only put in an appearance once a year (op. cit., reproduced in Drayton at p.26).

348 Her papers include a postcard addressed to her in 1915 at Wharf Studios, White Hart House, St Ives.

# SEA CHANGE : FINE AND DECORATIVE ART IN ST IVES 1914-1930

Figs. 6.6 - 6.9  Edith Collier

Top left : *A Cornish Woman of Spanish Descent*

Top right : *The Spanish Woman*

Bottom left : *The Pouting Girl*

Bottom right : *A Cornish Boy*

(All Collier Loan Collection, Sarjeant Art Gallery, except Fig. 6.6 Sarjeant Art Gallery, Wanganui)

Here the colour range has been reduced as well, leaving predominant the sharply contrasting colours of red and blue. This colour contrast was a feature of a considerable number of the works and, even when she executed portraits in watercolour, she was able to obtain the same strength of hue, as in *A Cornish Boy* (Fig. 6.9). However, it is her portrait, known as *The Pouting Girl* (Fig. 6.8), that demonstrates the influence of Hodgkins most, with its loose, fluid treatment and use of green for facial shadow.

A watercolour of an attic bedroom (Fig. 6.10) would seem to depict Collier's own room in St Ives, for it includes a red chair upon which a number of her models sat (see, for instance, the oil painting, *Jenny* Fig. 6.11). She also did a number of watercolour sketches of views of rooftops and chimneys, which may well have been of the vista from her attic window. In addition, she found the time to do numerous watercolours of the harbour and local streets, which are notable for their flattening of picture space, simplification of form, decorative impulse and soft colouring.

Aware that she had made real progress, Edith desperately wanted to accompany Hodgkins on a tour to the South of France in 1921, but her parents refused to pay for it. With her work not selling and having failed her teaching exams, she was left with little alternative but to give in to her parents' demands and return to New Zealand.[349] Frances Hodgkins wrote some words of comfort to her. "I am certain your fate will bring you back to England, as mine did. It will help your work a lot getting away from it, thinking over it from a distance and sorting out values and generally consolidating what you have absorbed.....don't mind the buffets or knocks. They are inseparable from the artist's life. Its an uphill tug all the way & its only the stout hearted who win through." [350]

Sadly, Hodgkins' predictions of a return to England and further success did not come true. Back in the provincial confines of Wanganui, Edith found herself, as the unmarried daughter, expected to look after elderly relations and a host of nephews and nieces. When she did exhibit at a prestigious exhibition put on in Wanganui in 1926, the New Zealand critics were completely unable to come to terms with her modernism. The slating her work received so upset her father that he inexcusably burnt some of her best work, particularly her nude studies. So discouraged, Edith only occasionally found the time and inspiration to paint and never developed the talent that had so blossomed in England. In 1980, the Sarjeant Art Gallery organised an *Edith Collier in Retrospect* touring exhibition and, in 1999, another exhibition, *Edith Collier and the Women of her Circle*, was accompanied by a biography by Joanne Drayton. As a result, her innovatory work in St Ives is now recognised in New Zealand. Because of her short visit, St Ives itself has yet to register that, here again, it provided telling inspiration.

Figs. 6.10 and 6.11 Edith Collier
*Attic Bedroom, St Ives* and (right) *Jenny*
(both Collier Loan Collection, Sarjeant Art Gallery, Wanganui)

---

349 She did manage to enrol in print-making and modelling courses at the London Central School of Arts and Crafts before leaving for New Zealand in December 1921.
350 Letter from Frances Hodgkins to Edith Collier, 18/2/[1921], quoted in Drayton, op. cit., at p.59.

## 6.4 The Simpson School of Painting

Whilst they may have given lessons to the odd student previously, the first reference in the local papers to either Charles or Ruth Simpson offering formal painting tuition in St Ives is not until May 1920, when Ruth Simpson advertised that she was giving lessons in portrait painting from the model at 5 Piazza Studios during June and July, with classes being three days a week, from 10 a.m. to 1 p.m. and fees being one guinea a week.[351] This suggests that the Simpsons' move to St Ives in 1916 was primarily for painting reasons, and was not motivated, as has sometimes been indicated, by a desire to set up a painting school. As noted above, Frances Hodgkins confirmed that, during the summer of 1920, St Ives was packed with students, and, presumably, the success of Ruth's venture persuaded Charles that they should set up a jointly run School that winter, with classes starting in October.[352] As Hodgkins had decided to leave St Ives, the field was left open to them, and the review of the year in the local paper that December indicated that the School had already become popular.

The prospectus for the Simpson School announced that all branches of painting and drawing would be taught and "especially the modern methods of handling oils, tempera, watercolour, etc and illustration work with a view to reproduction". Newspaper advertisements indicated that the subjects would include "portrait painting in oils (models daily), sketching in watercolour, tempera, etc; also the study of animal and bird life." The range of subjects taught and media utilised was, therefore, far wider than the original schools that had been run by Julius Olsson, Louis Grier and Algernon Talmage and, accordingly, the Simpson School lacked the distinguishing uniqueness that those early schools had had. In trying to appeal to a wide range of artists, it perhaps put off any student wishing to concentrate on a particular speciality. However, Simpson may have been right to broaden the curriculum, for the art world had changed and the most ambitious students of this era would not have considered the study of landscape and marine painting out of doors as a pre-requisite, in the same manner as it had been viewed at the turn of the century. The advertisements do not, in fact, place any emphasis on working outside but, being a keen *plein airist* himself, Simpson was still adamant that students should sketch out of doors, whenever possible, and a well-known photograph shows two girls, well wrapped up in thick coats, receiving tuition from Charles and Ruth on Porthmeor Beach. This was one of four photos promoting the School (another was Fig. 6.13), which were illustrated in *The Sphere* in September 1921 in an article entitled *The Artist Colony on the Cornish Riviera*.

Fig. 6.12 Charles and Ruth Simpson teaching on Porthmeor Beach

---

351 *St Ives Times*, 28/5/1920.
352 See advert in *St Ives Times*, 28/8/1920.

Fig. 6.13 The Simpsons entertaining in No 5 Piazza Studios in 1921

Charles Simpson is performing the honours with the bottle at the rear. On the easel is Ruth's portrait of the American, Rollo Peters, and she is sitting just to the right of this. To her left, are Eleanor Hughes, her bearded husband, Robert, and Ella Naper, friends from Newlyn and Lamorna, whilst the girl in the right foreground is unidentified. The elderly couple on the left of the photo are Professor Alfred Sidgwick and his wife, the author, Cecily Sidgwick from Lamorna. On the back wall can be seen Ruth's painting *A Company Commander*. Three students sit by this, with Kathleen Slatter immediately to the easel's left. Winifred Humphrey is likely to be one of the others.

The School was based in Nos 4 and 5 Piazza Studios, one above the other, and No 5 had specially constructed windows, which provided a wide view over Porthmeor Beach across the Bay, so that marine subjects could be painted indoors in adverse weather conditions. In the morning, sessions were led by either Ruth, who taught portrait painting, or Charles, whilst, after a picnic lunch, the students were left on their own in the afternoons to pursue a particular task. The School was run on a very flexible basis - it was open all year round, without any division into formal terms, and instruction in animal or landscape painting could even be taken via a correspondence course. The level of instruction was also negotiable - the normal fees were one guinea a week (with a minimum of four weeks), but additional private tuition could be obtained for three guineas a week. Students were often put up in the Simpsons' home, 'Loyalty Cottage', and joined in their social life, which invariably involved visits from old friends in Newlyn, such as Robert and Eleanor Hughes, who toyed with the idea of moving across to St Ives themselves.[353] Dinner and luncheon parties were not infrequent, for Simpson was renowned for his voracious appetite, whilst musical soirées were held from time to time, as another of Simpson's passions was Beethoven.

Fig. 6.14 The Piazza Studios and the overhanging window of Studio No 5 (St Ives Trust Archive Study Centre)

[353] In 1923-4, the *St Ives Times* mentions that three artists from Newlyn had decided to settle in St Ives - presumably, Arthur Hayward and Robert and Eleanor Hughes. Robert certainly participated in Show Day in 1924.

# SEA CHANGE : FINE AND DECORATIVE ART IN ST IVES 1914-1930

Fig. 6.15  Charles Simpson        *Phyllis and Vera Cuningham*        (Richard Green Ltd, London)

Fig. 6.16  Charles Simpson    *Phyllis and Vera Cuningham on Porthminster Beach*
(Private Collection)

Fig. 6.17   Charles Simpson   *Kathleen Bradshaw* (née Slatter)
(Private Collection)

In these congenial conditions, friendships soon grew between the students and their teachers, leading to a succession of portraits and other figure work in which the students acted as models.  Vera and Phyllis Cuningham studied for a while under the Simpsons in 1919.  Vera (1897-1955) was a wild child, who had been thrown out of her home by her father, because she was a bad influence on her elder sisters.  She had spent a few weeks at the Central School of Art in London, before deciding that the School had nothing to teach her and that she would try St Ives.  The two sisters feature in a number of Charles' paintings resting in the shade of one of the beach tents or leaning against the side of a boat in the harbour, at low tide.  Indeed, these paintings, clearly executed at some speed with considerable freedom, have proved to be Simpson's most popular works in the salerooms, as they combine the ever popular St Ives marine scene with the casual stylishness of the young women.  On her return to London, Vera took further lessons from Bernard Meninsky, becoming his model and mistress, before having a passionate affair with Matthew Smith, posing for the highly coloured nudes that made his reputation. She went on to enjoy some success as an artist herself, with her paintings of distorted female forms, exhibiting briefly with the London Group and later being promoted by the Creuze Gallery in Paris.[354]

One student, who ended up by staying in St Ives for the rest of her life, was Kathleen Slatter (1904-1997), the daughter of a well-known big game hunter, who had been brought up in Rhodesia.  However, after her father's death in the War, she had been sent to England under the guardianship of a great aunt, Lady Couchman, who lived in Gloucestershire.  Kathleen had wanted to study at the Slade School, but her guardian felt uncomfortable about a girl of her age and circumstances being on her own in London, and so selected St Ives.  She vividly recalled being picked up at the station by Simpson's father, an archetypal Major-General with a huge moustache, in his son's motor cycle and side car, thus forcing her to leap on to the back of the bike, whilst her trunk was placed at a jaunty angle in the side-car.  Her time at the School was enjoyable and rewarding.  She remembered a succession of 'bonny' Cornish models in straw bonnets, decorated with gaily coloured ribbon tied with a bow, or wearing other profusely decorated headwear, as was the fashion of the time, and being able to work on the draperies and backgrounds of portrait commissions that the Simpsons had received.

---

354 I am obliged to John Branfield for his summary of Vera's subsequent career.  See also R.Creuze, *Vera Cuningham*, Paris, 1984.

Fig. 6.18  George Bradshaw     *The White Barque*     (Royal Cornwall Museum, Truro)

One of Kathleen's fellow students was Winifred Humphrey (fl.1921-1959), who had work hung at the Royal Academy in 1921 and 1922, and whose portrait was painted by Ruth. Another was George Bradshaw (1887-1960), who not only was to become her husband in 1922, despite an eighteeen year age gap, but also the most successful of Simpson's students. As previously mentioned in Chapter 2, Bradshaw had served as a submarine commander during the War, but had managed during his leisure hours to pursue his interest in painting. When discharged from the Navy in acrimonious circumstances in 1921, he decided that he would like to study art further to see if he could make a second career out of it. Already with a keen interest in marine painting, St Ives seemed the obvious choice. He made progress remarkably quickly - the jagged, unrealistic seas of many of his submarine paintings giving way to the convincing swells and breaking waves of his early St Ives work. He had his first success at the Royal Academy in 1923, with a large canvas, *The White Barque* (Fig. 6.18 - Royal Cornwall Museum), showing a sailing barque driving through an ocean swell. This was also his first success at the Paris Salon in 1925. Having seen the old sailing ships so often during his Navy days, Bradshaw was acutely aware that their days were numbered and frequently included them in his paintings, having made endless and careful studies of their rigging, the set of their sails and their movement through water in all types of weather conditions.

The Bradshaws also sat as models for the Simpsons, Charles doing a portrait of Kathleen (Fig. 6.17) and Ruth one of George in his navy uniform, which Borlase Smart considered one of her greatest successes, showing "breadth of technique and spontaneity of touch".[355]

In 1923, adverts for the School changed. Charles was now the sole Principal, with Ruth merely listed as an assistant, whilst Bradshaw was now included as a further assistant. Perhaps Ruth had found that, with Charles perennially busy, she was being left with all the administrative tasks and that this was impacting on her own ability to paint. The topics covered were now briefly listed as 'Figure, Landscape, Marine, Animal', although the latter was soon discarded. A new 'mission statement' was concocted, which indicated that Simpson was responding to the increased interest in printmaking. "The object of the School is to teach Modern Methods of Painting in Oils, Tempera and Water Colours; Also Colour Printing from Wood Blocks etc and other methods of Reproduction."

Although the names of several other students, such as P.Lambe, L.S.Edmonds, Miss Bucknill, are recorded in the local press, none appears to have set the art world alight. Another was Donald Currie, a naval friend of Bradshaw, who acted as his best man. As the son of the owner of the Union Castle Line, he had little incentive to make art a career, and was summarily dismissed by Kathleen, with the words, "He played at art, but made a career of seducing other people's wives"!

---

355 *St Ives Times*, 17/3/1922.

Whilst learning much from Simpson, Bradshaw found his time as an assistant at the School less rewarding, as Simpson tended to use him as a dogsbody, sending him off to Scotland and Newmarket on matters relating to commissions received, without even covering his expenses. In fact, the issue of a financial reward for Bradshaw's time and effort became a serious bone of contention. Therefore, Bradshaw will have had mixed feelings, when the Simpsons decided to leave St Ives in 1924, bringing the School to a close. Both Kathleen and himself became integral figures in the colony's artistic and social life. Kathleen tended to concentrate on still life and portraiture, but had some success with her lampshades (see Chapter 10.4.5), whilst George developed a considerable reputation as a marine painter. Further successes during the 1920s included *The Western Ocean* (RA 1924, Paris 1926), *Crabbers Returning* (RA 1926), showing a white gig loaded with crab-pots coming round the Island in an attractive evening light, *Trade Winds* (RA 1927), again featuring a barque mid-ocean, and *At Sea* (RA 1929). However, Bradshaw became infuriated with the lack of direction that the colony displayed after Simpson's departure and was a key figure in the formation of STISA. The national exposure that he gained through STISA led him ultimately to become a founder member of SMA in 1939.

## 6.5 Arthur Hayward's 'St Ives School of Painting'

One suspects that Arthur Hayward's decision to open a new School of Painting, starting on Monday 5th May 1924, was taken in the knowledge that the Simpsons, whom he will have known from his Newlyn student days, would soon be departing. Calling his venture initially 'The St Ives School of Portrait Painting', Hayward offered his students "personal instruction in drawing and painting from the life, portraiture, still life, landscape etc". He ran this from 4 Porthmeor Studios until 1928, when he decided to link up with John Park. The School now became 'The St Ives School of Painting', with Park operating from 5 Piazza Studios, where the Simpson School had been held, and Hayward moving to the Harbour Studio, where the Olsson/Talmage School had been run.[356] Presumably, Hayward concentrated on portraiture and still life, working principally in the studio, whilst Park taught landscape and marine painting out of doors whenever the weather permitted. This arrangement lasted until the autumn of 1929, when Hayward was back operating on his own as 'The St Ives School of Painting', having moved once more - to the Shore Studio on The Wharf, Charles Simpson's old personal studio. In *Who's Who in Art* in 1934, Hayward still described himself as the principal of 'The St Ives School of Painting', but he had by then built himself a studio in the grounds of his home and converted Shore Studio into a Gallery for exhibitions by the Cornwall Group of Artists - a small group of friends comprising himself, Hugh Gresty, Harold and Gertrude Harvey, Ernest and Dod Procter, Alison Rose and Midge Bruford.

Given that Hayward ran the School for the best part of ten years, there is a remarkable lack of information about the students who studied under him. For instance, in the case of the Simpsons and John Park, Show Day notices often indicate that students are also exhibiting work in their principal's studio, but the only occasion when another artist is listed as exhibiting with Hayward was in 1928. However, the artist concerned, W.H.Fowler (d.1944), was a close neighbour, living in Carthew House, and was clearly practising art as a retirement hobby. Whilst Fowler contributed to the first STISA show at the Porthmeor Gallery in 1928, his work is rarely mentioned, and he is more often noted as a purchaser of works by artists such as Stanhope Forbes and Moffat Lindner. Notes in the local paper, such as that in June 1930, which stated, "Miss Bone, a pupil of Arthur Hayward, had two pictures accepted, but not hung, at the Royal Academy" are rare indeed.[357] Certainly, Bradshaw and Truman, who indicated the need for a School of Painting at the time of the STISA proposals in 1926, seem to have discounted Hayward's School, as did Borlase Smart, when later agitating for his old friend, Leonard Fuller, to come down to St Ives to set up an art school.

## 6.6 The classes of John Park

Even before Park moved permanently to St Ives, he appears to have taken pupils, whilst visiting the town, as an oil of a barn interior is inscribed "painted by J.A.Park by way of instruction to me, his pupil, at St Ives 1922, R.McNab".[358] Robert Allan McNab (b.1865) might have been a special case, as he came from Park's home town of Preston, but he went on to have some success at the Royal Academy between 1925 and 1933. Once he had settled in the town in 1923, however, Park place an advertisement that he would hold "a class for outdoor sketching this summer".[359] This soon led to classes being held on a more regular basis. One of his first students, who exhibited with him on Show Day in 1924 and 1925, was Frederick Uren, who was the Borough Surveyor from 1919 to 1926. Whilst being a chartered civil engineer and the author of the standard work *Waterworks Engineering*, he was also a chartered

---
356 He had probably been forced to move from 4 Porthmeor Studios, when STISA took No 5 as their Gallery, which led to Moffat Lindner moving from No 5 to No 4.
357 *St Ives Times*, 27/6/1930.
358 Ambrose, Loughton, Auction dated 27/7/1996 Lot 645.
359 *St Ives Times*, 20/7/1923.

Fig. 6.19 Gerard Wagner's Porthmeor Loft studio
(Gerard Wagner estate)

architect and wanted to develop his painting skills.[360] However, rather meanly, his application to join the Arts Club was rejected. Others to exhibit with Park on Show Day in 1924 included Mrs Sharpe, John J.Hart, who had work hung in Birmingham in the years 1925-8, and Mrs Fenn, who specialized in printmaking, becoming an ARE. She was a member of STISA until her death in 1946.

Another early student was Gerard Wagner (1906-1999), who became a highly regarded painter and art teacher for many years in Dornach, Switzerland, where he was inspired by the artistic legacy of Rudolf Steiner (1861-1925). Born in Wiesbaden, Germany, Wagner had moved back to the Manchester area with his English mother in 1912, following his father's death. In 1923-4, when he was in St Ives, he was merely a young seventeen year old art student, but he remembered John and Peggy Park, with great fondness. He took a small attic studio (Fig. 6.19) in the run of studios fronting Porthmeor Beach, between the Piazza Studios and the Island Studios, and recalled inviting fishermen to come and sit for him there. He followed up his time in St Ives with a year at the Royal College of Art, before settling in Dornach in 1926, where he lived until his death in 1999. The focus of his painting was how form came out of colour, a question that had fascinated Steiner, and, throughout his life, he remained truer to Steiner's ideas than any other painter. He was honoured with a retrospective at the Hermitage Museum, St Petersburg, in 1997 and, during 2006, numerous exhibitions around the world celebrated the centenary of his birth. Unfortunately, however, there is no extant work from his student days in St Ives.[361]

Park's move in 1924 into 5 Piazza Studios, following the Simpsons' departure, was clearly influenced by his painting classes, but, again, there is a frustrating lack of information about the students who came to study under him. Not being terribly organised himself, it was undoubtedly Peggy who dealt with the administrative matters, and he may well have run classes only when the mood suited or finances demanded. However, on several occasions, and, particularly in 1930, at the time of the death of William Paynter, the landlord of the Piazza Studios, Park is noted as the ratepayer of Studio No 7 as well, "for his students". Accordingly, after his brief involvement with Hayward, Park continued to give classes on his own, until his departure from St Ives in 1933.

## 6.7 Other art classes

There are occasional references to other artists holding art classes from time to time, such as Marcella Smith in the summer of 1920, Francis Raymond Spenlove in 1922 and Arthur White in July 1925. Quite a number of the artists will have been willing to give occasional lessons to visitors recommended to them, but it seems clear from this account of the classes run by the Simpsons, Hayward and Park that St Ives had ceased to be a destination for top quality students, from this country and abroad, in the way that it had been in the pre-War era. Whilst Frances Hodgkins had developed a special reputation amongst pioneering Antipodean female artists, which drew them to wherever she was operating from, St Ives itself, with its congenial climate for outdoors work and its attractive townscape and marine and rural surrounds, was no longer a draw for ambitious students of the day, whatever quality of teaching was available, as they were more interested in the new directions that art was taking. Landscape and marine painting out of doors was considered by them to be passé and, accordingly, the classes in St Ives became dominated discouragingly by the leisured female and the retired amateur.

---

360 See *St Ives Times*, 1/10/1926.

361 I am indebted to Caroline Chanter for drawing my attention to Wagner's time in St Ives and for biographical information about him and to the Gerard Wagner estate for the use of the image.

# PRINTMAKING IN ST IVES DURING THE ETCHING BOOM

## 7.1 Introduction

The 1920s witnessed an astonishing boom in the market for etchings, woodcuts, lithographs and other prints. The Society of Graphic Art and the Society of Wood Engravers were both set up in 1920, the Print Collectors' Club was formed in 1921 and a high quality publication *Fine Prints of the Year* was launched in 1923. These fuelled a collecting craze, and new print runs of etchings could often be sold at auction shortly afterwards for many times the initial price. No better example of the bubble that formed in the print market can be given than the good fortune experienced by Stewart Darmady, the Secretary of the St Ives Arts Club. In 1909, he had acquired, for ten guineas, an etching by David Cameron of *The Five Sisters, York Minster*. Although this was a fourth state, only three other proofs were taken of this particular state. When he sold it at Sotheby's in 1929, it fetched £630 - a result which Borlase Smart put down purely to American acquisitiveness, for Americans had become renowned for paying inflated prices to complete sets.[362] Darmady's timing was perfect, as the Wall Street Crash a few months later burst the speculative bubble, and the etching market for the next three decades was dead. Accordingly, the 1920s were a decade without rival in the history of printmaking.

## 7.2 Alfred Hartley

The reputation of St Ives as a centre for printmaking was largely due to Alfred Hartley (1855-1933). The son of a parson, the "gentle and rare-spirited" Hartley was born in Stocking Pelham, Hertfordshire, and had studied at the Royal College of Art. A severe accident, whilst he was a young man, left him lamed for life, and now "severely crippled with arthritis", he "could barely drag himself on two sticks across the Island to his studio".[363] However, Folliott Stokes observed, "No man could be more artistic than he looks. There is a glint of joyful alertness in his keen grey eyes which, combined with the delicate contours of his face and figure, would at once suggest the artist to the least observant." [364]

In his early career, Hartley was renowned for his landscapes and portraits, and he still produced and exhibited landscapes in St Ives. However, although he was elected an ARE in 1894, at the same time as Eve, Legros and Raeburn, and to full membership in 1897, it was only after he had settled in St Ives in c.1908 that he developed a reputation as a master printmaker. Albeit his first attempts with the needle were made at home prior to beginning his art training, Hartley ascribed most of the knowledge that he acquired about the craft to Sir Frank Short. An article on French colour-printing made a big impression on him, and he adopted this method, not only for colour etching, but also for monochrome work. He was also indebted to Charles John Watson for helping him overcome initial difficulties, when he started to do his own printing, and he became an accomplished printer as well. Indeed, Borlase Smart commented on his death, "To see him pull a proof from his press was like watching a magician. The sensitive manipulation of the star wheel and the flick of the printing blanket were part of a real etcher's ritual not to be deviated from so much as a hair's breadth, whilst the inking of the plate and the subsequent wiping with various grades of muslin were done with an unerring hand 'with the palm of a Duchess' ." [365]

Hartley, whom Smart described as "a perfect craftsman, who lived for his art alone", had twenty-nine works hung at the Royal Academy between 1914 and 1931, the vast majority of which were aquatints.[366] His subjects included landscapes, architectural studies and harbour scenes. Given his earlier career as a portrait painter, it is surprising that he did very few etched portraits, but one of a Cornish fisherman (Fig. 7.3) is very fine indeed. Not unnaturally, St Ives subjects were regular in his output. His 1914 exhibit was *Herring Boats, St Ives* (probably Fig. 7.1), an aquatint in an elongated landscape format, which depicted the fishing fleet at sunset just offshore in St Ives Bay, as waves, lit up by the last gleam of day, gently wash on to a beach. In 1918, he depicted that rare occurrence, *St Ives under Snow*, which Borlase Smart considered to be the cleverest work on display, when Hartley later had an exhibition of his prints at Lanham's Galleries.[367] In 1919, there were two further St Ives scenes. One of these,

---

362 See Borlase Smart, *The Romance of an Etching*, St Ives Times, 8/11/1929.
363 Averil Mackenzie-Grieve, *Time and Chance*, London, 1970 at p.37.
364 A.G.Folliott Stokes, *Alfred Hartley, Painter and Etcher*, The Studio, Vol 64, 1915, p.98.
365 R.Borlase Smart, *The late Mr Alfred Hartley, RE,RWA (An Appreciation)*, St Ives Times, 10/11/1933.
366 ibid.
367 *St Ives Times*, 10/12/1920.

# SEA CHANGE : FINE AND DECORATIVE ART IN ST IVES 1914-1930

Fig. 7.1  Alfred Hartley        *St Ives Fishing Boats*        (aquatint)

Fig. 7.2  Alfred Hartley    *Regatta Night, St Ives*    (RA 1924)        (aquatint)

Fig. 7.3  Alfred Hartley   *A Cornish Fisherman* (detail)   (etching)

Fig. 7.4  Alfred Hartley   *The Chapel Stairs, Eton College* (aquatint)

Fig. 7.5  Alfred Hartley   *Between Showers, St Ives*   (RA 1919)   (aquatint)

# SEA CHANGE : FINE AND DECORATIVE ART IN ST IVES 1914-1930

Fig. 7.6  Alfred Hartley    *Woodland by the coast*    (coloured aquatint)

*In St Ives Bay*, again featured the fishing fleet, but the other, *Between Showers, St Ives* (Fig. 7.5), a copy of which was acquired by the Victoria and Albert Museum, is a very different work. It depicts the view from the back of the West Pier across the harbour to Smeaton's Pier and John Bromley's home, 'Quay House', as storm clouds disappear across the Bay. An unusual feature is Hartley's decision to leave bare much of the immediate foreground of the stone surface of the pier but, by this means, he is aiming to show how the rain from the sharp shower has covered the paving stones, and how the light from the emerging sun is reflecting off this sheen of water.

Perhaps one of the most unusual of his depictions of the town is *Regatta Night, St Ives* (Fig. 7.2), an Academy exhibit of 1924, of which a copy is owned by the British Museum. This depicts a firework display on Smeaton's Pier, with the night sky lit up by a multitude of fireworks, whilst clouds of smoke hang in the air. Patterns are made by the rocket trails, whilst a final massive explosion takes place on the pier, lighting up the waters of the harbour. In fact, it looks as if the whole batch of fireworks had mistakenly gone off at once.

In 1925, the Canadian National Exhibition bought Hartley's coloured aquatint, *Harvesting*, for presentation to the Art Gallery of Ontario, Toronto. The British Museum also have a copy of this print, and of another coloured print called *The Capstan*. His coloured work also found favour in Italy, with one print being acquired by an Art Gallery in Venice and the King and Queen of that country being enthusiastic patrons. For these aquatints, Hartley usually limited himself to three plates - one for each colour, believing that the less colour elaborated, the better the result in this class of work. *The Glade*, which was illustrated in Folliott Stokes' article, is a good example, the subject - sheep grazing by woodland - being the sort of scene that Hartley tackled in his landscapes in oils, with the tree shapes being very reminiscent of the work of Alfred East, who may well have been an influence on Hartley's development both as an oil painter and a printmaker. However, the colours used in his prints tend to be a little drab, and I feel that his coloured prints are less successful. One of the better examples is *Woodland by the coast* (Fig. 7.6), again showing sheep grazing by woodland, but enlivened by the blue of sea and sky.

Hartley's landscape work in monochrome is also a little mixed. One of his finest accomplishments is *Early Morning Haze on a Swiss Lake* (RA 1929 - Fig. 7.7). An imposing range of snow capped peaks are picked out in the early morning sun, whilst their flanks and the waters of the calm lake, on which there is a single sailing boat, shimmer in the morning haze, the only sharply defined object being the buoy in the foreground. Here Hartley has created a superbly evocative atmospheric effect, and when it was exhibited on Show Day in 1929, Borlase Smart commented, "The extraordinary restraint in the 'Swiss Lake' reflects the high water mark of the art of the aquatint." [368] On other occasions, though, he

---

368 *St Ives Times*, 22/3/1929.

Fig. 7.7  Alfred Hartley    *Early Morning Haze on a Swiss Lake*    (RA 1929)
(aquatint)

tried to create such effects by leaving large areas of the plate open, and, whilst this novel approach was admired, works, such as *Mooring Post, Lake Como* or *At Low Tide*, a view of cloud formations over St Ives Bay, do seem rather empty.  However, his mountain scenes proved very popular and he had one of his greatest successes with an aquatint, *A Storm on the Alps* (RA 1929 - Fig. 7.8), which depicted a snow-capped peak lit up in sunshine on one side, just before a fearsome storm engulfed it.  This won a gold medal at the International Exhibition of the Printmakers' Society of California in Los Angeles in 1929, whilst, in 1932, he won a further gold medal in California for *Early Morning on the Alps*, a sparser more decorative design.

Fig. 7.8  Alfred Hartley    *A Storm on the Alps*    (RA 1929)
(aquatint)

Hartley's treatment of light passing through woodland was also exquisite, an early example being *The Bridge* (RA 1910), a scene at Asolo, in Italy. In 1926, he exhibited at the Royal Academy a subject with a similar theme, *A Shaded Stream* (Fig. 7.9 - Nottingham Castle Museum), showing cattle being driven over a two-arched stone bridge, which spanned a wooded stream. The sparse detail of the background hill suggests a scorching day, and parts of the bridge are lit up by a brilliant light and are reflected in the shallow stream. Yet there is welcome cool in the shade of the wood for the cattle and their young herdsman. The following year, he produced an aquatint version of his painting *In the Forest*, which he had exhibited at the Royal Academy in 1907, which simply depicted the attractive play of sunlight on trunks and branches, as it penetrated into a densely wooded area.

In the last years of his life, Hartley produced a number of architectural studies. These are some of his very best works, and, although full of intricate detail, his dexterous handling of the fall of light ensure that they are not merely dry representations, but are full of character. In 1928, he exhibited at the Royal Academy *Clare Bridge, Cambridge* - "charming bridge, limpid water, fascinating reflections" - and *The Gate of Honour, Caius College, Cambridge*, - "a work of distinction....beautifully drawn".[369] However, it was his aquatint *Christchurch Gate, Canterbury* (RA 1930 - Fig. 7.10), which, right up to his death, was hailed as his masterpiece. It "is a marvel of drawing, and an example of the best work in this medium. The extraordinary thing is, it is so light in tone, yet powerful in drawing and black and white values".[370] He returned to Canterbury for his final Royal Academy exhibit the following year, *West Window, Canterbury Cathedral*, in which "the loftiness of the Cathedral and the light through the window are wonderfully handled".[371] This was considered to demonstrate marvels in technique, as every chair was done with stopping out varnish in aquatint, not with line.[372]

In 1931, Hartley left St Ives on health grounds to move to Llandrindod Wells, but he died in Worthing in October 1933. A Memorial Exhibition was held at Lanham's Galleries in March 1934. In his review, Borlase Smart observed, "His art was so very personal, and his outlook on artistic matters reflected a dignity and bigness of appreciation that one will miss sadly in these days of hurry skurry...Every etching was a Hartley, of course, but every proof revealed a different outlook on Nature and was etched accordingly. This variety is not apparent in many etchers work today and that is one of the reasons that this noble artist will be missed artistically." [373] In addition to significant holdings of his prints at the British Museum and the Victoria and Albert Museum, there was at one juncture a good collection at Nottingham Castle Museum, but two thirds of this appears to have gone missing.

Fig. 7.9   Alfred Hartley    *A Shaded Stream*    (RA 1926)    (aquatint)

---

369 See *St Ives Times*, 24/5/1929 & 3/1934.
370 Review of 1930 Lanhams Galleries Spring Exhibition in *St Ives Times*.
371 *St Ives Times*, 25/7/1930.
372 See Review of Memorial Exhibition, *St Ives Times*, 3/1934.
373 *St Ives Times*,10/11/1933.

Fig. 7.10  Alfred Hartley    *Christchurch Gate, Canterbury*   (RA 1930)    (aquatint)

## 7.3  The etchings of Sydney Long

An artist, who owed much to Alfred Hartley, was the Australian, Sydney Long (1871-1955), who spelt his Christian name both with an 'i' and a 'y'. The posthumous child of James Long, an Irish commission agent, he was born and educated in Goulburn, New South Wales. In 1888, he moved to Sydney, where his teachers included Julian Ashton, and he began exhibiting with the Art Society of New South Wales in 1893. After an abortive attempt to visit England in 1905, when he fell foul of a confidence trickster, he left Australia for London in 1910, studying further at the art school at Kennington and at the Central School of Arts and Crafts at Holborn. His first visit to St Ives was in 1912, during which he exhibited some works at Lanham's Galleries and in Falmouth. These included not only watercolours of the harbour, but some unusual bird studies. The War years were tough for Long, who was living in straitened circumstances at 195 Ladbroke Grove in London, with a dancer from Covent Garden, called Catherine Brennan, whom he referred to as his wife. Initially frightened that he might be called up, he seriously contemplated enlisting purely to be able to eat on a regular basis! However, he managed to pay a further visit to St Ives and, in April 1918, he informed his Sydney agent, Adolph Albers, of his resolution to take up etching. "When I was in Cornwall, I showed photographs of my work to Alfred Hartley, one of the finest etchers in England. He advised me strongly to take up etching as my work would etch admirably, there being a decorative feeling for line in it." [374] One of his earliest aquatints is *Cornish Landscape*, showing two wind-blown trees on the coast, and this is dated 1919, suggesting a further possible visit.

Fired with enthusiasm for his new calling, Long studied under Frank Emanuel and Malcolm Osborne and told Albers, "I am going to learn the whole bunch of tricks in etching etc. so as to start a big school in that sort of thing when I get back." [375] In April 1920, he told Albers excitedly about the new Society of Graphic Art and commented, "It was a great compliment getting on the provisional committee but I really started the movement. It was my idea." [376] In fact, he was made Foundation Secretary and was also elected an Associate of the RE the following January. Suddenly, after a decade of hardship, he had become well-known. After a brief trip back to Sydney for eighteen months in 1921-2, he revisited St Ives in 1923-4. Three etchings of boats in St Ives harbour are known from this period. A print of the best of these, *St Ives, Cornwall* (Fig. 7.12), featuring boats on either side of the tower of the Parish church, is in the collection of the Art Gallery of New South Wales, Sydney, whilst the British Museum purchased a rather more impressionist image, *The Harbour, St Ives*, in 1924.

---

374  Letter dated 25/4/1918, see R King, *The Etchings of Sydney Long, the Richard King Collection*, Goulburn, 1990 at p.13.
375  Letter dated October 1919, see R King, ibid, at p.14.
376  Letter dated 23/4/1920, see R King, ibid, at p.15.

Fig. 7.11  Sydney Long    *St Ives, Cornwall*        (etching)

In 1925, just as the etching boom was about to take off in England, Long returned to Sydney. Nevertheless, he enjoyed much success in Australia, becoming President of the Australian Painter-Etchers Society and earning as much as £1,000 per annum from etching sales alone. After his death back in England in 1955, the Australian, Rubery Bennett commented, "Isn't it remarkable that we produce a man like Sid, that sees things with a different eye. He was a romanticist, he was a poet, he was a dreamer and yet his work was never sissy. It was always robust, virile and alive...No one else is a bit like him, not anyone." [377]

Fig. 7.12  Sydney Long    *St Ives, Cornwall*        (etching)

---

377 Quoted in R King, *The Etchings of Sydney Long, the Richard King Collection*, Goulburn, 1990 at p.17.

## 7.4 The 1919 visit of Donald Shaw MacLaughlan

Donald Shaw MacLaughlan (1876-1938) (whose surname is often mis-spelt MacLaughlin) is frequently called both a Canadian and an American. This is because he was born in Charlottetown, Prince Edward Island, Canada, but moved with his family, who were of Scottish descent, to Boston in 1890. However, he travelled widely throughout his career, particularly in Europe, and it was only after his death that his etchings came to be appreciated in both Canada and America.

After studying initially in Boston, MacLaughlan enrolled at the École des Beaux-Arts in Paris. He took up etching in 1899 and was influenced by Whistler. His best works are his depictions of townscapes, but he also produced numerous landscapes of Italy, France, Germany and England. Venice was a favourite destination. He paid his first visit to Cornwall in 1913, during which he produced two etchings, which he merely described as *Cornish Landscape No1* and *Cornish Landscape No 2*. Manchester Art Gallery have a copy of both, but, like many of MacLaughlan's landscapes, they are rather sparse and are lacking in interest. He returned to the Duchy in 1919 and did at least ten more subjects during that year. One of the first that he completed was *The Milk Round*, which showed a woman collecting milk from a pony and cart outside a house in a country location. His etching of *Lelant* (Fig. 7.13) is a fine work too, being largely concerned with the architecture of the village. *On the Hayle* (Fig. 7.14) is also an interesting subject, showing old mackerel boats drawn up on the sand on the edge of the estuary. The Lelant and Hayle etchings are part of a collection of eighty-nine of his works owned by the Smithsonian Institution, Washington, whilst a number of his other Cornish etchings are now in public collections - *Tregenna Wood*, a view of trees framing a gate into a field, at the Victoria Art Gallery, Bath, and *Gwinnear Lane* at Leeds, whilst the National Gallery of Canada's collection includes *Tregenna Pastures*.[378] There is also a work called *Gwinnear Fields*, and other titles include *Camborne Road*, *Roseworthy Cottages* and *Roseworthy Meadows*. In truth, none are particularly interesting examples of his work, his fascination with rather ordinary Cornish gateways and hedgerows leaving true lovers of the Cornish landscape a little perplexed as to his choice of subject.[379]

He appears to have made a number of return visits to Cornwall. In 1924, he exhibited *St Ives Harbour* at the New Salon in Paris, and his very last etching was called *By a Cornish Stream*. His work was included in the collection of the 'Chy-an-Drea Hotel' put together by Francis Wheeler and his widow.

Fig. 7.13  Donald Shaw MacLaughlan      *Lelant*        (etching)

---

378 MacLaughlan mispelt Tregenna as Tragenna.
379 A number of his Cornish works are illustrated in Harbor Gallery, *Donald Shaw MacLaughlan 1876-1938 - A Re-Introduction*, New York, 1986.

Fig. 7.14  D.S.MacLaughlan   *On the Hayle*   (etching)

### 7.5  Other specialist printmakers in the colony

In the winter of 1912, Alfred Hartley started a class for students interested in printmaking. This continued until the War, in any event, and generated considerable interest, but it appears that his declining mobility led him to give up holding formal classes.[380] Therefore, during the War years, Marcella Smith and Helen Stuart Weir opted to study etching under Fred Milner, who tended to favour mezzotints. According to Borlase Smart, these had "the bigness of outlook so prevalent in his paintings".[381] Nevertheless, it is generally understood that Christopher Nevinson's visit in 1920 was principally to obtain instruction from Hartley in printmaking, and so Hartley appears to have been happy to give advice and instruction to a few keen students. As the etching boom took off during the 1920s, his advice was also in demand from specialist painters, who wanted to expand into printmaking due to the astonishing prices being obtained. Accordingly, he gave a number of lectures on aspects of the subject at the Arts Club and to members of STISA.

One of the pre-War arrivals was Frank Moore (b.1876), who had been born in Watford and educated at Highgate School and University College, London. Having worked previously principally as a watercolourist, he appears to have come down to the colony specifically to study printmaking under Hartley and, having spent several previous winters in the town, he took up permanent residence during the winter of 1913-4, eventually living at 1 Draycott Terrace and working from 'Beach Studio', The Wharf, where he installed his own printing press. His etchings, drypoints and aquatints were first reviewed on Show Day in 1914, but he appears to have developed a preference for drypoint etchings. Certainly, when he held an exhibition of twenty-nine works at his studio in September 1922, most were drypoints. They covered a wide range of subjects - landscape, seascape, shipping and figure work - and were inspired principally by the scenery in and around St Ives. Borlase Smart considered that they held "a special appeal by reason of their simple treatment, artistic expression, and craftsmanlike printing."[382] A work which always provoked favourable comment was *Hayle from Lelant*. In 1925, a review of his works *Forest Sentinel* and *April Day* at the RWA, in the French Canadian magazine *La Revue Moderne*, hailed him as one of the best printmakers of the contemporary English School, endowed with precious gifts and rare qualities. He was elected an Associate of both the RWA and RCA, but, unfortunately, very little of his work has appeared on the market from which to form an independent judgement.

Fig. 7.15  Frank Moore   *St Ives Harbour*   (drypoint)
(David Lay, Penzance Auction House)

---

380 See Averil Mackenzie-Grieve, *Time and Chance*, London, 1970 at p.37.
381 Milner Obituary, *St Ives Times*, 10/1939.
382 *St Ives Times*, 8/9/1922.

Claude Francis Barry, who had studied under Frank Brangwyn, also exhibited a number of etchings on his return to the colony in 1917. Most of these were of Windsor, but he also did several of St Ives. Borlase Smart particularly liked his depiction of Windsor Castle, which he considered "a revelation in strong handling of forceful light and shade and a most scholarly work in its tonal detail".[383] Prior to George Turland Goosey's arrival in the colony, he had done some printmaking in America. Indeed, his etching *Moonlight on a Venetian Canal* had won the highest award at a printmakers' exhibition in New York in 1914. This was one of nineteen etchings that he exhibited on Show Day in 1922, a group which also included work done in Morocco. Borlase Smart commented, "His line is full of vigour and individuality, and a fine massing of light and dark tones seems to be the secret of his art." [384] Goosey produced a number of etchings of St Ives, but the majority were quite small. He had a further show devoted just to his etchings at Lanham's Galleries in 1930, when it was considered that he had made a marked improvement as a printmaker during his time in the town.

One of the most promising printmakers in the colony in the early 1920s was Dorothy Cooke (always known as 'Dossie'), who was hailed as a "fascinating and original talent" and praised for her imaginative interpretations.[385] She was one of the daughters of Arts Club stalwart, Norman Cooke, and lived with her family at 'Dunvegan', Carbis Bay, the house that Edmund Fuller had designed in 1900 and lived in for a decade. Her portrait by Nell Cuneo in 1923 was entitled *A Modern Botticelli*. Her greatest success was with an aquatint called *The Roadmaker* (Fig. 7.16), which was hung at the Royal Academy in 1922. This showed a mischievous expression on the face of the 'Spirit of the Road', as he puzzled two of the world's weary wayfarers with a road which had no end. It also received high praise in *Les Artistes d'Aujourdhui* when it was shown in France in 1925, and was a work that she continued to exhibit under her married name of Dorothy Bayley.[386] Another example of her imaginative outlook was her aquatint *Sorrow*, which featured the clever adaption of a sorrowing female to form the natural lines of a mountain. Tears of sorrow from the eyes of the woman ran down as rivulets, emptying into a pool fringed by weeping willows. In 1929, she won a first class diploma for her etchings at the North East Coast Exhibition at Newcastle-upon-Tyne. However, the collapse of the etching market in the 1930s led her to concentrate, after her marriage, on oils, which was a shame, as she was a more assured and innovative printmaker.

Fig. 7.16 Dorothy Cooke  *The Roadmaker*  (Private Collection)

---

383 *St Ives Times*, 4/7/1919.
384 *Western Morning News*, 16/3/1922.
385 *St Ives Times*, 17/3/1922.
386 Reproduced in *St Ives Times*, 14/8/1925.

A couple of artists specialized in colour prints. Matilda (Maud) Dorothea Hurst (b.1860, fl.1896-1927), the daughter of a barrister, who had been brought up in Horsham Park, Sussex, was involved with the colony between 1909 and 1920. Indeed, on Show Day in 1920, when she was exhibiting at Market Strand Studio, her small colour prints were hailed as "remarkable for their beauty of craftsmanship, colour and design" and considered one of the highlights of the day.[387] Annie Bliss Smith, originally from Hampstead, lived in the town between 1921 and 1925, exhibiting woodcuts and lino-cuts, which were considered "charming and restrained in quiet colour" and evidencing "breadth of feeling and expanse of design".[388] Having left St Ives, she had sixteen works hung at Liverpool between 1925 and 1933.

Lithography was the specialist medium of Winifred Burne (b.1877), the daughter of an actuary, who was born in Birkenhead, and trained in her home town, Liverpool, as well as in Munich. She used a Carbis Bay exhibiting address in 1914, and was living in 'Upalong' in that village in 1921, when she first advertised classes for the technical demonstration and study of lithography. She described herself as an exhibitor with the Senefelder Club, a London Society devoted to lithography, whose members included Joseph Pennell and Frank Brangwyn. However, later in the 1920s, she moved to 'Sunset' above Porthmeor Beach and ran her classes first at 'Balcony Studio', and then at 'Meadow Studio'. An article in the French Canadian magazine, *La Revue Moderne*, in 1925 praised her *Study of Boats* exhibited at Liverpool and *Stiff Breeze at Carthew Point* and *Summer Heat* exhibited at Derby, calling her a modernist, but adding, "son modernisme est sage et pondéré; c'est celui d'on peintre consciencieux et savant, honneté at expérimenté".[389] She had ten works hung at Liverpool and eighteen at the London Salon.

Another retired Naval officer, Francis John Roskruge (1871-1952), (surname pronounced 'Roskreeg') also made a telling contribution to the printmaking section, after he had settled in St Ives in 1921. He had studied art before joining the Navy in June 1894, as he won a bronze medal at the RCPS, Falmouth in 1891. He served as an engineer in both the Boer and First World Wars, although his involvement in the former was truncated by a bout of epilepsy. His Naval records reveal that he was very highly regarded, his talent as a draughtsman being recognised at an early juncture, and he came to be viewed as an exceptional officer - zealous, hard-working and tactful, with excellent powers of organisation and administration.[390] During the First World War, he served in *H.M.S.Hyacinth*, the flagship of the Cape and East Africa Station, and, in 1917, he was awarded the D.S.O. for keeping "the squadron and *H.M.S. Hyacinth* in a state of continual efficiency for over two years with the smallest possible allowance for necessary repairs".[391] In 1919, this was topped by the award of an O.B.E. "in recognition of valuable services rendered in connection with the War".[392] He was finally granted the title of Engineer-Captain.

Fig. 7.17  Francis Roskruge   *An Old Cornish Cider Press*   (Private Collection)

---

387 *St Ives Times*, 5/3/1920.

388 *St Ives Times*, 12/9/1924.

389 Reproduced in *St Ives Times*, 24/4/1925.

390 He was promoted to Engineer in 1900, to Engineer-Lieutenant in 1903 and Engineer-Commander in 1912.

391 For instance, his services were much needed in April 1915, when, chasing a vessel bringing much needed supplies to German troops, the starboard engine of *H.M.S.Hyacinth* blew up.

392 Extracts from Naval Records held in the National Archives at Kew.

Fig. 7.18 Francis Roskruge and his second wife, Maudie, at the entrance to his studio at 'Bosvean'

On settling in St Ives, Roskruge's multifold talents were soon put to good use. He became Secretary of the Arts Club in 1924 for three years, before being elected President for a further two. The finest actor amongst the artists, he played a significant role in transforming the entertainments at the Arts Club, even writing a number of plays, and he was also a key figure in the newly formed St Ives Dramatic Society. He was also Treasurer of STISA from 1928-1939. Wide erudition meant that he gave talks on a range of subjects, not only at the Arts Club but also to the Old Cornwall Society.[393] He, and his first wife, Lilian, whom he had married at St Keverne in 1904, lived at 'Bosvean' in The Belyars, and he had a studio/workshop in his home, for, in addition to art, he did woodwork, using his skill as an engineer to invent all sorts of gadgets. As an artist, though, he concentrated on printmaking, studying under Frank Moore and quickly gaining proficiency. His aquatints *Twilight, St Ives, Chelsea Reach* and *Selina's Cottage* were highly regarded for their poetic feel by the French magazine *Arts et Lettres*, when they were shown at the RWA in 1926.[394] His most successful work was *In the Track of the Moon* (Fig. 7.19), a superlative print of the moon gleaming over the waters of the Bay, which was first exhibited with STISA in the 1930 Summer Exhibition. Others to gain favourable comment were *The Old Slipway*, which captured that feature before it was demolished, *An Old Cornish Cider Press* (Fig. 7.17), *Rochester Castle* and *Norwich, in the gloaming*.

Fig. 7.19 Francis Roskruge    *In the Track of the Moon*
(David Lay, Penzance Auction House)

---

393 For instance, in November 1924, he gave a talk to the Old Cornwall Society on *Old Cornish Agriculture and Farm Implements*.
394 Reproduced in *St Ives Times*, 12/2/1926.

Fig. 7.20  Frances Ewan   *Portrait of a Fisherman*
(St Ives Trust Archive Study Centre)

## 7.6   The St Ives Print Society

In October 1922, Frank Moore, then President of the St Ives Arts Club, proposed the formation of a new exhibiting society devoted solely to printmakers. This was to be the first of its kind in West Cornwall and was called the St Ives Print Society. Alfred Hartley was unanimously voted as President, and it held its inaugural exhibition in April 1923. There were, by then, fourteen members, and sixty-five works were shown in the exhibition, demonstrating a wide range of printmaking techniques; there were coloured aquatints by Alfred Hartley, drypoints by Frank Moore and Frances Ewan, etchings by Bernard Leach, Francis Roskruge and Edith Walters, aquatints by Dorothy Cooke, a mezzotint and a drypoint by Fred Milner, woodcuts by Charles Simpson and Edmund Fuller, a lithograph and a lino-print by Marjorie Ballance, and lino-cuts by Annie Bliss Smith and Miss D.G.Webb.

Borlase Smart, who reviewed the exhibition, felt that some of the finest etchings on show were those by Edith Walters, who was only involved with the colony that year. "Her strength of line is so decisive and sure, and the composition dignified. She has an eye, too, for arrangement of masses." [395] He also liked the work of Bernard Leach, who had set up his pottery in the town in 1920, having spent the previous eleven years in Japan (see further Chapter 10). Leach, though, had originally gone to Japan to teach etching, having studied under Frank Brangwyn, and, on Show Day in 1922, one of the Lanham's Galleries was devoted exclusively to his work and was hung with a collection of his etchings done before and during his time in Japan. Whilst describing his Japanese soft ground etchings as "visionary in conception", Smart and other reviewers preferred the earlier Brangwyn-esque *Coal Heavers, Earl's Court* and *The Gothic Spirit*, which featured angels hovering on either side of St Luke's, Chelsea, a Catholic church built in the Gothic style. The latter print was felt to combine "great power and classical feeling" with "beauty of design".[396] However, with the travails of the Pottery, Leach produced few new etchings after his arrival. Fred Milner's mezzotint, *A Dorset Landscape*, with its effect of rising moon, was considered one of the most romantic prints, and was a rare state, being the only print with the plate destroyed. The exhibition also included Frances Ewan's portrait of a fisherman (Fig. 7.20). An ex-Bushey student, she had been, prior to the War, principally a magazine and book illustrator, but, in the early 1920s, she settled in the colony and rented one of the Porthmeor Studios for over forty years.

---

395 *St Ives Times*, 6/4/1922.
396 ibid.

Fig. 7.21  Borlase Smart  *The Sloop Inn*  (Private Collection)

Fig. 7.22  Borlase Smart  *The Rialto, Venice*  (Private Collection)

Fig. 7.23  Borlase Smart    *Mont St Michel*    (etching)
(Private Collection)

I have not found any reference to the second exhibition of the St Ives Print Society, but the third exhibition was held in September 1924. There were now seventeen members - Edith Walters having left and Borlase Smart, Averil Mackenzie-Grieve, E Sykes and the Newlyner, Geoffrey Garnier, having joined. Garnier's involvement demonstrates that the Society was open to printmakers in other parts of West Cornwall. However, Garnier seems to have been the only one - certainly, he was the only artist in Newlyn to dedicate himself to printmaking. His exhibits with the Society were his early religious scenes, full of melodramatic effects, but the death of his son, Jeremy, aged two, in 1926 led to a loss of faith.

From his review of the first exhibition by the Society, Borlase Smart clearly knew quite a bit about the techniques of printmaking, but it was only during an extended visit to Venice in 1924 that he developed his own printmaking skills, and his exhibits at the exhibition included a powerful etching *The Rialto, Venice* (Fig. 7.22), a copy of which was acquired by Bristol Art Gallery, as well as *Start of the Herring Season, St Ives*. Santa Maria della Salute was another famous landmark that he etched, and one source indicates that half of the thirty etchings that Smart produced during his life were done during his time in Venice. He also did a number of aquatints, such as *Evening on the Grand Canal, Venice*, which he exhibited on Show Day in 1925. Subjects in St Ives included *The Sloop Inn* (Fig. 7.21), *St Ives from the Malakoff*, *Tommy Thomas' Boatyard* and *The Old Curiosity Shop* (Fig. 7.24). Smart's skill as a draughtsman meant that he was well-suited to this genre, and his election to membership of the RWA was based solely on his etched work. Furthermore, when he was invited to contribute to the RBC's exhibition at the Prince of Wales Museum, Bombay in 1933, he sent two etchings - perhaps his best. His depiction of *Mont St Michel* (Fig. 7.23), with the church rising over ancient houses, was considered by *The Times of India* to be "strangely Arthurian in the appeal of its towering spires and crowded angles". His other exhibit, *Reconstructing the Implacable*, was the fine etched version of his 1926 Royal Academy work (see Fig. 5.37).

Fig. 7.24  Borlase Smart   *The Old Curiosity Shop*   (drawing)
(Private Collection)

Averil Mackenzie-Grieve came from a wealthy family and had spent the happiest years of her childhood at Castle Hill House in Torrington. In 1918, she studied in Florence and her interest in book illustration led her to take up wood engraving. On settling in St Ives in 1920, her mother created the Fire Station Studio for her use and, prior to her marriage in 1925 to Cyril le Gros Clark, which took her off to Sarawak, she produced some interesting wood engravings, the most significant of which was *The New Italy*, which was "a study of Facisti on the march", which had "fine qualities of expression and massing".[397] It was the rise of Fascism in Italy, which had led her mother and herself to return to England and settle in St Ives. Averil continued to exhibit her woodcuts in the town on her return trips, but these now had oriental themes and subject matter. She went on to become better known as a writer, but her wood engravings were used to illustrate both her own and other people's books.

Fig. 7.25 Averil Mackenzie-Grieve engraving

---

397 *St Ives Times*, 12/9/1924.

Fig. 7.26  Frank Short    *Seine Boats, St Ives*    (etching)
Alfred Hartley's printmaking master and friend paid a visit to the colony in the late 1920s

There is no further mention of the Society, which is strange given the manner in which interest in etchings took off after 1925. In the Cheltenham exhibition of 1925, whereas Hartley was represented by twelve prints (including *Sunny Morning, St Ives*, *Polperro Harbour* and *A Cottage near the Lizard*) and Bernard Leach by two (*Coal Heavers, Earl's Court Road* and *The Gate of Peking*), none of the other printmakers were represented at all, which may not have been well received. Departures in the middle of the decade were probably also a key factor, as Simpson, Fuller and Smart all left, and there is little mention of Moore, Bliss Smith, Webb and Ewan. When the St Ives Society of Artists held their first exhibition in the Porthmeor Gallery in 1928, the only printmakers exhibiting were Alfred Hartley, Francis Roskruge, Dossie Cooke, Geoffrey Garnier, Averil Mackenzie-Grieve (now le Gros Clark) and a young Terence Cuneo. The absence from all these exhibitions of the etchings of George Turland Goosey demonstrate further his lack of interest in promoting his work.

Former members of the St Ives Print Society, such as Fred Milner, Annie Bliss Smith and Frances Ewan, did contribute some prints to STISA exhibitions before the end of the decade, and others to exhibit prints in this period included Beatrice Vivian, Hugh Gresty, Arthur Hambly, Shearer Armstrong, Anna Findlay and Joan Ellis. Anna Findlay (d.1947) was the daughter of Colonel James Marshall Findlay (d.1945), the former Commander of the 8th Scottish Rifles, who had come down to St Ives in 1925 to act as the property agent for the Hain family's Porthia Estate. She was an engraver and a linocut artist and her coloured prints are first mentioned in STISA's Winter Exhibition of 1928 and, although later moving to Glasgow, she remained involved with STISA until her death. Eleanor Joan Ellis (b.1904) was rated a young artist of considerable promise at this juncture. Born in Putney, she had studied under Leon Underwood before coming down to St Ives, and she worked in a variety of media. She first attracted attention with a portrait of local boy, Edward Craze, in the *Daily Express* Young Artists Exhibition in 1927 and then that November, she held a joint exhibition with Marjorie Ballance at Gieves Art Gallery in London, where she showed not only "some very clever - and very modern - oils", which included a sketch of St Ives, but also some woodcuts, featuring studies of Cornish fishermen.[398] She continued to exhibit with STISA until 1930, but, having become Mrs White, her artistic career came to an end.

In the early 1930s, the black and white section of the colony, despite the economic malaise, came to feature prominently in STISA exhibitions, with the arrival in St Ives of Job Nixon, who had taught etching at South Kensington, and Raymond Ray-Jones, whilst Royal Academician, Sydney Lee, also joined the Society.

---

398 See two articles in *St Ives Times*, 18/11/1927.

# VISITORS OF NOTE IN THE TWENTIES

## 8.1 Introduction

The cessation of the publication in the local paper of Visitors' Lists during the summer months means that it is far less easy to track visitors to the colony during this period than it is prior to the War. St Ives, though, became an increasingly popular holiday destination and, although this might have been off-putting for some, there was still a steady flow of artists from both home and abroad, who came to paint in the colony. Many former residents also made pilgrimages back. As before, some visiting artists were inspired to produce some of the seminal works of their careers.

## 8.2 The visit of Effie Charlton Fortune in 1922-3

Euphemia Charlton Fortune (1885-1969) was an American landscape painter, born in Sausalito, California, and was yet another artist whose work made enormous progress during her time in St Ives. In fact, her paintings of St Ives are now considered some of the finest of her career. Her father, who died when she was nine, was a Scot and, in 1898, she returned with an aunt to live in Scotland. She was educated at St Margaret's Convent, Edinburgh, but her cleft palette did not make her childhood easy. In 1904, she enrolled at St John's Wood School of Art but, the following year, she returned to California to study at the Mark Hopkins Institute in San Francisco. However, all her early work was destroyed in the earthquake of 1906. She then moved to New York and studied further at the Arts Students League under William Merritt Chase until 1910. That year, she came over to Scotland again, and visited Paris, before returning to the States, where she moved between studios in San Francisco and Monterey. She won a silver medal at the Panama-Pacific Exposition in 1915.

Between 1921 and 1927, Effie, as she was known to friends, and her mother, Helen, toured Europe, and they took a studio in St Ives in January 1922. This was 'The Cabin' on Westcott's Quay, which offered fine views over the harbour. Effie, who was made a member of the Society of Scottish Artists that year, was both passionate and knowledgeable about art. Writing to her friend and former student, Ethel McAllister Grubb, shortly after her arrival in St Ives, she commented, "You can see Henry Poor all over England... There are the half baked Cezannes...and a dozen schools that have completely supplanted them and made them seem older...than Landseer, and quite as out of date...the more you see, the more damn sure you are that nothing whatever can be gained by outside influence (movements) but that anything new must come from within." [399] Enthused by her new surroundings, she added, "I am at last doing some decent stuff, for the first time since I came over....This place would make a sick cat paint. You never saw such ripping stuff in your life to do." [400] The vigour of her work was noted when she exhibited on Show Day that year in 'Beach Studio' with Frank Moore. Borlase Smart was most impressed, feeling that her work would enhance the reputation of the colony and "stimulate those around her with a deeper sense of regard for painting in the open air. Her canvases radiate vitality of outlook, and her vigorous technique, but searching tonalities, offer a lesson in expression to more timid members half afraid of their own powers".[401] The handling of the clear morning light in *Sunny Landscape, Phillack* placed the work among the best on show.[402] As Smart intimated, whilst in St Ives, she became an enthusiast for *plein air* painting, exhorting her friend, Ethel Grubb, to "paint as much as you possibly can out of doors" and to avoid at all costs what she termed "the MADE PICTURE" - the studio composition.[403] However, she admitted "It is impossible to take large canvases out of doors here, as the light changes so rapidly, but I am doing some of the best stuff I have ever done now." [404]

The aspect of St Ives that most attracted her attention was the harbour. In November 1922, she commented, "I have spent almost a year here, studying the harbour and the people on the quays, not as studies in psychology ....but as color and movement. When the tide is in, the harbor is generally a sheet of melted silver. Against it are silhouetted the figures of fishermen, girls, dogs, children and rows of washing.... When you look at the results the artists get, you see that St Ives has to be swallowed and digested before you can paint it." [405]

---

399 Letter dated 29/1/1922 - Fortune papers, Monterey Peninsula Museum.
400 ibid.
401 *Western Morning News*, reproduced in *St Ives Times*, 24/3/1922.
402 *St Ives Times*, 17/3/1922. The work has also been exhibited as *Spring Morning, Phillack* and *Cornish Town - After Rain*.
403 Letter to E A Grubb dated 20/11/1922 - Fortune papers, Monterey Peninsula Museum.
404 ibid.
405 ibid.

SEA CHANGE : FINE AND DECORATIVE ART IN ST IVES 1914-1930

Fig. 8.1  Euphemia Charlton Fortune       *Summer Morning, St Ives*
         (Monterey Peninsula Museum of Art, gift of Monsignor Robert E. Brennan)

Fig. 8.2  Euphemia Charlton Fortune    *Harbour Floor, St Ives*     (Private Collection)

## VISITORS OF NOTE IN THE TWENTIES

In November, she experienced, for the first time, the sight that had captivated many artists before her - the herring fleet returning at night. "Just now the Herring fishing season is in full swing....I wish you could see it. The whole fleet of boats, the big black herring boats with red sails and the smaller mackerel boats (all white) leave the harbour in the evening. They have engines now, which most of the older artists deplore, but to me they are beautiful, as the increased speed makes them look like swallows when they fly out of the harbour entrance ....Sometime in the night they return with their catch, and if the tide is out, and the Harbour empty, you get down to the sands about nine o'clock and the beauty of it all simply knocks you flat. Hundreds of little carts pulled by little Exmoor ponies run back and forth to the boats... These carts either carry gasoline in bright green tins to the boats, or stand alongside, the water well above the ponies' knees, while the boxes of herrings are loaded on the carts. The color of it all is too amazing for words. When we first came here, everyone spoke of the grayness of St Ives. It is like a Claude Monet but never gray. The ponies are red mostly, and occasionally black and very shaggy, the carts have rose-madder wheels, the petrol cans are pure Sinn Fein. The fishermen wear oilskins and, after they have been working in the barking sheds on their sails, they are pure terra cotta and venetian red. Along the quays, hundreds of girls in blue red and mauve are packing herrings in rock salt, all screaming to each other at the tops of their voices." [406] A vibrant sketch *Herring Season* (Monterey Peninsula Museum of Art) attempts to capture the scene.[407]

During her time in St Ives, Effie's painting developed immeasurably and she produced two particularly fine works towards the end of her stay. The first - *Harbour Floor, St Ives* (Fig. 8.2) - shows mackerel boats and fishermen in the harbour at low tide in a brilliant light, the unseen blue sky brought down to earth in the shimmering reflections in the pools of water on the sands. Definition is abandoned in the cause of light, vibrant colour and atmosphere. However, her master work was *Summer Morning, St Ives* (Fig. 8.1) - again a depiction of the harbour beach. However, on this occasion, the fishermen and their boats are joined by inquisitive summer visitors and their children, whilst the sky is filled almost entirely with gulls. Charlton Fortune mentioned the effect of this phenomenon on colour to Ethel Grubb; "...gulls, literally millions of them, looking like a snowstorm seen through a telescope, hang in a dense cloud over the town, the whole harbour is dappled with the shadows of them, like the shadows of a tree in leaf, only all moving and wheeling so rapidly that the colors take on life." [408] She exhibited the painting on Show Day in 1923 in Loft Studios, along with a portrait of Henry Jenner, of the Old Cornwall Society, and it made quite an impact at the Royal Academy. A London critic described it as "impressionism beating futurism at its own game in the amount of complex suggestion that it provides, without straining the imagination to interpret a lot of arbitrary forms and, best of all, without any lapse from beauty of colour and brushwork." [409] In 1924, she submitted the same work to the Paris Salon, where it won a silver medal, the French mistakenly making out the diploma to Monsieur Charlton Fortune. She also submitted paintings of St Ives Harbour to the Carnegie Institute at Pittsburgh in 1923 and 1925.

Effie and her mother left St Ives in 1923 and settled for a couple of years in St Tropez, where her colour became even richer and stronger. On her return to Monterey in 1927, she exhibited work from her European trip. Although panned by modernists, she received some considerable accolades. Florence Lehre, Assistant Director of the Oakland Art Gallery, commented that she had "retained the soundness, the comprehensibility of the academicians, ...the methods and colors of the impressionists, ...and some of the organisation of the moderns", whilst the *San Francisco Chronicle* saluted her as "the ablest thinker and producer among living California women artists....Her work has been uncontaminated by cults and isms." [410]

In the 1930s, she gave up easel painting altogether in order to devote her life to liturgical mural painting for the Catholic Church, becoming a founder member of the Monterey Guild, a group that crusaded for sane liturgical art. In 1990, an exhibition of her early work was organised by the Monterey Peninsula Museum of Art and this included eight paintings of St Ives.[411] This exhibition has re-established her as one of California's foremost women Impressionist painters, as demonstrated by a price of $800,000 being obtained recently for one of her small St Tropez sketches. St Ives is blissfully ignorant of her very existence.

---

406 Letter to E A Grubb dated 20/11/1922 - Fortune papers, Monterey Peninsula Museum.

407 This work seems now to be known incorrectly as *Pilchard Boats*.

408 Letter to E A Grubb dated 20/11/1922 - Fortune papers, Monterey Peninsula Museum.

409 *The Gentlewoman*, 23/6/1923.

410 F W Lehre, *Oakland Tribune*, October/November 1927 and Gene Haley, *San Francisco Chronicle* 21/10/1927.

411 In addition to the work mentioned in this section, these included *Autumn in Harbour, Down Along, St Ives, Mackerel Season, Red Sails, St Ives*. The catalogue for this exhibition *Colors and Impressions - The Early Work of E Charlton Fortune*, Monterey, 1990 has been the primary source for this section and contains colour images of five St Ives works.

### 8.3  The 1923 visit of Wilson Henry Irvine

During his trip to Europe in 1923, which lasted ten months, the American artist, Wilson Henry Irvine, maintained a Journal, which provides a fascinating day by day record of his experiences during the three and half months that he worked in St Ives.[412] Born in Illinois, Irvine became known for his impressionist landscape paintings. After schooling in Rockford, Illinois, he moved to Chicago in 1888, starting out as a commercial artist, using the new airbrush technology. In April 1891, he married Lydia Weyber, the daughter of a language Professor at Purdue University, Lafayette, Indiana, and, in 1893, he started working for the Chicago Portrait Company. Between 1895 and 1903, he took evening classes at the Art Institute of Chicago and was a founder member, in 1895, of the Palette and Chisel Club. He started exhibiting at the Institute in 1900. In 1908-9, he spent some time in Europe, working in the colonies of Pont-Aven and Concarneau and it is possible that, during this trip, his wife and himself visited St Ives for the first time.[413] On his return to America, Irvine based himself again in Chicago and continued to exhibit there and in Pennsylvania. In 1915, he won a silver medal at the Panama-Pacific Exposition, San Francisco. However, having spent the summer in Connecticut in the years 1914-7, he moved there permanently in 1918 and became associated with the Old Lyme Colony, which had developed into a centre for American Impressionism and was the home of several artists, such as Guy Wiggins and William Chadwick, who had previously worked in St Ives.

Irvine, who was always keen to experiment with his art, confirmed that the purpose of his European trip in 1923 was to seek new challenges so as to avoid getting into a rut. "I determined to get new impressions and to start afresh in all things when I went abroad. I left my palette, brushes and paints at home. In London, I bought new square brushes. Before that, I used round ones. I found a different palette and chose a new make of colors and a new easel. Everything was different." [414] His wife, Lydia, and himself arrived in St Ives on 20th February and stayed until 1st June.[415] He commented, "I understood at once what it was that drew the artists to that odd little old village, and its picturesque characters. The shore and the sea held me...Every day had something new for a picture. The associations are extraordinary."[416]

It took them just two hours to find a studio flat in a loft on The Wharf, which he described as "hardly more than a barn, but roomy, airy (very) and good north light for work".[417] He considered the view from their window to be the best vista of the harbour and described it as "a never-ending joy", for, even when the men were not going out on the boats, there was constant work to be done, as they overhauled sails, nets, anchor chains and ropes, whilst there were always "groups of men talking, talking".[418] He was soon outside at work on a low tide scene, with pools of water in the sand and an old man raking seaweed, and realised that he would need to work quickly. "Got to get this harbor on the run for each tide lays the boats, pools and seaweed differently." [419] His descriptions of fishermen pacing up and down, boats swaying in the groundswell, children playing on the sand and dogs scampering through the pools of water make fine word pictures as well. Unfortunately, almost from the outset, he was dogged by bad weather, which hampered his efforts to paint *en plein air*, but he made forays out whenever he could, even if he was beaten back inside within an hour or two. Comments such as "Corking sky today" or "The harbor was simply glorious" are more than outweighed by curses over the incessant rain.

In addition to harbour subjects, which drew him back time and again, he records a number of sketches that he worked upon. He was attracted by a smithy near the Tregenna Castle Hotel, he painted the houses in The Warren in an afternoon light and the end of Fore Street, with James Cockings in his usual pose, hands deep in his pockets. He did a big canvas of the houses on the waterfront under a gray light and also one of the "stunning" outside of his studio flat, with its mottled coat of patched plaster and exposed brick, revealing windows filled in here and others opened there. A corner street scene,

---

412 See my book *St Ives 1860-1930 - The Artists and the Community*, Tewkesbury, 2009 for further extracts from the Journal.

413 I believe that Mr Irvine (or Irving) and his wife signed into the Arts Club in January, April and December 1909 are likely to refer to Wilson Henry Irvine and his wife, but he gives no indication in his Journal that he has visited the town before and there is no mention of a 1909 visit to St Ives in his biography.

414 From undated and unattributed review of Irvine's 1925 Carson exhibition - Archives of American Art, Smithsonian Institution, Wilson Henry Irvine papers, Reel 1233.

415 On several occasions, he pays tribute to his wife, "Is there another wife that would do what Lydia is now, put up with the many discomforts of this studio, the fact of our being alone - no one for her to talk to, no interest but that of the strangeness of it all, but the good of the cause." - Journal of Wilson Henry Irvine, 22/3/1923, Archives of American Art, Smithsonian Institution, Irvine papers, Reel 3564.

416 From undated and unattributed review of Irvine's 1925 Carson exhibition, ibid.

417 Journal of Wilson Henry Irvine, 20/2/1923, ibid. The landlord was a Colonel James and the rent 13s 5d per week, which Irvine considered cheap.

418 Journal of Wilson Henry Irvine, 26/2/1923, ibid.

419 Journal of Wilson Henry Irvine, 3/3/1923, ibid.

Fig. 8.3  Wilson Henry Irvine     *St Ives, Cornwall*     (Collection of Clement C Moore II)

This work was used as the cover illustration for the catalogue of an exhibition of Irvine's European works at the Wadsworth Atheneum, Hartford, Connecticut, in November 1925.

Fig. 8.4  Wilson Henry Irvine     *Boats of St Ives*     (Private Collection)

that he refers to on occasion, is likely to be of Norway Lane, and this resulted in a work called *Rooftops*.[420] Towards the end of his stay, he worked on a painting of Lelant Church and a landscape at Phillack - "cottages along under Cliff creek, in spring dress, apple blossoms and redening trees".[421]

Irvine had been impressed by the village of Zennor, as he passed through on the way to St Ives, and, on a Sunday in late March, he and his wife returned to view the cliff scenery. "We walked to the Zennor Head - about 15 minutes. In the clear afternoon light, it was all tremendously impressive. Headlands 150 or 200 feet high, great chasms leading down to the sea, their sides broken with grey rocks, gorse and reddish stone debris, all in shadow with fascinating lines of light picked out here and there, water breaking at their foot and the sun in such a position to sparkle on the water. And against these great, rich dark masses, gulls flying way below us giving it all scale." [422] So impressed were they by the scenery that they immediately determined to spend some time based there and they booked a fortnight in mid-May in a cottage in the village near to the Inn. It was very basic. "We have to pick up gorse brush to kindle our fire, meat man once a week, baker twice, coal man seldom. Water at the town pump by the roadside. Privy up three of the dampest stone steps one ever negotiated. Stone floors." [423] The cottage creaked at night and was very cold. However, he loved the desolation of the moors and the rich gold of the gorse. On his first day, he spent five hours battling the wind and rain on Zennor Head. "It was rotten but the intermittent bursts of the sun on the fierce seas, as they broke against the head, was simply great and it was worth all the discomfort." [424]

Fig. 8.5  Wilson Henry Irvine         *Early Morning Light, Zennor*              (Bonhams and Butterfield)

---

420 This was No 30 in the retrospective exhibition *Wilson Henry Irvine and the Poetry of Light* put on by the Florence Griswold Museum in Old Lyme in 1998.
421 Journal of Wilson Henry Irvine, 26/4/1923, Archives of American Art, Smithsonian Institution, Irvine papers, Reel 3564.
422 Journal of Wilson Henry Irvine, 25/3/1923, ibid.
423 Journal of Wilson Henry Irvine, 10/5/1923, ibid.
424 Journal of Wilson Henry Irvine, 11/5/1923, ibid.

Fig. 8.6  Wilson Henry Irvine      *The Cornish Coast*      (Bonhams and Butterfield)

Two days later, he explored Gurnard's Head as well. "Its south slope is easy on the water and there are motifs simply great. A fine surf today. The view to the south - great gashes in the rocks black against the sun, sparkling surf below, gulls soaring in the chasms. It's titanic cosmos unspoiled through the ages."[425] He considered these heads to be the finest that he had ever seen, and he braved the elements to do a number of small and large works, finding the glare off the sea of the sun, when it did condescend to shine, painful to the eyes. There seems little doubt, therefore, that his painting, *England's Shores*, which he showed at the National Academy of Design, New York, and Chicago in 1924, was a depiction of one of these headlands. A fine work depicting a sailing boat pulling two dinghies off a rocky headland on the Cornish coast, (Fig. 8.6) is also likely to have been painted in this region. In 2005, it achieved $70,000, the highest price at auction for a work by the artist.[426]

Irvine mentions painting on occasion with an artist called Hilliard, probably his fellow American, F. John Hilliard (b.1886), a portrait painter and etcher, who came from Massachusetts. Irvine's first mention of him reads, "Hilliard around, when I was working, in his swank tweeds and light gloves, tan socks. Backed into him with my palette - smear."! A couple of days later, he records, "Hilliard along with me. He improves fast in his painting." [427] However, Hilliard may not have stayed in St Ives, as there are references to him "coming over". A favourite destination after they had finished sketching was the 'Sloop Inn', whose old port they both rated as "corking".

Albeit waiting six weeks for one of the St Ives artists to introduce himself, Irvine ended up by becoming friendly with Lowell Dyer and John Douglas, with whom he shared an interest in photography, and, on his departure, he bought a considerable number of Douglas' photos, which he may well have found useful in finishing off his paintings, given the poor weather that he had experienced. Indeed, one of Douglas' photographs of a sailing ship off a rocky headland may well have been the inspiration for Irvine's *The Cornish Coast* above.[428]

425 Quoted In Harold Spencer, *Wilson Henry Irvine and the Poetry of Light*, Old Lyme, 1998 at p.27. I am indebted to this book for much of the information about Irvine.
426 Bonhams and Butterfield, Auction dated 8/8/2005, Lot 23. The work was listed as *Low Tide, St Ives*!
427 Journal of Wilson Henry Irvine, 8/3/1923, Archives of American Art, Smithsonian Institution, Irvine papers, Reel 3564.
428 See Archives of American Art, Smithsonian Institution, Paul Dougherty papers, Reel 950, "reference photos".

# SEA CHANGE : FINE AND DECORATIVE ART IN ST IVES 1914-1930

From St Ives, the Irvines moved on to Clovelly, then to Betwys-y-Coed, before going up to the Outer Hebrides as guests of Lord Leverhulme. They then paid a return visit to Brittany, spending some time painting in Pont-Aven and Concarneau, before returning home by the end of the year. He had various exhibitions of his European work, including a joint show with Guy Wiggins at Carper Galleries in Detroit. Cornish titles included *Low Tide, St Ives*, *The Ragged Coast, Cornwall*, *Harbor of St Ives*, *The Fishing Fleet* and *The Cornish Coast*. The trip was felt to have had a profound influence on his work. Known previously for his bright and happy palette and his spirited handling of paint, some reviewers felt that his European work evidenced "a resolve to subdue his paint handling to conform to a more sober palette. Here and there, especially in the foreground of some of his landscape paintings, are to be found his old fireworks, but generally speaking, the paint is more methodically and carefully placed with a new care for drawing and values...The effect of this has been to give to these pictures more air of reality and actuality." Of the St Ives works in particular, the critic said, "It is evident that he has had to deal with colors gauged and subdued and bound together into a tonality by a light perhaps filtered through Atlantic mists." [429] This is likely to be the result of the excessively wet weather that Irvine encountered, for he mentions that, even when the weather cleared, there was often a fine haze over the harbour, but, in an interview in 1924, he admitted that he liked to paint best "when there's a kind of hazy beauty in the air".[430] Fig. 8.3 captures this effect magnificently.

In 1926, Irvine was elected an ANA and the following year he exhibited there *Dick 'Awkins of Cornwall*, his portrait of the local hunchback and his donkey. Cornish titles, such as *St Michael's Mount* and *Cornish Coast*, also featured later amongst what he called his 'aqua-prints', printed on marbleized paper made by an old Japanese process. A retrospective exhibition *Wilson Henry Irvine and the Poetry of Light*, which contained five paintings of St Ives, was put on by the Florence Griswold Museum in Old Lyme in 1998.[431] Yet again, the well-documented visit of this fine artist and the splendid paintings that he was inspired to produce have received no attention at all in St Ives.

Fig. 8.7  Arthur Powell    *In St Ives Harbor*                                  (Doyle's, New York)
Arthur James Emery Powell (1864-1956) was born in Vanwert, Ohio, and studied at the San Francisco School of Design, the St Louis School of Fine Art and Julian's Academy in Paris. He lived in New York. He appears to have visited St Ives in the mid-1920s, as a painting *In St Ives Harbor* was exhibited at the NA in 1927.

---

429 *Irvine Seen in New Guise in Carson Show*, Chicago Herald Examiner, 13/4/1924.
430 Journal of Wilson Henry Irvine, 5/3/1923, Archives of American Art, Smithsonian Institution, Wilson Henry Irvine papers, Reel 3564. Interview - *Detroit News* 16/3/1924.
431 Catalogue nos 24-6 and 31 contain 'St Ives' in the title, whilst No.30 *Rooftops* is clearly of Norway Lane, St Ives.

Fig. 8.8  Charles Bryant    *Landing Fish, St Ives*
(Art Gallery of New South Wales, Sydney)

## 8.4    Return visits by former colonists

Long-standing members of the colony frequently found themselves entertaining friends from past years, as fond memories drew former residents of the colony back on return visits.

A fairly regular guest was Julius Olsson, who had remained a J.P. of the town.  Frances Hodgkins recorded that he was staying with the Lindners in July 1915, albeit she was not very complimentary. "He is a bloated A.R.A. & is spreading himself, large & pink, having just sold his big marine (*The Night Tide*) to the Sydney Gallery." [432]  He was back again that September, when he organised the dinner on the 8th at the Queen's Hotel in honour of Elmer Schofield, following his decision to enlist, and, later in the month, signed the letter to the local paper complaining about the new sketching restrictions.  Paintings by him were often hung at the exhibitions at Lanham's Galleries and so, for example, that in June 1917 contained his works *Morning Sunshine* and *Silver Moonlight* (Fig. 8.11 - Southampton City Art Gallery), one of his finest depictions of moonlight on St Ives Bay.  He was probably back in 1919 as well, as his Royal Academy exhibits of 1920 included *Summer Moon, Cornish Coast*, a view over St Ives Bay to Godrevy.  Furthermore, in February 1920, his work *The Wet West Wind*, depicting "that mysterious quality of forced light that plays on the sea just before a heavy squall of rain", was considered the best work in the Lanham's show, combining "simple technique and searching analysis of wave form".[433]

His presence in the town was again noted in July 1921 and, during this visit, he not only took a keen interest in the work being produced locally, but also sat as a J.P. . The following April, a correspondent to the *Weekly Despatch* commented, "I saw Mr Olsson painting some of his beautiful sea pictures in Cornwall.  No matter how busy he was, the great artist was always willing to find time to give a friendly hint to amateurs staying in his hotel."  This prompted the editor of the *St Ives Times* to comment that Olsson's many friends in St Ives would agree with this accolade.  "His personal interest, especially in the younger section of the St Ives art colony has often been remarked upon...He is truly a 'great' man in every sense".[434]  As already seen, as President of the ROI, he was able to help the careers of former students, such as John Park and Borlase Smart.

In 1925, Olsson was one of the early colonists to send work to the St Ives artists' exhibition at Cheltenham - two typical paintings, *Moonlight on the Cornish Coast* and *Sunset on the Cornish Coast* - and one of his Royal Academy exhibits of the following year was *The Night Mail from Cornwall*, another depiction of the coastline at Carbis Bay bathed in moonlight.  Olsson was also, of course, one of the first Royal Academicians to be offered honorary membership of STISA.  Given that the Porthmeor

---

432 Letter to her mother dated 22/7/1915 - Ed. L Gill, *Letters of Frances Hodgkins*, Auckland, 1993 at p.307.
433 *St Ives Times*, 20/2/1920.
434 *Weekly Despatch*, 30/4/1922 & *St Ives Times*, 5/5/1922.

Gallery of STISA had been created out of part of his original Porthmeor Studio, he came down to open the inaugural exhibition in June 1928. Mindful of the fact that the Society's decision to have its own gallery had ended Lanham's forty year monopoly on the sale of paintings by local artists, he passed comment, at the opening ceremony, on the happy associations that had been enjoyed in the past between business people and artists in St Ives, a point picked up by Martin Cock, the then owner of Lanham's in his other role as editor of the *St Ives Times*, who recalled how Olsson's "own personal affability to the community was well remembered".[435] A touchy subject was, accordingly, well handled. Olsson decided to stay on in the town for some months, and it was probably during this period that he completed works such as *Cloudy Moonlight* (Doncaster Art Gallery). He even found time to sit as a J.P. and get involved in the local general election campaign.

Terrick Williams, another of the leading artists of the day to be made an honorary member of STISA, was also a regular visitor to the colony during this period, as he had been from 1889.[436] Dated paintings of St Ives place him in the colony in 1915, 1917, 1923 and 1924, and he also was invited to open STISA's Spring Exhibition in 1930. I have written previously about Williams' technique in oils, but, in the 1920s, he started experimenting with working in pastels and wrote a book on the subject, which featured *Breaking Waves at St Ives, Cornwall* (Fig. 8.10), about which he recorded, "It was made one afternoon when there was a considerable amount of movement in the water, and in brilliant sunshine. This effect on a rock-bound coast, such as one finds in Cornwall, is quite wonderful. The waves here, however violent, are always of a very fine greenish colour, as there is little sand and no mud to be stirred up by the movement of the water....The colour is thus of a curiously irridescent quality."[437] This work, and the other pastel illustrated, *On the Cornish Coast* (Fig. 8.9), which features Gurnard's Head, make distinctive use of the colours purple and orange, and Williams highlighted the quality given to a colour by the juxtaposition of its complementary. "Thus purple, which is the complementary of orange, will have a surprising effect of increasing the apparent brilliance of the latter if placed alongside it. I have often noticed this when painting out of doors an effect of sunshine and shadow. If the edge of the shadow just touching the sunlit part be made a very positive tone of purple it will make the warmth of the sunshine far greater, and, if the edge of the sunlit part where it touches the shadow be somewhat forced in its orange quality, the purple of the shadow is correspondingly intensified."[438]

As already seen, former Olsson student, Charles Bryant, seems to have returned to the town in 1917, as his work was included in a show at Lanham's Galleries that year. He also returned in 1922, as various fine paintings of the harbour from this visit, including *Landing Fish, St Ives* (Fig. 8.8), are owned by the National Gallery of New South Wales, Sydney. Another work, *The Harbour, St Ives*, was exhibited at the ROI in 1923. However, between 1924 and 1930, he settled back in Sydney, but he was clearly well-liked in St Ives, as notes of his various achievements were recorded in the local paper during this time. On returning to England, he paid a number of further visits to the colony during the 1930s, becoming a member of STISA. Another Australian former student to return was Richard Hayley Lever, who, since his emigration to the United States in 1912, had inspired many Americans to visit St Ives, due to his countless paintings of the town. An American attorney, who was a keen collector of his work, whilst staying at the Tregenna Castle Hotel in 1923, wrote to a friend, "As I look out over this beautiful harbor of St Ives, I am thrilled and reminded of Lever's pictures; these boats don't dance more, neither are the reflections more beautiful than they are on Lever's canvases!"[439] Lever himself came back in 1925 to pick up a collection of his work, which he had left behind, and he exhibited these in a solo exhibition at the Macbeth Gallery in New York in 1926.

Several other American painters made return visits. Elmer Schofield's great friend, Walter Norris, who had stayed a year in St Ives in 1904-5, returned again in the early 1920s, as he exhibited St Ives scenes at the National Academy of Design in 1921-2. This probably means that Schofield accompanied him, and, in 1924, he settled for a few years near Perranporth. George Gardner Symons, whose wife, Sarah Trevorrow, came from a St Ives family, made a number of return visits during the 1920s, including quite a prolonged one in 1929, and he included some St Ives scenes in his joint exhibitions with Schofield at the Stendahl Galleries in Los Angeles in 1928 and 1929. A further planned visit for the following year was unfortunately scotched by his untimely death. Herbert Faulkner, who had also married a St Ives girl, Mary John, was a guest at the Arts Club in June 1924. Charles Chapel Judson and his wife, Helen, whose first stay in 1914-5 had been curtailed by the sketching ban, returned for a further visit in late 1924 with their daughter, following his retirement from teaching at University College, Berkeley, and

---

435 *St Ives Times*, 22/6/1928.

436 In my book *Pioneers of St Ives Art at Home and Abroad 1889-1914*, I indicated that Williams' first visit to St Ives was in 1890, as he himself indicated in his speech when opening the 1930 Spring Exhibition of STISA (*St Ives Times*, 18/4/1930). However, I see that a watercolour *Summer Holidays, St Ives* dated 1889 was sold at Christies, London on 8/3/1990 Lot 36.

437 Terrick Williams, *The Art of Pastel*, London, 1937, at p.51-2.

438 ibid, at p.45-6.

439 *St Ives in America*, *St Ives Times*, 19/9/1924.

Fig. 8.9  Terrick Williams  *On the Cornish Coast*  (Private Collection)

Fig. 8.10  Terrick Williams  *Breaking Waves at St Ives, Cornwall*  (Private Collection)

Fig. 8.11  Julius Olsson    *Silver Moonlight, St Ives Bay*    (Southampton City Art Gallery)

were re-elected as members of the Arts Club in November. The Smithsonian record an oil *St Ives, Cornwall* in private ownership, but no other work from their stays has been traced. This may be due to their home in San Francisco being destroyed by fire in 1926. This is a shame, as on his death, an obituary commented, "His lyrical landscapes of California qualify him as one of the state's finest painters of his time." [440]

Another American, who was based in the town on a couple of separate occasions, was Vernon Ellis (1885-1944), about whom little seems known. He was first signed into the Arts Club by Edgar Skinner in February 1918 and took part in Show Day in 1919, when his exhibits in 'Norway Studio' were considered to have "with a strongly marked sense of colour" - his Italian landscapes "vibrating with intense southern sunshine".[441] In 1923, a Mr Ellis, presumably him, was again exhibiting on Show Day, this time at 'The Little Studio', his works being two local scenes - one of Porthmeor and one entitled *Taking the Nets Aboard* - and an Isle of Man interior subject. He exhibited occasionally at the Carnegie Institute in Pittsburgh, the last occasion being 1929, but his work is rare.

The Austrian-born artist, Rudolf Hellwag, now a Professor of Art in Germany, and his wife, Annie, who had lived in St Ives between 1900-1902 and been regular visitors over the next decade, were recorded as working in the town again in July 1925. Hellwag was credited with having organised a number of exhibitions on the Continent, which had resulted in works by English artists, such as Arnesby Brown, being bought by European public galleries, whilst it was noted that a number of his own Cornish works had been acquired by "various National Galleries on the Continent".[442]

## 8.5    Some temporary residents

Amidst the large number of artists, who visited St Ives for relatively brief periods of time during the 1920s, a few merit mention. One well-known artist, who became a resident of the colony in 1919-1920, was the Scot, David Murray Smith (1865-1952), a landscape artist, who exhibited extensively, particularly at the RBA and RWS. The first specific reference to him is in February 1920, when he showed a small canvas *Bereaved* at Lanham's Galleries, which was felt to be very distinctive and full of quiet power. "A woman in deep mourning stands in an upland over which hangs great cumulous clouds suggestive of a troubled state of Nature in keeping with the emotions of the figure. The low horizon gives a happy feeling of space to the picture and the bigness of the sky emphasizes the rich quality of the blacks in the dress." [443]

---

440 Edan Hughes, *Artists in California, 1786-1940*, San Francisco, 1986.
441 *St Ives Times*, 14/3/1919.
442 *St Ives Times*, 24/7/1925.
443 *St Ives Times*, 20/2/1920.

However, Murray Smith appears to have been working in St Ives during 1919, as his exhibits at Harris and Sons, Plymouth, in June 1920 included *August in Harbour, St Ives* and *Summer Afternoon, St Ives*, both of which were felt to reveal a vivid sense of colour. Borlase Smart also rated his Royal Academy exhibit that year. "Mr D.Murray Smith of St Ives, has one of the most sympathetic medium-sized landscapes in this year's Academy in No.281 *Golden Glow of Afternoon*. The picture does not owe its success to any particular scheme of composition. It is just a distant range of rolling hills, with meadow land and field leading to their bases. It is the tone of lighting and colour which raises the canvas to a such position of first rate importance. It is a simple landscape, simply painted; hence its artistic value." [444] The work was bought by the National Museum of Wales. By the time that Murray Smith exhibited a number of Cornish scenes at the RWS that November, he had left the colony, but he continued to exhibit Cornish scenes for a while and a work *In the Hayle* was included in a Fine Art Society show in 1925.

An artist, whose visit will have overlapped with that of Murray Smith, was Christopher Richard Wynne Nevinson (1889-1946), for he and his wife are recorded as guests of Nora Hartley at the Arts Club in February 1920. Nevinson, who had studied at the St John's Wood School of Art and the Slade School, had made his name with his futurist paintings during the War years. The purpose of his visit appears to have been to study printmaking techniques under Hartley, and he went on to become a fine etcher, featuring in the *Modern Masters of Etching* series in 1932. However, the work that he did in St Ives was in other media. An oil, *The Old Harbour, St Ives* (Fig. 8.12), must rank as one of the earliest, and best, naive depictions of the harbour, in which elements of the town's architecture are incorporated into a decorative circular design. Two sailing barques provide the principal interest in the centre of the composition. A watercolour sketch of the view from above Porthminster Beach across to the harbour was included in his memorial exhibition in 1947 as well.

Several artists with strong New Zealand connections visited the colony in the early 1920s. Francis McCracken (1879-1959) had been born in Ireland, but his parents had emigrated, when he was a young boy, first to Australia, where he lived on a cattle station, and then, in 1903, to New Zealand. On the outbreak of War, Francis had been studying art at the Elam School of Art in Auckland under Claus Fristrom for some years. However, he decided to join the New Zealand Expeditionary Force, but was severely wounded at Ypres, losing a leg. After being invalided out of the Army, he studied at the Royal Scottish Academy Life Schools. He appears to have worked in St Ives in or prior to 1920, as his watercolour, *Fishing Fleet, St Ives* (Fig. 8.14) was acquired by Auckland City Art Gallery in June that year from a successful touring exhibition of New Zealand, with two other Kiwi servicemen, which became known as 'The Soldiers' Exhibition'. Accordingly, there is the possibility that he had been drawn down to St Ives by the classes of his compatriot, Francis Hodgkins.

Fig. 8.12  Christopher Nevinson  *The Old Harbour, St Ives*  (Private Collection)

---

[444] *St Ives Times*, 14/5/1920.

# SEA CHANGE : FINE AND DECORATIVE ART IN ST IVES 1914-1930

Fig. 8.13  Hendrik Jan Wolter      *Boats by the West Pier, St Ives*      (Sotheby's, Amsterdam)

Fig. 8.14  Francis McCracken    *The Fishing Fleet, Saint Ives*
(Auckland City Art Gallery Toi o Tamaki)

Persuaded by the success of the exhibition to return to Edinburgh, McCracken was taught for a while by the Scottish colourist, S.J.Peploe, and the award of the Carnegie Travelling Scholarship enabled him to study in Paris, under André Lhote, and in Florence. As a result, he adopted a more modernist approach. He spent most of his career based in Edinburgh.

During 1920-21, McCracken painted a couple of posthumous portraits of Kiwi soldiers, who had received the Victoria Cross, and it was a similar commission that persuaded Annie Elizabeth Kelly (1877-1946) and her artist husband, Cecil Kelly (1878-1954), to visit Europe for a year in 1920-21. Both were tutors at the Canterbury College School of Art, where Elizabeth had studied from 1891-1901, and she went on to become one of New Zealand's leading portrait painters and the only female to be awarded the CBE for services to art. She also exhibited regularly in Britain. However, all that is known from their visit to Cornwall during the summer of 1921, when they painted both in St Ives and Penzance, are some watercolours of St Ives street scenes (see Fig. 8.15).[445]

Another visitor to the colony in 1921 was Hendrik Jan Wolter (1873-1952), one of the few Dutch artists to embrace Impressionism, whose visits to Cornwall before and after the War are considered to have had a major impact on his development. Born in Haarlem, he moved to study in Antwerp, when he was twenty-two, and then spent some time in Paris, where he was influenced by the work of Georges Seurat, Claude Monet and Paul Signac. His main theme became the representation of boats either in harbour or on rivers, as he was fascinated by the play of light on water and the impact of the boats' reflections. In the early part of his career, he often painted the seaside town of Amersfoort, which was close to where he lived, but, having moved to Amsterdam shortly before the War, he was constantly drawn to that city's waterways, particularly the view of the Amstel from his studio window. However, a number of his Cornish works capture the harbour scene at low tide, when pony and carts were on the beach and the boats, showing their colourful hulls, were leaning over at assorted angles. Dated works place him in Polperro in 1911 (see Fig. 8.18), and it is believed that he also visited St Ives and Lynmouth at this time. His presence in St Ives in 1921, the year after he had suffered a serious illness, which tempered the exuberance of his painting style, is revealed by two dated works - one a pastel of boats in St Ives harbour at low tide and the other a depiction of the church. Therefore, it is likely that one of his master works, *Misty October Morning, St Ives* (Fig. 8.17) was also completed during this visit. It is certainly a post-War scene, as two of the boats have wheelhouses, indicating that they have been fitted with motors. John McWilliams believes these to be *Perseverance* (SS 40) and *Excellent* (SS 122). Towards the right of the picture, with a blue hull and yellow funnel, is one of the few steamboats that operated from St Ives, possibly *Gleaner*. Dated works reveal that Wolter was back in Polperro in 1922, and another looser, luminous oil of boats by the West Pier, St Ives (Fig. 8.13) is thought to date from 1924. However, there is nothing in the usual sources recording his presence at any particular juncture. In 1924, Wolter was appointed professor at the State Academy in Amsterdam, a position that he held until 1938, and this impacted greatly on his painting output. Whilst he did start to paint again after his retirement, his health deteriorated and, accordingly, his Cornish work is some of the best of his career.

Fig. 8.15 Annie Elizabeth Kelly
*Houses on The Wharf, St Ives*

Fig. 8.16 Francis McCracken
*St Ives Harbour*

(both Jonathan Grant Galleries, Auckland)

---

445 A watercolour of Westcott's Quay, featuring the Arts Club and 'The Cabin' studio, was sold at the International Art Centre, Auckland on 25/7/2002 Lot 99.

Fig. 8.17  Hendrik Jan Wolter     *Misty October Morning, St Ives*     (Sotheby's Amsterdam)

Fig. 8.18  Hendrik Jan Wolter     *Low Tide, Polperro*     (Sotheby's Amsterdam)

Fig. 8.19  Lucy Kemp-Welch     *Low Tide, St Ives*          (Walker Art Gallery, Liverpool)

The year 1923 seems to have brought a large number of artist visitors to the colony. One of the most well-known was the animal painter, Lucy Kemp-Welch (1869-1958), who had been Principal of the Bushey School of Painting since 1904. She had enjoyed a most productive period in Cornwall in 1919, when she brought her sister, Edith, who had had a masectomy, to recuperate on the Lizard Peninsula. Between August and October that year, she produced eight fine paintings, whose colouring had an intensity not matched in her whole oeuvre. Apart from the superb *The Glory of the Setting Sun*, which featured the waters of Cadgwith Cove, the paintings were principally of horses at work on the cliff edges at harvest time. Her return visit to Cornwall in 1923, when she stayed in St Ives, is less well documented. However, it resulted in at least two fine paintings depicting the use of ponies and carts on the harbour beach (Figs. 8.19 and 8.20). *Low Tide, St Ives*, showing the carts being pulled past the end of the West Pier, was bought by the Walker Art Gallery, Liverpool.

Fig. 8.20  Lucy Kemp-Welch        *St Ives Harbour*           (David Messum Fine Art Ltd)

# SEA CHANGE : FINE AND DECORATIVE ART IN ST IVES 1914-1930

Fig. 8.21 Dorothea Sharp  *On Porthmeor Beach*
(Toy family collection)

Fig. 8.22 Dorothea Sharp  *Mother and Child*
(Toy family collection)

Kemp-Welch was not the only distinguished female artist in the colony that summer, for Vera Hemmens, in her article on St Ives, *A Cornish Chelsea*, records meeting in the town both the President and Vice-President of the Society of Women Artists. The President was Charlotte Blakeney Ward (fl.1898-1939), who painted the portraits of fashionable London. Hemmens commented, "Armed with her palette and paint-box, she was revelling in the glories of Cornwall". Her Vice-President was Dorothea Sharp, down in the colony on one of many visits that she made during the 1920s. When Marcella Smith had moved up to London to live with her in Maida Vale, she had retained the lease of 3 Porthmeor Studios, whilst Sharp's sister's husband had bought, from Frances Horne, 'Tremorna', the impressive mansion in Carbis Bay designed by Edmund Fuller. Hemmens found Sharp "painting on the Porthmeor beach, surrounded by children, mostly the daughters of fishermen, for these are her chief sitters. How they love to dress up in the pretty frocks from the children's wardrobe she always carries about with her!" [446] There seem few sources to gauge precisely when Dorothea and Marcella were back in the colony, and few painting titles by either of them are of much assistance. However, the local paper indicated that *Jack, Jill and Peter*, her Royal Academy exhibit of 1925, depicting three children in sunshine amidst flowering plants, was a St Ives scene.[447] This work did not sell and, clearly somewhat dissatisfied with it, Sharp painted on the other side of the canvas, in 1929, a work entitled *Where Children Play and Seagulls Fly*, which is now owned by Leamington Art Gallery. However, Figs 8.21 and 8.22, originally from the collection of the local builder, Robert Toy, who died in 1928, are both Porthmeor Beach scenes and are excellent examples of her colourful, distinctive style of this period.

Ernest and Esther Borough Johnson, who were both first signed into the Arts Club by Alfred Hartley in December 1914, came back to the colony for an extended visit in the autumn of 1923, when they were photographed working *en plein air* for the December edition of *Eve*, the ladies pictorial (see Fig. 8.23). They took part in Show Day in 1924, after which they announced that they were extending their visit. Ernest Borough-Johnson (1866 -1949) had been born in Shifnal, Salop, and had studied at the Slade School and Bushey. He was a well-regarded art teacher at various schools - Francis Hodgkins having been one of his pupils - and had written a book on the technique of pencil drawing. Whilst best known for his portraits, he also produced landscapes and worked in a variety of media. Like Simpson and Park, he had been fascinated by the bustle of 1923's particularly successful herring season, and his major picture on Show Day was an oil depicting the busy scene on the Wharf at that time, with girls packing the fish and a cart, loaded with barrels, setting off on its way. However, he also had an interest in Japan, and he seems to have linked up with Bernard Leach, for his other exhibits included a portrait of his kiln builder, Tsuranosuke Matsubayashi, in Samurai costume, with a bright red background, and a charcoal study of three famous Japanese ladies seated around a tea table. Whilst based in St Ives, Borough Johnson had a large figure painting, *La Creche*, exhibited at the Paris Salon, a Venetian scene hung at the Venice International Exhibition and a specially invited portrait shown at the Wembley Exhibition.

Fig. 8.23 Esther Borough Johnson painting on the harbour beach in 1923.
(St Ives Trust Archive Study Centre)

---

446 Vera Hemmens, *A Cornish Chelsea*, *Daily Graphic*, reproduced in *St Ives Times*, 3/8/1923.
447 See *St Ives Times*, 5/6/1925.

Fig. 8.24  William Lionel Wyllie          *St Ives*

Esther Borough-Johnson (fl.1896-1940) had been born at Sutton Maddock, Salop, and had studied at Birmingham, Chelsea and Bushey, where she had met Ernest. She was also principally a portrait painter and her exhibits on Show Day included a painting of a child playing with coloured balloon balls. Both enjoyed considerable success in Paris, with Ernest winning a Mention Honorable in 1923 and a silver medal in 1925 for his portrait of Esther, whilst she won awards in 1925 and 1929.

An artist, whose time in St Ives will have overlapped with the Borough Johnsons, was the Swedish-born portrait and landscape painter, Alexander Akerbladh (b.1886, fl to 1940), who had studied in Glasgow, St John's Wood (1916) and Munich (1917). His name is first mentioned in a list of St Ives artists successful at the Paris Salon in 1924, where his exhibits included a self-portrait, and his 1925 Academy exhibit was an interior of 'Skiber War Voir Studio', on The Wharf in St Ives, in which the quality of the outside lights and the reflected light on the ceiling was felt to have been ably rendered.[448]  He was also successful again in Paris that year with *Veillard Méditant*. Despite exhibiting at a wide range of societies, including having eighteen paintings hung at the Academy and fifty-nine at the Fine Art Society, his work rarely appears at auction.

Another artist to work in St Ives in 1925 was the famous marine painter, William Lionel Wyllie (1851-1931). Asked for his impressions of the town, he wrote, "A tangle of lanes and steep alleys. Granite built cottages and studios. A busy quay and Smeaton's Pier protect the haven from the great Atlantic rollers. The motor drifters jostle together in their hundreds. Towards evening, boat after boat slips into the bay, and soon their lights stud the dark water, rivalling the stars above in brightness and multitude. On the morrow, the craft return with their catch. Thousands of gulls, screaming, whirling, and fighting, make an animated snowstorm and almost blot out the forest of masts and spars. No wonder artists abound. Here they make their studios right amidst the bustle. There is neither annoyance nor curiosity, and the packing of herring and the skinning of dog-fish goes on without intermission." [449]  Wyllie was particularly struck by the view from John Bromley's home, 'Quay House', right by Smeaton's Pier, and did an elaborate sketch of it, which he utilised for his Academy exhibit of 1926, *St Ives*, which measured 53" x 27" (Fig. 8.24).[450] He also did an etching of the fishing fleet passing Godrevy lighthouse.

The most celebrated visit to the colony during this decade is that of Christopher Wood and Ben Nicholson in 1928, during which they discovered the paintings of Alfred Wallis, and this is considered in detail in the next chapter.[451]  Although this was Nicholson's first visit, he was well aware of Wood's prior spell in the colony in 1926, and may well have heard accounts from his father, William Nicholson, of his own stay in the colony in 1927, during which he completed, amongst other things, an oil of the old pier.[452]

---

448 *St Ives Times*, 5/6/1925.

449 *St Ives Times*, 18/12/1925.

450 See review of Show Day, *St Ives Times*, 19/3/1926 & *St Ives as an Art Colony*, 22/4/1927.

451 Some other visitors are revealed by dated paintings; 1921 - Alfred Aaron Wolmark (1871-1961), W.H.Ludlow (1852-1921); 1923 - George Soper (1870-1942), whilst local scenes were exhibited that year, at the RBA, by John Littlejohns and Frank Swinstead and, at the ROI, by Charles D Ward and Gyrth Russell; 1924 - E.Rowley Smart (1887-1934), John MacSymon (b.1876); 1925 - Frank Sully; 1926 - Mary Sutherland Hunter (b.1899); 1927 - Dora Holmes; 1928 - John MacSymon, the New Zealander Marion Tylee (1900-1980); 1929 - Frank Mole, Lewis Mortimer; 1930 - Harold Fletcher Trew (b.1888).

452 See Phillips Auctions dated 22/11/1994 Lot 40 and 21/11/2000 Lot 27.

# THE NOVELTY OF THE NAIVE VISION

## 9.1 A meeting hailed as "one of the great milestones in 20th Century British art"

In August 1928, a chance encounter in the streets of St Ives led to significant consequences, not just for the history of the colony, but also for British modernism. As Ben Nicholson and Christopher Wood, two young artists interested in the avant-garde, came off Porthmeor Beach, they noticed, through an open door, as they walked along Back Road West, some naive paintings of ships and houses nailed haphazardly on the walls. On entering, they found a small, semi-literate, irascible old man, who told them that he had just taken up painting "for company", following his wife's death. His name was Alfred Wallis, and the pair of friends at once recognised that they had stumbled on a phenomenon. Here was a man, who had received no training in art, and yet had a most extraordinary, seemingly simplistic vision of things, which he set down with cheap paint in an apparently haphazard manner on any piece of material that he could lay his hands on. This vision at once struck chords with Nicholson and Wood, who were part of a growing band of artists, who felt that most paintings were merely illustrative and had become too academic, too sophisticated, too highly finished and too concerned with a narrative, and who believed that they must start afresh from the beginning, looking first at the instinctive creativity of primitives and children.[453] Nicholson and Wood, therefore, had already been experimenting with their own attempts to present a naive, child-like view of their chosen subjects. The fact that Wallis' approach was entirely unconscious made it even more significant, for there was also a feeling that creativity was innate, leading to strength of expression and vitality of working, and that the imagination was fettered by training. Here then was a prime example of instinctive, untutored creativity. Furthermore, due to Wallis' unusual choice of materials to paint on and to paint with, his pictures assumed a character of their own, with unique textures and shapes. This, coupled with a lack of any observation of proportion or perspective, meant that his paintings made their own statement and were not merely representations of something else.[454]

Ben Nicholson, in particular, indicated that his attitude to art was revolutionised by this meeting, and, as he went on to become a leading figure on both national and international stages, his subsequent championship of Wallis as an authentic primitive has resulted in this encounter being hailed as "one of the great milestones in 20th Century British art". This, though, has drawn attention away from the significant influence that Christopher Wood had on Nicholson, for Wood had worked out a naive approach himself, including novel methods of paint application, some two years prior to the meeting with Wallis, particularly during a lengthy stay in St Ives in 1926. When Ben and Winifred Nicholson first saw these works, they walked home "in the high skies", believing that they had chanced upon "England's first painter". Having become firm friends, they proceeded to work, and correspond, with Wood, over the next twenty months, leading up to the meeting with Wallis, during which time they absorbed some of the influences that had inspired Wood's development, in the very different surroundings of Paris, in the company of such luminaries as Pablo Picasso and Jean Cocteau. Whilst Wood met a tragic end at an early age, and thus only shone briefly, like a meteor, this book, by pressing the pause button in 1930 - coincidentally, the year of Wood's death - brings into sharp relief Wood's far greater critical and commercial success at this juncture, fully deserved by his production of an extensive and varied range of interesting and innovative work. However, as Wood's paintings of St Ives are essentially representational, even he has received little attention in the colony.

## 9.2 The first St Ives visit of Christopher Wood in 1926

Christopher Wood (1901-1930) was born at Knowsley, near Liverpool. His father was a doctor on the Earl of Derby's estate there, but his mother, Clare, whilst coming from a rich Lancastrian family, had forbears, the Pellews, who had owned a large house overlooking St Ives harbour.[455] At the age of fourteen, after just one term at Marlborough School, Wood contracted polio. With his father serving as a medical officer in France, he spent the next three years at home with his mother, as he battled

---

[453] For instance, Henry Moore, when talking of the 1920s, commented, "There was a period when...I thought that the Greek and Renaissance were the enemy, and that one had to throw all that over and start again from the beginning of primitive art." D.Hall, *An Interview with Henry Moore*, Horizon, vol 3 no 2, New York 1960.

[454] In this section, I am indebted to Charles Harrison's article, *The Modern, the Primitive and the Picturesque*, in *Alfred Wallis - Christopher Wood - Ben Nicholson*, Scottish Arts Council, 1987.

[455] See Richard Ingleby, *Christopher Wood - An English Painter*, London, 1995 at p.15. Robert Morton Nance indicates that Edward Pellew, who became 1st Viscount Exmouth, was educated for a while at the St Ives Free Grammar School in the mid-18th century - see *St Ives Times*, 3/9/1948. Thanks to Janet Axten, St Ives Trust Archive Study Centre.

the debilitating illness, eventually emerging with a slight limp and a faint, but almost incessant, pain in his leg. During this time, his mother nurtured his self regard and his imagination, and they became very close. His desire to repay her devotion is felt to account for the extraordinary ambition that he later displayed. Accordingly, his letters to her, which are such a vital source, are full of confident, even arrogant, statements so as to ensure that she is pleased with his progress, albeit other letters to friends at the same time reveal considerable doubts and uncertainties.

On his father's return from the War, he was keen for his son to take up a profession and, accordingly, Kit, as he was known to all, enrolled at Liverpool University to study architecture in the autumn of 1919. However, before the end of his first year, he moved to London, promising his father, whose dull, middle-class values, he came to abhor, that he would work in an office, only pursuing his artistic interests in his spare time. A meeting with the Paris-based financier and patron of fledgling artists, Alphonse Kahn, put paid to this resolve, and led to Wood moving to Paris in March 1921, where he enrolled in a number of ateliers. There, he met the wealthy Chilean émigré, Antonio Gandarillas, and, being good-looking, smartly dressed, immensely personable, unworldly and not scarred by war-time experiences, he was drawn, with open arms, into a circle of men, who were wealthy, influential and homosexual. Gandarillas, in particular, with whom he lived for six years, became a close friend, patron and, presumably, lover. Wood, however, was "conveniently" bisexual.[456]

Wood set his sights high. In June 1922, he declared to his mother, "You ask me what I am going to be: I have decided to try and be the greatest painter that has ever lived...You were quite correct when you say I have a lot of work before me." [457] A month later, he indicated that he was attracted by the trend towards a child-like vision of things. "Do you know that all the great modern painters who we may not quite understand through their pictures, are not trying to see things and paint them through the eyes and experience of a man of forty or fifty or whatever they may be, but rather through the eyes of the smallest child who sees nothing except those things which would strike him as being the most important? To the childish drawing they add the beauty and refinement of their own experience - this is the explanation of modern painting." [458] However, his role as the companion of a rich man, with a penchant for gambling, who travelled extensively and moved in fashionable circles, interfered with his dedication to his art, and this came to trouble him more and more.

Fig. 9.1  Christopher Wood  (Redfern Gallery)

---

456 Anthony Powell, in *Messengers of the Day*, London, 1978 at p.58, commented, "He was the only British artist found acceptable in the Paris Monde of Picasso and Cocteau, a convenient bisexuality being no handicap in that particular sphere."
457 Letter dated 6/1922.
458 Letter dated 28/7/1922.

In 1923, Wood was introduced to Pablo Picasso, whom he called "the greatest painter of the day", and was honoured by Picasso being complimentary about his work, when visiting his studio. Picasso proved a major influence, but it was work from his pre-Cubist period that most interested Wood. He told his mother, "Our painters now don't understand colour as they should - colour to him is always the first law long before form. I rarely go outside three combinations. I use a lot of black, white brown and blue together, then mauve, pale green and grey, yellow and black and pink and black. Colour is not colour unless it is properly chosen." [459]

In 1924, Wood was also introduced to the infamous poet-impresario, Jean Cocteau, who may also have been a lover. Certainly, Wood was starstruck, calling him "not only the greatest poet alive, but the greatest genius" and also "a God".[460] Through him, he mixed in the circles of the *Ballet Russes* and had the opportunity of producing designs for a new ballet, but these did not find favour with Diaghilev. Whilst Wood valued highly Cocteau's critique of his work, his advocacy of opium was ultimately to prove Wood's undoing. The drug was thought not only to aid creativity, imagination and memory, but also to induce a sense of harmony, self-possession and clarity of mind. Gandarillas, and many of his circle, were regular opium users, and so Wood will have smoked it socially before, but Cocteau seems to have persuaded him to use it as an integral part of the creative process. In any event, he became ever more reliant on the drug, and never had the mental strength to wean himself off it. Withdrawal symptoms included vivid hallucinations and dreams, which accelerated and fragmented experience, and led to other malevolent side effects, such as a sense of duplicity, and Wood did constant battle with these, as his addiction took hold.[461]

Whilst Wood's time in Paris made him dismissive of English modernism, such as that of the Bloomsbury Group, he decided in the mid-1920s that his work needed to display English character. In December 1925, he told his mother, "I am going through a very difficult period at the moment as I must decide what I am going to do in the future. All the pictures that I paint now will be fatal, one way or another, to my career. They must be personal, quite different to everyone else's and full of English character." [462] A few months later, bolstered by a visit from Frank Dobson, he demonstrated renewed confidence in his ability to make an impact, confiding in his mother, "Everyone seems to think that I am going to be the best painter in England and I am gradually getting known through one reason or another, although I have not shown anything. My exhibition will have to be a terrific success and done in the right gallery... Dobson, who has known Augustus John since he began, says I am the only person in England who has begun with as much talent and the same greatness in his mentality and work. John is finished, dead, it rests apparently with me to carry on and go further. I hope all this will prove true for it is a big thing to attempt." [463]

Perhaps encouraged by Frank Dobson and/or another friend, Cedric Morris, both of whom had worked briefly in Newlyn, Wood decided that he ought to explore his Cornish roots, and he visited West Cornwall with Tony Gandarillas in August 1926. He immediately told his mother, "Cornwall is beautiful, rather austere, but I think that if I am here long enough I shall paint good things and I hope unlike other people's work." [464] They based themselves at the Mount's Bay Hotel in Penzance initially, but explored the surrounding area each day and paid a short visit to the Scilly Islands, which Wood found barren and not conducive to work. On 25th August, they settled in St Ives, taking a little wooden bungalow, in the grounds of Pedn Olva House Hotel. This had only two rooms, with no hot water or toilet, but these rooms possessed big windows affording splendid views over the rocks of Pednolva Point out to Godrevy. The bungalow also had an enchanting small rock garden, so that Wood felt little need to go out. He bathed on Porthminster Beach once a day. They took their meals in the hotel, and Wood considered the food first-rate and cheap. Gandarillas left on 20th September and so, for the first time since 1922, Wood was left on his own for a few weeks to paint to his heart's content. During this period, he produced a series of works that saw the evolution of a distinctive style, combining a naive vision, with powerful colour passages. Away from the superficiality of a metropolitan environment, Wood discovered, for the first time, his passion for the sea, something that Winifred Nicholson felt "had lurked in his Cornish spirit", and, over the course of the rest of his life, he produced his finest work when he was based in rural settings on the coast.[465]

---

459 Letter dated 6/7/1923.
460 Letters to his mother dated 1/11/1924 & 14/11/1924.
461 See Virginia Button, *Christopher Wood*, London, 2003 at p.28.
462 Letter dated 29/12/1925 - TGA 773.5.
463 Letter dated 2/5/1926 - TGA 773.6.
464 Letter dated 24/8/1926 - TGA 773.6.72-3.
465 Letter from c.1930 quoted in Jon Blackwood, *Winifred Nicholson*, Cambridge, 2001 at p.60.

Fig. 9.2  Christopher Wood        *Ship leaving a Cornish Port*        (Private Collection)

One of the most typical of the dozen or so works that he completed during this first visit was *Ship leaving a Cornish Port* (Newton 179 - Fig. 9.2). Dead centre of the image is a barque, with billowing sails, setting off past the end of Smeaton's Pier over a deep, ultramarine sea. The stark black and white of the foam-washed rocky foreground, upon which seagulls perch, is matched by a glowering sky - black over a solid bank of white cloud. Two spots of deep red set off this powerful, but limited, palette - one, a flag flying from the ship's mast, and the other a marker on a rock on the very right of the composition, probably intended to delineate the end of the old wooden pier. The whole has an eerie, foreboding feel to it, perhaps indicating the influence of opium. Eric Newton passed the following comment on the whole of Wood's oeuvre, but it seems particularly appropriate to this work. "His best paintings are at the same time radiant and faintly sinister...There is an unclouded purity, at times a rapture, in his pictures, but there is also a thunderstorm somewhere in the neighbourhood. Sometimes it is the inky blue-black of the sea, sometimes a leaden sky, more often a series of sinister shapes that cannot be analysed, that set the mood." [466]

Similar deep and harsh colours were used by Wood in *The Harbour, St Ives* (Mercer Art Gallery, Harrogate). Here the harbour is presented in a U-shape, with the chapel on the Island presiding over the scene. In describing their abode to his mother, Wood commented, "Opposite is the little port, full of fishing boats, and the little grey houses go up and up behind it and are topped by a little green hill with a small chapel on it, which adds greatly to the interest and the composition." [467] Again, the sea is painted a dark blue - so dark, in fact, that the presence of a black steamer coming into port is easily missed. Blue played an important part in his palette for the rest of his life, and Winifred Nicholson, after his death, commented, "Blue was his colour and the evolution of the use of blue in his work was the evolution of the driving power of his life." [468] Again, in this work, red is used, as a counterpoint to blue - on the base of the lighthouse, in the chimneys and roofs of the houses, on the rigging of the steamer and in the fish laid out in the foreground.

The most interesting work that Wood completed on this visit was *China Dogs in a St Ives Window* (Newton 168 - Fig. 9.4), for, even more than the other works, this includes features, such as a cone-shaped Godrevy and a naively drawn steamer, placed without regard to perspective or proportion, that

---

466 Eric Newton, *Christopher Wood 1901-1930*, Redfern Gallery catalogue, London, 1938 at p.46.
467 Letter dated 6/9/1926 - TGA 773.6.75.
468 Quoted in Richard Ingleby, *Christopher Wood - An English Painter*, London, 1995 at p.143.

merit direct comparison with the motifs used by Alfred Wallis. However, there is absolutely no doubt that this work was completed in 1926, a full two years before the fabled first meeting with Wallis in 1928.[469] There is no suggestion that Wood saw the work of Wallis during his 1926 visit and, so, one must conclude that Wood arrived at this approach off his own bat. The painting is discussed in further detail below, as Nicholson made an unsuccessful attempt at copying the subject, but its colour scheme again rests on the vibration between vivid blues and reds, albeit Wood's attempt at painting the red chair upon which the china dogs sit was unsuccessful. As Ingleby mentions, the ill-judged perspective has rendered the chair almost an abstract patterned background, but this does not enhance the picture. The humorous aspect of the subject - china dogs sitting on a chair taking in the vista out to sea - was quite unusual in Wood's work. It was a painting that was held dear by two of Wood's closest friends, being owned initially by his lover, Frosca Munster, before being given by her to Winifred Nicholson, who described it a "haunting picture".[470]

A painting, whose subject location has been difficult to place, is that owned by Manchester Art Gallery entitled *Loading the Boat, St Ives* (Newton 190 - Fig. 9.3). Albeit always known by this title, it can safely be stated that it is <u>not</u> of St Ives. In fact, it is unlikely to be of anywhere in particular, but, instead, be an amalgam of scenes witnessed by Wood, as he explored the area with Gandarillas.[471] The metal bridge, over which people are walking in the background, should be the best clue, and this is felt to bear similarities to the original Ross swing bridge, or even to the narrow walkway above the harbour gates, at Penzance. An alternative view is that the glimpse of houses seen through the arches of the bridge has resonances with the railway viaduct at Hayle. In any event, the painting is likely to have been done back in St Ives purely from memory. Matthew Rowe has expressed the view that the painting's "overall rich tonality, highly textured surface and free-flowing outlines recall the work of Cedric Morris, whose paintings of the previous summer present a similar impression of a hard-working, earthy Cornwall." [472]

Fig. 9.3   Christopher Wood          *Loading the Boat, St Ives*          (Manchester Art Gallery)

---

469 The painting is not only listed as a 1926 work by Newton but also is specifically mentioned by Winifred Nicholson as one of the masterpieces that Wood showed them at the end of 1926.

470 Other Cornish subjects completed in 1926, listed by Eric Newton in the catalogue for the Redfern Gallery's 1938 exhibition of Wood's complete works, include *Cove, Cornwall* (128), *Window in Cornwall* (129), *Fishing Village, Cornwall* (131), *Cornish Landscape* (143), *The Valley, Cornwall* (148), *St Ives* (167), *The Sloop Inn, St Ives* (184 - Auckland Art Gallery) and the watercolours *Cemetery by the Sea* (671) and *Atlantic Beach, St Ives* (679).

471 They did some further exploring after settling in St Ives, for Wood mentioned in a letter to his mother dated 6th September that he had used the car quite a bit in the previous week.

472 A.Cariou and M.Tooby, *Christopher Wood - A Painter between Two Cornwalls*, London, 1996 at p.30.

Tony Gandarillas returned to St Ives on 9th October, but immediately went down with 'flu, which Wood then caught. With both of them poorly, the lack of hot water and a toilet made the bungalow impossible, and they decided "to get back to town or die in the attempt".[473] Back in London by 21st October, Wood told his mother of the considerable progress that he felt that he had made, "I know that my stay in St Ives has been a great profit to me as I have at last learnt how to finish my work, which is the most, and was especially to me, the most difficult part. I feel that I have thought a lot and assimilated much and that now really I feel that I am an artist and could never have done anything else in my life, which is a great comfort to me. For when I see how much others struggle and labour, and how much more natural it all is to me and fluent and easier, I know that I was born an artist and have not just become one. I am absolutely mad about my work and sit and think about it and do nothing else all day...Those who have seen what I have done lately are bewildered by the progress and sometimes I think that I do the things by accident, but I am not quite sure it is so, and nothing in art that is good is done by accident - only by very hard work." [474]

Shortly after returning to London, where he occupied Gandarillas' flat in Cheyne Walk, Wood was taken by Cedric Morris to dinner at the home of Ben and Winifred Nicholson. Winifred, who, on a number of occasions, was prone to premonitions, sensed a strong connection with him, merely from the sound of his voice, without having laid eyes on him. Impressed by his company, the Nicholsons took him up on his offer to show them his latest work, at Cheyne Walk, the next day. Winifred later recorded their initial impressions. "Crowded together in his small bedroom were an amazing array of canvases. He produced masterpiece upon masterpiece. The Red Dogs; the White Ship, the portrait of Tony, a nude, a number of still and dark Cornish landstrips...we walked home in the high skies. Here was England's first painter. His vision is true, his grasp is real, his power is life itself." [475] Wood was delighted by the enthusiasm shown by the 'Nickies', as he dubbed Ben and Winifred, but they were not the only ones to be impressed, as he proudly boasted to his mother. "My work of this summer has caused a perfect uproar of admiration from those who have seen it and I am getting better known each day. Augustus John could not express himself sufficiently to say how much he liked my work and the extraordinary progress in it...Something came over me this summer which opened new fields before me and shed light on my hitherto rather confused brain. It is wonderful and I hope that I won't be disillusioned. I have made lots of new friends for all the artists like my work and I am almost acknowledged the best of the young painters." [476]

Fig. 9.4   Christopher Wood        *China Dogs in a St Ives Window*
(Private Collection, on loan to Pallant House Gallery, Chichester)

---

473 Letter dated 21/10/1926 - TGA 773.6.82.
474 Letter dated 8/11/1926 - TGA 773.6.85.
475 In Winifred Nicholson, *Kit - An Unpublished Memoir*, TGA 723.100.
476 Letter dated 13/12/1926 - TGA 773.6.91.

# THE NOVELTY OF THE NAIVE VISION

Fig. 9.5  Ben Nicholson   *1928-1931 (St Ives Bay, sea with boats)*
(Manchester Art Gallery, © Angela Verren Taunt 2010. All rights reserved, DACS)

## 9.3   Ben and Winifred Nicholson

Although already planning to take control of, and transform, the Seven & Five Society, to which he had been elected in 1924, Benjamin Lauder Nicholson (1894-1982) was still struggling, when he met Christopher Wood, with the direction that he wanted his own art to take, albeit he had acquired an appetite "to bust up the sophistication around me". This desire stemmed most directly from a reaction against his father. Nicholson was the eldest son of William Nicholson (1872-1949) and Mabel Pryde (1871-1918), who had met whilst studying art together under Hubert Herkomer at Bushey and who had married in 1893. William came from a monied family, his father being an industrialist and Conservative M.P. for Newark. He enjoyed a successful career, first, as an illustrator, producing striking woodcuts and other graphic work, (often operating in conjunction with Mabel's brother, James Pryde, as the Beggarstaff Brothers), and, secondly, as a painter of glossy Edwardian portraits and conversation pieces, as well as luscious still lives. As he mixed with ever more fashionable members of society, his inherent self-centredness led him to pay less and less attention to his wife, who became increasingly withdrawn, and his children. Affairs soon held sway as well, and Ben, who was close to his mother, considered him to be a poor husband and father.

Having not excelled academically at school, Ben was sent to study at the Slade School of Fine Art, when aged only sixteen, and worked there on and off under Henry Tonks from 1910-1914. As his drawing ability was so poor, Tonks could see little future for him as an artist, and his father was appalled at some drawings that Ben sent to him for comment in 1914, labelling them frightening, "so abnormal" and "the work of an untrained eye, both in colours and form".[477]

On the outbreak of War, Ben volunteered, but was rejected initially on health grounds, but with conscription looming in 1917, he was sent by his mother to America. Accordingly, he was mortified to hear, whilst there, that she had died in the flu outbreak in 1918. On his return, he then learnt of the death of his brother, Tony, in France. He soon resumed his friendship with Edith Stuart-Wortley (née Phillips), a young, wealthy, artistically-inclined war widow, whom he had known from the Slade, and the pair became engaged, only for Edith to decide instead to marry Ben's father. The unexpected loss of his dear mother, coupled with his father's snatch of his fiancée, in such close succession, unsurprisingly had a devastating effect on the frail Ben - one that impacted on all his future relationships. Accordingly, when a keen art student, Winifred Roberts, daughter of Charles Roberts, a Liberal M.P. and grand-daughter of the 9th Earl of Carlisle, whose family seats included Castle Howard in Yorkshire and Naworth Castle in Cumberland, demonstrated in 1920 that she considered him not only attractive, but also talented artistically, Ben did not resist a hasty wedding.

---

477 Letter from William Nicholson to Ben Nicholson post-marked 7/10/1914.

Albeit well-off, the happy couple nevertheless enjoyed working closely together in spartan conditions, firstly in a lake-side villa in Switzerland bought for them by her father. They became "utter paint fiends", painting all day in silence until each had finished, and experimenting with a range of styles and techniques. Winifred, in particular, had a special interest in trying ways of making colour lose its subservience to form. When, after giving up the villa in January 1923, they held an exhibition of their work in Bond Street, Frank Rutter acclaimed Winifred for inventing "a new sort of flowerpiece", where the blooms were seen on a window-sill, not against the frame of the window, but against the vista outside. This required "the foreground flowers and the distant background to be held together formally and tonally, but primarily by colour harmonies".[478] Rutter was not alone in his admiration for these works, for all Winifred's flower paintings sold. However, none of Ben's portraits of Winifred, his still lifes, "with a peasant flavour" or his landscapes, looking "like desert places", attracted a purchaser. Later, Ben decided to destroy all the work from this period, but influences mentioned in letters are wide-ranging and included tribal art and the naive painter, Henry Rousseau.

In 1924, Ben and Winifred bought a grey stone farmhouse, Bankshead, built over the remains of a Roman mile-castle on Hadrian's Wall, close to Boothby in Cumberland, which was to be the inspiration for their next intensive spell of experimentation. However, by the time of his first one-man show at the Twenty-One Gallery in March 1924, Ben had already produced his first completely abstract paintings and these sufficiently impressed Ivon Hitchens to lead him to invite Nicholson to become a member of the Seven & Five Society, an association of artists, which, when founded in 1920, comprised seven painters and five sculptors. Once elected, Nicholson worked to convert the Society into his own power base, arranging for both Winifred, and even his stepmother, Edith, to be elected.[479] Having been appointed Chairman in 1926, he organised a change in the voting rules so as to get rid of the 'duds'. Accordingly, his first reaction to the sight of Christopher Wood's paintings of St Ives was to invite him to join the Society, and four works by Wood, including one St Ives subject, were included in the January 1927 exhibition. Frank Rutter, in his review of the show, singled out, for particular mention, the work of Wood, the Nicholsons and Cedric Morris. Wood also was represented in the joint show that the Nicholsons had with the potter, William Staite Murray, in April that year, which resulted in Winifred being hailed by *The Times* as "a genius" as a flower painter.[480] Wood's contributions included his fine self-portrait, which showed him in a harlequin jumper (a nod to Picasso's self-portrait as a harlequin), set against the rooftops of Paris. As Wood considered this work was his best to date, he was rather disappointed that it failed to elicit praise at the time. However, for most of 1927, Wood was in the company of Tony Gandarillas, either in Paris or in the South of France, and contact with the Nicholsons was largely by letter. Winifred, in particular, started to send him her news and reflections on art, as well as flowers from the garden. Whilst enjoying carefree times with Gandarillas, Wood began to envy the Nicholsons' lifestyle, in which they were able to dedicate themselves wholeheartedly to art.

Around the time that she first met Wood, Winifred Nicholson discovered, most unexpectedly, but delightedly, that she was pregnant. Told by her gynaecologist previously that she would not be able to have children, this was considered a 'miracle' by him, whilst Winifred felt it owed much to her recent conversion to Christian Science. However, during her pregnancy, she had a serious accident, breaking her back when she fell through a trap door at an exhibition. At first, it was felt that both she and the child would die, but, against the odds, she was able to give birth on 16th June 1927 to a strong and sturdy boy, whom they called Jacob (soon Jake). This sequence of events made her an avid believer in the teachings of Christian Science.

## 9.4 The 1928 visit and the discovery of Alfred Wallis

Having seen the mutual support that the Nicholsons afforded each other, Christopher Wood indicated to them his desire to find a "real woman" like Winifred to share his life, as an artist-lover-companion. Whilst in Cannes in late 1927, he fell madly in love with Meraud Guinness, a pretty, artistically-inclined, heiress, whom he described as "the sweetest, gayest, smartest thing in the world". However, their plans to elope and marry were thwarted at the last moment by her parents, who suggested a year's separation. Distraught, and a little embarassed, Wood decided to return to England, and took rooms in Chelsea, whilst Winifred attempted to play the role of sister to both Wood and Meraud. At Easter, Wood joined the Nicholsons at Bankshead. Winifred later compared his arrival to that of a meteor, and recalled, "inspiration ran high and flew backwards and forwards from one to the other".[481] In particular, Wood passed on ideas about elimination of detail that he had learnt from Picasso and Cocteau, and introduced 'the Nickies' to his practice of covering old canvases with a thick white paint called coverine,

---

478 Judith Collins, *Winifred Nicholson*, London, 1987 at p.15-6.
479 Edith Nicholson worked under the name Elizabeth Drury.
480 *The Times*, 6/7/1928.
481 Tate Gallery, *Winifred Nicholson*, London, 1987 at p.86.

which dried fast and gave the new surface a rich and varied texture - a technique which particularly appealed to Ben, for whom the physical characteristics of the picture surface became increasingly important. Certainly, the month spent together sealed the trio's friendship. In addition to her own 'love' for Wood, Winifred later recalled, "Ben and Kit had made friends with a friendship and fellowship in their work which brought the very best of them to flowering point - It was great fun to see - the zest and vitality and life in it meant everything to us all." [482] Interestingly, however, Wood destroyed much of the work that he did at Bankshead, feeling it substandard.[483] The inspiration, therefore, may have been mainly travelling one way - from Wood to Nicholson.

Wood linked up with the Nicholsons again in August that year on a trip to Cornwall, initially staying with Ben's friend and patron, Marcus Brumwell, at Feock, a village on one of the estuaries leading to Carrick Roads, near Falmouth. They occupied separate tiny, white cottages, and Winifred described the area as "a sleeping beauty's countryside of southern foliage, sheltered creeks and wide expanse of placid water".[484] Wood, who had joined them by 13th August, also called it "a very beautiful place" and told his mother, "I love Cornwall - it feels very familiar to me." [485] Amongst the resulting works based on local subjects were two paintings by Ben of nearby Pill Creek, and Kit's *Church at St Feoch, Cornwall* (Newton 294) and three paintings of Portscatho (Newton 258, 308 & 310), one of which featured a yacht race, which Wood found exhilarating (Fig. 9.6). Wood's paintings *Card-Players, Falmouth* and *Fishermen, Falmouth* (Newton 258-9) may also have been completed in this section of the trip. Winifred also worked diligently during this period.

After a few weeks, Ben found that the woods adversely affected his asthma, and so it appears that Wood suggested to him that they might go to look for some rooms in St Ives.[486] Ben later recalled, "This was an exciting day, for not only was it the first time I saw St Ives, but on the way back from Porthmeor Beach, we passed an open door in Back Road West and through it saw some paintings of ships and houses on odd pieces of paper and cardboard nailed up all over the wall, with particularly large nails through the smallest ones. We knocked on the door and inside found Wallis, and the paintings we got from him then were the first he made." [487]

Fig. 9.6   Christopher Wood        *Yacht Race, Portscatho*
(Private Collection/ Photo © Crane Kalman Gallery, London, UK/ The Bridgeman Art Library)

---

482 Letter to Frosca Munster, late 1930, in Richard Ingleby, *Christopher Wood - An English Painter*, London, 1995 at p.184.
483 See letter to his mother dated 20/4/1928 - TGA 773.8.29.  He kept "some 5 or 6 things".
484 In Winifred Nicholson, *Kit - An Unpublished Memoir*, TGA 723.100.
485 Letter dated 3/9/1928 - TGA 773.8.47.  His first communication with her from Cornwall was a postcard sent on 13/8/1928.
486 See Wood's letter to his mother dated 5/9/1928 - TGA 773.8.49, in which he says, "BN not so well with asthma here and so I went over to St Ives once or twice to see if there are any rooms there."
487  Ben Nicholson, *Alfred Wallis, Horizon*, vol.7 no.3, 1943.

Fig. 9.7  Winifred Nicholson     *The Island*     (Dartington Hall Trust)

Fascinated by Wallis' work, they asked him about his life, and were told that he had been a mariner for many years, some of his voyages taking him as far as Newfoundland, before dealing in marine stores. However, he indicated that, after being robbed of £40 some years earlier, he viewed his fellow men with suspicion and had become reclusive. Now that his wife had died, his paintings, which drew on memories from his career, and his two books - *The Bible* and a *Life of Christ* - were all that he required.

Having found some accommodation, the Nicholsons and Wood had moved to St Ives by mid-September, and they were joined there by Wood's exotic new lover, Frosca Munster, a White Russian, now living in Paris and married to a Polish count in an open relationship. The Nicholsons rented 5 Channel View, whilst Wood and Munster took 'Meadow Cottage' on Back Road West, which they found dirty, flea-ridden and, to Frosca's chagrin, with no bath. However, having spent a week cleaning and re-painting the place and having put in fresh curtains and bedspreads, Wood told his mother that, although very simple, it was charming and gay. "It has a lovely, lovely view of a beach with pale green waves and seagulls; ideal and very, very restful." [488] After a succession of servants initially, he settled on a hunchback, who was "very quick and good-tempered".[489]

Despite having Jake to look after, who "ran with bare baby feet by the sea", Winifred managed to find time to paint herself "with keenest delight", and completed a number of works, which included a painting of a boat being tossed on a stormy sea and one of pilchard nets drying on the Island. The latter (Fig. 9.7) was bought by Leonard and Dorothy Elmhirst of Dartington Hall from her successful Leicester Galleries exhibition in 1930, where she sold twenty-six of the thirty-one exhibits. It was probably painted from St Nicholas' Chapel, and depicts nets being laid out by the coastguard station on the northern side of the Island, with Godrevy in the distance, as a storm sweeps into the Bay. Additional interest results from the pencil arcs, that Winifred always used in planning her compositions, being still visible in many areas of the painting. Judith Collins explained her practice, "She made sweeping gestures with a pencil or crayon in her hand, and these gestures resulted in a series of interlocking or overlapping graphic arcs. They do not necessarily relate to the composition as painted, but they helped her to stake out the web of connections revealed by looking at coloured objects in a certain light." [490]

Unfortunately, despite Ben being inspired by his meeting with Wallis, very few of the paintings that he completed during this visit have survived his later cull of his early work. The most well-known is *1928*

---

488 Letter dated 28/9/1928 - TGA 773.8.51.
489 Letter to his mother dated 6/10/1928 - TGA 773.8.54.
490 Judith Collins, *Winifred Nicholson*, London, 1987 at p.81-2.

*(Porthmeor Beach, St Ives)*, an unusually large work that features a cone-like Godrevy and a sailing ship on a grey sea with white breakers in a style that clearly owes a debt to Wallis, but Nicholson has also included a naively drawn horse, a motif, without, seemingly, any local significance, as it featured frequently in his works that year, and, dominating the right hand side of the composition, an architectural feature, with an arch. This has caused considerable puzzlement over the years, until Chris Stephens of the Tate Gallery worked out recently that the painting, despite its title, is actually of Porthminster Beach and that the arch refers to a short railway tunnel. As the art critic, Paul Konody, commented, "all objects [here] are reduced to 'mere symbols' distorted to the point of forming a decorative rebus."[491] However, these introduced elements have little positive impact on the limited decorative scheme of the work, which is not made any more appealing by a colour scheme that is unremittingly drab.

The period in St Ives was not an unqualified pleasure for the Nicholsons, as the presence of Frosca Munster, with her "glittering frocks", upset the balance of the group relationship, for she resented the warmth and depth of the friendship that Winifred enjoyed with Kit. Whilst there was great mutual admiration on the artistic front between Kit and Winifred, there are suggestions that there was a physical attraction as well. Winifred was certainly obsessed with Kit, and she herself admitted that her love for him had "meant going through fire, but fire purified it". However, she also commented that, whereas she would have given Kit "anything", she would "not have been faithless to Ben".[492] Kit, for his part, indicated in a letter to her, that his feelings for her were "everlasting" and "far above all the little sensuous ins and outs of the world".[493] Nevertheless, he became aware that Frosca was not happy with the situation and, on 20th September, he told his mother that, although his painting was going well, he was looking forward to the Nicholsons leaving: "as a matter of fact it would be much nicer when the Nicholsons go as they are round here on and off all day". Eventually, Frosca said some harsh words to Winifred, which she recalled "cut like a dagger into my love and I walked along the brink of the sea in bitter anguish".[494] Shortly afterwards, Winifred decided to "cut out" and leave, but the Nicholsons, in any event, had to attend a family wedding on 9th October. Frosca, in fact, proved a good influence on Wood, stimulating him into intense periods of work, and, after her departure on 16th October, he told her, "I have never been so happy as during these last few weeks....You have shown me the beauty of life. You have taught me the worth of so many things and you have taught me to paint what is good taste." [495] By then, the Nicholsons, or, in any event, Winifred, were back, as she accompanied Kit on a walk to Clodgy to help him get over Frosca's departure. However, it seems that further relationship problems resulted in the Nicholsons deciding to leave on 1st November. Comments by Kit suggest that Winifred was very keen to stay on to work, but that Ben had a "difficulty".[496] Ben, in any event, in a symbolic gesture, left Kit his palette - presumably, assumed Wood, because from now on he planned to mix his colours "on box lids" like Picasso and Wallis.[497]

Wood was not too dismayed to see 'the Nickies' leave, grumbling to his mother, "I think they love having a hand in the lives and intrigues of others, as if they hadn't sufficient for themselves with that child, Christian Science, vegetarianism, killing themselves with self-sacrifice and painting as well." [498] He was now left to make "the last big effort" on his own for a couple of weeks, before returning in mid-November first to London and then to Paris.[499] He revelled in St Ives in the winter, telling Winifred, "I seem to live on the very edge of the world. But what an edge it is. I love this place and could stay here for ever if I had those around me for whom I care. Each day there is a new thrill here, wonderful sunshine, terrific storms - each thing is at its best for this is a picture gallery of only the good pictures and one feels the good qualities so much that one hardly wants to seek another...You seem to feel this place as I do. I feel that it belongs in a sense to me....One can't tell the seasons for there is not a tree, but there is a great feeling of intensity and usefulness like a garrison that is working in real earnest after a lazy peace. All the summer things have disappeared. The beach huts all gone. The windows on to the sea boarded up in the houses." [500]

---

491 Quoted in Ed. Chris Stephens, *Ben Nicholson - A Continuous Line*, London, 2008, at p.26.
492 Quoted in Sarah Jane Checkland, *Ben Nicholson - the Vicious Circles of his Life & Art,* London, 2000 at p.78.
493 Undated letter to Winifred Nicholson #2, November 1928 - TGA 8618.1.43. However, he indicated that his feelings for Frosca were the same!
494 In Winifred Nicholson, *Kit - An Unpublished Memoir*, TGA 723.100.
495 Letter to Frosca Munster, October 1928, quoted in Richard Ingleby, *Christopher Wood - An English Painter*, London, 1995 at p.196.
496 See undated letter to Winifred Nicholson #2, November 1928 - TGA 8618.1.43.
497 See Sarah Jane Checkland, *Ben Nicholson - the Vicious Circles of his Life & Art,* London, 2000 at p.78.
498 Letter dated 31/10/1928 - TGA 773.8.59.
499 Although Wood had taken the cottage until the end of December, he tells Winifred in the undated letter TGA 8618.1.43 that he intends to leave St Ives to spend a few days in London on Monday - probably Monday 12th November - as Frosca, in Paris, was "prepared to go anywhere with him on the 20th". He was certainly in Paris when he wrote to his mother on 26th November.
500 Undated letter to Winifred Nicholson #2, November 1928 - TGA 8618.1.43.

Fig. 9.8  Christopher Wood     *Porthmeor Beach*     (Anthony Hepworth Fine Art, Bath)

Wood also appears to have paid one visit to Mousehole, for Newton lists *The Red Cottage, Mousehole, Cornwall* (292) and *Mousehole, Cornwall* (295) as dating from this visit.[501] Certainly, he popped in to see Cordelia Dobson, the ex-wife of his friend, Frank Dobson, at her mother's house in Newlyn, and then entertained her and her sister, Mary Jewels, back at 'Meadow Cottage'.[502] He often saw 'Admiral Wallis', and, on one occasion, took him "some baccy and a few papers".[503] Indeed, he told Winifred, "More and more influence de Wallis, not a bad master though." [504] When Winifred asked him to send her some drawings of St Ives so that she could use these for her own work, Wood responded, "Why don't you simply paint St Ives from memory. I don't make drawings any more - now all out of my head. I find it more valuable to use my eyes instead of a pencil. I remember just as much that is important." [505]

Becoming lonely on his own, Wood tried to get his mother to join him. "I have this house and it's doing nothing and it seems almost a waste to have a cook when I hate eating and fires when I live in my bedroom...It would be so wonderful to see this place together - we have certain associations with it as you say and which I feel." [506] However, illness prevented her from joining him, and so he had a final period of intense work. Believing that he had made significant further progress, he told his mother, "I am working very well and doing the best I have ever done. It must sell as it's good and I know it....It is a great moment in my life, I feel things are becoming really vital and the studentship has passed, my work is forming something quite personal and sure, unlike anybody else's, and I don't think anyone can paint the pictures I am doing. This time of quiet has come at the right moment as before I didn't know enough to need it, but now it is essential as it is now or never, and I am making a big dash for it." [507]

---

501 This work was sold for £108,500 at Christies, London on 16/11/2007 Lot 45.

502 He commented, "Delia is so essentially a woman of this country - she gives me so much the spirit of the place, the enormous capacity and hardiness for suffering, the extraordinary devotion and yet the revengeful attitude at the end". However, he felt that he did not understand her sister, Mary, whom he felt was "like a poor female imitation of Cedric and Lett" and whose drawings he considered were poor. Undated letter to Winifred Nicholson #2, November 1928 - TGA 8618.1.43.

503 Undated letter to Winifred Nicholson #1, November 1928 - TGA 8618.1.42.

504 Undated letter to Winifred Nicholson #2, November 1928 - TGA 8618.1.43.

505 Undated letter to Winifred Nicholson #1, November 1928 - TGA 8618.1.42.

506 Letter dated 31/10/1928 - TGA 773.8.58-9.

507 Letter dated 28/10/1928 - TGA 773.8.56-7.

# THE NOVELTY OF THE NAIVE VISION

Given that both Kit and Winifred felt that he produced his best work to date during this 1928 visit, it is a little disappointing that so few of the nearly forty Cornish works from this trip, listed by Newton, in the Redfern Gallery catalogue in 1938, have been located.[508] The best known is a painting that tends to be referred to as *Porthmeor Beach* (Fig. 9.8).[509] Whilst the background of the Island, with Godrevy in the distance, and the beach flanked by the long run of studios is relatively conventional, the principal novelty is the decorative scheme employed in the foreground - one that appears to bear the influence of Van Gogh, an artist for whom Wood had deep admiration. The grass of the headland is broken up by snaking stone walls and a winding path, up which an old fisherman laboriously makes his way. Some rocks are delineated merely by black and white stripes, and a strange creature, probably intended to be a horse, is silhouetted on the edge of the headland against the sand. The bright yellow and white of the beach could have divided the painting into two distinct halves, but Wood has introduced in the very bottom left corner a single patch of brown which picks up on the colour used to depict the Island. One, but only one, roof of the studios run is also depicted in a brown, as well. The painting is one of Wood's finest accomplishments.

Another well-known work from this visit is *The Fisherman's Farewell* (Newton 254 - Fig. 9.9), which, in fact, features the Nicholson family. Young Jake Nicholson is held up by Winifred, whilst Ben seemingly plants a farewell kiss on his cheek. These three figures dominate the work. The pepperpot lighthouse in the middle of Smeaton's Pier emerges from the centre of the group. To the right is the second lighthouse on the end of the pier and a group of moored boats, whilst, to the left, is depicted the top of the pier, with its distinctive three arches, and several groups of fishermen busy on the harbour beach. The high vantage point adopted gives the impression that the farewell is occurring in an interior, with the background scene being seen through the room's window. The unusual elongated horizontal format of the painting (11" x 27.5") may be a response to a Wallis work. Overall, however, the painting does not convince.

Wood's letters to Winifred at the end of his stay make a number of references to the violent storms that battered the town, one of which made a huge whole in the harbour wall by The Warren and "knocked a house down".[510] These conditions brought home to Wood the harsh life of the fishermen, whom he came to admire immensely. He features them in *Cornish Fishermen, The Quay, St Ives* (Aberdeen Art Gallery) (Newton 282 - Fig. 9.11), in the area known as 'The Castle', a raised walled area above the entrance to

Fig. 9.10  Christopher Wood    *The Fisherman's Farewell*    (Tate, London, 2010)

---

508 Other work listed by Newton, not referred to in the main text, with titles confirming that they were done, or based on sketches completed, during this visit, include *Girl and Lamp in a Cornish Window* (261), *Beach and Town, Cornwall* (262), *Cornish Farmhouse* (280), *Daisies in a Lustre Jug, St Ives* (281), *Farm near St Ives* (283), *St Ives* (284), *Horses on the Cliff, St Ives* (288), *A Cornish Window* (291), *St Ives* (298), *Ships and Lighthouse, Cornwall* (300), *Entrance to the Harbour, St Ives* (301), *Cottages in Cornwall* (302 - Sydney Art Gallery), *St Ives, Cornwall* (307), *From the Artist's Window, St Ives* (309), *A Cornish Sailor* (315), *House on the Hill, Cornwall* (317), *Cornish Harbour* (320), *Cliffs and Beach, St Ives* (321), *Beach, St Ives* (322), *St Ives* (323), *Fishing Boats and Lighthouse, St Ives* (324), *Cornish Harbour* (328), *Nasturtiums in a Glass, Cornwall* (333), *St Ives, Cornwall* (334), *Green Hills, Cornwall* (335) and *Flowers and Lamp in a Cornish Window* (338).

509 There is no work of this title listed by Newton. Ingleby records it as *From a Cornish Window* (Newton 285), a work of the right size, but, as the viewpoint from which the scene is depicted is in the region of Man's Head, where no properties exist, and as there is no indication of a window in the work itself, this seems a little odd. More likely is *Cliffs and Beach, St Ives* (Newton 321), which, again, according to Newton, would be of the right dimensions.

510 Undated letter to Winifred Nicholson #1, November 1928 - TGA 8618.1.42.

Smeaton's Pier. This was a popular look-out point from which to gauge the weather. Despite the fierce sky and the choppy seas, several men make their way down on to the pier to join their boats, as other vessels in the fleet set off into the Bay. On the very left, Wood has introduced a tall building in which he depicts women, safe from the elements, mending nets. The painting seems to have been inspired by a scene that he described to Winifred, "St Ives is like a terrific roulette table at the moment. There is a terrific storm. The sea is dead white and angry white all over. The sea gulls and fishing boats are blown about like bits of paper and the women scuttle into their houses like frightened rabbits. The fishermen are heroes - they look like pirates with their big jack boots up to their thighs...they look very brave and dashing." [511]

Wood also continued with his fondness for views from or of windows. In these paintings, either he used the window itself as a frame for his depiction of the external vista, often with a vase of flowers by the window to increase spatial complexity, or he employed the bars of the window as a geometrically-patterned backdrop to a still life arrangement set up on the window seat. A number of works clearly featured the fenestration of 'Meadow Cottage'. An oil lamp, with black base and a white china section in its middle, was regularly part of the still life arrangement, as were flowers and gaily coloured pieces of pottery.[512] His new interest in flowers in his work may be the result, not only of having a female companion, but also of witnessing, at Bankshead, Winifred paint her flower pictures. Several titles also make reference to a girl sitting in the window. This might be Frosca, but Wood does tell Winifred after everyone has gone, "I have a little model who has a lovely body but she is rather a nuisance as I want to paint the place." [513]

Fig. 9.11  Christopher Wood     *Cornish Fishermen, The Quay, St Ives*
(Aberdeen Art Gallery & Museums Collection)

---

511 Undated letter to Winifred Nicholson #1, November 1928 - TGA 8618.1.42.
512 A more unusual still life subject was *Under the Kitchen Table, St Ives* (Leeds Art Gallery) (Newton 330), depicting a basket of vegetables.
513 Undated letter to Winifred Nicholson #2, November 1928 - TGA 8618.1.43.

## 9.5  Alfred Wallis' true background

Whilst various aspects of Wallis' background were teased out of him by Nicholson over the years, the earliest detailed research was done after Wallis' death by the artist and writer, Sven Berlin, who published a biography in 1949. Subsequently, however, a good deal of myth has developed. More recently, a full investigation of public records by Peter Barnes has revealed important information, whilst the wider availability of Dr Roger Slack's recorded interviews with relatives of Wallis in the 1950s and 1960s has provided fascinating anecdotal accounts of the man. The area of most doubt has been the extent of Wallis' experiences at sea, and this has been the subject of claim and counter-claim over the years. In a biography published in 2001, artist and mariner, Robert Jones, argues convincingly that Wallis' paintings themselves evidence an intimate knowledge of boats and seamanship.[514] Despite all this research, there are still areas of doubt.

Whilst Wallis' parents, Charles and Jane, who had married in 1844, came from Sennen and Madron, both in West Penwith, Wallis himself was born, in 1855, in Devonport. Records describe his father as a labourer (1849), a street paver (1861 and 1866) and a journeyman mason (1871). Wallis claimed, and several relatives interviewed by Dr Slack believed, that he had first gone to sea as a cabin boy, aged just nine, one of his initial trips being to the Bay of Biscay. However, his life between the ages of seven and seventeen is still shrouded in mystery, albeit that it is is known that his mother died in 1866. Robert Jones, however, mentions a painting of *The Flying Scud* (PZ 11) (registered 1867, broken up 1893), on which Wallis had written "this is the number that I was on about 65 years ago I was sea-sick I never eat anything un till we got to Scarbro from Newlyn". The boat, which appears to have followed shoals of mackerel and herring around the coast, features in a number of his other works, but this inscription suggests that Wallis worked on her from an early age.

By the time of the 1871 Census, the family had moved back to Penzance, with Alfred being recorded as an apprentice basket maker. Objecting to the drinking habits of his brother, Charles, and his family, with whom he had been living, Alfred, who was a small man, under five foot in height, decided to lodge with the family of a friend, George Ward, in New Street, Penzance. Accordingly, his marriage to George's mother, Susan Ward, in April 1876 will have set tongues wagging, as she was 43 and he a mere 20 - especially when she gave birth to a child that July! By this juncture, though, Alfred described himself as a mariner in the merchant service and, a few weeks after his marriage, he joined *The Pride of the West* on a voyage to Newfoundland, via Cadiz, before leaving St John's in August on the *Belle Aventure*, a ship which featured in a number of his paintings, arriving back in Teignmouth in November. Therefore, he missed both the birth in July, and the death in September, of his son. In May 1879, a second child, Ellen, was born to the couple, but she also died young, aged only fifteen months. These losses, and the large age difference, cannot have made the relationship any easier, but Susan and he were apparently very happy together during a marriage that lasted forty-six years.

Wallis was recorded on Ellen's birth certificate and in the 1881 Census as a labourer, which again casts doubt on the length of time he spent at sea. However, Robert Jones has researched the boats named by Sven Berlin as being ones upon which Wallis crewed, and he believes that it is very likely that he did indeed serve from time to time during the 1870s on the *Alpha* and the *Beta*, owned by George Bazeley of Penzance - the former sailing to the Channel Islands, Antwerp, Palermo and Gallipoli, and the latter going to Cardiff, Swansea, London and Chatham. He also supports Berlin's contention that, after his move to St Ives in the early 1880s, Wallis served over a period of five years on the *Faithful* and *Sisters*, both owned by Thomas and Richard Clarke. Names of particular ships, such as *The Golden Light*, included in titles of paintings by Wallis, might also indicate other boats upon which he may have crewed. Furthermore, Robert Jones argues that his paintings display an intimate understanding of the different types of sail layouts of a variety of craft, of how boats would cast their nets in certain conditions, and of the importance of the rigging, the ratlines and the reef points, confirming that he did spend quite some time at sea.

After the family's move to St Ives, where they lived initially at 4 Bethesda Hill, Alfred was asked by a businessman, Joe Denley, for whom Alfred's brother, Charles, ran a marine stores in Penzance, to set up a similar store in St Ives. Alfred established this in 1887 on Back Road West, before moving it to The Wharf. In the main, the stores relied on second-hand and salvaged goods, and Wallis collected items in a small cart. His rag-and-bone-man's cry 'Old Iron' became his nickname. He was industrious, but the perils of his trade are revealed when he was fined £10 in 1894 for receiving stolen goods, when items from the wreck of the *Rosedale* were found in his cart. Like everyone else involved with the fishing industry in St Ives, Wallis will have noticed the ever-decreasing numbers of boats operating from the harbour, as catches became less and less dependable. Nevertheless, in 1908, Susan and himself were able to buy 3 Back Road West as their home. He continued with the marine stores until 1912, a truly terrible year for the fishing industry in St Ives, when over one hundred fishermen were

---

514 Sven Berlin, *Alfred Wallis - Primitive*, London, 1949; Peter Barnes, *Alfred Wallis and His Family - Fact and Fiction*, St Ives 1997; Robert Jones, *Alfred Wallis - Artist and Mariner*, Tiverton, 2001; Slack recordings at St Ives Trust Archive Study Centre.

sued for non-payment of rates. By this juncture, Susan was 78 and was glad to retire, whilst Alfred continued to do odd jobs. For ten more years, they lived happily at 3 Back Road West until Susan's death in June 1922. It appears, though, that the couple kept their wealth in coins, and Alfred claimed that £40 in gold and £5 in silver were taken after his wife's death by his stepchildren, leaving him short of funds. It is possible that his wife had made promises to them, for she too was the subject of his ire. Accordingly, he was obliged to sell his home to a Mr Spink in September 1924, with the proviso that he could remain there for the rest of his life for a nominal rental of one shilling per annum. On his own, most probably after a lifetime of being mothered by his much older wife, and, in his view, undeservedly impoverished, it is not surprising to find him being portrayed often as reclusive, bitter and irascible, and yet other accounts refer to him as being pleasant, chatty and entirely un-mercenary.

Wallis indicated that he had taken up painting after his wife's death in 1922 "for company", whilst Ben Nicholson's account of the discovery of Wallis in 1928 contends that "the paintings we got from him then were the first he made".[515] However, interviewees of Dr Slack, particularly Jacob Ward, confirm that Wallis was painting whilst he was still running the marine stores (i.e. before 1912), sketching initially in pencil, before moving on to colour. His wife, though, scoffed at his efforts, and relatives got fed up with receiving jars upon which he had painted. A number of artists, such as Cedric Morris and Alethea Garstin, claim to have known about Wallis' paintings before he was discovered by Wood and Nicholson, but none seems to have taken any significant interest. It also appears that Wallis had been offering his paintings in exchange for goods or services and that a few locals, such as the grocer, Mr Baughan, the watchmaker, Mr Edwards, and the antique dealer, Mr Armour, did appreciate them, and gave him some encouragement. There are also many accounts of Wallis merely giving works away to children or anyone else who showed a semblance of interest.

### 9.6  Ben Nicholson's promotion of Wallis

Nicholson, having bought numerous examples of Wallis' work from him, wasted no time in telling his friends of his find. Most were perplexed at his enthusiasm, something that Wood did not consider was unexpected. "I am not surprised that no one likes Wallis, no one liked Van Gogh for a long time did they?"[516] However, one friend, H.S. (Jim) Ede, then at the Tate Gallery, was equally smitten, and arranged, as early as December 1928, for a Miss Bromby, who lived in St Ives, to keep an eye on the old man. Ede reported her account to Nicholson: "He's evidently turned over a new leaf as she's found no fleas - she finds him a dear quiet dignified person with the most unmercenary mind she's ever met. She's got lots of cardboard 'cos he said he had no more...He says he will have to do less as it was only a hobby & he now sits in too much - what with all these 'orders' - his life he says is out of doors, so you must not overwork him, poor thing. He says he's going off his food with overwork!!!...Your next batch are all grey - he's feeling grey it seems."[517]

Encouraged by the interest now shown in his art, Wallis continued to produce an extraordinary body of work. He could not afford artist paints, but merely used household paint, bought in small tins. This limited the colours that he could use to black and white, blue, what Nicholson described as "a particularly pungent Cornish green", some yellow and a little red. However, before painting, he would sketch out the subject in some detail in pencil, and might use a pencil again to re-emphasize some aspect after his application of paint. Being totally unschooled, he did not bother with the niceties of proportion or perspective, and his designs were largely the consequence of the shape and size of the piece of material that he was working on. He tended to paint on whatever there was to hand - one painting owned by the Tate Gallery (Plate 9.12) is painted on an undated advertisement for an exhibition of the St Ives Society of Artists, whilst another work is painted on the back of a railway timetable. In the main, though, he used cardboard, as this was widely available and free, and he was quite happy to improvise on pieces that were not square. The thickness of the cardboard, its absorbency, its colour and whether it had a glazed finish all impacted on the effect that could be obtained, and Wallis seemed to demonstrate considerable skill in adapting to each variety. Nicholson recorded, "He would cut out the top and bottom of an old cardboard box, and sometimes the four sides, into irregular shapes, using each shape as the key to the movement in a painting, and using the colour and texture of the board as the key to its colour and texture."[518] Accordingly, he was happy to leave sections of the card unpainted, thus making use of its original colour, explaining to Jim Ede, "i Thought it not nessery To paint it all around so i never Don it."[519] There are several accounts of Wallis talking at length about his work, but the extent to which he gave serious thought to his art, and the manner in which it developed over time, have both been underplayed, due to the desire to portray him as an unconscious 'primitive'.

---

515 Ben Nicholson, *Alfred Wallis*, Horizon, vol.7 no.3, 1943.
516 Undated letter to Winifred Nicholson #2, November 1928 - TGA 8618.1.43.
517 Letter from Ede to Nicholson dated 13/12/1928.
518 Ben Nicholson, *Alfred Wallis*, Horizon, vol.7 no.3, 1943.
519 Letter to Ede dated 24/4/1929.

Fig. 9.12 Alfred Wallis *The Hold House port meor square island port meor Beach* (Tate, London, 2010)

Fig. 9.13 Alfred Wallis *Houses at St Ives, Cornwall* (Tate, London, 2010)

If Wallis ever did paint on canvas, then this was normally another artist's rejected work, and, in such instances, he could achieve unusual effects by blending part of the original work into his own composition. One of his earliest known works on canvas, *Seascape* (Kettle's Yard, Cambridge), showing a schooner passing between three sailing ships and Godrevy lighthouse, is likely to have been given to him by Christopher Wood, as he was its first owner. Matthew Gale has pointed out that, whereas Wallis often started by placing his principal motif in the middle, he employs a different tactic in this work, with each of the motifs hugging the edge of the canvas' two inch stretcher.[520]

Whilst he would keep an eye open for contemporary motifs on his sorties out from his house, referring in one early letter to Nicholson, in November 1928, to a painting of a steam drifter driven ashore by Hayle Bar, he never sketched out of doors, telling Ede "all i do is hout of mery [memory] i do not go out any where To Draw".[521] Indeed, in the main, the subjects of his pictures were, as he put it himself, "what use To Bee out of my memory what we may never see again".[522] Accordingly, in addition to local scenes, there were vaguely remembered images from his early years in Devonport, his trip to Newfoundland and his voyages on coastal trading vessels. When painting the local townscape, Wallis might depict cottages all leaning in one direction, as if buffeted by a wind, and even upside down, when the street turned a corner. Painting from memory, he was not interested in what could actually be seen from any viewpoint, but the way his streets buckle round tend to suggest that he had a particular direction in mind. One house that features repeatedly in his output is the property now known as 'Norway Cottage', but which Wallis called 'Hold House, Porthmeor Square' (Fig. 9.12). Its remarkable door, which rose up between its first floor windows, clearly fascinated him. Ships, though, were his principal passion, but his boats often rode the waves at forty-five, even ninety degree angles, or could be dwarfed by giant shoals of fish. Lighthouses frequently played an important role in the composition, and that of Godrevy was normally represented by a cone shape. The brigantines and other sailing ships that he had seen during his days as a mariner were regularly featured, often with their rigging being depicted in a surprising amount of detail. This, though, may, in part, be the result of Nicholson's gift to him of F.W.Wallace's *In the Wake of the Wind Ships*, which some see as an infringement of the primitive isolation in which he had worked previously. Nicholson also sent Wallis a book on the untrained French painter, Henri Rousseau, having clearly made the connection between the two, but Wallis seems to have dismissed this with the comment, "At any rate he knew nothing about boats." [523]

Fig. 9.14　Alfred Wallis　　*The Blue Ship*　　(Tate, London, 2010)

---

520 See Matthew Gale, *Alfred Wallis*, London, 1998, at p.41.
521 Letter dated 1/4/1936.
522 Letter to H.S.Ede dated 6/4/1935.
523 Letter from Wood to Winifred Nicholson dated 28/10/1928.

Nicholson and Ede soon made arrangements to buy up a large percentage of what Wallis produced and, in response to these 'orders', he sent off parcels of paintings to them, wrapped up in string. Nicholson described the unveiling of each work as an "event", for one could not predict, for instance, what material Wallis had used, what shape it was, what unusual ways he had organised his motifs into his composition, how he had applied the paint and what novel colour scheme he had adopted, for he was just as likely to paint a street blue, as he was the sea.

With Winifred now as Chairman and with Ben and Kit on the hanging committee, it was no surprise to find a couple of Wallis' works - listed as *Mount's Bay* and *Lugger* - included in the 1929 exhibition of the Seven & Five Society. As the show also contained a number of St Ives works by Ben, Winifred and Kit, the presence of works by Wallis was, in the words of Matthew Gale, "an affirmation of the immediacy of feeling and a guarantee of authenticity".[524] The plan backfired, however, as, whereas Wallis' work inspired a certain degree of interest for its unconscious vision, it merely served to demonstrate the self-conscious attempts at a cultivated faux-naif style in the work of the others. As one critic put it, the works of "a genuine illiterate, a St Ives fisherman now well into his second childhood" afforded "too refreshing a contrast with the would-be unalphabetic attempts of some of the group".[525] Using the terminology adopted by Bernard Leach and his Japanese friends at this time, the work of Wallis was more noteworthy for being "born not made".

## 9.7 Breakdown

Although Nicholson did not revisit Cornwall until 1932, he did produce over the next couple of years, a few paintings that were based on sketches or remembered scenes from the 1928 trip. However, despite his considerable continuing interest in Wallis, he does not appear to have produced many paintings that show a clear Wallis influence. *1930 (Cornish Port)* (Kettles Yard, Cambridge) might have a Wallis-type sailing barque in it, but it has more of the feel of the landscapes that Nicholson had been doing at Bankshead, whilst, with *1928-1931 (St Ives Bay, sea with boats)* (Fig. 9.5), the influences seem to stem more from Wood, than from Wallis. If one compares this work with Wood's *China Dogs in a St Ives Window* (Fig. 9.4), one finds that each is a view, through a half-open window, over rocks in the foreground, to a steamship off Godrevy and its lighthouse. On most counts, though, Nicholson's work, in my view, is inferior to that of Wood. To make an attractive decorative arrangement, Wood has foreshortened the distance to Godrevy so that the steamship and the lighthouse appear at close quarters, whilst the vivid reds and oranges of the china dogs, and the chair upon which they are placed, vibrate against the blue of the sea. Nicholson, however, uses more correct perspective, so that the steamship and the lighthouse appear as relatively inconseqential notes on the horizon. Instead, he has to give greater emphasis to the foreground rocks, which, painted a uniform grey colour, provide little by way of interest. Whilst both artists place important emphasis on the window furniture, Wood's window stay is boldly shown in black, picking up the colour and strength of the steamship, whilst Nicholson resorts merely to pencil and produces a contorted shape that is foreshortened and does not sit comfortably on the wood. In fact, the whole of the opening section of the window is utterly unconvincing. Modernist art historians may argue that his use of pencil demonstrates a further challenge to the high level of finish expected by sophisticated art, but, to me, it has no positive benefit at all, merely making the picture look unfinished, particularly given the poor quality of the drawing. Nicholson's painting, principally a mix of blue, grey and white, also lacks any strong colour note, such as the orange used by Wood, to pick it up. Quite clearly an imitative work, it has little to commend it.

A more interesting painting is *1930 (Porthmeor window - looking out to sea)*, but this is again a window picture owing a debt to Wood. In this, the viewer is placed further back in the room, so that the whole of the frame of the window, with its curtains to each side, is visible and, as the window surround, including a central pillar, is thick and heavy, the vista outside is restricted, and is broken into rectangular segments. Although, again, a naively drawn barque is seen in the distance, the painting is largely a geometrical pattern picked out in soft pastel colours, with a dusky orange livening up the pale blues and yellows. It is a delightful piece, but far removed from a Wallis.

During 1929, Christopher Wood discovered Brittany, which held considerable attractions for him, due to its similarities and close ties to Cornwall. He worked feverishly during the summer in Dinard, St Malo, Douarnenez and, particularly, Tréboul, and on the basis of what he produced, he was offered an exhibition in Paris in May 1930 by the highly-regarded dealer, Georges Bernheim. He told Winifred proudly, "I think I am almost the first English painter to exhibit at a big Parisian gallery like this since Whistler." [526] However, the need to make certain that the show was a success brought additional pressure, as did

---

524 Matthew Gale, *Alfred Wallis*, London, 1998 at p.28.
525 Unidentified press cutting quoted in Richard Ingleby, *Christopher Wood*, 1995 at p.208.
526 Letter dated 19th October 1929.

the realisation that the Wall Street Crash at the end of 1929 had dealt severe blows to a number of his patrons and supporters, particularly Tony Gandarillas, so that he needed to become self-financing. Furthermore, Frosca's allowance from her brother-in-law was cut significantly, so that Wood felt obliged to help her as well.

In early March 1930, Wood returned briefly to Cornwall, staying on this occasion in Mousehole, so as to produce some further Cornish work for the Bernheim exhibition.[527] Lodging at 'Colvellan', he told Ben Nicholson, "Mousehole has quite a different aspect from these two wonderful rooms - there is a huge window running right across the sitting room which sticks out over the harbour. The sea is very rough and bright dark blue and lovely French sailing boats foam past that rock lifting themselves almost out of the water. Behind there is hilly country...and all the cliff is covered with daffodils and anemones, lovely green fields, beige farms etc. It's too wonderful.....I won't write more as I am working at an enormous pace and absolutely deliriously happy painting. Never have I had such a delicious sensation from life before...It's wonderful to be able not to consider anything but ones want to work and work and not to sleep and eat just when one wants." [528] Despite staying only some fourteen days, he did, indeed, work at an extraordinary rate, producing at least ten oils and several wash drawings. However, these were not sketchy pieces, and a number included a considerable amount of observed detail. One of the best works is *Cornish Fisherman in a Cap* (Newton 398 - Fig. 9.15), a fine portrait of an old salt, probably in front of the large sitting room window of his lodgings, which again has an extended horizontal format. There is nothing naive in this representation - it is just a cracking portrait. By now, in his depictions of boats, Wood was not featuring groups of vessels, but, instead, he tended to concentrate on one particular boat, noting in greater detail the equipment on deck and its sails and rigging. Accordingly, *P.Z.134* (Newton 433 - Fig. 9.16) is again quite a realistic depiction of the boat by the quay in Mousehole, with its cabin, and gear neatly stored on the deck, whilst another boat sails across a somewhat threatening Mount's Bay to the rear. Scratching out enlivens the water in the foreground. As usual, he also painted some still lifes, such as *Anemones in a Cornish Window* (Newton 408 - Leeds Art Gallery).[529] He may even have paid a quick visit across to St Ives, as *Still Life with Boats, St Ives* (Newton 399) is listed as a 1930 work. A further meeting with Wallis during this visit is suggested by the existence of a canvas by Wood of a Breton scene that Wallis has used for the basis of one of his works, for Wood had not visited Brittany when he had met Wallis before. As Wood was trying to kick his opium habit during his Mousehole visit, there is no hallucinatory feel to the works, and they are as close to standard representational art as Wood gets, which is presumably why modernist art historians find them disappointing.

Fig. 9.15  Christopher Wood    *Fisherman in a Cap*
(Private Collection/ © The Fine Art Society, London, UK/ The Bridgeman Art Library)

---

527 In a letter to his mother dated 5/3/1930 (Wednesday), he said that he was going down to Cornwall that week. TGA 773.10.
528 Letter dated 12/3/1930 - TGA 8618.1.71.
529 Other works listed by Newton with Cornish titles include the oils, *P.Z.416, Cornwall* (395), *Salvation Army Band, Mousehole* (396), *The Ship Inn, Mousehole* (397), *Still Life with Boats, St Ives* (399), *Newlyn, Cornwall* (421),*The Red Funnel, Mousehole* (422), *Drying Sails, Mousehole* (437) and the wash drawings *P.Z.613, Cornwall* (826) and *Drying Sails, Mousehole* (828).

Fig. 9.16  Christopher Wood    *P.Z.134*    (Towner Art Gallery, Eastbourne)

Fearing that he did not have enough work for the Paris show, Kit persuaded Bernheim to include work by Ben as well. However, when Nicholson's work arrived, Bernheim detested it and was "simply beastly" to him, refusing to exhibit more than ten paintings. None of these sold, but Wood managed to find purchasers for eight on the first day and eleven in all, which pleased Bernheim immensely, as he had not managed to sell a single work in the previous six months, due to the economic situation. The friendship between the artists was also placed under strain by the Nicholsons, shocked at Kit's physical decline, upbraiding his lifestyle, whilst Kit objected to the way that they refused to adapt to the Parisian mode of life and tried to convert his friends to Christian Science.

On 1st July 1930, Wood was able to tell his mother that he had managed to sell all bar five of the works in the Bernheim exhibition and that he had earned £500 from his painting since the start of the year. For this, he was particularly indebted to a single purchaser, Lucy Carrington Wertheim, who had initially been recommended to his work by Frances Hodgkins, and who bought a significant number of paintings both during and after the show. Having been introduced to the artist, she became ever more enamoured of his paintings and his personality, and Wood saw her as a potential saviour, encouraging the idea, first put into her head by Hodgkins, that she should open a gallery. With the prospect of exhibiting in her very first show, Wood returned to Tréboul, where he indulged in an extraordinarily intense period of painting. This, though, was combined with long sessions smoking recycled opium and a series of homosexual encounters, when Frosca was not around. He hardly left his room for weeks and completed some forty pictures in a month, a number of which are disturbing. Back in England in August, in a very troubled state, he fell under a train at Salisbury station. Deeply shocked, Winifred felt that the effort put into those last paintings had meant that he no longer had the strength to fight his worsening opium addiction.

## 9.8  Afterglow

Wood's death caused an unseemly wrangle between Lucy Wertheim, who had funded, to a significant degree, his last painting extravaganza, and his family, advised by Jim Ede, over ownership of Wood's last paintings, as Wertheim did not have a contract in place. This meant that these works were not shown until 1932, but, as the 1930s wore on, the myth of Wood, the brilliant, but flawed, genius, took hold. He began to be hailed as a lyrical poet-painter of essentially English character, and his work started to fetch more than Old Masters. The 1938 exhibition of his complete works at the Redfern Gallery probably marked the zenith of his reputation, as, after the War, the advance of British Modernism towards complete abstraction meant that the figurative aspect, ever present in his works, led them to fall out of favour.

Because representational work has been held in such low regard by modernist sympathisers ever since, Wood's early pioneering work has received only occasional bursts of attention. However, his three visits to Cornwall can be seen to have proved important periods in his development, resulting in some fine innovative and original work. Furthermore, the part that he played in Nicholson's development has been considerably underplayed, due to Nicholson's emphasis on the far more 'authentic' influence of Wallis.

The death of Wood seems to have led Nicholson to reconsider his own outlook, given that he had had limited success with his naive approach. The interest in the childish vision had become something of a fashion or cult in the late 1920s and was now losing support. Wyndham Lewis, former leader of the Vorticists, condemned it, as early as 1927, as the product of the "irresponsible Peterpannish psychology" then in vogue among the " 'revolutionary' rich". Why, he asked wearily, did its supporters want to remain children?[530] Having met and fallen in love with the sculptor, Barbara Hepworth, Nicholson became more interested in paintings as three-dimensional objects, and started to produce his carved abstract reliefs, which saw him rise to the forefront of British Modernism.

Wallis, though, remained as a unique phenomenon and, whilst there was a pause in his contact with Nicholson and Ede in the period of 1930-32, due to the Nicholsons' marriage break-up and Ede's mental breakdown, Wood's dealer, Lucy Wertheim, also became enamoured with his work. In 1931, she mounted an exhibition of twenty of Wallis' paintings, recording that he demonstrated, at that time, a preference for working on Quaker Oats boxes. However, she recalled, "They did not cut much ice with either the public or the critics." [531] She also commented that, whereas she had often heard it remarked that Wallis had influenced Wood, she was inclined to wonder whether the influence was not the other way around, recording how she owned a Wallis painting done on the back of a photograph of a Wood work.[532] Because such a conclusion would impair the 'unconscious primitive' status of Wallis, it is not a topic that I have seen discussed at all, but, remembering how *China Dogs in a St Ives Window* predates Wood's meeting with Wallis, the viewpoint merits consideration.

In 1932, Nicholson and Ede, resumed contact with Wallis, and, with the old man producing some of his most complex work in the period 1932-7, they were able to ensure that a few others in intellectual avant-garde circles began to take an interest, including the art critics, Herbert Read and Adrian Stokes. Towards the end of his life, though, Wallis began to have dementia problems and spent his last years in the workhouse at Madron. On his death in 1942, artist friends secured a grave plot for him and his grave stone is covered with glazed tiles designed by Bernard Leach, depicting a tiny man climbing the steps through the door of a tall white lighthouse.

---

530 Wyndham Lewis, *A Brief Account of the Child-Cult*, in *Time and Western Man* 1927, quoted in Sarah Jane Checkland, *Ben Nicholson - the Vicious Circles of his Life & Art,* London, 2000 at p.80.
531 Lucy Carrington Wertheim, *Adventure in Art,* London, 1947 at p.84.
532 ibid.

# THE DAWN OF THE CRAFT TRADITION IN THE COLONY

**10.1  Introduction**

In the period prior to the First World War, the Decorative Arts, more commonly referred to at the time as Handicraft, had barely featured at all in the art colony at St Ives. Indeed, the only craftsperson highlighted in that period was Annie Hellwag, the French wife of the Austrian-born painter, Rudolf Hellwag, who, between 1900 and 1902, ran a School of Art Needlework in St Ives and Penzance.[533] The 1920s, however, saw an explosion of handicraft activity in the town. Because this was dominated by the Leach Pottery, no attention has been given to the other handicraft makers in the colony, many of whom were sufficiently accomplished to hold London shows of their work. Furthermore, whereas the primary influences on the Pottery derived from Leach's experiences in the Far East, the other artists specializing in craft work were reacting to trends in Britain. What was the background, therefore, to this surge of interest in handicraft?

The name of William Morris is inextricably linked with crafts in Britain. His vision of a "glorious art, made by the people and for the people, as a happiness to the maker and the user" remained the underlying tenet for most craftspeople.[534] As a result of the burgeoning Arts and Crafts Movement inspired by Morris, the Central School of Arts and Crafts was established in 1896 in London, with the architect, William Richard Lethaby (1857-1931) as its first Principal, a position that he held until 1911. Its aim was to provide specialist teaching for students interested in the craft industries. In 1908, the Royal Female School of Art was merged with it, and the School did attract a large number of female students, as it became more acceptable for women to pursue an artistic career. A series of technical handbooks on various crafts, edited by Lethaby, published between 1901 and 1916, encouraged direct processes and small workshops, with the designer also being the maker. Lethaby believed that such enterprises could be run economically, but it transpired that few craftspeople could make a living merely from work created solely by their own hands. They needed to use a machine either in the design and/ or in the production processes. The big debating point by the time of the First World War concerned the commercialisation of craftwork and there were heated arguments, which went on through the 1920s, as to whether machines should be used at all and, if so, how they could be used sensitively, so as not to impair artistic credibility.[535]

The Arts and Crafts Exhibition Society, which venerated the memory of Morris, began to flounder in the War years, as some members broke off in 1915 to form the Design and Industries Association, which aimed to bring together designers, craftsmen, manufacturers and retailers, whilst its own exhibition at Burlington House in 1916, the brainchild of its President, Henry Wilson, was widely felt to be too wedded to past fantasies of rural idylls and to be directed solely at the prosperous middle-classes. The Society had ceased to have contemporary relevance. No-one, though, was clear as to a way forward. Arthur Richard Orage, best known as editor of *The New Age*, and the letter cutter and sculptor, Eric Gill, both championed a guild system and hoped, in different ways, that the trade unions could play a role. Roger Fry, who was to play a pivotal role in shaping English modernism, proclaimed on setting up the Omega Workshops that they aimed to keep "the spontaneous freshness of primitive or peasant work while satisfying the needs and expressing the feelings of the modern cultivated man."[536] However, whilst having an anti-industrial aesthetic, Omega had few underlying craft principles, with artists painting on objects, even machine-made ones, rather than making them.

In some quarters, the War, strangely, was felt to have boosted the craft movement significantly, by giving it a political and social agenda. Firstly, there were a large number of wounded and disabled troops, for whom craftwork was seen as therapeutic, recuperative and educational. Secondly, there was concern that many discharged soldiers, after their novel experiences in the War, would find it hard to settle back into the same dead-end, tedious jobs that they had accepted without question previously. In 1919,

---

533 On a brief return visit to the town in 1925, she was hailed as having "founded the Artists' Costume Balls with which were connected Sir John Lavery, Poynter and Walter Crane." - *St Ives Times*, 24/7/1925.

534 From *The Art of the People* (1879), quoted in Tanya Harrod, *The Crafts in Britain in the Twentieth Century*, Yale, 1999 at p.16.

535 Morris was frequently portrayed as having a complete antipathy to machines, but he stated, "It is not this or that tangible steel or brass machine which we want to get rid of, but the great intangible machine of commercial tyranny, which oppresses the lives of all of us." From *Art and its Producers* (1888), quoted in Tanya Harrod, *The Crafts in Britain in the Twentieth Century*, Yale, 1999 at p.16.

536 From pamphlet, Omega Workshops, Artist Decorators, c.1915.

a book of essays, *Handicrafts and Reconstruction*, was published by the Arts and Crafts Exhibition Society, which deplored the decline in vernacular crafts and the cultural poverty of rural and village life, and sought to encourage small workshops in rural places manned by fulfilled ex-servicemen making affordable hand-crafted goods. Whilst a number of worthy institutions, such as St Dunstans, for blind servicemen, were founded and did useful work, the idealist visions of rural communities of craftspeople did not materialise. Nevertheless, this was the backdrop against which Frances Horne decided in 1919 to set up the St Ives Handicraft Guild.

## 10.2   Frances Horne and the St Ives Handicraft Guild

The St Ives Handicraft Guild was officially opened at Hazelbury House, 1 Draycott Terrace, on Tuesday 29th April 1919, and the local paper reported,

> "Guilds on the line of the new St Ives venture have been established for many years in various parts of the country and the pioneer work done by some of the earliest is now bearing fruit, and today we see a steadily increasing demand for good well-made and artistically designed articles for the home as well as materials for personal attire.[537]
>
> The object of the Handicraft Guild is to stimulate and encourage the creation of handmade objects for use in the home, or for personal requirements. Utility, good material, simplicity and beauty of form and design being the essential of all good handcraft, it will be the endeavour of the Guild to maintain these ideals. The activities of the St Ives Guild will, at first, be confined to hand-loom weaving, basket-making and embroidery, but it is hoped that these activities may be extended and other branches developed as circumstances allow.
>
> Work from other centres of Great Britain will also be on exhibition and for sale, so that it will be possible to keep in touch with what is being done elsewhere, thus forming a larger brotherhood."[538]

Fig. 10.1   David and Frances Horne
(St Ives Trust Archive Study Centre)

---

[537] Ventures that the reporter was likely to have been referring to were the Haslemere Weaving Workshops, run by Joseph and Maude King, and the Peasant's Art Society, run nearby by Maude's sister, Ethel, and her husband, Godfrey Blount. Under the banner of the Fellowship of the New Crusade, this sought to promote the revival of handicrafts, "country life and country labour", folk music and dance.

[538] *St Ives Times*, 16/5/1919.

Fig. 10.2  Bernard Leach
*Self-portrait* (etching)
(Private Collection)

The St Ives Guild was the brainchild of Frances Horne, the wife of David Macfarlane Horne, a wealthy rice merchant, who had been born in Edinburgh in 1874. They had lived for some years in Siam, where their daughter, Margery, was born in 1902. During the War, they spent a year in Carbis Bay, which Frances enjoyed immensely, and, despite David needing to be based in London for his work for at least half the year, they decided to move their principal home from Richmond to Cornwall. After a short spell renting, they acquired in 1919, 'Tremorna', the substantial home on the cliff edge at Carbis Bay, designed by the artist, Edmund Fuller, in 1901, for the building contractor, Albert Lang.[539]

Frances was some thirteen years older than her husband, having been born in 1861, and, with the prospect of her husband being away from home for significant periods, her daughter recorded that "she thought it would be a nice interest for herself to have a handicraft guild".[540] She had always been keen on embroidery and design, and, having been brought up in Germany by two aunts, had already run a similar venture there. In St Ives, she employed Rosie Gillett to be in charge of basket-making, whilst the energetic Florence Welch supervised the weaving room.[541] It is noteworthy that philanthropic objectives, which had been the basis for many of the other Guilds set up around the country, were not mentioned at all in the initial press coverage, the emphasis instead being placed on "utility, good material, simplicity and beauty of form and design". Nevertheless, it appears that Frances Horne did hope that, in addition to helping wounded servicemen, some of the fishwives, who could no longer find employment due to the collapse of the fishing industries, might learn new skills and be able to supplement their husbands' uncertain income. The opening exhibition also included Dorsetshire Ware, Peasant Pottery, toys and lace, but it is not certain from whom these articles were sourced.

When Frances Horne decided that the Guild should also include a resident potter, it was Edith Skinner, who recommended Bernard Leach, as she was an old family friend.[542] Margery Horne recalled that Leach and her mother had a considerable amount of correspondence. "He sent us some absolutely beautiful little tiny pots that he'd made and various books that he'd published and there was one that had a self-portrait of him looking absolutely wild and his hair all over the place and looking terribly fierce, and Mother thought "Good Heavens, what have we let ourselves in for!" [543]

539 It is possible that they rented 'Tremorna' for a couple of years before buying it, as Mrs Horne is recorded as organising a garden fete there in August 1917. See *St Ives Times*, 17/8/1917.
540  See transcript of interview with Margery Horne by Dr Roger Slack p.2 - St Ives Trust Archive Study Centre.
541  ibid at p.3.
542  Bernard Leach, *Beyond East and West*, London, 1978 at p.139.
543  See transcript of interview with Margery Horne by Dr Roger Slack p.2 - St Ives Trust Archive Study Centre.

Any further grand plans had to be shelved, when David Horne's business failed and then he died unexpectedly in 1923, aged only 48.[544] Forced to live off her own capital, Frances immediately sold 'Tremorna' and its contents, and moved into the Guild's headquarters at 'Hazelbury House'. Leach, whilst appreciating her initial generosity, could not hide his views on the Guild. Margery Horne recalled, "Poor Bernard - he was such a very funny contradiction in terms, because he disapproved of everything at the Handicraft Guild, so terribly, because he thought it was all a compromise, because we used machine spun warps for our weaving, or Indian machine made cotton, and the baskets hadn't got vegetable dye raffia, it was just ordinary raffia, you know, with different colours, and he thought all this was shocking. And he thought the embroidery was pretty dim too, which was rather sad for Mother, because she designed all that." [545] The Guild also failed to attract any fishwives, the only worker from outside the Horne's own circle being a man who had been badly gassed during the War, who made baskets. Apart from Rosie Gillett and Florence Welch, the only other persons recorded by Margery Horne as working there were her friends, Dorothy and Irene Turner, the daughters of the artist, Herbert Turner, who lived in Carbis Bay. She commented, "Dorothy did all the embroidery, and Irene was a weaver." [546] Margery herself became Secretary of the Guild for a year or so, but then it folded in 1925, when Frances moved to 'The Grey House' in Steeple Lane.

Despite Frances Horne's venture folding so speedily, with seemingly little in the way of success, two people that she attracted to the Guild - Bernard Leach and Florence Welch - were to be prominent figures in the town for decades. Indeed, the Leach Pottery not only ensured that handicraft would in future play a central role in artistic activity in St Ives, but also secured for the colony an international reputation as a centre for pottery. Without Frances Horne, this would not have occurred.

### 10. 3  The Leach Pottery - Introduction

Despite the status that Bernard Howell Leach (1887-1979) eventually acquired, his first decade in St Ives was by no means easy. Hand-made pottery was not in fashion and, indeed, was in danger of dying out. The prevailing taste in ceramics in Britain was for fine porcelain made by factories such as Chelsea, Derby, Spode and Worcester. By comparison with the translucency and delicate quality of this, hand-made pottery seemed rough and often imperfect. Low-fired earthenware was porous when unglazed and chipped and broke easily, whilst high-fired stoneware, whilst watertight and stronger, was often heavy and rough, and scratched polished surfaces and silver. Leach was not the only potter, who was attempting to demonstrate that he deserved to be considered more an artist than a craftsman, but such pioneering spirits were a select few and, unfortunately, in the 1920s, collectors of their work were a select few as well. The pioneer potters distinguished themselves from the producers of 'art pottery' in the late nineteenth century, as they attended to every part of the ceramic process themselves and were more particular about the authenticity of their sources.

Leach did not make his task any easier by being a poor businessman and taking some bad decisions, perhaps the worst of which was to set up in St Ives in the first place! For much of the 1920s, his financial position was desperate. Nevertheless, he drew to St Ives, during this first decade, a number of potters, who were influenced by his ideas and who also went on to secure international reputations. As he strove to survive, he became dissatisfied with the concept of pottery as purely an art object and, by the end of the decade, had started to formulate his ideas concerning affordable, well-designed functional pottery, which eventually led to him being considered to be the father of the studio pottery movement. Recently, the Pottery at St Ives has been refurbished and re-opened, not only for production, but also as a display centre. Whilst painters had ensured that the art colony at St Ives was well-known in most Western countries, Leach, who had worked in Japan and China before settling in St Ives, gave it a strong link with the Far East, which has endured.

### 10.3.1  Bernard Leach's background in the Far East

The distinctive outlook on art and life of Bernard Leach derived from his unusual background. The son of a barrister, who subsequently became a Colonial judge, Leach was born in Hong Kong in 1887, but, as his mother died at his birth, he was brought up initially by his grandparents, who were missionaries in Japan. At the age of four, however, he returned to Hong Kong to live with his father, who had re-married. As he had no siblings, his childhood was lonely and, at the age of ten, he was sent back to England to be educated at the Jesuit College of Beaumont, Windsor. In 1903, on learning that his son only excelled at drawing, elocution and cricket, his father allowed Bernard to enrol at the Slade School, where he

---

544 In the interview, Margery comments, "Mother, you see, had quite a bit of money on her own, while Father was still alive and before his business went, and before he was so ill."- see transcript of interview with Margery Horne by Dr Roger Slack at p.13.
545 ibid at p.5.
546 ibid at p.6.

was taught by Henry Tonks. However, after only a few terms, on learning that his father had terminal cancer, Bernard obediently left his studies to share his final days and, in accordance with his father's last wishes, tried a career as a bank clerk. He hated it. Nevertheless, living in Chelsea, he maintained contact with friends from the art world, particularly the South African born Reginald Turvey, whom he had met at the Slade, and Henry Lamb, whom he knew from time spent with his aunt in Manchester. It was at Lamb's studio that he met Augustus John, of whom he became a great admirer, considering him "one of the best draughtsmen England has produced".[547] Chelsea also harboured associations with Whistler, whom Leach admired for "an unfamiliar asymmetrical Oriental sense of composition and a highly refined taste" and from whom he felt that he had caught some "dream of Japan".[548] On leaving the bank after nine months, he studied further under John Swan at the London School of Art. He also had two invaluable terms learning etching under Frank Brangwyn, for line, rather than colour, was his metier. It was Brangwyn, who, on hearing that he had completed, all told, five terms of study, advised, "Enough, get out! Go to nature!". Leach, despite having recently got engaged to his cousin, Muriel, decided that Japan should be his destination, as he wanted "to try to understand Eastern art and the life behind it".[549]

Leach left for Japan in the spring of 1909 and took his etching press with him. What he might have lacked in competence was made up for by supreme confidence, for he quickly secured the publication of an article *The Introduction of Etching into the Art World of Japan*, claiming that the use of light and line in etching would appeal to young Japanese artists, for one of the fundamental characteristics of Japanese Art was "not dynamism, but the development of the exquisite decorative concept".[550] Leach's arrival coincided with a surge of interest in Japan in Western art and so, although he could only speak with some authority on Tonks, Brangwyn and John (and did so repeatedly), he was immediately feted in artistic circles. He soon made friends with Yanagi Soetsu, a young art critic, and became part of the Shirakaba (White Birch) movement, a small group of artists, intellectuals and poets, who were searching for a new way of artistic life, blending approaches from both Western and Oriental cultures. Edmund De Waal, one of Leach's biographers, has commented, "They were privileged young men of the same mould as Leach: passionate, discursive and often enthusiastically muddled."[551] Topics that were covered in the movement's magazine, which was edited by Yanagi, included European medieval mysticism, Van Gogh, Walt Whitman and William Blake. Indeed, in relation to the latter, Yanagi was sufficiently inspired by his discussions with Leach, who felt that Blake was "in profound harmony" with Post-Impressionism and Walt Whitman, that he produced a biography.

Fig. 10.3 Leach family in their Tokyo home c. 1913 (Emmanuel Cooper)

Fig. 10.4 Leach and Yanagi in 1912 (Emmanuel Cooper)

---

547 Bernard Leach, *Beyond East and West*, London, 1978 at p.31.
548 ibid, at p.32.
549 ibid, at p.36.
550 Quoted in Edmund de Waal, *Bernard Leach*, London, at p.8.
551 Edmund de Waal, *Bernard Leach*, London, at p.9.

Fig. 10.5 Tomimoto and Leach in 1913 (Emmanuel Cooper)

On the artistic side, an important influence was Kenkichi Tomimoto, who had studied architecture and interior design at the Tokyo School of Fine Arts and who had spent two years at Goldsmiths' College in London studying stained glass, during which he had spent days sketching metalwork, glass and ceramics at the Victoria and Albert Museum. On his return to Japan by boat in the spring of 1910, he had met Leach's great friend, Reginald Turvey, who had been induced by Leach to pay him a visit. Leach and Tomimoto became great friends, and it is somewhat paradoxical that it was Tomimoto who introduced the ideals of William Morris and the Arts and Crafts movement to Leach, rather than vice versa. They often went sketching together, and Leach commented that the resultant "quick, concentrated notes of fern or flower, of cloud or bird, or building, greatly simplified, were the sources of many patterns we each used in later years on our pots".[552] The pair became like brothers, sharing research, ideas, everything.

A trip with Tomitoto to Tokyo in February 1911 to discuss a joint exhibition of Leach's etchings and Tomitoto's woodcuts resulted in Leach having a career changing experience, for they were invited to take part in a *raku yaki* tea-party, where the guests had the opportunity of painting low-fired earthenware ceramics. Enthralled by the process, Leach decided on the spot to take up pottery. He took tuition from Urano Shigekichi (1851-1923), who was known by his adopted title Kenzan VI, and produced initially pots, decorated not only with imagery drawn from the Kenzan tradition, which dated back to the seventeenth century, but also with a wide range of other motifs, including lettering, oriental calligraphy and even poetic stanzas, often reflecting the discussion topics of the moment. Despite his technical shortcomings, he quickly acquired a good reputation for his aestheticism and, in an article about his art which accompanied a 1914 exhibition, Yanagi praised his taste as being "rich in decorative quality" and his designs for their "naive power and warmth of colouring".[553] Already, Kenzan VI had made both Leach and Tomimoto joint heirs of the Kenzan title, so that Leach was entitled to, and did frequently, call himself Kenzan VII. As his obituary later recorded, this was "the equivalent, in the world of ceramics, of an English Pope".[554]

Just as Leach had begun to make a name for himself in Japan, he decided to spend extended periods in the years 1914-16 in China, as he had been convinced by the arguments of Dr Westharp, a Prussian Jewish writer, based in Peking, who was a student of the teachings of Confucius, that "my whole attitude towards Life and Art suffers from the curse of Dualism - a separation of thought and act, will and deed, which I believe is at the root of the rottenness of our Western Life." Whilst enjoying his immersion into Chinese culture and gaining a deeper knowledge of Chinese pottery, Dr Westharp did not prove to be the leader for whom Leach had craved, and he was easily persuaded in 1916 by Yanagi to give up any

---

552 Bernard Leach, *Beyond East and West*, London, 1978 at p.54-5. For Leach, Tomimoto excelled in particular "as a rare maker of patterns, an originator". - ibid, at p.59.
553 Yanagi Soetsu, *Leach in Japan: Collected Works*, vol 14, p.66.
554 *The Times*, 19/11/1979.

notions of becoming a philosopher and to join the artistic community that was developing in his home village of Abiko, attractively situated on Teganuma lagoon just outside Tokyo. Leach built himself a Chinese style studio (Fig. 10.7) and had Kenzan VI's kiln rebuilt alongside. Whilst interested in the folkcraft of the locality, Leach's pots of this era reveal a new influence - English slipware, discovered as a result of a book, *Quaint Old English Pottery*, bought by Tomimoto from a Tokyo bookstore!

By 1919, Leach was beginning to develop his own views as to the role of the modern craftsman in the light of the impact that factories, city life, science, education and travel had had on traditional ways. In an article in a Japanese newspaper, he commented, "All the folk-law, the country traditions which determine the shape, size and pattern of all decorative objects is dying out." [555] Therefore, the modern craftsman, whilst alive to archaic traditions, needed to devise new decorative objects for every aspect of contemporary living, and Leach turned his attention to the design of furniture as well as pottery.

Leach's time at Abiko came to a tragic end in May 1919, when a spark from his kiln destroyed his studio and all his belongings, including his drawings, prints, notes on glazes and such-like as well as work, including furniture, intended for exhibition. It was a bitter blow, however much his friends rallied round. However, for his last year in Japan, an aristocratic patron, Viscount Kuoroda, offered Leach the use of a kiln in Tokyo, along with assistants to help him. As a result, the 2000 or so pots that were produced from this kiln in his final year were better quality than any that he had produced previously, for, having given his assistants appropriate instructions, he was not involved in the throwing of the pots and concentrated purely on their decoration. His final exhibition in Japan was a huge success, critically and commercially, and both his Japanese friends and Leach himself anticipated that his return to England, prompted principally by his desire to educate his children there, would lead to immensely significant developments. In his tribute to Leach, written shortly before his departure, Yanagi felt that Leach's understanding of Japan was far greater than most visitors, for it "had soaked into him through the experience of entering deeply into our inner life". He also considered that Leach understood "the needs of New Japan: he shows in his art what they are. Living with us, he has felt our yearnings, our thirst, our struggles and our labours." He concluded that "his mission in his own country [was] pregnant with the deepest meaning. He is trying to knit the East and West together by art, and it seems likely that he will be remembered as the first to accomplish as an artist what for so long mankind has been dreaming of bringing about."[556] Having journeyed to Japan in 1909 alone and in third class, Leach left with his family in 1920 in first class, with hundreds of tearful wellwishers lining the quay.

Fig. 10.6  Bernard Leach at an exhibition of his work in Tokyo in 1920        (Emmanuel Cooper)
The table, and probably also the textiles, were designed by Leach.

---

555 Bernard Leach, *Democracy in Art*, The Japan Advertiser, 22/6/1919.
556 Yanagi Soetsu, *Leach as I know him*, from *An English Artist in Japan*, 1919, reproduced in Bernard Leach, *Beyond East and West*, London, 1978 at p.133-4.

Fig. 10.7 Leach's self-designed studio at Abiko with round door (Emmanuel Cooper)

## 10.3.2 Shoji Hamada's background

When Leach left Japan for England in the summer of 1920, he was accompanied by Shoji Hamada (1894-1978), the son of a Tokyo industrialist, who wanted to become an artist potter and who sought to gain experience in the West. Hamada had initially intended to become an artist, but had been persuaded to change his objective by a comment made by Renoir that it would be better all round if more would-be painters became craftsmen. He recalled that he asked himself, "Why not be a potter? Pots can be used, they have a function. Even a bad pot has some use, but with a bad painting, there is nothing you can do with it except throw it away."[557]

Hamada trained initially at the Tokyo Institute of Technology, where he studied ceramics under Hazan Itaya, but the course was geared towards industrial pottery, and the section relating to the potter's wheel lasted a mere two weeks. He then spent four years at the Kyoto Ceramic Testing Institute, during which time he did some 10,000 tests imitating old Chinese glazes.

Whilst a student, Hamada was an avid reader of art books and a regular visitor to exhibitions. He developed a particular interest in the work of Leach and Tomimoto, for this reflected new ideas and approaches resulting from their exposure to Western culture. Indeed, he concluded "that the two 'grand champions' of pottery were Leach and Tomimoto. There were no others who equalled these two."[558] Accordingly, he made arrangements to visit each one and was invited by Leach to his workshop at Abiko - shortly before it was destroyed by fire. It was not just Leach's pots, etchings, drawings and furniture that Hamada admired, but the whole ambience of the Chinese style studio, particularly its circular doorway - "No Japanese could ever have thought of this".[559] Even the way that he ate his food, Hamada considered interesting and unique. Leach, on the other hand, was impressed by Hamada's sensitivity, his technical knowledge and his broad and easy flowing mind.

In his last year in Japan, Leach visited Hamada in Kyoto and saw some of the pots that he had begun to make. He also asked his advice on a number of technical issues. Eventually, when Hamada heard that Leach was returning to England with the aim of establishing a new pottery, he asked if he might accompany him. Hamada's sponsors were not at all convinced that he had made the right decision, for they thought that experience in China would have been better. Leach, though, having got permission from Frances Horne, readily agreed, as he was aware that Hamada's technical know-how would be invaluable.

---

557 Bernard Leach, *Hamada Potter*, Tokyo and New York, 1975 at p.93.
558 ibid, at p.94.
559 ibid, at p.98-9.

### 10.3.3 The establishment of the Leach Pottery by Leach and Hamada

It is unclear whether Leach, buoyed by the tributes bestowed upon him by his Japanese friends, truly appreciated the scale of the task facing him on his return to England, and what, if any, research he had done as to the suitability of St Ives as a base for his new venture. Leach's status in Japan did not, by any means, guarantee him success in England. As he himself wrote later, "Japan is a potter's heaven: all the waves of Far Eastern culture have broken upon its shores. Pots are understood through the senses: from the outset people bought even mine. The background of Zen and Tea provided a highly developed perceptivity of truth and beauty, and there was no hard dividing line between arts and crafts." [560] The situation in England was totally different. The general public had no particular sensibilities towards pottery, and craftwork, in any event, was considered to be inferior to painting. Leach's work was only likely to appeal to a cultured elite in metropolitan centres. St Ives, though, was tucked away in a remote part of the country in a county that had no major towns and was about as far away from London as it was possible to get. Despite its status as an art colony, it had no history as a decorative arts centre at all. Whilst Leach might have heard tales of St Ives from fellow students Reginald Turvey, Reginald Brundrit, a future Academician, Annie Fearon (later Walke) and Milford Norsworthy, all of whom had worked in St Ives previously during its heyday, the vigour of the colony in 1908, prior to Leach's departure to Japan, was very different from its somewhat directionless state in 1920.[561] It is a pity that the correspondence passing between Leach and Frances Horne has not survived. Her grand plans for the St Ives Handicraft Guild must have been very persuasive. However, perhaps it was merely the offer of finance that Leach found irresistible, as he does not even appear to have made any enquiries about the two most essential ingredients for a pottery - the availability of appropriate local clay and firewood.

On their arrival in London, Hamada, who was welcomed by two Japanese friends, was most surprised that no-one at all came to meet Leach. Whilst Hamada spent three happy weeks immersing himself in London's Museums, Leach went to his wife's father's home in Cardiff - his father-in-law, Dr. William Evans Hoyle, an expert on cephalopods, being the first director of the National Museum of Wales (1909-1924). Here, a few days later, Leach's long-suffering wife, Muriel, gave birth early, and unexpectedly, to twins - their fourth and fifth children. After ensuring that she was comfortable, Leach and Hamada journeyed down to Cornwall, lodging initially in 6 Draycott Terrace. They immediately walked over to Carbis Bay to visit the Hornes in their splendid home, 'Tremorna'. Unusually nervous, Leach was relieved to discover that Frances Horne was "kind and sensitive" as well as "charming and enthusiastic about craftsmanship". She confirmed that she would lend him the capital sum of £2,500 to enable land to be acquired and the pottery built, and pay him £250 per annum for the first three years to cover running expenses. He commented, "I could not have had a better partner".[562] She also became a friend and Leach asked her to become godmother to one of the twins, Jessamine.

Prior discussions had led Leach and Hamada to the conclusion "that making and planning round the individuality of the artist was a necessary step in the evolution of the crafts. So, at St Ives, at the outset, we based our economics on the studio and not on the country workshop or the factory." They compared themselves with William Staite Murray in London, Decoeur in Paris and Tomimoto in Japan.[563] The first decision to be taken, therefore, was the location of this studio. A hundred-yard strip of land in the upper part of The Stennack, between the main road and the stream, was eventually selected, for Leach required not only water, but a slope for the climbing kiln which he wished to erect. A position right at the edge of town at the top of a steep hill was not, however, best suited to attract tourists or less curious residents. The original workshop, built in natural granite, was a small 'L' shaped room, with a fireplace in the corner, large enough for two wheels, a glazing and decorating room, and a small room where Hamada lived. Part of the building was open to the rafters, but the other part was ceiled, so that pots could be dried overhead on beams in the attic. The plans, roughly drawn by Leach and Hamada, were knocked into shape by the Borough Surveyor, Frederick Uren, who, as noted in Chapter 6.6, had artistic ambitions himself, as he later became a student of John Park. Permission was duly given.

Whilst work commenced on the pottery, Leach and Hamada looked for suitable fuel and clays in the locality. This involved a considerable amount of walking up hills to view the surrounding countryside through field glasses, and their initial findings were not promising. They soon realised that West Penwith was short of both woodland and wood cutters, and the provision of adequate fuel was to prove a major expense for the pottery over the years. However, they did discover a number of dead fir trees in

---

560 Bernard Leach, *Beyond East and West*, London, 1978 at p.128.

561 It appears that Leach also knew the Australian artist, Will Osborn, who worked in St Ives for a number of years in the 1890s, as he retained in his papers a note of the inquest into his death in 1906, from an overdose of chloroform, which Osborn had been using to induce sleep, as he suffered from insomnia. For the previous six months, Osborn had been a friend of Henry Lamb, through whom he will have met Leach. See Craft Study Centre, Farnham, Leach archive no 10040.

562 Bernard Leach, *Beyond East and West*, London, 1978 at p.137 & 139.

563 Bernard Leach, *The Leach Pottery (1920-1946)*, The Berkley Galleries, June 1946.

Tregenna Woods close to Knill's Steeple. These were owned by the Great Western Railway, and Leach realised that the swathe of rhodedendrons that would need to be cut down to enable these trees to be moved would provide further fuel for which he did not need to pay. Accordingly, for £20, he got about 200 tons of wood, but the cost of transportation, even this short distance, proved to be £100. They then had to chop it all up, which was a major undertaking in itself. Nevertheless, it did provide fuel for three years.

Their hunt for suitable clay was also not very successful. They soon found a small pit of red clay, which had just enough plasticity and stiffness, which they were able to use as a start, and then spied from Trencrom some yellowish clay deposits at St Erth. On investigation, this was on land belonging to the local parson, who initially only asked ten shillings a ton, and they were able to use this for their slipware. However, they could not locate any high-temperature clay with the right plasticity. Accordingly, they had to obtain ball clay from either Devon or Dorset and fire clay from below the coal seams of the Midlands - yet further expense that the fledgling venture could have done without. The experience was not lost on Hamada, who later opined, "Considering the nature of pottery, the primary consideration is the selection of the clay...When you discover a natural clay that suits your work, you should immediately pack up and move to the place where that clay is available." [564]

Leach's decision to construct the first Sino-Japanese style climbing kiln in the Western world was based on its versatility. There were three chambers in the kiln, each chamber measuring six feet in height, six feet in width and four feet from front wall to back wall, and Leach explained how it worked. "It was the use of the slope (a forty degree angle) that created the right kind of draught and enabled the potter to fire one chamber after another. The fire enters, meets with a wall of saggars, which forces it up and over the top and down into the space at the back; and then it goes through passages in the lower part of the wall into the next chamber and so on, so that each chamber can be varied in temperature or atmosphere at will. Several temperatures can be used in different chambers if one so wishes."[565]

Hamada and Leach undertook the construction of the kiln themselves. They acquired some second-hand firebricks from the National Explosives Company at Hayle and, with these, made a small temporary kiln in which to fire blocks for the climbing kiln. These were made of a mixture of ball clay from Devon and impure china clay from the first preliminary diggings of the newly formed Porthia China Clay Works two miles away. This was run by the Hain family, who made no charge. Instead of bamboo, which was traditionally used to support the roof and arches of the kiln during construction, they improvised with curved staves from large barrels used to pack salted herring. It was a lengthy task and Hamada indicates that it was almost a year after his arrival in England before they were able to fire the first pots.

The kiln, however, had a number of defects. The bricks that they made proved unable to cope with the heat in the kiln and began to deteriorate. They also made mistakes in their use of wood to fire the kiln. They did not dry or cut the timber properly and their tendency to over-stoke it led to deposits of ash on the walls. As a result, there was an extraordinarily high percentage of losses from that first kiln - 20-30%. Hamada recalled, "There were all kinds of losses; accidents, dunting, skipped glazes, deformed shapes, fallen saggars, all sorts of things. Besides that, after a firing, even a good one, we would go through the pots and take out a certain number of our own that we did not like, put them up on the keel of an old boat next to the river, and when we were disgusted with our own work, or wanted a little exercise, we would get a rock or two to throw at these pots - it was a grand, clean sound when they broke and fell into the stream."[566] Another problem that they had was that the saggars began to bend. Nevertheless, there were some successes and Hamada did do some good glaze tests. Indeed, Leach commented, "The last firing that Hamada ever did in that kiln was one of the best that I can remember - effects for which you might have waited twenty years in vain, though it was responsible for most of the damage to the old kiln." [567]

## 10.3.4 George Dunn

George Dunn was one of the workmen that built the pottery. Illiterate and barely five foot tall, he had also worked as a miner and as a fisherman. After the pottery building was completed, Leach and Hamada were surprised the next day to see Dunn standing in the gateway, arms folded, and asked him why he was there. Leach recalled, "He looked me square in the eye and replied, with an extended hand: "Cap'n, I'm staying put." I took his hand with all that he had to give." [568]

---

564 Quoted by Satoshi Yokobori in *Bernard Leach and Shoji Hamada - Journey to St Ives, England : Kinship Beyond East and West*, exhibition catalogue 2003.
565 Bernard Leach, *Hamada Potter*, Tokyo and New York, 1975 at p.113.
566 ibid, at p.118.
567 ibid, at p.114.
568 Bernard Leach, *Beyond East and West*, London, 1978 at p.139 & 141.

Fig. 10.8  Hamada building the first kiln
(Craft Study Centre,
University for the Creative Arts)

Fig. 10.9  Hamada by the first kiln in 1923
(Leach archives)

Fig. 10.10  Leach studying a slip-combed dish
by the fireplace in the Pottery in 1923
(Pitshanger Manor, Ealing)

Fig. 10.11  Bernard and David Leach loading up the new
kiln in 1924
(St Ives Trust Archive Study Centre)

The first job was to furbish the interior of the pottery and to make or acquire "tables, benches, damp and other cupboards, shelving etc". After that, Dunn proved invaluable as a general handyman, chopping wood for the kiln and laboriously grinding the clay between two metal plates. In the early years, his pay was higher than the monies that Leach himself was able to draw from the venture. However, his contribution was valued, Leach recording, "When the roof of George's house threatened to fall in, I had another cottage built for him at a nominal rental - with a bathroom. The bath, however, he filled with coal. Baths were evidently considered new-fangled in the countryside, but coal was precious." [569] This was Penbeagle Cottage, and Dunn lived there with his wife and "a rabbit warren of young Dunns".

One of Leach's first students, Katharine Pleydell-Bouverie, recalled her impressions of Dunn. "He was like something out of a book about buccaneers; stocky, very short, indestructively good-tempered and devoted to Bernard...When he approved of anything he said 'handsome'. When he disapproved, he spat." [570] Wrecking, looting and smuggling were the topics upon which he was most knowledgeable and, in tune with the dubious moral values of such practices, when he heard that the Pottery was in financial difficulties, he offered to torch the place so that Bernard could claim on the insurance! He remained a crucial cog in the venture until his death in 1940.

### 10.3.5 Edgar Skinner

Given that she was an old family friend and had been responsible for recommending Leach to Frances Horne in the first place, Edith Skinner, and her husband, Edgar, took a considerable interest in the Pottery. Realising that finance and paperwork were not Bernard's forté, Edgar, having a banking background, offered his services. In April 1922, Leach indicated that Skinner was joining the Pottery the following month as "business manager and assistant craftsman", but he is generally referred to as the Secretary.[571] In order to be closer at hand, the Skinners sold 'Salubrious House' and built right opposite the pottery, 'Chy-an-Creet', now a hotel appropriately known as 'Edgar's'.

Katharine Pleydell-Bouverie recalled, "Skinner had, I think, spent his youth in a bank and his age in Italy. The bank had given him a sense of order that must have been very useful to the pottery, and Italy had added a philosophical outlook that was undoubtedly very useful to himself. Kind and polite, a painter of water-colours upon which Bernard cast a baleful eye, he trotted in and out of the sheds, wrote the business letters, and usually cooked the midday meal which we all ate by the big open fire in the main shed. My chief memories of these meals are of curry and rice, interminable arguments, black treacle and Bernard making sauces over the open fire." [572]

In those difficult early days, Skinner's business know-how was invaluable. Skinner's major task will have been to secure the survival of the Pottery, when the collapse of David Horne's business was closely followed by his untimely death in March 1923. This meant not only that further funding of the venture by the Hornes ceased, but raised the possibility of the monies loaned to date - £2,500 - having to be repaid, as Frances Horne was left financially strapped herself. Negotiations were not made easier by the fact that Frances Horne had become very deaf, with the result that her daughter, Margery, who had only just left school, had to bellow sensitive financial information into her ear. Clearly, here was a moment, when the fledgling enterprise could easily have folded. Buoyed by some legacies and some support from Muriel's father, Leach determined to battle on.

Fig. 10.12 Frederick Beaumont
*Portrait sketch of Edgar Skinner*
(1918) (Chy-an-Creet Hotel)

---

569 ibid at p.141.
570 Katharine Pleydell-Bouverie, *At St Ives in the Early Years*, quoted in Bernard Leach, *Beyond East and West*, London, 1978 at p.150-1.
571 *St Ives Times*, 7/4/1922.
572 Katharine Pleydell-Bouverie, *At St Ives in the Early Years*, quoted in Bernard Leach, *Beyond East and West*, London, 1978 at p.151-2.

When it became apparent that the Pottery was attracting interest from students, it was Skinner who suggested to Leach that they should pay for the privilege, whilst at the same time providing free labour. He also had to deal with another major financial crisis in 1925, when the future of the venture again looked bleak. This time, he suggested that, in return for upfront payments for 'shares' in the Pottery, patrons and collectors were given first choice at discounted rates on the next batches of pots. This alleviated the problem, but Skinner died from heart failure during a bout of pneumonia in December that year. His obituary recorded "the kindliness of his disposition,....his genial courtesy and his charitable outlook,...his ever-ready sympathy.... and a rare sincerity", and Leach adorned his grave in Barnoon Cemetery with tiles, bearing the wording, "He went through life with outstretched hand of help".[573]

### 10.3.6 Shoji Hamada in St Ives

Shoji Hamada initially found the Cornish countryside a shock. He had imagined that England was soft, but, in Cornwall, he found nothing but stone and harsh jutting rocks, with any trees bent and wind-blown. It was "As if all the skin and flesh were taken away and only the bones remained."[574] In time, though, he got to like stern and austere Cornwall and found its appeal more enduring than, say, the softness of the Cotswolds. Leach, on the other hand, had been attracted to "the bare landscape - folded hills and stern cliffs" from the outset, something that he attributed to the Celtic blood that coursed through his veins as a result of some Welsh ancestry.

Hamada lived very simply, in basic conditions, during his time in St Ives. His room at the Pottery was only eight by ten feet, and most of this was taken up with a bed that he made out of the dead wood from Steeple Hill, to a design inspired by a four poster bed that he had seen in Pendeen Manor, when Robert Morton Nance and members of the Old Cornwall Society had taken them on a tour of that property. A small table, chair and chest of drawers were its only other pieces of furniture. He had to cook using a small gas ring or the corner fireplace in the workshop, where there was a table and chair. There was no bathroom, just the sink and a basin in the pottery section. If he wanted a bath, he had to make arrangements with the Skinners over the road or with Leach at 'The Count House'. The only toilet was an earth closet in the garden. He ate bread in the morning and bread in the afternoon, but found some Javanese rice to cook for his evening meal. His attempts at propogating Japanese vegetables from seed were not too successful, but Edgar Skinner taught him how to grow some English vegetables.

Hamada was described by Leach's first student, Michael Cardew, as "rather silent, quick moving, with an air of always knowing exactly what he wanted to do and being determined to do it at all costs".[575] His silence was not only due to natural Japanese reserve in unfamiliar surroundings, but also because he had had an early training in meditation, which had helped to solve a health problem. Accordingly, he still meditated for an hour a day, and this affected his whole outlook - the inner directing the outer. As a potter, he was still experimenting and, in judging mixtures, he was keen to test his own instincts rather than rely on formulae learnt. Indeed, Leach recorded that, "he could hardly bring himself to use a weighing machine in making our first tests of clays and glazes", as such equipment would not have been available to the old master potters.

Hamada's speciality was glazes and he spent a considerable amount of time testing local materials to see if they could be used in a glaze to good effect. Leach recalled one occasion, in particular, when they had tried out a bracken ash glaze recipe that Tomimoto had translated from an early Chinese document, using bracken gathered in the autumn from Rosewall Hill and burnt slowly so as to produce black rather than white ash. This was then mixed with feldspar and quartz and "made a creamy white, big-crackled glaze, which we have never since equalled. It was velvety white, it took pigment on its surface with gentleness, it did not look mechanised, it was hard and it was soft at the same time."[576] The inability to replicate it, though, reveals the hit and miss nature of a number of the experiments. Hamada, anyway, was not convinced, as a whole roomful of bracken made only a bucketful of ash.

Another test involved using the ash from the sawdust that was used for smoking kippers in a local factory. Again, as Hamada relates, it was not an easy option. "The heads and tails of the fish fell into the sawdust, so we had a stinking mess to sieve and wash to kill the smell. Not only this, but the kipper factory burned a load of sawdust for only one night, so that much of it was not completely burned - it was really crude stuff."[577] It also transpired that the high salt content of this ash meant that a stable firing could not be obtained, and so the experiment was abandoned.

---

573 *St Ives Times*, 12/1925.
574 Bernard Leach, *Hamada Potter*, Tokyo and New York, 1975 at p.110.
575 Michael Cardew - *Bernard Leach - Recollections* in *Bernard Leach - Essays in Appreciation*, Wellington, 1960.
576 Bernard Leach, *Hamada Potter*, Tokyo and New York, 1975 at p.120.
577 ibid, at p.121.

More successful were black glazes made from the cruder pine ash that was left in the kiln after a firing, to which iron was added. This was good for tenmoku and celadon glazes. Celadon, which was first used in China and was especially associated with the Sung Dynasty, was a pale grey-green to grey-blue glaze, which Hamada and Leach used for their stoneware. The colour was created by a small amount of iron oxide and, being translucent, was often combined with a carved decoration which showed through the glaze (see Fig. 10.16). Another Chinese glaze, tenmoku, in the words of Leach, a "lustrous black iron stoneware glaze sometimes running to a red rust on the thinner parts", also became popular with them (see Fig. 10.13).[578] By August 1923, Leach indicated that they had used some thirty glazes, most of which derived from Chinese or Japanese recipes.[579] Watching the way that Hamada operated in these glaze tests enabled Leach himself to develop an intuitive approach to such matters, based on practical experience rather than theory, which he believed was infinitely preferable.

Hamada, who was quite happy to share his expertise, also helped William Staite Murray, who was to prove Leach's great rival. Having met at the Artificers' Guild exhibition, Staite Murray came down to St Ives in 1923 to see the pottery, and Hamada not only taught him about Chinese glazes but also how to put footrings on bowls, for Murray, having only seen Oriental pieces on Museum shelves, had not realised that they should have footrings! For Leach and Hamada, though, the enduring memory of Staite Murray's visit was his going as red as a turkey-cock as he battled with, but refused to be beaten by, Leach's Oriental hand wheel. Cardew described this as "a beautiful piece of nicely balanced wood spinning on a porcelain cup-bearing which turned on a long spike of hardened wood or bamboo".[580] It could only be spun clock-wise, whereas most English wheels spun anti-clockwise, which explains the problems that Murray had. It also added to the exotic aura of the Pottery.

In relation to Hamada's own output, Leach recalled, "I do not remember a flow, exactly, of pots from him, either stoneware, raku or slipware: I remember experimental ones that were successful. He did not exhibit them until his third year in England." Michael Cardew only overlapped with Hamada briefly, but was impressed. "He made the most lovely raku out of red clay. Well, it was slipware, but it was fired with raku glaze. Red clay dipped in white. Sgraffito decoration. Dashes of copper green. Lovely stuff." [581] It combined Chinese peasant ware, with sgraffito on red clay from Hupei Province, and English peasant ware. Interestingly, the principal influences on both Hamada and Leach, during these early years, were from Chinese rather than Japanese pottery.

When he needed a break from the Pottery, Hamada would often wander down to the harbour and, there, he got talking to an elderly fisherman, known as Old Bassett, "grandfather of a whole tribe", who became a good friend. One night, Hamada went out with Bassett and his crew on his fishing boat, when they caught 5,000 herring per net. He recalled, "Watching their start from the quay and their quiet work in the dark sea impressed me very much. They still have the right mind and true love for their fatal hard work. Some of them, with straight-looking eyes and heavy voice, in their old costume, were splendid."[582] Old Bassett would often walk up to the Pottery, just before it closed, with a lobster or a crab, saying merely "You can use that". He would then sit in silence and watch Hamada, as he completed his day's work at the wheel. Sometimes, he was persuaded to stay and join them for supper. Leach recalled, "Gradually he emerged from his silence, and later in the evening would begin to express ideas that were remarkably intelligent. But his intelligence was of a man who had learned his wisdom from a craft of life."[583] It was from Old Bassett that they learnt of the sawdust ash at the kipper factory, and Leach made him an earthenware cup and saucer, with slip decoration and the inscription 'Edward Bassett'.

At weekends, Hamada would invariably go off, with sandwiches and a bottle of cold tea, to the moors or the cliffs to spend time on his own, cleansing his mind from the travails of the previous week. One day, he was lying on a slab of stone on the cliff, silent and motionless for a long time, when he became aware that a cuckoo had come very close to his head. Suddenly, the bird cried out 'Cuckoo' and Hamada at once knew the course that he must take in life. He could not explain it more succinctly - he just *knew*. This course involved rejecting the creation of novel, refined art objects and, instead, concentrating on "making correct and healthy things, pottery that is practical and not forced, that responds to the nature of the materials. I did not want to make something outwardly beautiful, but to begin from the inside; health and correctness were more important to me." [584]

---

578 Bernard Leach, *A Potter's Book*, London, 1940 at p.280.

579 *St Ives Times*, 10/8/1923.

580 Michael Cardew, *A Pioneer Potter*, London, 1988 at p.31.

581 Bernard Leach, *Hamada Potter*, Tokyo and New York, 1975 at p.136.

582 ibid, at p.127.

583 ibid, at p.126.

584 ibid, at p.151.

# THE DAWN OF THE CRAFT TRADITION IN THE COLONY

Top left & Top right from Milner-White collection -
York Museums Trust - York Art Gallery

Middle left & Middle right -
Craft Study Centre, University for the Creative Arts

Bottom right - Royal Cornwall Museum, Truro

Figs. 10.13 to 10.17    Shoji Hamada

Top left :    Mei Ping Vase (26cms high)  1923
              tenmoku glaze with iron-oxide random decoration

Top right :   Mei Ping Vase (27.4cms high)  1923
              cream ash glaze flecked with iron

Middle left : Stoneware Teapot (19 cms high) 1923
              with white slip overall decorated with sgraffito
              feather curves between scallops

Middle right : Stoneware Bowl (21.6 cms wide) 1923
               inlaid white slip decoration under a celadon glaze

Bottom right : Stoneware Vase 1923
               tenmoku glaze

Financial constraints meant that Hamada could not travel around the country as much as he would have liked, but he joined Leach on a trip to Ditchling in Sussex and was very impressed by the experiment in communal living there, which was based on self sufficiency, craft and prayer. Inspired by an intense Catholicism, its guiding principles were simplicity, gentleness, peacefulness and domesticity.[585] Key members at this time were the artist and sculptor Eric Gill, the weaver Ethel Mairet and the writer, Edward Johnston. At dinner with Ethel Mairet, Hamada was impressed that she used only her best dishes - slipware made by Fishley. The quality and style of life that Hamada witnessed here had a significant influence on the community that he formed at Mashiko. He was also pleased to meet Leach's old etching master, Frank Brangwyn, who lived nearby.

### 10.3.7 Refining an underlying philosophy

Initially, Leach restricted any indication of the philosophy behind the venture to the words, "The object will be to take the old ideas of the East and the West as applied to pottery, and adapt them to present day needs".[586] This objective of effecting a "meeting of East and West" was the fundamental driving force behind Leach's entire career. The problem, on his arrival in St Ives, was that he knew very little about Western pottery traditions. Accordingly, he needed to learn fast about English folkcraft pottery. This involved visits to Lake's in Truro, as well as to the Fremington Pottery. Pottery seen in local houses was discussed, and even shards of pottery unearthed by gulls in the fields adjoining the Pottery were examined. If any style or form appealed, attempts were made to replicate it. Their most exciting discovery was English slipware, about which they could find little written and of which even leading Museum curators appeared ignorant. By repeated tests, however, they regained many of the old techniques of slipware decoration and it was the one English technique that Hamada took back to Japan, where it was translated into applications for stoneware.[587]

The second fundamental plank to Leach's philosophy was a rejection of industrial pottery, where standardisation of form and hardness, whiteness and translucency were seen as virtues. Instead, he sought to champion the artist potter, for whom each pot was an artistic response to the challenges that the medium posed in form, design, colour and texture. The artist potter showed "an appreciation of nature, of the natural effects of raw materials." [588] Accordingly, for instance, Hamada and Leach consciously used "impure materials that were considered by the Westerner to be second rate or faulty… as we delighted in the natural subtleties wood ash and other impure materials can have when fired at stoneware temperatures." [589] Inspiration might often be derived from folk art, but "the artist potter cannot pretend to be a folk potter; the potter of today is inevitably travelled, educated and conscious, even self-conscious".[590]

Leach distinguished the approach of Hamada and himself from that of the Arts and Crafts Society, which was wedded to the ideals of William Morris. "To both of us the movement contained something antipathetic and somewhat sentimental. However strong their reaction to the utter dominance of the machine over the hand, I think we both felt that the work done by many of the members was tinged with self-conscious efforts towards a medievalist revival rather than the real thing...There was an element of sophisticated imitation quite different from inevitable birth." [591]

Incorporating ideas and approaches from the East in pottery for use in the West presented its own problems. The Western consumer regarded pottery as principally utilitarian and, even if he was prepared to consider the possibility of pottery as art, had completely different artistic sensibilities. Pottery designed against a backdrop of Japanese quiet and austerity was unlikely to prove attractive to someone brought up to admire Victorian exuberance. Furthermore, many forms of pottery, such as that used in the Japanese Tea Ceremony, were inappropriate in England, whilst there were many new forms of pot, which were integral features of Western lifestyle, that Leach and Hamada had to learn to make. For instance, Leach had not put handles on his cups previously and struggled at first to do so elegantly.

---

585 See further *Ditchling, Eric Gill and the Nobility of Craft* in John Edgeler, *Michael Cardew and the West Country Slipware Tradition*, Winchcombe, 2007 at p.42-9.

586 *St Ives Times*, 19/11/1920.

587 Hamada records that the breakthrough came when, one teatime, he saw the effect that his knife had made when he cut through bread which had been layered with butter, jam and clotted cream! Bernard Leach, *Hamada Potter*, Tokyo and New York, 1975 at p.125-6.

588 Bernard Leach, *Hamada Potter*, Tokyo and New York, 1975 at p.119.

589 ibid.

590 ibid.

591 ibid, at p.133.

The very different ambience and lighting of an English home also made certain Eastern pottery practices inappropriate. Hamada recalled, "Someone ordered a panel to decorate the wall of the room. We used our local clay and raku glaze, which we brought from Japan. The piece came out all right, the glaze and colour were also good, but the panel seemed strange when hung on that stone wall of an English house. It lacked something. The soft raku glaze colours blend well in the Japanese room of wood, paper, grass and clay, but it did not harmonize with a room of stone walls and glass windows; the surroundings were too hard...We had to try something else. We decided to experiment with galena glazes of the traditional English earthenware...to our surprise, the glaze was successful on the first try. At last, we had something indigenous - the earth was indigenous and the glaze was indigenous. We decided to work with these materials.... A great lesson to me was that if a thing is not indigenous, it just does not work. The clay and the glaze must come from the area in which one is working." [592] Hamada, therefore, began to query the whole concept of East and West combined.

## 10.3 8  Educating the locals

The arrival of Leach, and his Japanese colleague, in St Ives not unnaturally aroused considerable curiosity, but there was widespread misunderstanding as to their objectives. At a time when work was scarce, there was hope that this new "industry" would provide much needed jobs, and Leach's repeated statements that he was not planning a large factory or workshop, but merely a studio for some private work, took time to be believed.

There was no doubting the exotic flavour of the venture and an early journalist visitor from Manchester was fascinated by the ambience, as he witnessed Hamada working at the wheel, whilst Leach expounded upon his influences and objectives in the presence of the "poetess" Edith Skinner, and her "artist" husband Edgar. "And the talk linked with subtle invisible bands the early endeavours of the Chinese, the skill of the Egyptians, the spirit of the Greeks, and so on to the artistry of medieval Europe, and the research of modern chemists, English, French, and German; and finally, to the hope, sincerely re-echoed, that we may find here the germ of a new Cornish industry." [593]

Nevertheless, in view of the complete lack of local knowledge about pottery in the West, let alone the East, Leach was forced on a number of occasions to explain what he was trying to achieve and to convince locals that his often imperfect pots were indeed more interesting than factory produced pottery.

Leach images ©
Leach Pottery/Craft Study Centre,
University for the Creative Arts

Figs 10.18 and 10.19    Bernard Leach

Raku plate (22cms wide) and vase (6.5cms high) in white body with blue, yellow and green pigments bought by Sidney Greenslade from the 1925 Red Rose Guild Exhibition in Manchester for Aberystwyth University Ceramics Collection

---

592 *Bernard Leach and Shoji Hamada - Journey to St Ives, England : Kinship Beyond East and West*, exhibition catalogue 2003.
593 A.R.Trelawny, *A Beautiful Trade*, *St Ives Times*, 31/3/1922 (reproduced from *Manchester Daily Despatch*).

In 1923, he wrote, "The aim of my work in St Ives is to continue making pottery from my own designs with our local Cornish materials. The technique remains very largely oriental, except in the Galena slip-ware, which derives from the old Devonian and Staffordshire pottery of a century and more ago. I regard this type as the backbone of English pottery. Besides these brown and cream Galena pots fired at 1000°C., two other types of pottery are made: first, stoneware of a great variety of quiet textures and colours fired at 1300°C., and second 'Raku'-ware, a soft Japanese faience, with a much brighter colour scheme, fired at 750°C. My chief endeavour is to produce a high temperature stoneware of various types, somewhat resembling the early Chinese and Corean work of the Sung and Korai periods. This pottery is very different from any which has been made in England until quite recently, and as it has the advantage of being hard and strong, it can be used for practical purposes." [594]

Despite the limited success that they had had in sourcing materials locally, Leach felt it important to emphasize how the pots produced would assume a special local character. "In regard to the clays used, we obtain them as locally as possible, china clay and fire clay from Towednack, and two or three red and blue plastic clays from the St Erth deposits. Besides these, we get Cornish stone and feldspar from St Austell, and a ball clay and white slip clay from Devon. These are mixed in various proportions for different wares. I hope to depend more and more on local materials, not only because it saves expense, but because it enables one to choose on the spot exactly what one needs and to develop in the finished pottery a basic local character. The same applies to the glazes for stoneware, which are composed of various wood or vegetable ashes, such as pine, oat, wheat, bracken, rhododendron, etc; feldspar, lime and quartz; and mineral colouring agents, like ochre, tin and copper." [595]

He also described the ways of the unique climbing kiln. "It is fired entirely with wood fuel (pine) and works admirably. When fully packed it holds about 500 pieces in three chambers and takes just about 24 hours to fire up to 1300°C., burning between two and three tons of wood. Wood is superior to coal as fuel, as it imparts a finer quality to the glazes, which I cannot afford to sacrifice, in spite of increased cost and labour of production. A firing is a very critical time, as it represents two or three months work. The kiln is almost like a living thing. One has to pack it with the utmost care, and know its ways and humour them with continual alertness and foresight, for there are always unforeseen dangers ahead. Not only is an even distribution of heat necessary..., but the nature of the flame and the gases in the kiln is a matter of the utmost importance. Smoke will produce in some glazes blood-red, while a clear flame will give apple-green." [596] Leach gave an example of the sort of problems that could arise in his memoirs. "I remember one firing in about 1924 which lasted twice as long as usual - 72 hours. In all that time I had only two hours off, and could hardly stand up at the end...The fire-bars below the mass of white-hot ember became choked with mixed ash and a flux from saltpetre with which, unknown to us, some of the wooden railway sleepers we were using as fuel had been saturated. Eventually, raking desperately at the fire-mouth, I drew out long streamers of slag-glass, freeing the air passages once more, and the temperature soared." [597]

### 10.3.9 Bernard Leach's early Cornish pots

After the completion of the pottery building, Leach and his large family continued to occupy 6 Draycott Terrace for a while, but then moved to No 14 as it was larger. In late 1922, however, Leach acquired 'The Count House' in Carbis Bay, the old mining property that had been converted into a home by Havelock and Edith Ellis in the 1890s. He paid £1,100 for this, but re-sold much of the land to raise funds for alterations and repairs. Hamada made an interesting observation that Leach, during the early days in St Ives, had so many appointments and other commitments, given his new business, new house and young family that "he had no opportunity to settle down to throwing and decorating....Frequently he longed for the days spent in Japan, when he could immerse himself in work." [598]

Of the three principal types of pottery that he produced initially - high-fired stoneware, lead-glazed earthenware, often referred to as galena-ware, because of the glaze used, and low-fired raku - Leach considered stoneware more 'noble', because of its association with Chinese wares. He was also aware that Art Galleries were more interested in exhibiting it than earthenware and that it commanded higher prices. He considered his own personal interpretations of the early Chinese and Korean work of the Sung and Korai periods to be distinctive. He was particularly taken with Sung dynasty (960-1279) ceramics, about which little had been known until the end of the nineteenth century. Unearthed during railway construction, their strong, simple forms, with plain, deep glazes and little decoration, were far removed

---

594 Letter to Editor, *St Ives Times*, 17/8/1923.
595 ibid.
596 ibid.
597 Bernard Leach, *Beyond East and West*, London, 1978 at p.145.
598 Bernard Leach, *Hamada Potter*, Tokyo and New York, 1975 at p.118.

from the dazzling porcelain of later periods. Their discovery was a revelation to ceramic cognoscenti, and their austerity resulted in new evaluations of beauty. Indeed, their reliance purely on abstract values of form and colour touched chords with those who championed that painting and sculpture should move away from representation. Leach was not the only English potter to be influenced by Sung pots, for they had caused a stir when included in an exhibition of early Chinese pottery held at the Burlington Fine Arts Club in 1910. Other artist potters, such as Staite Murray, Charles and Nell Vyse and Reginald Wells, had been reacting to them as well, with the latter even producing an imitative range which he called 'Soon' ware. Leach's experience in the East, however, gave him a more instinctive feel for weight and form. He also enjoyed adapting Eastern shapes into pots for Western lifestyles. Leach promoted his pots as "both homely and beautiful, simple and sensible in shape, and sober in colour and decoration".[599] Unfortunately, whilst knowledgeable collectors were intrigued by their Eastern influences, the general public tended to find them desperately dull.

More popular were the large earthenware slip-decorated plates and chargers, which Leach had started to make in Japan, having seen the late seventeenth century work of Thomas Toft illustrated in the book *Quaint Old English Pottery*. Toft's plates featured stylised historical, mythological or biblical scenes as a pictorial image in the centre, with borders of cross-hatched lines of trailed slip that often incorporated lettering, such as the date or even his own name. On being shown the carving of a mermaid on a pew in the church at Zennor, Leach immediately recalled Toft's 'Mermaid' charger (Victoria and Albert Museum) and produced his own version, with the words 'Mermaid of Zennor' incorporated into the trailed slip border (Fig. 10.29). Another charger, dating from 1923, (Victoria and Albert Museum) has as its central image 'The Tree of Life', a favourite subject for Leach who considered it symbolic (see Fig. 10.22). The design was taken from Chinese temple stone-carvings of the Han period. Stylised depictions of the mountains that he had sketched during summer breaks in Japan, when he did some rock-climbing, also featured regularly. Leach recalled, in *Beyond East and West*, "the peaks of the high Japan Alps became part of a dreamland which I often drew or even painted on pots. That picture has remained with me all through life." Well-heads, griffins (Fig. 10.23), hairs, owls and the Gemini twins were other subjects for such chargers, whilst Hamada produced one of a stylised bull, which was bought by Henry Bergen (Potteries Museum, Stoke). These pots are successful, for they were more colourful and enabled Leach to give freer rein to his painterly abilities.[600]

Fig. 10.20 Leach family and Shoji Hamada outside 'The Count House', Carbis Bay in 1922
(Private Collection)

---

599 Catalogue note to the Exhibition by the artists of St Ives at Cheltenham Art Gallery in 1925.

600 Cardew, who threw a number of these large plates for Leach to decorate with slip trailed designs, commented, "We biscuit-fired them, and then dipped them in galena glaze and fired them at 1000°C, set face downwards in a small updraught kiln built for the purpose." Michael Cardew, *A Pioneer Potter*, London, 1988 at p.39.

# SEA CHANGE : FINE AND DECORATIVE ART IN ST IVES 1914-1930

Despite Leach's training as an etcher, he tended to favour brushwork for his slipware decoration, rather than sgraffito. However, both sgraffito and removed slip techniques were used from time to time. Despite the very favourable reaction that he received for his slipware pieces in Japan, Leach, having considered that Hamada and he had rediscovered some eighty per cent of old slipware techniques, became less and less interested in it.

Leach's raku-ware was also quite popular, as raku tended to lend itself to more brightly coloured decoration. Blue, yellow and green were the pigments that he used most, and designs were often based on Dutch delftware. One of Leach's more highly decorated pieces of raku-ware is a plate, 22cms wide, which was acquired by Sidney Greenfield from the Red Rose Guild exhibition in Manchester in 1925 for the University of Aberystwyth collection (Fig. 10.18). Leach, however, reduced the production of raku later in the decade, partly because its bolder, brighter decoration did not fit in with his changing aesthetic and partly because of his greater interest in function and utility. Because raku, being low-fired, was porous, it needed a craze-free glaze, if it was intended to hold liquid, and these were not always successful. It was also easily chipped.

One of Leach's deficiencies as a potter is that he was not a skilled thrower, and showed little resolve to attempt to improve. He admitted later in life, "I am better as a decorator than as a thrower. I am not, in my own opinion, a first-class thrower, and I have never achieved a complete mastery of throwing."[601] Unlike during his last year in Tokyo, he did not in St Ives have the luxury of having skilled assistants, who could throw pots to his design. Accordingly, when coupled with the early difficulties with the kiln and suitable clays, his own thrown pots are often disappointedly imperfect, wobbly or uneven. His better work, therefore, tends to be when he has been responsible for the decoration on pots that had been thrown by Hamada, or later by Michael Cardew, who were much better skilled in this art.

Figs. 10.21-10.23 Bernard Leach

Top left : Stoneware Teapot (12.8 cms high) c.1927
brown decoration over brown ground

Top right : Teapot stand (15.8 cms wide) c.1927
with 'Tree of Life' decoration
in cream and brown glazes

(both from Milner-White collection
York Museums Trust - York Art Gallery)

Bottom left : Slipware plate with Griffin
decoration and slip-trailed border
(image Cotswold Living Publications/
John Edgeler)

Leach images ©
Leach Pottery/Craft Study Centre,
University for the Creative Arts

---

601 In John Furleigh, *The Creative Craftsman*, London, 1950 at p.69.

## 10.3.10 Early patrons

Recalling the start of the Pottery, Leach commented, "For some years, our main revenue came from enthusiasts and collectors in London and Tokyo. We worked hard, but with irregularity of mood. We destroyed pots, as artists do paintings and drawings, when they exhibited shortcomings to our own eyes. We only turned out 2000 to 3000 pots a year between four or five of us and of these not more than 10% passed muster for shows. Kiln losses in those days were high - quite some 20% The best pots had to be fairly expensive." [602]

Discounting Frances Horne, who, in addition to her financial support, was an enthusiastic purchaser of his pots, Leach recorded, "An American collector, Henry Bergen, by profession a lifelong student of Middle English, became our first patron and friend. He was an expert in Japanese art, especially pottery, and not content with collecting Oriental art on a modest income from the Rockefeller Foundation, used to come down to stay in St Ives, solemnly model and cut raku pots and also take a full turn at firing kilns during long, hot nights." [603] Leach later could not recall how he met Bergen (1873-1950), thinking that it might possibly have been at some exhibition, but it does appear as if Bergen was already a friend of Ernest Morton Nance, presumably because of Nance's interest in South Wales pottery.[604] Certainly, one of the earliest extant letters from Bergen to Leach confirms that he was staying with Nance to take some photographs.

Figs. 10.24 to 10.26   Bernard Leach

Top :   Stoneware Sugar Bowl
grey matt glaze with
brown and blue decoration
(Red Rose Guild 1925)

Michael Cardew, with whom Bergen also worked at Winchcombe, described him as "a tall, powerful man with a rather square head and an athletic build", whilst Leach found him "good company, learned and enthusiastic".[605] He left his collection of some six hundred pieces to The Potteries Museum, Stoke-on-Trent, and, in addition to an hexagonal earthenware trinket box, with gold-painted interior, which he hand-made himself at St Ives, this includes an interesting bowl by Hamada, with sgraffito decoration to the interior, comprising a stylised floral pattern cut through a cream-coloured slip coat.

Middle : Globular Stoneware Vase
buff body with yellow-
brown wood ash glaze
(Red Rose Guild 1926)

(both Aberystwyth University Collection)

Bottom:  Stoneware Vase
crackled grey glaze
(National Museum of Wales)

Bergen also introduced Leach and Hamada to some important museum people, particularly Robert Lockhart Hobson of the British Museum and Bernard Rackham of the Victoria and Albert Museum, who bought Leach's 'Tree of Life' Galena dish from the second exhibition of the British Institute of Industrial Art held at the Museum in 1923. This proved a perennially favourite motif for Leach, who always incorporated animals, birds and fishes into the design (see Fig. 10.22). It was also presumably Bergen, who organised early sales to the Metropolitan Museum of New York and the Boston Fine Arts Museum. It was Bergen too, who introduced Leach to George Aristides Eumorfopoulos (1863-1939), a Liverpool born banker, who lived in London, and who was hailed at the time as "the greatest collector in

---

602 Bernard Leach, *The Leach Pottery (1920-1946)*, The Berkley Galleries, June 1946.
603 Bernard Leach, *Beyond East and West*, London, 1978 at p.144.
604 See text of Interview between Dr Roger Slack and Margery Horne 1/7/1981 (St Ives Trust Archive Study Centre), in which she says about Ernest Morton Nance, "He was very interested, not really in Bernard's kind of pottery, but he had an American friend who was very fond of Bernard and they were interested in a sort of way, and they, I think, put money into the pottery, and were paid in having been given pots."
605 Michael Cardew, *A Pioneer Potter*, London, 1988 at p.94 & Bernard Leach, *Beyond East and West*, London, 1978 at p.144.

Europe", due to his extensive collection of Chinese, Korean and Near Eastern art. Leach recalled that he was "a very quiet man, short of build, and with innate modesty and love for art", and he had shown off his collection to Leach and Hamada, offering to do the same to any student of Leach's who cared to visit.[606] He also came down to St Ives to view the Pottery and wanted to buy the fluted Tz'u-chou bowl of the twelfth century that Leach had been given as a farewell present by his Japanese friends. However, this was one of Leach's most prized possessions. Leach, though, did not help his cause with Eumorfopoulos by selling him a vase, which was not waterproof, thus ruining the surface of his grand piano! One piece that Eumorfopoulos did acquire was a bowl in tenmoku glaze, with iron-red decoration of three six-dot floral motifs within and pine-needle decoration without, which was clearly modelled on an Oriental form (York Art Gallery). When, during the 1930s, Eumorfopoulos was forced by the effects of the Depression to dispose of parts of his collection, this bowl was bought by Eric Milner-White (see below).

Sidney K. Greenslade (1866-1955) was another important patron and was responsible for acquiring the significant collection of the early work of Hamada and Leach at the Museum of the University of Aberystwyth. This had been set up in the mid-1870s, but a donation in 1918 of £5,000 by Gwendoline and Margaret Davies of 'Gregynog', who were also major supporters of Leach's father-in-law at the National Museum of Wales, enabled a systematic approach to be adopted to the accumulation of specimens of fine and decorative art. In the same year, Sidney Greenslade, who had been the initial architect of the National Library of Wales and who was a keen exponent of the Arts and Crafts ideal, was appointed Consulting Director. Greenslade is highly likely, therefore, to have known Leach through his father. He acquired at least eight pieces from Hamada's Paterson shows in 1923, including a stoneware teapot and several stoneware jugs and bowls, but the finest piece (price £4) was a large plate, 39 cms wide, in light buff body, with leaf and flower sgraffito decoration in brown slip, covered with a heavy galena glaze. In 1925-6, he also bought a number of pieces by Leach, shown at the Red Rose Guild in Manchester. These included a number of pieces of colourful raku-ware (see Figs. 10.18 and 10.19), and several pieces of Leach's more sober stoneware, the pick being a small stoneware pot, covered in matt grey glaze, with some interesting brushwork decoration in brown and blue, into which Leach incorpoated his initials 'BL' and the date '25' (see Fig. 10.42). Michael Cardew recalled that, when he first turned up for work at the Pottery in 1923, Greenslade was there, along with Leach, Hamada, Staite Murray, Skinner, Dunn and Old Bassett, and had pulled him to one side to say how pleased he was that Cardew was joining this group who were "so full of enthusiasm".[607]

Another important collector, albeit his interest was only first aroused in 1925, was Eric Milner-White (1884-1963), who was Dean of King's College, Cambridge. He was described by Staite Murray as "the acknowledged Spiritual Father of the Studio Potters", and he developed a particular interest in the pottery of Murray, Leach and Hamada, calling them "the three Master Potters of the Century".[608] However, he only bought stoneware, believing it to be the aristocrat of ceramics. He later admitted that, in the 1920s, the number of people who were interested in collecting studio pottery could be counted on the fingers of one hand, naming Eumorfopoulos, Rackham and himself, with interest also being shown by Charles Marriott, the art critic of *The Times*, who had fraternised with the artists in St Ives during his residence in the town between 1902 and 1909.[609]

By the time that Milner-White started collecting, Hamada had returned to Japan, but he went on to acquire fifty-four examples of his work, by far the largest collection outside Japan, and this collection included five pieces done in St Ives. Two of these are tall, thin vases in a classical Oriental shape, called 'Mei Ping' by the Chinese, one in tenmoku glaze and the other in a cream ash glaze, flecked with iron (see Figs 10.13 and 10.14). Interestingly, he was particularly attracted to any pots by Hamada, where he felt that he could trace a hint of Western influence. He also was an avid collector of Leach's pots, acquiring eighty-three in all. A particularly fine piece is a vase, that was exhibited at Paterson's in 1926, which features cut-away T'zu Chou type decoration into a grey slip (Fig. 10.27). Another interesting piece is an oriental style tea-pot, with decoration comprising six-petalled flowers and two double 's' and dot motifs over a light brown ground (Fig. 10.21). A somewhat similar tea-pot was also acquired by Henry Bergen. Milner-White's collection also contained later work by Leach's students Michael Cardew, Katharine Pleydell-Bouverie and Norah Braden. The majority of the collection is now housed at York Art Gallery, Milner-White having become Dean of York in 1941, but a number of pieces were given to Southampton Art Gallery in 1939 in memory of his father, and these include a Celadon dish and a Globular pot produced by Hamada in St Ives and a number of Leach pieces from the 1920s.

---

606 Bernard Leach, *Hamada Potter*, Tokyo and New York, 1975 at p.139.
607 Michael Cardew, *A Pioneer Potter*, London, 1988 at p.31.
608 Sarah Riddick, *Pioneer Studio Pottery : The Milner White Collection*, London, 1990 at p.7.
609 ibid, at p.14.

# THE DAWN OF THE CRAFT TRADITION IN THE COLONY

Fig. 10.27  Bernard Leach
Vase (22.4cms high)  1926
grey slip with cut away
T'zu Chou style decoration
(York Museums Trust - York Art Gallery)

Fig. 10.28  Shoji Hamada
Stoneware Vase (16.5 cms high) 1923
iron glaze with painted decoration
(Craft Study Centre, University for the Creative Arts)

## 10.3.11  First Exhibitions

Leach recorded that the very first showing of his pots in England was in 1921 in Conduit Street, London in a group show at the Artificers' Guild, and it was here that he first met William Staite Murray.  Sidney Greenfield, however, at this juncture, whilst considering Staite Murray's work excellent, felt that Leach's pots were "just in the experimental stage - and clay and colours and glazes are uncertain".[610]  Later in the year, Leach showed work at Lanham's Gallery in St Ives for the first time, but it was not a success.  His first one-man show was at the Cotswold Gallery in Frith Street in November 1922, and this did generate considerable interest in the press, with the *Pottery Gazette* carrying an illustration of twenty-eight pieces displayed on six shelves.  Most of the exhibits were jugs, bottles and bowls.

In early 1923, Leach took up Yanagi's suggestion that he should hold an exhibition of his work in Japan - at the Ruisseau Gallery in Tokyo.  It was an enormous success, with the finest pieces selling in the first two days.  Interestingly, it was work reflecting English, rather than Japanese, culture that sold best - tea or coffee sets, rather than tea bowls or tea ceremony objects - and the novel galena-ware aroused considerable interest.  Aware of Leach's financial travails, Yanagi ensured that no sales commission was taken and was able to remit to him 3,000 yen (about £300), a sum that far exceeded total sales in England and which arrived just when the Hornes' support of the venture had come to an end.

Hamada's first solo exhibition was at the Paterson Gallery, 5, Old Bond Street in the spring of 1923.  The Gallery, up till then, had not usually staged pottery shows, but the elderly Paterson had been impressed with Hamada's personal application.  Hamada recalled, "I was very pleased with the way it went - men like Eumorfopoulos came the first day, and each bought something, not like Japan where they come in gangs.  These men bought thoughtfully.  The exhibition sold very well - it was reported in the newspaper, the clipping was sent from one person to another in letters, telling each quietly that such an exhibition was being held, and slowly but surely the news spread and the whole show went quite well."  Henry Bergen, who felt that the pots on show were the best Hamada had yet done, reported that the young connoisseur, William Wilberforce Winkworth (1897-1991), came early and bought some nice pots and that Edgar Skinner, Robert Morton Nance and Margery Horne had all made the effort to come up from St Ives to view it.  Winkworth, in fact, gave some of his collection of Leach and Hamada pots to the Victoria and Albert Museum as early as 1924.[611]

---

610 Malcolm Haslam, *William Staite Murray*, Crafts Council, 1984, at p.17.
611 See Obituary in *The Burlington Magazine*, Vol 133, No 1062, September 1991.

It was at Bergen's instigation that Leach combined with Staite Murray, also in 1923, to send a selection of pots for exhibition in America, but a disastrous set of breakages, coupled with poor sales, made it an "edifying experience". An exhibition in Leipzig was also a disappointment, as the Germans found his work dull. However, a London exhibition in November 1923 received good notices. *The Morning Post* commented, "Quiet charm and strength are the distinguishing features of the pots, vases, bowls, etc, particularly in those pieces in cobalt blue and celadon, and in the warmer glazes, ranging from rich red to deepest brown", whilst *The Times* felt the exhibits were "remarkable for dignity of shape, depth of colour and quality of surface." [612]

Feeling that Bond Street was too expensive, Leach then exhibited at the Beaux Arts Gallery in nearby Bruton Street. He also tried the Three Shields Gallery in Church Street and joined with the Ditchling group at the New Handworkers' Gallery in Bloomsbury. After initially being rejected, Leach also became a member of William Morris' Arts and Crafts Society, which held triennial exhibitions in London and of the Red Rose Guild in Manchester, which Leach described as "the northern branch of Morris' counter-industrial movement".[613]

### 10.3.12  Hamada's return to Japan

In September 1923, the Great Kanto Earthquake shook Japan. Yokohama was wiped out and two-thirds of Tokyo was burnt down. The death toll was 250,000. Incredibly, it took three months before Hamada heard whether his family had survived. Hamada's father owned a small factory employing fifty people in a crowded area of Tokyo near the river. Aware of the danger of fire, following such shocks, they escaped to a large area of open ground, into which 50,000 people were crammed. However, severe winds drove the flames so that they encircled the field and bore down on the defenceless crowd, and 32,600 were burnt alive. Hamada's father only escaped as he was close to the river. Friends of Leach to die in the catastrophe included his master, Kenzan VI, and Yanagi's brother. Hearing that his father's business and home had been destroyed, Hamada, as the eldest son, felt duty bound to return home, although Tomimoto and others urged him to stay away until some stability had returned.

In December that year, Hamada held his second exhibition at Paterson's in New Bond Street, which proved an even greater success than the first, with only three pots unsold. Paterson presented him with a fine Persian pot, as a gift at the end. As he journeyed home, Robert Morton Nance arranged for all the proceeds from the premiere of his third Cornish dialect play, *The Kite in the Castle*, to be earmarked for the Japanese Disaster Fund and this, coupled with an appeal in the local paper by Leach, helped to raise £77 - a gesture that was much appreciated in Japan.[614]

Reflecting on his time in St Ives, Hamada commented, "By the time I left St Ives, the technical standards, using local materials, had reached the level we had planned", and both he and Leach had achieved recognition through their exhibitions in London. As far as his own personal development was concerned, he reflected, "The first year abroad everything is interesting, everything is new and exciting. The second year, nothing is any good, nothing is of any value, nothing Western is exactly favourable or virtuous; you begin to negate what you have experienced. But the third year everything starts coming in without resistance. You just absorb what comes and goes without particular emotion, and this is when you begin to understand the true nature of a country." He was taken by "the quiet, conservative, thoughtful English tradition....I realised that what I myself had mastered before was merely the decoration, the surface colouring, and that I had missed the more important heart of the English and their customs. Coming from the opposite side of the world in the East to the far West, I decided to do away with what I had hitherto learned and to start completely anew." [615]

On his return to Japan, Hamada, working closely with Yanagi and his old student friend, Kawai Kanjiro (1890-1966), was instrumental in founding the artistic and philosophical movement, the Mingei, or Japanese Folkcraft Association. Influenced by his visit to Ditchling, he set up his pottery in a remote rural village, Mashiko, which had a folkcraft pottery tradition. He soon secured for himself a reputation as one of Japan's leading potters, with a style that combined robustness and simplicity of form, with delicate brushwork and complex glaze techniques. His pots were purely functional and utilitarian, never simply art objects. On purpose, he had left behind in St Ives his pottery seal and, thereafter, did not seal

---

612 Reproduced in *St Ives Times*, 7/12/1923.
613 Bernard Leach, *Beyond East and West*, London, 1978 at p.145-6.
614 In a letter from Henry Bergen to Leach dated 22/4/1924 (Crafts Study Centre, Farnham), Bergen says that Hamada, before he left, had indicated that Nance could have the pick of those pieces returned from the show at Paterson's. Nance did not appear to take him up on this, largely one suspects because there was nothing left! Bergen indicates in the same letter that he had been promised the bull at Kimber's - presumably the Bull platter now at the Potteries Museum, Stoke.
615 Bernard Leach, *Hamada Potter*, Tokyo and New York, 1975 at p.141.

or sign any of his work. He objected to over-individualism in art, and did not want people to buy his pots just because of his name. He took the view that if a prospective purchaser could not tell a Hamada pot, either it was bad or he was blind. Whilst his experiences in St Ives had played a significant role in the evolution of his philosophy, the influence, on his subsequent output, of English pottery, other than, for a time, slipware, was minimal.

**10.3.13**      **The first students - Michael Cardew and Katharine Pleydell-Bouverie**

Michael Ambrose Cardew (1901-1983) was the first student to be taken on by the pottery. He was the son of Arthur Cardew, a successful London civil servant, whilst his mother, Alexandra, was the daughter of the Dean of Winchester. However, the family had a holiday home at Saunton in Devon, and his father had become an enthusiastic collector of the work of Edwin Beer Fishley, whose pottery at Fremington was nearby. Michael, therefore, as a result of day trips to Fremington whilst on holiday, had been enthused by pots from an early age. In 1919, he won a scholarship to Oxford University to read "Greats" (ancient literature and philosophy), but, as his "pot-madness" meant that he spent a lot of his time learning to throw, he was nearly rusticated.

In January 1923, having seen some examples of its work that intrigued him, Cardew visited Lake's Pottery in Truro and, whilst there, decided that, if there was a train to St Ives, he would go. There was, and he arrived in St Ives late in the afternoon. On climbing up The Stennack to the Pottery, he met George Dunn, who introduced him to Hamada. Leach, however, was at his home, and so, in deep discussion about Ethel Mairet, Hamada and Cardew walked in the dark the two miles across the fields to Carbis Bay. During the evening meal that they shared with Leach's family, Cardew's enthusiasm for reviving the English slipware tradition appealed to Bernard. In the precarious state that the Pottery was in, he had not actively been thinking about taking on students, but later wrote about that first meeting with Cardew, "He strode in, nose and brow straight, handsome as some young Greek god, eyes flashing blue, hair waving, gold, and within the hour announced that this was where he wanted to work." [616] Leach, who had just acquired a Martinside motor-bike and side-car, drove him up to Saunton, ostensibly to see if his family approved. In truth, Leach wanted to inspect Cardew's father's collection of Fremington pottery. However, instead of admiring the decorative pieces on display in the main rooms, Leach disappeared into the kitchen and sought out the comb-decorated oven dishes and plain water pitchers, which led him to describe Edwin Fishley as "the last vital peasant potter left in England".[617] Cardew recalled, "It did not take me long to move over to seeing the Fremington pots in the way he saw them: the green-glazed 'decorative' ware as a modern deviation and the plain kitchenware as the authentic channel of expression." [618]

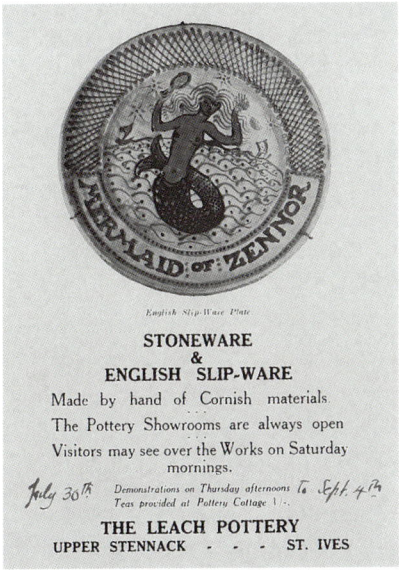 

Fig. 10.29 Bernard Leach Slipware plate with 'Mermaid of Zennor' design (Museum of Ohara, Japan) & Pottery poster using its image (Craft Study Centre, UCA)

---

616 Quoted in Garth Clark, *Michael Cardew - A Portrait*, London and Boston, 1978 at p.16.
617 Bernard Leach, *Beyond East and West*, London, 1978 at p.148.
618 Michael Cardew, *A Pioneer Potter*, London, 1988 at p.32.

Cardew, who had been told by Leach not to expect a salary, as the Pottery's capital was almost exhausted, started in July 1923, but was then tempted by a friend to join him for eight weeks in the Mediterranean. He arrived back in November, shortly before Hamada left, and so had limited contact with him, which was a lasting regret. Unable to get on with the wheels at the Pottery, Cardew installed his own Devon kick wheel, which he had commissioned from a carpenter and blacksmith at Braunton in 1921, whilst he had been taking lessons from William Fishley Holland.

Leach recalled, "From the first Cardew showed definite character; he galloped on impulse, then pulled up to think. He could also reach red-heat and fury in a moment - even throw a pot at some offender! But Michael was lovable. I can see him taking his first slipware pots out of the third kiln-chamber - having waited with barely hidden impatience whilst we unpacked the first two, glance at them and in immediate dislike send them flying in an arc into the Stennack stream behind him; also him wading into the water to retrieve them later that afternoon! More than with most people, these two aspects of Cardew's personality were difficult to marry." [619] Cardew's intellect and his knowledge of ancient philosophy will have ensured that Leach and himself had fascinating debates. Leach recalled, "Michael was a good talker, illustrating his points with broad gestures, flashing eyes and a fine row of white teeth."[620] However, although Cardew was only fifteen years younger than Leach, he did not feel totally at ease with him, for he considered him "a perfectly preserved example of an English Edwardian".[621] Leach, of course, being in Japan, had been shielded to a large degree from the horrors of the Great War.

Cardew recalled that the two new techniques that he learnt, which were particularly exciting, were the Japanese method of spiral wedging, which helped to remove bubbles and make the clay smooth, and throwing "off the hump". He set aside fifteen minutes per day before breakfast for trying to master these new skills. In return, he taught Leach the Devon method of 'bowing' or handle-making. Following Leach's enthusiasm for the work of the Sung dynasty, Cardew worked hard at trying to incorporate Sung purism in his work. However, when he threw a lidded jar, which he felt had been a success in this respect, Leach had passed the comment, "My goodness, Michael, isn't it strange. Whatever you make is so extraordinarily English." [622] Although interested in Leach's fascination with all things Oriental, Cardew, who took a long time to warm to stoneware, was never completely won over, and was happy to label himself a "Western barbarian".

Cardew's knowledge and love of North Devon pottery was a major influence on the work that he did in St Ives, and he produced a number of jugs and tankards for the tourist market that drew on these traditions. These were put on a table outside the Pottery, in the hope of drawing in passing motorists. Following the Devon practice, these often had verses incised into the slip covering. John Edgeler argues that the seriffed lettering employed by Cardew was influenced by Eric Gill at Ditchling.[623] Fig. 10.30 is a wheel thrown earthenware Harvest Jug in the North Devon manner, with scroll handle, the red body slipped white, with incised seriffed lettering proclaiming, *Fill me up & drink about / & never leave till all is out / & if that will not make you merry / fill me again & sing down derry*.[624] Another earthenware Harvest Jug by Cardew from 1925, with a golden brown galena glaze, fetched £7440, at Bonham's, New Bond Street, in November 2008. This had the incised slip wording, *Despise me not because I'm made of clay / but make me welcome when I come this way / My belly fill with good strong punch (or beer) / & I will make you merry all the year*. Cardew also produced earthenware tankards, with inscriptions in similar vein, sometimes in Latin. An order for two dozen beer mugs from a friend in Oxford made him appreciate the difficulties of throwing 'in series' - i.e. of getting the mugs even roughly the same size and shape and with level rims. Clearly, there is no Eastern influence here; what is being propogated are old English folkart forms and traditions.

In January 1926, Cardew wrote an article, *New Pots for Old*, in the local paper, in which he championed pots, which preserved the best qualities of old peasant pottery and reflected instinctive craftsmanship, over cheap industrially produced ware, which tended to have superficial or meretricious effects. Such a stance was quite standard, but, interestingly, he highlighted one particular new type of potential customer - the mistress of the house who no longer had any maids to help her. "More and more people, who are using their own kitchens, are trying gradually to convert the kitchen cupboard and dresser from a dismal array of soul-less jam pots and pudding-bowls into something more homely and sympathetic and civilised." [625]

---

619 Bernard Leach, *Beyond East and West*, London, 1978 at p.148.
620 ibid, at p.149.
621 Michael Cardew - *Bernard Leach - Recollections* in *Bernard Leach - Essays in Appreciation,* Wellington, 1960.
622 Quoted in Garth Clark, *Michael Cardew - A Portrait*, London and Boston, 1978 at p.16.
623 See John Edgeler, *Michael Cardew and the West Country Slipware Tradition*, Winchcombe, 2007 at p.61-2.
624 I am indebted to John Edgeler of The Long Room Gallery, Winchcombe for this description and the image.
625 M A Cardew, *New Pots for Old, St Ives Times*, 22/1/1926.

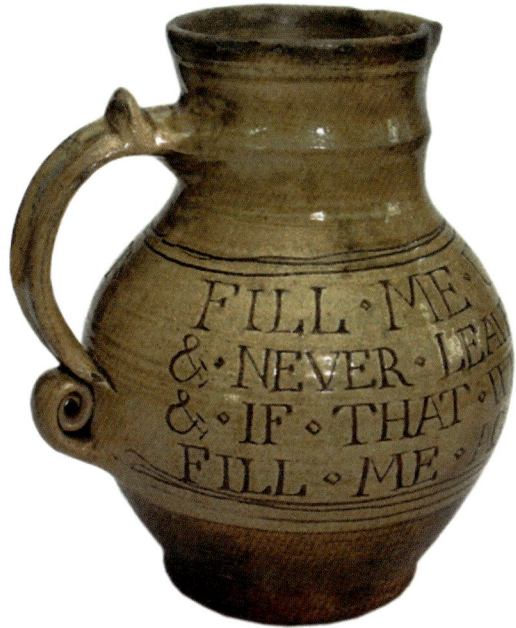 

Fig. 10.30  Michael Cardew
Slipware Harvest Jug
*Fill me up & drink about
& never leave till all is out
& if that will not make you merry
fill me again & sing down derry*

(image Cotswold Living Publications/John Edgeler)

Fig. 10.31  Michael Cardew
Slipware Jug with sgraffito decoration of mermaid, sea-horse, and ship
(Royal Cornwall Museum, Truro)

Leach's second student was Katharine Harriot Duncumbe Pleydell-Bouverie (1895-1985), who came from an aristocratic family that lived at 'Coleshill House' in Berkshire, an impressive property built to the design of Inigo Jones in 1660. Her interest in pottery started when she visited Roger Fry at his Omega Workshops, which led her to attend the Central School of Art and Crafts to study the subject. She first met Leach at one of his early exhibitions in 1923 and, although considering him "a long spidery man, giving a curious impression of shagginess in a Norfolk jacket and an extensive moustache", was taken with his "quiet-coloured, gentle-surfaced pots with a pleasant sense of peace about them".[626] Accordingly, she asked to become his student straight away, but, as Cardew had just joined, Leach turned her down. Edgar Skinner, though, later persuaded him that the Pottery might well be able to use a paying stooge and, after a fortnight's trial, she was allowed to join in January 1924. She was always known as 'Beano' and "had a very telling and communicative laugh like the neigh of a horse, especially if she disagreed".[627] Cardew found her "very beautiful and also very big, with a large frame like a French peasant's; and yet at the same time somehow petite, because her features were so curiously fine".[628] She stayed for a year, living with a friend in an empty miner's cottage in Halsetown, a mile along the Penzance road. Leach had warned her that it would be hard work, "as we do everything with our hands from the wood splitting and mixing of clays to throwing and packing", and that "unusual enthusiasm" would be necessary to get though the periods of being "dirty and tired, hot and cold".[629] She did indeed have to endure a lot of "general stooging", recalling, in particular, interminable periods of grinding cobalt, but she picked up knowledge from careful observation and from "Bernard's erratic but mainly genial tutelage".[630] She was impressed that there were no 'trade secrets', and that Leach was ungrudgingly generous with information and suggestions. Certainly, her overriding interest in ash glazes, upon which she became an acknowledged expert, was sparked by her time in St Ives, whilst her work also demonstrated truth to materials and a minimalism that can be linked to Leach's Oriental perspective.

---

626 Katharine Pleydell-Bouverie, *At St Ives in the Early Years*, quoted in Bernard Leach, *Beyond East and West*, London, 1978 at p.151.  See also *Ceramic Review*, No 58, July-August 1979.
627 Bernard Leach, *Beyond East and West*, London, 1978 at p.149.
628 Michael Cardew, *A Pioneer Potter*, London, 1988 at p.34.
629 Letter from Leach to Pleydell-Bouverie dated 20/1/1925.
630 Barley Roscoe, *Katharine Pleydell-Bouverie : A Potter's Life 1895-1985*, Craft Council, London, 1986 at p.8.

Fig. 10.32 Tsuranosuke Matsubayashi by the fireplace in the Pottery
(Craft Study Centre, University for the Creative Arts)

### 10.3.14  Tsuranosuke Matsubayashi

Realising that the kiln that Hamada and himself had built initially was defective, Leach arranged in 1922 for Tsuranosuke Matsubayashi, an old fellow student of Hamada, who was a specialist in kiln construction, to come across to St Ives. Then in his late twenties, he came from a well-known Kyoto family that had been making pots for thirty-nine generations, and was a very competent chemist and engineer. Cardew recalled, "He was totally conventional and sometimes frighteningly correct in his manners, but most of the time managed to be charming, humorous and sympathetic." [631] His room, in the opinion of 'Beano', resembled "the bed-sitting room of a Victorian spinster with Oriental accretions".[632]

The old kiln finally became unusable after the firing for Hamada's last Bond Street show in 1923. Leach recalled that he was able to put his hand right through a bulging crack in one of the internal walls. Matsubayashi produced a detailed drawing of the Kyoto type kiln that he recommended and worked tirelessly and assiduously on its construction. The newly arrived Michael Cardew was useful manual labour, hammering the stiff, crude local kaolin rock into wooden moulds for the fire bricks. Pleydell-Bouverie recorded the momentous occasion, when Matsubayashi's expertise was first put to the test in May 1924.

> "The first firing began, I remember, with a ceremonial offering of salt on the fire arch. And gradually, through the long day's slow stoking, an atmosphere of tension developed that would have been quite suitable on a battlefield. The rate of firing increased, and the kiln grew hotter. So did we. There was a great deal of black smoke billowing out of the chimney, making an acrid fog in the shed. We got blacker. Night came, and, in the flickering light of what Matsu called 'bro holes' and the crackle and flare of the logs in the fire mouth, we moved about like creatures out of the sinister creations of Hieronymous Bosch.
>
> And then in the grey dawn, something began to go wrong. Matsu took out a spy brick, and as the wicked little flame that jumped out at him died down, peered into the incandescent kiln and let out a ghoulish roar. 'Oh-ho-ha-ha-hay-awful sings happen', sang Matsu with every appearance of enjoyment, as a six foot bung of saggars leaned slowly forward and collapsed on to the front wall, blocking up the draft." [633]

---

[631] Michael Cardew, *A Pioneer Potter*, London, 1988 at p.34.
[632] K.Pleydell-Bouverie, *At St Ives in the Early Years*, quoted in Bernard Leach, *Beyond East and West*, London, 1978 at p.151.
[633] ibid, at p.152-3.

Little was able to be salvaged from the firing. Cardew, surveying the disaster, was bold enough to quote an eighteenth century proverb, "Experience keeps a hard school, but fools will learn in no other", to which Leach had at once retorted, "Experience may be a hard school, but anyone who *expects* to learn in any other would be a fool".[634]

Despite this initial set back, the new kiln proved infinitely superior to the previous one and has remained in place ever since. Nevertheless, Janet Leach, Bernard's third wife, later recorded, that it "was actually not the proper type of kiln for Bernard's new pottery concept. It is a Kyoto type kiln built for hundreds of small porcelain pots, reduction fired, but it was never designed for a pot of 12" in diameter. It is a precious pot kiln (court taste) and not a stewpot (folkcraft) kiln. We struggled to adapt and fire the pots that Bernard was making." [635]

As regards Matsubayashi's own work as a potter, Pleydell-Bouverie commented, "his pots were rather terrible; and Bernard looked on them with a withering contempt which he was at no pains whatever to hide. It seemed a little hard on Matsu, who made him a beautiful kiln and quantities of very fine saggars, lavishing on his building all the artistry that he never got into his pots. But Matsu, wrapped in a cloak of complacency that was so impermeable as to be comic and rather endearing, remained quite unperturbed by all the things that Bernard said." [636]

On Show Day in 1924, Matsubayashi's portrait in samurai costume by Ernest Borough Johnson was exhibited, and he also showed some of his own original drawings, but Cardew confirmed, "Mr Matsubayashi was no artist, but a very accomplished craftsman and technologist. During the winter, he gave us evening lessons in the theory of pottery. His best pupil was Katharine Pleydell-Bouverie, who took conscientious notes of his lectures. At that time, I thought the theory of ceramics did not matter, and I took almost no notes at all. (I lived to regret this missed opportunity). Leach himself attended the lectures, rather as a philosophical critic than as a student." Pleydell-Bouverie recalled that the lectures covered kiln construction, chemical formulae and the plasticity of clay. " "Velly important the cray should have the plasty", intoned Matsu, who never learned the difference between the letters L and R, but shook them up in a bag and took what came. "For which put in tub with water till smell bad, yes lelly strike your nose too much, when have the plasty and perfect condition for make the cray body." " The lectures, she recalled, were full of good sense whenever it was possible to disentangle their remarkable English.[637]

When, after a year at the pottery in St Ives, Pleydell-Bouverie decided that she would like to set up a pottery at her family home, 'Coleshill House', she invited Matsubayashi to come and give advice about a suitable kiln. Whilst there, he performed a Japanese Tea Ceremony, which Leach recalled with some amusement. "He preceded this by dressing in best formal Japanese clothes and going out into the rose gardens to select two or three blooms as a background for the ceremony. Looking at them with a calculating eye as they grew, he squatted first on one foot and then the other, quite unaware of the tiptoe curiosity of the gardeners peeping over the hedges at his antics! The magnificent old drawing-room was the last place to think of as a background for Japanese Ceremonial Tea. He proceeded to arrange the old furniture to simulate a small Tea room, with a very low entry for the poor dears to crawl in humbly on their knees and in their English skirts. They took their positions sitting on their heels, whilst he pontificated with boiling water, rinsing out each of his bowls, emptying the water into some receptacle, then wiping them ceremonially. He then opened a *cha'ire* (tea-caddy), took a couple of bamboo teaspoonful of green tea which he emptied into a bowl, and over which he poured a bare cup of boiling water. This brew he then frothed with another fine tool, a bamboo whisk, before presenting the front of the bowl towards the principal guests, whom I presume had been invited to nibble a special Japanese sweet to enhance the austere flavour of this peculiar drink....My mind boggles at the thought of those English ladies composing their faces to this solemn ordeal presented by the Master." [638] Margery Horne recalled that Matsubayashi and Hamada had put on a similar ceremonial at 'Tremorna'. Again, Matsubayashi went out into the garden to find something for a flower arrangement. "He wandered round the garden for ages and he finally came back with one little bit of Veronica, one little twig of Veronica! And then he spent about a quarter of an hour in the sitting room, stroking it, to make it lie just as he wanted it, and then he put it in a little pot and he thought that was really beautiful, and we were a bit bemused by that!" However, she recalled enjoying the Tea Ceremony itself. "There were the most wonderful claws

---

634 Michael Cardew, *A Pioneer Potter*, London, 1988 at p.40.
635 Janet Leach, *Tribute to Bernard Leach - The Leach Pottery and Bernard Leach's Later Years*.
636 Katharine Pleydell-Bouverie, *At St Ives in the Early Years*, quoted in Bernard Leach, *Beyond East and West*, London, 1978 at p.151.
637 Katharine Pleydell-Bouverie, *At St Ives in the Early Years*, quoted in Bernard Leach, *Beyond East and West*, London, 1978 at p.152.
638 Bernard Leach, *Beyond East and West*, London, 1978 at p.153-4.

that Mr Hamada produced and there was a very artistic way in which you had to fold them with certain movements; it would only be a certain number of movements, and each movement was significant, and that was lovely, it was very, very beautiful, it was so graceful, it was like a ballet, although they were hardly moving." [639] In such ways did Leach's presence in St Ives result in novel experiences for its inhabitants.

Having advised Pleydell-Bouverie about kiln construction at 'Coleshill House', Matsubayashi went to Paris before returning to Japan. On leaving St Ives, though, he tellingly drew Michael Cardew to one side and remarked, "I hope you will stay here with Mr Leach, and always help him with his work, because - ah - I think - ah - Mr Leach - ah - rather poetical".[640] At that time, Cardew had no thoughts of leaving, and assured Matsubayashi that he intended to stay for many years.

Cardew recalled that Matsubayashi "wrote charming letters from home, telling us he was intending to marry 'the most beautiful woman in Japan'. But something went wrong: the marriage never took place, and we heard later the sad news that he was dead." [641]

### 10.3.15  Robert Morton Nance

Very little attention has been given to the influence of Robert Morton Nance (1873-1959) in previous accounts of the Leach Pottery. Leach mentions that Nance was the first friend that he made in St Ives, and this friendship lasted for life, being further enhanced by the marriage of Robert's son, Dicon, to Leach's daughter, Eleanor. Robert, albeit labelled a recluse by Leach, clearly took a great interest in the Pottery from the outset, possibly because he had developed an earlier interest in pottery in South Wales, having been born in Cardiff. Certainly, his brother, Ernest Morton Nance, a London solicitor, who also had a house in Carbis Bay, was an expert on the pottery and porcelain of Swansea and Nantgawr, being included in *Who's Who in Art* in 1929 solely due to his collection, and later, in 1942, publishing the definitive history of this pottery. Ernest, who was known by Frances Horne as 'Black Nance', because he was a very dark, swarthy looking individual, also took an interest in the St Ives pottery, albeit Leach's pots were not entirely to his taste.

Despite their birthplace, the Nance brothers came from a family with long-standing St Ives connections; indeed, their forbears gave sanctuary to John Wesley in the town. Robert was an erudite man, with a remarkable range of knowledge. He started out with the objective of being an artist, and trained at Bushey and, in 1898, in St Ives. He went on to enjoy some success with marine paintings, which tended to feature medieval ships on the high seas, and a sketch for his 1904 New Gallery exhibit, *On the Wings of the Wind*, which was illustrated as a Picture of the Year, is owned by St Ives Arts Club. However, after his wife, Beatrice, died in 1902, he devoted himself to a study of sailing ship models, leading ultimately to the publication in 1924 of what has become the definitive book on the subject. Having settled, in 1906, with his second wife, Annie Maud Cawker, a weaver, in Nancledra, close to St Ives, he wrote, for the local schoolchildren, a play, *Duffy and the Devil*, which sought to carry on the West Penwith tradition of guise dance drolls - local folk-tales turned into plays for Christmas acting, which incorporated the local speech and broke, from time to time, into rhyme or song. This attracted considerable interest and was performed on a number of occasions in St Ives in the early 1920s. Building on the work of the Celtic scholar, Henry Jenner (1848-1934), it also fostered renewed interest in the Cornish language and in Cornish history and folk-lore, and led to the formation of the Old Cornwall Society in 1920.

The formation of the Leach Pottery inspired Robert Morton Nance to utilise, once again, his artistic skills, in the decoration of pots. In a letter dated 20th November 1922 to Leach, who was away from the Pottery at the time, Hamada states, "We have started raku and hope to finish firing about one hundred pots by the end of next week. Mr Nance came last Saturday with Dicon and will come Friday again to paint some." [642] One raku dish decorated by Nance (Fig. 10.34) is owned by the Craft Study Centre, Farnham and features one of Nance's beloved medieval ships in the centre, brushed in with iron oxide, with the words 'Measure is Treasure' around the rim in sgraffito lettering through the iron oxide. This would appear to be a reference to the play, *Magnificence*, written by the then poet laureate, John Skelton, in c.1515-1521, in which he dramatized "personified qualities of human relations in order to moralize politics and thus politicize those moral and economic issues". Measure, therefore, is the character in the play that demonstrates financial and political prudence.[643]

---

639 See text of Interview between Dr Roger Slack and Margery Horne 1/7/1981 (St Ives Trust Archive Study Centre).
640 Michael Cardew, *A Pioneer Potter*, London, 1988 at p.43.
641 ibid.
642 Bernard Leach, *Hamada Potter*, Tokyo and New York, 1975 at p.127.
643 Tai-Won Kim, *"Measure is Treasure" : Financial and Political Prudence in John Skelton's* Magnificence, Sungshin Women's University, published on the internet.

Figs. 10.33 & 10.34  Shoji Hamada / Robert Morton Nance (decorator)

Left :  Raku Bowl with decoration in blue slip
*The True Figure of Troy Town*

(images Cotswold Living Publications/John Edgeler)

Right :  Raku Dish with brushed decoration in iron oxide and sgraffito lettering
*Measure is Treasure*
(Craft Study Centre, UCA, Farnham)

Another Nance-decorated raku dish (Fig. 10.33) is even more fascinating, as it features Nance's depiction of the unicursal maze on St Agnes, Scilly Islands, with lettering in blue slip on the rim reading 'The True Figure of Troy Town'. Nance had originally presented his study of unicursal mazes in and around Europe to the Royal Institution of Cornwall, Truro in 1913 and, at the time of decorating this pot, was preparing a paper, *Troy Town*, which was published in the Journal of the RIC in 1924 and for which he received the Henwood medal in 1926.[644] Mazes of turf and small stones, such as that at St Agnes, frequently had names incorporating "Troy" in them, presumably because, in popular legend, the walls of the city of Troy were constructed in such a confusing and complex way that any enemy who entered them would be unable to find their way out. That at St Agnes was called "Troy Town" and followed the classical labyrinth pattern, as found on coins from ancient Knossos, Crete. It was laid out in 1729 by the son of the local lighthouse keeper, and the wording on the pot indicates that Nance had discovered its initial plan.[645]

It is not certain how long Nance continued his pot decorating activities, as he became increasingly tied up with the activities of the Old Cornwall Society. However, both Cardew, who had Cornish forbears, and Leach, who liked to play on his Celtic background, decided in the autumn of 1924 to enrol in the Cornish language classes that Nance ran once a week on behalf of the Society. Cardew commented, "I had been wanting to learn the language for a long time, chiefly I think because it fed two of my ruling emotions - romanticism and a passion for words. The idea of it tantalized me; there was this ancient language, idiomatic and idiosyncratic, which yet possessed an almost Roman dignity." [646] Amongst the small class of four or five people was Richard John Noall, an elderly recluse, who was Cornish to the core, and so, as they walked back up The Stennack together, Cardew felt that he was hearing the true sound of the language, which had hardly been spoken for one hundred years. Unsurprisingly, Cardew began to include Cornish words and sayings into his pots. A stoneware pitcher, owned by the Royal Cornwall Museum, has an inscription in Cornish with English translation, reading "First was shaped by potter's hand / in Cornwall near where ends the land / If to the ground I be not hurl'd / I hope to last till ends the world." If this were not enough, Cardew adds, "Indebted to R.M.N. for writing this Cornish-English. This pitcher was made myself in the year one thousand nine hundred and twenty six. M.A.C." In gratitiude for Morton Nance's assistance, Cardew also presented him with a mug, with the incised inscription *Rag Yeghes Ha Carensa* (For good health and love), and a Jug, inscribed *Ty Podick Byghan Meur My Ath Gar rag R M N* (Little pot, I dearly love thee. For R M N). For Richard Noall, he designed a two-handled mug, with the inscription 'May you from misery be free / Blest with health and prosperity / My wish to you one and all / Your humble servant R.J.Noall'. Through their involvement with the classes, both Cardew and Leach took part in the Old Cornwall Society's production of *St George and the Dragon* (Fig. 10.35).

---

644 I am indebted to John Edgeler, of The Long Room Gallery, Winchcombe, for his research into Nance's study of unicursal mazes.

645 See Wikipedia entry under 'Troy Town'.

646 Michael Cardew, *A Pioneer Potter*, London, 1988 at p.41-2.

Fig. 10.35  Cast of the Old Cornwall Society's performance of George & the Dragon c.1924 featuring A.K.Hamilton-Jenkin, Phoebe Nance, Richard J. Noall, Bernard Leach, Michael Cardew and Robert Morton Nance
(Royal Cornwall Museum, Truro)

In 1928, the Society organised the first Cornish Gorsedd at Boscawen-Un just outside Penzance, with members of the Welsh Gorsedd present to confer the requisite authority. The title of Grand Bard was bestowed on Henry Jenner and, amongst the other Bards elected that day were not only Nance but also, despite having left the county, Michael Cardew, described as a "student of Cornish", who took the bardic name Myhal an Pry (Michael of the Day). Nance was elected Grand Bard in 1934, on Jenner's death, and retained the title until his death in 1959. During this time, he published numerous books on the Cornish language and was at the forefront of research into Cornish history.

### 10.3.16 Pottery demonstrations for the locals

Whilst securing the interest of some distinguished collectors during his first few years, Leach had still failed to inspire the enthusiasm of more than a handful of the locals. Remembering how he himself had first been entranced by the potter's art, he decided that it would be a good idea to hold pottery demonstrations, so that the public could appreciate the skills involved and the difficulties that needed to be overcome. In 1924, he decided to hold these demonstrations in the week that included Show Day, so as to catch the crowds that came into town for that event. However, he had already learnt that few people were likely to make the long walk up The Stennack to visit the Pottery itself, and so he hired the Drill Hall. Michael Cardew was due to play an important role in these demonstrations, but, after the first day, he was diagnosed with pneumonia, resulting from the austere lifestyle that he had decided to follow, which included bathing solely in the cold waters of the Stennack river! Nevertheless, Leach demonstrated some of the basics of pottery making, including the use of slip, how pots were engraved and how raku-ware was decorated and fired, using a portable kiln.

The demonstrations were well received and, the following year, having arranged for the construction of a further small round kiln, about a yard in diameter inside and a yard in height, for low temperature ware, he set aside Thursday afternoons at the Pottery for demonstrations to the public. However, in these sessions, visitors were encouraged to have a go themselves. Plain biscuit-ware was available to purchase, and they could then decorate it, and see it glazed and fired whilst they waited. Margery Horne could still recall, in 1981, the excitement of such afternoons. "We all used to go there and there were all these pots, already thrown,...and then all the paints labelled because, of course, they're quite a different colour when you paint them on, and then we would all do our different designs and feel awfully thrilled about them." [647]  An added attraction were excellent shilling teas, put on by Leach's wife, Muriel. Leach, however, was not certain whether the afternoons had really been a success. "Year by year people returned, doing their dreadful decor on our pots, from which they certainly gained pleasure, but we doubted whether our dwindling finances or reputation were much helped." [648]

---

647 Text of Interview between Dr Roger Slack and Margery Horne 1/7/1981 (St Ives Trust Archive Study Centre).
648 Bernard Leach, *Beyond East and West*, London, 1978 at p.142.

Attracting more visitors to the Pottery was one thing, but cultivating their taste was rather more difficult. Many visitors considered Leach's pots uninspiring. They wanted bright colours - blue, nasturtium orange or bright apple green - and symmetrical designs. Any slight deficiency in texture or form was not passed off as a natural incident of the potter's art, but was branded an imperfection, which certainly militated against the payment of a premium price. Leach admitted, "It was years before we could get people to appreciate the quiet innate kind of colours of the raw materials themselves and of nature in its quieter moods - a certain amount of freckle of iron in the clay or the tinge of grey-green in a celadon." [649]

### 10.3.17  Further exhibition in Japan

In 1925, Leach had a further exhibition in Japan - this time at the newly refurbished Ku-Kyo-do Gallery on Ginza - , which was again successful. However, Yanagi indicated that he felt that the stoneware was "too black and grey in tone for the present psychology of Tokyo people after a disaster" - a friend's polite way of saying that it was a little dull. On the other hand, he enthused again about the yellow galena-ware and said that the Japanese found this most appealing, for its "pure Western quality...suited for the psychology of modern Japanese who live in Western buildings, manners and styles". It was, he said, "born-pottery, not made-pottery", a comment that Leach said had struck home, but his production of slipware tailed off.[650] Unfortunately, despite commissions on sales again being waived, movements in the exchange rate led to Leach only receiving £136 from the show.

### 10.3.18  Norah Braden

Dorothy Kathleen Norah Braden (1901-2001) was the third student taken on at the pottery. Born in Margate, she had studied between 1919 and 1921 at the Central School of Arts and Crafts. She had then moved to the Royal College of Art, and Leach had received a letter from Sir William Rothenstein, saying, "I am sending you a genius". In addition to working as an unpaid assistant, she assumed the duties of Secretary, after Edgar Skinner's death in 1925, and so ordered materials and arranged such matters as the carriage and packing of pots for exhibitions. Attractive and vivacious, with piercing blue eyes, Leach recalled, "Norah was perhaps the most sensitive of all the students who have spent time at the Pottery. She drew beautifully, she played the fiddle and had the sharpest eye for any falsity in art or character I have ever known." [651] That eye did not ignore Leach himself, whose general air of fogyism she satirised mercilessly and whom she accused of being sentimental about both his Japanese friends and English slipware. Despite this, Leach was enthralled by her critical understanding of his work and was totally smitten by her. For once, though, his amorous advances were rebuffed.

Fig. 10.36 On the steps of 'Coleshill House' 1929 (Private Collection). From the left
standing : Bernard Leach, Yanagi Soetsu, Shoji Hamada
sitting : Henry Bergen, Katharine Pleydell-Bouverie, Michael Cardew,
Katharine's mother and Nora Braden

---

649 Bernard Leach, *Hamada Potter*, Tokyo and New York, 1975 at p.122.
650 Letter from Yanagi to Leach dated 2/11/1925.
651 Bernard Leach, *Beyond East and West*, London, 1978 at p.155.

Cardew also came to like Norah Braden immensely, although he described her as "in build, appearance, and even in character,...more like a guinea-hen than any other creature".[652] She also turned her critical eye on his big, fat pitchers, with long necks, with which he was rather pleased. "They are like proud, strutting peacocks. Why do you have to make such proud peacocks?"[653] Cardew, who played the clarinet, and Braden shared an interest in classical music, and he recalled one occasion, when they played Mozart sonatas with Will Lloyd, now living in Zennor, but a stalwart of the St Ives music scene for many years. Lloyd, in fact, became an avid collector of Cardew pots.

Braden also proved a good saleswoman and it was a great loss, when she decided to join Katharine Pleydell-Bouverie at 'Coleshill House' in 1928, playing an integral role in her study of ash glazes. She acquired a good reputation as a potter, before turning to teaching in 1936. She remained lifelong friends with Leach and her fellow students.

### 10.3.19    Leach's efforts to form a creative community

Leach believed that pottery was not just an art form but also a way of life. As Cardew explained, he felt that "Every touch by the potter is *physiognomic* - that is, it is an infallible guide to his real character, to the state of his mind (or his soul)".[654] Still fighting "the curse of Dualism", Leach believed that the inner life directed the outer life, and felt that his inner being would be improved if he were able to encourage other like-minded craftspeople to settle in the town, in the hope of reproducing to some degree the ambience and communal spirit that had impressed him at Ditchling. As it was, he felt that the pottery, and all it stood for, was somewhat isolated.[655] Accordingly, he attempted to set up in St Ives a Craft Guild, which was to operate from 'Skidden House' on Skidden Hill and was to be open only to professionals. A number of weavers, who had been pupils of Ethel Mairet in Ditchling, were invited to consider the proposal. Leo and Eileen Baker, who later set up in that other well-known craft centre of the period, Chipping Campden, and Luned Jacobs, the second daughter of the author, William Wymark Jacobs (1863-1943), and an equally attractive female companion, were amongst those who came down to stay with Leach to explore the idea further. Michael Cardew was smitten at first sight by Luned Jacobs, who, with her bobbed dark hair, he considered looked like a grave and serenely beautiful fifteenth-century page. On hearing that she had already gone back to Ditchling, and having no money, Cardew found a free but uncomfortable passage on a boat from Newlyn. Luckily, Luned was charmed by his pursuit of her. She had had many admirers, including an adolescent Evelyn Waugh, who did not appreciate being dropped by her, whilst her sister, Barbara, who was also artistically inclined, had married Waugh's brother, Alec, only to discover that he was a homosexual.[656] Cardew indicated that Jacobs himself did not pay much attention to his daughters' bohemian activities, and Luned introduced him amongst others to Ethel Mairet and the writer and printer, Hilary Pepler. On his return to St Ives after a week, she followed him down and lodged with Leach at 'The Count House'. She continued with her weaving, and Cardew recalled gathering crottal (lichens) from rocks on walks to Zennor for use in dyeing her yarns. However, at the crucial moment when Muriel Leach felt that, in the light of their lengthy sojourns together, convention dictated that they should get engaged, Luned announced, after a visit from her formidable feminist mother, Eleanor, that she was going to marry Kenneth Hamilton-Jenkin, a stalwart of the Old Cornwall Society, with a particular interest in Cornish mining, who was not only handsome and settled, but wealthy. Whilst there are references to her weaving activities thereafter (see Chapter 10.4.2), there is no record of her linking up with Leach. Furthermore, as an ardent feminist herself, she became very involved, along with the Arnold-Forsters and Gussie Lindner, in the League of Nations Union, of which she was joint Secretary.[657]

The heartbreak caused by this broken relationship led Cardew to review his position in St Ives, as it was hard to see Luned and Hamilton-Jenkin frequently around town. He had become frustrated at Leach's concentration on stoneware, which he considered was not only difficult to make because of the high temperature required but also difficult to sell, as it was perceived to be unattractive in colour and too expensive. Slipware, his own passion, he felt had been relegated to a side-show in St Ives, and he realised that there was neither space nor equipment there for serious slipware production.[658] An

---

652 Michael Cardew, *A Pioneer Potter*, London, 1988 at p.53.

653 ibid, at p.54.

654 ibid, at p.30.

655 ibid, at p.46.

656 See John D. Cloy, *Pensive Jester - The Literary Career of W.W.Jacobs*, London, 1996.

657 Her mother, Eleanor, who had been imprisoned for her activities as a suffragette, came to live in St Ives in the 1930s, after separating from her father. Residing in a small flat overlooking the harbour, she continued to espouse social causes, but was often ill and died from an overdose of tablets in 1945. See John D. Cloy, *Pensive Jester - The Literary Career of W.W.Jacobs*, London, 1996.

658 Michael Cardew, *A Pioneer Potter*, London, 1988 at p.52.

unexpected legacy of £300 from an aunt proved the catalyst for a change, and he decided to leave in 1926 in order to revive the pottery at Greet, near Winchcombe, where he made a significant reputation, which ultimately closely equated to that of his master.

Despite failing to get the Craft Guild concept off the drawing board, Leach, perhaps buoyed by better sales figures, decided in September 1927 to build a significant extension to the Pottery, which he called the 'Pottery Cottage', so as provide further much needed space for himself and his students.  This merely precipitated a further financial crisis, but when it was eventually completed in April 1928, Leach wrote in the local paper about the showroom, which was the principal feature of the development; "It is furnished with textiles, furniture, metal-work, book-binding etc of a few contemporary craftmakers, with the object of showing how far a group can express a new artistic unity, and, at the same time, remain closely connected with tradition." [659]  The work on show was all by exhibitors at the Mairets' New Handworkers' Gallery, which had just opened, and the rationale was to demonstrate how Leach's pots fitted in with the best of contemporary design.  At the time, Leach was also influenced by Philip Mairet's attempt, promoted by the weekly magazine, *New Age*, to set up, following the General Strike, a 'Circle of Reformers', rekindled from "Distributionists, Labourists, Craft Idealists, Ruralists and Credit Reformers".[660]  This all kindled Leach's desire to foster a craft community in St Ives. However, it does not appear as if the inclusion of other craftwork was a great success.  Sales were certainly insufficient to tempt exhibitors to move to the colony, and the New Handworkers' Gallery itself closed in 1931, after just three years.

Fig. 10.37  The Leach Pottery tableware range launched December 1928
(*The Studio*)

---

[659] *St Ives Times*, 4/1928.
[660] *New Age*, 21/4/1927.

### 10.3.20 Changes in approach

As general critical and financial success continued to elude him, Leach was forced, reluctantly, to re-think his underlying approach and philosophy. In *A Potter's Outlook*, which was published in 1928, as part of a series of pamphlets issued by the New Handworkers' Gallery, Leach recalled wistfully, "In Tokio, I made shapes and patterns with the same enthusiasm as I spent on drawings and etchings, without thinking very much at first about utility and price. The pots were bought by people who looked, and were accustomed to looking, for the same essential qualities in handicraft as in so called pure art. By degrees, I paid more attention to use, but it was only when I returned to England that I found, as in so many ways, an opposite tendency, a valuation as a matter of course of the utilities first and the spirit second. It was impossible to continue here in so 'idealistic' a condition as to make just what I liked with only kiln and saggars as my limit." [661] Later, he called into question the value of any of the 'art pots' that he had created in the early years, and took a swipe at the collectors that had bought them. "Working by hand to please ourselves as artists first, and therefore producing only limited and expensive pieces, we have been supported by collectors, purists, cranks, or "arty people", rather than by the normal man or woman...we have tended ourselves to become abnormal, and consequently most of our pots have been still-born: they have not had the breath of reality in them: it has been a game." [662]

Furthermore, Leach indicated in *A Potter's Outlook* that one of his greatest erstwhile enemies, the machine, might, in fact, have a role to play. This was a complete *volte face*, for it was only in the spring of 1926 that Cardew and he had criticised the views of the furniture maker, Gordon Russell, that machines could be used sensitively. Perhaps Leach had seen the role of machines at Crysède that had recently moved to St Ives, or had been persuaded by Tomimoto's decision to become mechanised. In any event, Leach now proclaimed, "The machine is an extension of the tool; the tool of the hand; the hand of the brain; and it is only the *unfaithful* use of machinery which we can attack." [663] Leach, though, never really overcame his dislike of machines, and it was some years before the Pottery became more mechanised.

Influenced by the philosophy that Yanagi and Hamada were now propounding with regard to the fledgling Mingei movement, "that plain things made for the use of humble people had more *mana* or power than articles of luxury", Leach's new approach focused on utility.[664] Accordingly, he sought to produce "sound hand-made studio pots sufficiently inexpensive for people of moderate means to take in to daily use".[665] By then, Leach had already launched in March 1927 at the Three Shields Gallery at 8 Holland Street in London a new more regular range of tableware in earthenware, which could be sold relatively cheaply and which could be made by the ever-increasing numbers of students, who were applying to gain experience in the Pottery. In December 1928, he had a further show of 'utility pieces' at the New Handworkers' Gallery, which he publicised extensively in *The Studio* and *Pottery and Glassware* with a photograph of the tableware, in use at breakfast time (Fig. 10.37). As Emmanuel Cooper has stated, "With its mood of tasteful and discerning living, the photograph could easily have been taken forty or fifty years later. The rounded friendly forms with comfortable handles still look fresh, uncluttered, practical and inviting." [666]

At much the same time, Leach began to start producing tiles with hand-painted brush decoration. Subjects included flowers, birds and animals in stylised form, kilns, well-heads and landscape in a combination of western and oriental themes. During firing, the brushwork softened and married pleasingly with the cream or grey glaze used. Cheap and simple to produce, functional but allowing rein to Leach's pictorial vision as an artist, these proved to be another good line, and an illustrated brochure was produced showing a tiled fireplace. Fittingly, one was installed in 'Tremorna' by Mrs A.R. Trevithick, Dorothea Sharp's sister, whose husband had purchased the property from Frances Horne for £3,750. Two panels of tiles, one forming a view of a well head and mountains, a favourite theme, and one featuring a range of individual subjects, were bought by Eric Milner-White and are now owned by York City Art Gallery (Figs. 10.38 and 10.39). In *A Potter's Work*, Leach wrote of the landscape scene that "the design is imaginary but derived from things seen and felt in the mountains of Japan, although the various elements had, to me a long-term significance of a pictorial kind."

---

661 Bernard Leach, *A Potter's Outlook*, London, 1928.
662 Quoted by Tanya Harrod in *Bernard Leach and Shoji Hamada - Journey to St Ives, England : Kinship Beyond East and West*, exhibition catalogue 2003.
663 Bernard Leach, *A Potter's Outlook*, London, 1928 at p.29.
664 Michael Cardew, *A Pioneer Potter*, London, 1988 at p.30.
665 Bernard Leach, *A Potter's Outlook*, London, 1928 at p.29.
666 Emmanuel Cooper, *Bernard Leach - Life and Work*, London and New Haven, 2003, at p.170-1.

Fig. 10.38  Bernard Leach     Panel of tiles - *Well Head and Mountains*  (68.5 cms)
(Milner-White collection - York Museums Trust - York Art Gallery)

Fig. 10.39  Bernard Leach     Panel of small tiles (84 cms)
(Milner-White collection - York Museums Trust - York Art Gallery)

Leach images © Leach Pottery/Craft Study Centre, University for the Creative Arts

Without a seasoned production thrower after Cardew's departure, Leach also started to use hump moulding, a low-tech method used widely in the slipware traditions of the Midlands, North Wales and Northern England. Whilst he still continued to produce a number of 'art pots', such as the famous *Leaping Salmon* (Fig. 10.40), he tended to exhibit these separately, and to mixed reviews. However much potential his new ranges had, the Wall Street crash of 1929 devastated the world-wide economy and Leach was not alone in finding the following years very difficult. Luckily, Leonard and Dorothy Elmhirst at Dartington came to his rescue, but the long-term plan during the 1930s, when Leach was teaching at Dartington, was for the complete transfer of production to there from St Ives. Accordingly, as the decade ended, the future of the St Ives Pottery was in considerable doubt.

### 10.3.21  Leach and his fellow artists

Due to his later involvement with the St Ives modernists, Leach is often presented as having had an uneasy relationship, during his initial years in St Ives, with other members of the art colony. This seems, in part, to be based on the preconceived notion that an 'original' artist, such as Leach, with a good intellect, cannot have had much in common with the second-rate reactionary representational artists that, in the view of modernist historians, were the sole other colonists at the time. A more realistic assessment suggests that, whereas Leach clearly did make a number of friends in the colony and took part in various aspects of its social life, a number of difficulties were caused by aspects of his personality.

Just before Leach's arrival, a Literary Society was formed in St Ives, with Edgar Skinner being elected its first President. Unsurprisingly, Leach soon became a member and his influence can immediately be seen by the choice of Walt Whitman and William Blake as subjects for discussion. Leach himself gave the talk on Blake, no doubt mentioning the impact that he had had on Yanagi and his other Japanese friends, whilst, in March 1926, he spoke on *The Influence of European Literature in Japan*. The local paper reported, "It is not possible here to do justice to the way in which Mr Leach took his hearers from the life and thought of the West and led them into another world of ideas of a different attitude towards life and its meaning." [667]

Leach also joined the Arts Club shortly after his arrival, gave a Tea Talk on Oriental Art and took part in performances from time to time. For instance, in December 1926, both his wife and himself had leading roles, along with George Bradshaw and Stewart Darmady, in a mystery play, *Father Noah*. His deep friendship with Robert Morton Nance, which has already been discussed, led him to join the Old Cornwall Society, and he acted in their performances as well (see Fig. 10.35).

Leach also appears to have become friends with Greville Matheson, who was the greatest literary buff in the town, for he designed a roof-ridge tile, with a figure on horseback, for the roof of his new library at 'Boskerris Vean'. Matheson certainly praised Leach's initiative of holding pottery demonstrations to educate the locals. Cardew mentions another friend as being Will Arnold-Forster, who lived at Eagle's Nest and who was still practising irregularly as an artist. However, it was likely to be his political views, which will have interested Leach, for Arnold-Forster was a fervent socialist, standing as St Ives' first Labour Party candidate in 1928. Indeed, Leach is noted as the Chairman of the Grand Labour Party Rally in 1929.

The above suggests that Leach mixed fairly well with many of the intellectual members of the community. The Visitors' Book of the Pottery also reveals that many other artists, particularly females, enjoyed the pot-making afternoons that he organised. Starting in 1924, the year when the Thursday sessions commenced, the first few pages of the Visitors' Book record the presence, for instance, of Georgina Bainsmith, Pauline Hewitt, Mary Williams, Annie Falkner, Kathleen Bradshaw, Ellen Fradgley, Lucy Bodilly, Dossie Cooke, Averil Mackenzie-Grieve, Alice Drey, Shearer Armstrong, the widow of William Fortescue and the wife of Francis Roskruge. Ernest Morton Nance, the visiting American artist, Herbert Faulkner, the Darmadys, the Mathesons and Charles Pugh are also signed in.[668]

Whilst this clearly demonstrates a good deal of interest in Leach's project, it would not be surprising, however, if some other members of the colony found Leach himself a trial. Leach liked an audience and enjoyed pontificating at length on art, philosophy, religion and life in general, always keen to cultivate an aura of intellectual exoticism. Staite Murray was probably not the only one to find his constant "theorising on Pots and Art...a little tiresome".[669] Even his students felt that Leach was "still to a great extent living in a dreamworld of his pre-1914 coterie of Japanese artists" and that this was "an unavoidable patch of

---

667 *St Ives Times*, 5/3/1926.
668 The Visitors Book is held at the Craft Study Centre, Farnham (ref: 2047). Frances Horne makes certain that she is the first entry, albeit, by that juncture, she had had to give up funding the Pottery.
669 Malcolm Haslam, *William Staite Murray*, Crafts Council, 1984, at p.25.

absurdity in Bernard's make-up".[670] His constant references to the way of life in Japan, which sought "to establish a combination of the various arts to culminate in a complete artistic unity", must have begun to grate after a while.[671] In the discussions leading up to the formation of the St Ives Society of Artists, Leach stressed the need for a "common faith". This was really at odds with all that St Ives art had stood for in the past. Individuality was what was prized, not adherence to some common creed. There had been no 'St Ives School'. A sense of common purpose was certainly required, but not a common faith. It is hard not to conclude that a number of locals, particularly those whose outlook on life had been transformed by their wartime experiences, must have considered him, with some reason, to be a self-opinionated dreamer, whose views were rather 'alternative', and removed from reality.

Leach will have been desperately disappointed at the decision taken by the new Society that there was no place in its exhibitions for the decorative arts. This marked a change in stance, as Leach had exhibited twenty-eight pots and two etchings at the most prestigious exhibition that the St Ives artists had put on that decade - in Cheltenham in 1925. However, Leach had only included in the exhibition one 'art pot' - a Toft-inspired galena dish similar to the 'Tree of Life' one that had been bought by the Victoria and Albert Museum the previous year. All the other pots - jugs, jars, bowls and vases - had been priced at £1-10s or less, other than a greystone pilgrim bottle at £2-10s. Whereas Staite Murray, who was invited by Ben Nicholson to join the Seven & Five Society in 1927, consistently promoted his pottery as high art, gave his pots artistic names and agreed with Herbert Read that pottery was "plastic art in its most abstract form", Leach vacillated between 'art pots' and utilitarian ware.[672] The Society also needed to have regard to the fact that Leach was not the only craftsperson in town. If they offered space in their exhibitions to Leach, would there not be an outcry from all the other practitioners of the decorative arts in the colony? Admittedly, the change in stance might have been the result of a resurgence of the general prejudice against craftwork that tended to be prevalent in Fine Art Societies, but, in my opinion, it could also have been prompted, in the difficult economic conditions of the time, by a desire not to distract prospective purchasers of paintings by having lower priced craft-work for sale. Certainly, this was one reason why the Society decided to move its exhibitions away from Lanham's Galleries, where all sorts of craft-work was on display. Clearly, this decision will have had some impact on Leach's decision in 1927 to build a showroom for himself at the Pottery.

Fig. 10.40

Bernard Leach

Stoneware Vase -
*Leaping Salmon* (32.7 cms high)

(York Museums Trust - York Art Gallery)

---

670 Michael Cardew, *A Pioneer Potter*, Oxford 1988 at p.53-4.
671 *St Ives Times*, 5/3/1926.
672 See Tanya Harrod, *The Crafts in Britain in the Twentieth Century*, Yale, 1999 at p.33-4.

There must also be a distinct possibility that most artists in the town did not sympathise with Leach's sparse, colourless aesthetic. As already indicated, the overriding interest amongst the artists in the colony at the time was the use of heightened colour to gain a greater emotional response. Leach's approach, which would later become more acceptable when minimalism came to the fore, was out of step with his colleagues.

One artist with whom Leach enjoyed a deep friendship was Reginald Turvey, his original student chum, who had originally worked in the colony in 1904. Having sold his farm on the south coast of Natal, Turvey arrived in St Ives in 1925 with his new bride, Frances Waddell Gunn, who was twenty-two years his junior and the younger sister of a married woman, with whom Turvey had been having an affair. She was nicknamed 'Topsy' and, immediately on her arrival, was rushed to hospital with appendicitis. They took Alison Studio initially, before building a house and studio, 'Wheal Speed', in Carbis Bay opposite the Leaches, which Leach helped to design. As in South Africa, Turvey did not have great success with his art, although he was elected to the St Ives Society of Artists. The local paper commented, "He has a style of his own, and if his draughtsmanship at times leaves something to be desired from an Academic point of view, he has the right colour sense and his brushwork is 'slick'." [673] Turvey proved to be a fervent disciple of Leach, following his ideas without question, and they planned in his home a small white room for meditation - "a sanctuary of the spirit wherein the pursuits of truth and beauty meet".[674] The Turveys even moved to Dartington to be close to Leach when he took a post there in 1932. This makes Leach's fling with 'Topsy' particularly reprehensible. Leach, however, proved himself to be a serial philanderer, and this may well have been the character trait that was frowned upon most in St Ives society.

### 10.3.22 Eloquent visionary versus shambolic businessman

With considerable assistance from Yanagi and his other Japanese friends, from Leonard and Dorothy Elmhirst at Dartington, and from Harry Davis and Leach's son, David, in St Ives, the Leach Pottery somehow stumbled on during the 1930s, enabling Bernard to refine his ideas, which he expounded eloquently in *A Potter's Book*, published in 1940. With its promise of a spiritually fulfilling way of life, this became the 'bible' of studio potters, leading Michael Cardew to reflect, in his memoirs, that "the landing of Bernard Leach and Shoji Hamada on the island of Britain in 1920 was for craftsmen potters the most significant event of the twentieth century", due to the power and influence of the ideas that Leach imparted.[675] However, what would have been the verdict on his career if he had died in 1930, the end of the period covered by this book?

This account of the first decade of the Leach Pottery has drawn to a significant degree on memoirs of the principal protagonists written many decades later, when all had acquired significant reputations. At that distance in time, it was easy to look back through rose-tinted spectacles, forgetting many of the mistakes made and the travails endured, whilst casting a humorous light on those recorded. All were able to gain further kudos by recording close associations with people who had become leading figures in the pottery world.[676] In truth, all were entitled to wear a badge, which read "Leach Pottery - I survived the shambles of the 1920s". The accounts of the pottery reveal the truly appalling state of its finances. In the first four years, it lost £2,534. Income of a mere £29 in 1921 rose to a peak of £1,030 in 1927, but then fell back in 1929 to just £383. Average sales in the years 1925-1930 were just £262. The 1920s were a difficult time, but these figures demonstrate limited success and incompetent management.

Leach's first, and principal, mistake was to commit himself to establishing a pottery in a specific location, whilst still in Japan. Financial considerations were clearly the reason for him doing this, as he was returning to an uncertain future with a pregnant wife and three children. Accordingly, Frances Horne's offer proved irresistible. However, Leach had been away from England for eleven years, during which time there had been a devastating, and financially debilitating, conflict that had changed lives and lifestyles for ever. Therefore, he had no real feel for the state of English society, or of the contemporary art market. Furthermore, Leach had left England as an etcher, rather than a potter, and so had no past, let alone present, knowledge of the market for ceramics in this country or of his potential rivals. He also knew very little about indigenous pottery at all. What, in hindsight, Leach should have done was to

---

673 *St Ives Times*, 2/12/1932.

674 Letter from Leach to Yanagi, 16/1/1926.

675 Michael Cardew, *A Pioneer Potter*, London, 1988 at p.29. The fact that William Staite Murray was caught in Rhodesia at the commencement of the Second World War and decided to stay there for the rest of his life, never making another pot, left the field open for Leach to become the sage for the next generation of potters.

676 By way of example, Katharine Pleydell-Bouverie recounted that "the team at St Ives" during her time included Hamada, and this is duly trotted out by dealers/galleries that hold her work. However, she only joined the Pottery permanently in January 1924 after Hamada had left the previous month. Accordingly, she would only have experienced working with Hamada, if at all, during her two week trial period.

# THE DAWN OF THE CRAFT TRADITION IN THE COLONY

Fig. 10.41  Bernard Leach  Yellow glazed earthenware Vase
(19 cms high)
Acquired in 1924 by Leach's father-in-law, W. Hoyle,
for National Museum of Wales, Cardiff

stay with or close to his father-in-law in Cardiff for a few months, which he could easily have afforded, having made a profit of £1,000 from his last Japan exhibition, and used this time to do some research, so as to form a reasoned judgement on the state of the market, what he wanted to do and where he wanted to do it.  Instead, he found himself committed to St Ives, which was totally unsuitable not only because of its lack of clay and fuel, but also because it lacked a decorative arts tradition.  It was also much too far away from any metropolitan centre, but particularly from London.  Many of the travails encountered during the first decade resulted from this initial blunder and, although there were several occasions when Leach could have 'cut and run', albeit with a loss of both face and finance, he chose, obstinately, to flounder on.

Due to Yanagi's entrepreneurial talents and his championship of both men, Leach and Hamada shared many international platforms and remained life-long friends, but Hamada's principal education in St Ives was how NOT to do it.  He realised immediately that the most important factor in setting up a pottery was the availability of local materials.  Accordingly, one should choose one's preferred clay first, and site one's pottery nearby.  He also came to appreciate that local requirements dictated appropriate forms, with utility and function key considerations, whilst the use of local materials gave work an unique local character, as well as ensuring 'truth to nature'.  Accordingly, he was not convinced at all by Leach's overriding philosophy of a meeting between East and West.  In his view, pots with Eastern designs sat uncomfortably in Western households, and his own solid, utilitarian ware reflected his own detailed research into Japanese folk-ware and showed very little trace of his Western experience.

The second major decision that Leach took was to utilise a Sino-Japanese climbing kiln.  This again was taken before he had set foot in England and had any knowledge of the manner in which indigenous pots were normally fired.  However, it was a central plank of his East meets West philosophy, and its uniqueness in the Western world and its exotic flavour have certainly proved a useful marketing tool.  The decision to build it himself, with Hamada's help, and to use home-made bricks, when neither had any expertise in these fields at all, was foolhardy and proved a costly mistake, which set the venture back several years.  If Janet Leach is correct, he then chose the wrong type of climbing kiln when Matsubayashi came over to build a new one.  Furthermore, whilst the separate chambers of such kilns allowed pieces to be fired at different temperatures at the same time, the process required great skill, obtained through experience, neither of which Leach had.  Consequently, losses from over-firing or under-firing merely added to the percentage of losses incurred as a result of all the other problems.  Even in the 1930s, such losses were occurring, with Dicon Nance being particularly scathing about the way in which Leach would ruin pots because, in his eagerness, he would open the kiln too soon.[677]

---

677 From a 1991 interview - see Tanya Harrod, *The Crafts in Britain in the Twentieth Century*, Yale, 1999 at p.167, note 184.

Fig. 10.42 Bernard Leach Stoneware Pot (6 cms high) in grey body covered in matt grey glaze with brushwork decoration in brown and blue. Acquired by Sidney Greenslade from the Red Rose Guild Exhibition, Manchester 1925 (Aberystwyth University Ceramic Collection)

Another unfortunate decision, largely as a consequence of Leach's desire to use a climbing kiln, was the siting of the pottery at the top of a steep hill on the very outskirts of town. It is not known what other options were available, and clearly the planners may not have been happy with a kiln in the town centre, but the pottery's location did not encourage casual tourists to visit it, a serious problem that the newly refurbished building still faces.

Leach also demonstrated that he was no businessman. Hamada admitted that, in the beginning, there was not "any overall organisation in the pottery, we did what we were enthusiastic about", whilst Leach rarely put in an appearance before mid-day.[678] Edgar Skinner soon picked up on this, and ensured some form of proper housekeeping whilst he was Secretary, but his death in 1925 resulted in matters deteriorating so that Cardew complained that there were often insufficient materials with which to work. The clay-making arrangements he found were "chaotic and always inadequate for our needs".[679] As Matsubayashi intimated, Leach was "poetical". He loved an audience and to talk about art and philosophy, which was good for his students but not for his business. Even his friend and patron Henry Bergen realised that Leach was blind to economic realities and, amidst a series of put downs made whilst he strove to introduce some semblance of financial feasibility into *A Potter's Book*, commented "No-one can take you seriously as *producers*".[680] For someone in the 1920s still to be railing against the machine, and unable to appreciate how it might be used to advantage, seems old-fashioned and quaint, rather than at the forefront of modernism. However, it was Harry Davis, who later laid bare the true reason why both Leach and Cardew hated machines. "I realised that this was because their ignorance of them was total. Coming from middle-class backgrounds, tools for them were alien things and machines something worse." [681]

What one cannot take away from Leach, however, is his eloquence, which was combined with a good intellect and an interest in philosophical matters. No-one had had such a grounding in the ways of the East as he, and so his expositions on Eastern art and philosophy were found interesting and unable to be challenged. However, whilst he proved stimulating to successive intakes of students, the lack of a clear strategy from the outset meant that he was constantly having to adjust his stated objectives, which did not help his reputation amongst dealers and collectors. Was his pottery 'art pottery' or utilitarian ware, and how did one classify functional objects that reflected his unique interpretation of East meets West? To begin with, Leach aimed at the 'art pottery' market, but the austerity of many of his pots failed to ignite the interest of collectors who were experiencing the excitement of Art Deco, with its strong colours and geometrical forms. Whilst Leach may have been interpreting Oriental art in a far more refined way than earlier copyists, the wave of interest in all things Oriental had ebbed away, whilst there was always the danger, foreseen by Hamada, that any such combination of East and West would merely prove a poor or rather odd relation of the originals. Leach's subsequent concentration on home-ware later in the decade merely cast doubt on the artistic value of his earlier work. Such variations in strategy were often forced upon him by his lack of success in St Ives, but, rather than consider a move from St Ives, he changed his approach. By contrast, Staite Murray never wavered in his objective of producing high quality, high priced 'art pots' for the wealthy connoisseur and, as a result, had no doubt that he needed to be in London. In the end, supported by others, Leach found his niche and made a significant and lasting impact, but the first decade of the Pottery was financially disastrous and a difficult learning experience. Nevertheless, Hamada, Cardew, Pleydell-Bouverie and other students all emerged from the shambles enriched in one way or another and were able to forge successful careers, forever friends with and in debt to their somewhat idiosyncratic Master.

---

678 Bernard Leach, *Hamada Potter*, Tokyo and New York, 1975 at p.118.
679 Michael Cardew, *A Pioneer Potter*, London, 1988 at p.35.
680 Letter from Bergen to Leach dated 3/9/1937.
681 Harry Davis, *Handcraft Pottery - Whence and Whither*, Ceramic Review, 93, May-June 1985 at p.12.

## 10.4 Other handicraft makers in the colony

The ultimate success of the Leach Pottery, and Leach's dismissive attitude to other handicraft makers in the colony, has led to their very existence being overlooked, and yet a number of these artists were sufficiently well-regarded to hold London exhibitions of their craft work. The range of work produced in the colony was very wide. In addition to the hand-loom weaving of Florence Welch, Irene Turner and Luned Hamilton-Jenkin, there was the art embroidery of Doris Barry, Ruth Davenport and Lucy and Vera Bodilly, the painted lampshades of Kathleen Bradshaw, the raffia hats of Marcella Smith and the painted models of Marjorie Ballance. Ruth Davenport also produced jewellery and leather work, whilst Pauline Hewitt, Nell Cuneo, Peggy Park and Annie Bryant also exhibited handicraft items from time to time.[682]

All these other handicraft makers were females, reflecting a whole range of different trends. There were more females deciding to become art students, and more women artists thinking that the crafts offered the possibility of greater artistic equality, given that painting and sculpture remained male dominated. Handicraft also offered a broader range of artistic practice in a period where the division between fine and decorative art was far less than previously. In times of economic hardship, it was easier to sell lower cost utility items than paintings, which many had to consider a luxury. The demographic effect of the War's huge death toll also meant that the percentage of females amongst both the consumers and the makers was higher than it had ever been. Accordingly, many of the handicraft works were not only made by women, but also directed at the female market.

With surviving examples of such works rare, it is very difficult to assess the underlying influences upon them, the extent of any novel approach and the quality of their finish and design. All that remains are a few reviews, which at least give some idea of the work produced and the favourable reception that it received locally. It is also noticeable how craftwork, during the 1920s, was included in exhibitions of paintings more readily than before or since. So, for example, the Newlyn exhibition of 1924 included leather work, repoussé copper, raffia, beaten silver and pottery.

### 10.4.1 The Art Needlework of Doris Barry and Lucy and Vera Bodilly

Doris Barry was the wife of Claude Francis Barry, whom she had met at Bournemouth Art College in 1900. They had got engaged in 1903, but despite her family, the Hume-Sprys, being descended from the Duke of Rutland, the match was not approved by Barry's father and stepmother, firstly as Doris did not have any money, and secondly, because Barry's mental state was still cause for concern. In the five years that they had to wait before Barry broke free from his stepmother's grasp, the cause of his problems, they had each broken the engagement a number of times, but the relationship had somehow endured. The marriage, though, was never particularly steady, for Barry was a serial philanderer, later declaring that an artist should never marry: "He must be completely free to give all his time and energy to his painting; art is a jealous and possessive mistress and demands...everything the artist has to give."[683]

Immediately after their marriage in December 1908, they settled in St Ives and Doris's portrait was painted by both Louis Sargent and Mabel Douglas. After spending the early years of the War near Barry's family home at Windsor, they settled back in St Ives in 1917. Doris, by this juncture, had acquired a fine reputation for her art needlework, where she embroidered landscapes and seascapes in delicate silks on the finest of linen, and she had exhibitions of her work, alongside her husband, at St Leonard's Studio, Porthmeor Square in both September 1918 and August 1919. However, her needlework may well have been overpowered by her husband's first pointillist searchlight paintings. Her art was seen to better advantage, when, in February 1919, she held a joint exhibition at the Upton Slip Studio in Falmouth, with another needlework artist, Lucy Bodilly, about whom little is known, except that she was the wife of Arthur Bodilly, who lived at 'Rosemorran', St Ives. The show was then mounted in St Ives in April. The critic of the *Western Daily Mercury* was most impressed, saying that all and sundry had congratulated the ladies on "their brilliant work". Unusually, he has given us titles and a brief description of some of the principal exhibits, albeit not indicating authorship:-

---

682 In July 1923, Cuneo and Hewitt held an exhibition of "unique handicraft" at Cuneo's home, 'Downalong House'. They held a further one in December 1925, aiming for the Christmas market. In April 1927, Peggy Park held a 'Special Easter Show of Local Arts and Crafts' in the Bay Studio, The Harbour, whilst, in February 1928, Annie Bryant, an irregular visitor, who was wife of the Rector of Clyst St Lawrence, Devon, showed at the Bay Hotel "some hand-embroidered crepe-de-chine shawls and bridge coats".
683 Quoted in Katie Campbell, *Moon Behind Clouds - An Introduction to the life and work of Sir Claude Francis Barry*, St Helier, 1999, at p.23.

"The exhibition is really a revival of the old needlework art, and the wonderful colour effect in most of the pictures is striking and realistic. A set of four pictures depicting spring, summer, autumn and winter are remarkably realistic and decorative designs. Included in the large and beautiful collection are *In the wake of the moon*, a brilliant colour effect; *The Italian Garden*, a scheme of reds, turning from deep Indian to delicate pinks, and set off by deep olive greens; *Evening Glow*, a most attractive design in low tones; *Cornish mine shafts*, which should find a place in the home of mining men, *Golden Glory*, *Afterglow* and *The Sentinels*, three splendid specimens of needlework art; *The Mill*, extremely decorative; *In the Garden*, luminous in colour and realistic; *Tanned Sail*, showing St Ives fishing boats on a breezy day in full sail; *Varenna, Lake Como*, a pretty and fascinating bit of work; *Fishing Boats*, showing them up on moonlit waters and a calm sea; *Moonbeams*, a futuristic design; *The Cottage Door*, a typical specimen of the Cornish cottage of bye-gone days, with its thatched roof and beautiful display of flowers near the front door; *An Eastern Street*, one brilliant mass of colour; *August*, a noteworthy and picturesque picture; *Yellow Roses*, the height of perfection in the art of needlework; *A Quiet Evening*, a bold and strong design and remarkably effective; *Venetian fishing boats*, showing sail of wonderful design; and many others." [684]

What is particularly striking about this list is not only the variety, but also how the subjects are far more akin to those chosen by painters than by standard needlework artists. Brilliancy of colour coupled with fascinating designs suggest some interesting, innovative work.

Unlike other handicraft makers, Doris Barry's needlework pictures invariably get a mention in reviews of Show Day. Indeed, in 1920, the *Daily Chronicle* highlighted her work as being novel and attractive and often delightfully picturesque, and mentioned that two examples, *Cornish Mine Shafts* and *Reflections*, were on show at the Society of Women Artists' exhibition in Suffolk Street.[685]

In 1921, Barry finally deserted his family, and Doris moved to 126 Lexham Gardens in Kensington. She appears to have changed tack, as, in both September 1921 and September 1923, she came back down to St Ives to hold exhibitions at the Tregenna Hill Studio "of her inexpensive Paris and London Autumn Models", which included "jumpers, frocks, coats etc".[686] There is very little information about her subsequent life, but she was stated to be living in New York, when she was signed into the Arts Club by Cecil Magnus in November 1926.

Fig. 10.43 Doris Barry　　　　　　　　　　　(David Capps)

---

684 Reproduced in St Ives Times, 14/2/1919. See also *St Ives Times*, 25/4/1919.
685 Reproduced in *St Ives Times*, 5/3/1920.
686 *St Ives Times*, 30/9/1921 & 7/9/1923.

Fig. 10.44 The Malakoff Studios (Herbert Lanyon)

After Doris Barry's departure, Lucy Bodilly continued to show her work both in St Ives and at the specialist craft shows held in Newlyn. She also began to hold exhibitions jointly with her daughter, Vera, who had become a student member of the Arts Club in 1913. During the War, Vera worked as a War Hospital nurse.[687] She exhibited at Lanham's in 1920 and then went on to train at St John's Wood under Walenn, winning a scholarship to the Royal Academy Schools in 1922. In 1925, her portrait of her mother was hung at the Paris Salon. However, in addition to her painting, Vera also enjoyed her mother's speciality, art needlework. In August 1925, they held a joint show of their art needlework at the Malakoff Studio, which so impressed Borlase Smart that he wrote an extemely laudatory review - one of the only detailed accounts of such an exhibition, which is worth reproducing in full, as Smart not only lists the range of objects produced, but also passes comment on the originality and artistic quality of the designs.

"It is a delight to visit the Malakoff Studio just now, where Mrs and Miss Bodilly are holding a most artistic exhibition of art needlework. It speaks volumes for what we may describe as the pioneering quality of originality, which is the keynote of the display. The amount of thought (should we say research) that these two have put into the designing of each piece, the originality of conception and the very high quality of workmanship raises such an exhibition to a standard hitherto unapproached in St Ives....

The firescreen designs arrest the eye with splendour of colour and contrasting styles of expression. One of a fiery dragon against a black background forms a rich note of dramatic vigour in design and spacing. The dragon is picked out in gold wire, over-sewn occasionally with scarlet thread, giving a rich subtlety of vivid tone. The other motif is a bold flat treatment of a peacock but totally unlike the usual conception of the conventionalised peacock which one knows so well by heart. The treatment of massed effect in luscious flat colour planes of material cleverly embroidered, is almost a revelation in originality.

Then there are some new ideas in raffia bags with naturalistic treatment of flowers and landscape in this delightful medium. One receptacle is especially worthy of note and shows an effect of a lily pond, dragon fly and reeds and has all the quality of a painting. Colour gems of rich wool embroidery are provided by designs for purses. Table runners by reason of their flat display provide original ideas in design, and the material used. One in particular has a rich poppy scheme, relieved by the coarseness of a material resembling silky hessing. A couple of ladies' jumpers in charming colour schemes are worthy of attention, especially a grey one with floral border to neck opening and sleeves. The broken edge of the design formed by the floral shapes is a happy inspiration. The simplicity of the little golden straw work-basket, with its quaint grape design made of cut wood, leaves and button moulds for the grapes are most alluring in originality.

To those who prefer fine detail similar to church embroidery, the small silk bag with its volute design in fine gold thread will appeal. This intricate pattern provides a contrasting note to the more simplified forms of the larger patterned parts. There are several scarves, providing splashes of glittering colour with such motifs as love birds, and with an Egyptian decoration, cleverly worked in

---

687 Her scrapbook, which contained not only photos of her war work but also paintings by Edmund Fuller and Herbert Babbage, was sold at auction in 2006.

pure colour. One of the cleverest schemes is a beach bag, trimmed with opalescent shells, and the embroidered patterns of decoration being symbolical of the sea-shore, in fish and seaweed forms. Then there are those delightful needlework pictures, with which we are already familiar, but here are some new schemes on view in which the blending of half tones in silk is nothing short of marvellous. One dainty picture of spring-time has all the quality of light and tone of a real painting. Some artistic necklaces and something new in sunshade decoration completes a rough review of just a few of the fine things to be seen in this exhibition."[688]

It is interesting that Smart, in his role of art scribe in the colony, should have been inspired to write such a complimentary article on this branch of handicraft, whilst on no occasion being moved to pass comment on the output of the Leach Pottery.

Vera Bodilly married Charles Connington Oxland at Illogan on 30th July 1927 and both her and her mother joined the St Ives Society of Artists, exhibiting paintings until the mid-1930s. Surprisingly, however, there is no other reference to their art needlework.

### 10.4.2 The hand-loom weaving of Florence Welch, Irene Turner and Luned Hamilton-Jenkin

Upon Frances Horne's sale of 'Hazelbury House', the headquarters of the St Ives Handicraft Guild, Florence Welch set up on her own and, certainly from 1930, was operating from premises on The Wharf (see Fig. 10.45). Whilst she appears to have kept on display Leach pots for sale, Leach felt that she was not working in a true, authentic manner, by her use, for instance, of Indian machine made cotton, and so discounted her presence, when trying to attract other hand-loom weavers to the colony. However, she clearly found herself a niche market, with both locals and tourists, as, thirty years later, Denys Val Baker recorded that she was still thriving in business. Indeed, she had been able to train a number of young Cornish girls to help her, so that she had three looms operating in her workshop. Her range of products included scarves, cushion covers, aprons, skirts, stoles, wraps, ties, table-cloths and mats, whilst some indication of the type of designs that she offered can be seen in Fig. 10.45.[689] Although she may not have satisfied Leach's idealistic vision of craftwork, she was able to run for many decades a successful business, without financial support from wealthy patrons and without machines, whilst at the same time training up a number of local girls in this ancient craft. Accordingly, she deserves a considerable amount of credit, given how few craft operations were able to operate economically during this period.

Fig. 10.45 The interior of Florence Welch's weaving shop on The Wharf
(estate Denys Val Baker/St Ives Trust Archive Study Centre)
Note the Leach pottery on top of the dresser

---

688 *St Ives Times*, 7/8/1925.
689 Denys Val Baker, *Britain's Art Colony by the Sea*, (originally 1959), 2000 edition at p.91-3.

Irene Turner, who was also involved in the weaving activities of the St Ives Handicraft Guild, also continued working after the collapse of the Guild. In November 1923, she advertised dressmaking classes and her work was included in the Newlyn exhibitions of 1924 and 1927.

Albeit Bernard Leach's attempts to entice to St Ives a hand-loom weaver trained in the practices advocated by Ethel Mairet did succeed, after a fashion, by virtue of Luned Jacobs settling in the colony after her marriage to Kenneth Hamilton-Jenkin, Luned's treatment of Michael Cardew, which resulted in Leach's best student leaving the Pottery, seems to have militated against any form of partnership between Leach and herself, albeit that she did set up a hand-loom weaving shop on the Harbour and continued to follow Mairet principles. When she contributed to the 1927 exhibition in Newlyn, a reviewer passed comment on her hand-woven clothes. "In her Harbour weaving-room may be seen fleeces as they come straight from the sheep of the Pyrenees or the Shetland Isles; also silk spun on the spindles of native women of Assam. Lichen from Cornish rocks and wild mignonette from the Towans are used in the dyeing processes." [690] Luned was one of the group of students and apprentices at Ethel Mairet's that K.R.Drummond classified as "gentlewomen under no particular pressure to earn a living", and her marriage had rendered her under even less pressure.[691] Authenticity of this scale came at a price that did not invite longevity.

### 10.4.3 The craftwork of Ruth Davenport

Ruth Davenport appears to have settled in St Ives in 1917, having trained at South Kensington and having worked previously in Oxford Street.[692] She both lived and worked in 6 Piazza Studios. She held an exhibition of art needlework, designed and executed by herself, at Lanham's Galleries in February 1919 and shortly afterwards placed an advert in the local paper, indicating that she took students and inviting commissions. Exhibits on subsequent Show Days also included hand-beaten pewter and copper work and jewellery. Despite developing a reputation for being difficult amongst her fellow artists, she seems to have continued to attract students throughout the 1920s and 1930s. One, a Miss Northwood, even came from Canada to study under her.

Davenport's one close friend was Helen Knapping, a wealthy artist whose father had run a successful brickworks at South Shoebury, Essex, and who had rented a studio in the town from 1897. In December 1927, they held a joint exhibition at 6 Piazza Studios, which included needlework pictures, pewter works, gloves, jewellery and many other items, as well as some studies of flowers and plants painted by Ruth Davenport in Tresco Gardens.[693] Shortly, thereafter, adverts started appearing in the local paper for the 'St Ives Handicraft Studio', which was said to be situated at both Back Road West and 6 Piazza Studios. Although Knapping's studio was really in Porthmeor Road, rather than Back Road West, it is difficult to think of Davenport having any other partner in this venture. Items for sale, in addition to oil and watercolour paintings, included needlework pictures, designs, pewter work, hand-woven goods, lacquer-work and raffia goods, and the advertisements continued for several years.

After Knapping's death in 1935, Davenport seems to have taken an additional studio in the Piazza Studios block (No 7) for her students and held another exhibition there of work by herself and her students in March 1936. The work of Miss Cobbold Sawle of St Austell was highlighted as being particularly clever. By this juncture, Davenport was driving her fellow tenants to distraction with her anti-social behaviour, and she was eventually evicted from the studios in 1939.[694]

### 10.4.4 The millinery of Marcella Smith

Having moved to live with Dorothea Sharp at 22 Blomefield Road in London in the early 1920s, Marcella Smith turned her attention to millinery. Explaining her decision, she commented, "People are so fond of chasing about for week-ends and living at restaurants that they have no time to think of making their homes beautiful. They all have heads and they all must wear hats." [695] She had two exhibitions of her raffia and hand-painted hats at Lanham's Gallery in 1924 and 1925, and an article in *The Illustrated Country Review* in 1925 indicates that her 'Marcella Hats' had acquired a considerable reputation amongst the social elite. The article commences by outlining the fashion of the day and by highlighting the attractions of raffia. "A hat which completes the style and colour scheme of the dress is now considered the acme of fashion. It is not always possible for a hat to be made of the same material. In

---

690 *St Ives Times*, 22/7/1927.
691 Margot Coutts, *A Weaver's Life, - Ethel Mairet 1872-1952*, Crafts Study Centre, 1983 at p.60.
692 See her advert for commissions and students in *St Ives Times*, 28/3/1919.
693 *St Ives Times*, 23/12/1927.
694 See David Tovey, *St Ives (1860-1930) - The Artists and the Community - A Social History*, Tewkesbury, 2009 at pp.161-4.
695 *The Daily Graphic*, reproduced in *St Ives Times* 14/11/1924.

such a case, the wearer has to choose a straw, raffia, silk or some other medium which harmonises with the fabric of which the dress is made. Raffia is one of the most adaptable materials for hat construction. It is a kind of dried grass, not unlike straw, but pliable and strong. It has been increasingly used in recent years in the millinery trade, and has been popularised by the variety of shades and artistic models it adapts itself to." [696]

Smith produced a wide variety of hats made in raffia and was renowned for her artistic designs and attention to detail. Some of these were hand-painted and many had silk trimmings, which were also hand-painted. She did not confine herself to raffia, however, and specifically designed hats for well-known social events, such as Ascot and Henley Regatta. The article commented, "Some of the Ascot models, which have already appeared, are transparent models of lace tulle and net. A pretty beige lace and net hat may be seen with the lace design delicately picked out in gold." She also specialized in mourning hats "in a variety of materials and fashionable shapes", which gave "a dainty and smart appearance to the wearer".[697] In the late 1920s, however, Smith returned to painting.

### 10.4.5 The painted lampshades of Kathleen Bradshaw

As noted above, Kathleen Bradshaw (née Slatter) came to St Ives to study under Charles Simpson and, in addition to her figure and still life painting, enjoyed some success with her lampshades, which she designed and painted herself. These were first mentioned on Show Day in 1925 and she recalled some embarrassment about her early efforts, as she discovered that the glue she used came unstuck as the lamp heated up. Accordingly, she resorted to stitching them. However, she went on to hold an exhibition of them in the De Vere Hotel, London in November 1928 and enjoyed some commercial success, supplying Heal's in London. She was particularly thrilled by a sale to an Indian Princess. The subjects that she painted on the lampshades varied enormously - some were inspired by medieval motifs, some featured ships and the sea or rather beatific whales, whilst others featured flowers. She was also prepared to incorporate more modern designs as well. They made good wedding presents, and she gave one to Martin Cock's son, Gerald, on his marriage in 1928. She was still producing these lampshades in 1944, as she gave one to H.M.S. Farnham Castle, when she was asked to launch the vessel.

Fig. 10.46 Kathleen Bradshaw and her mother with a selection of her lampshades in 'Ship Studio'

### 10.4.6 The painted tableaux of Marjorie Ballance

Marjorie Heudebourck Ballance (1898-1969) was the sister of Percy Ballance and shared his Piazza Studio. She had trained at the Slade, but had an especial interest in medieval textiles. Her paintings, therefore, tended to be primarily decorative arrangements, in which clothing and textiles of the past featured prominently. Accordingly, her one success at the Royal Academy in 1922, *Merchants*, was an interior scene set in the fifteenth century, showing a lady selecting fabrics. Later in the decade, she turned to making painted wooden models, which she ordered into tableaux, like figures on a stage.

In November 1927, she had a show at Gieves Art Gallery in London, which featured decorative watercolours, bookplates and some of her tableaux. One of these, *Joust - 15th Century*, included knights on horseback and crowds of gaily coloured spectators. Very original were other little groups designed for menu-holders.[698] Whilst continuing to produce painted models throughout the 1930s, Ballance found her metier as a designer of theatre sets not only for the Arts Club and the Minack Theatre at Porthcurno, but also for various Birmingham repertoire companies and Midlands schools. Exhibitions of her designs of costumes and settings for the stage were held in Downing's Bookshop, St Ives, in 1948 and 1949.[699]

---

696 Reproduced in *St Ives Times*, 24/7/1925.
697 ibid.
698 See *Two Artists from St Ives*, *St Ives Times*, 18/11/1927.
699 For more on an extraordinary life, which involved a considerable amount of social and community work, see her obituary in *St Ives Times and Echo* 7/3/1969 and David Tovey, *Creating A Splash - The St Ives Society of Artists (1925-1952)*, Tewkesbury 2003-4 at p.196.

## 10.5 The heyday of Crysède hand block-printed textiles

### 10.5.1 "The most complete independent achievement of our time"

In 1926, the fledgling hand block-printed textile business, Crysède, established by Alec Walker in Newlyn in 1920, was, at the instigation of Martin Cock, the owner of Lanham's, transferred across to St Ives, where a new factory was built over old fish cellars on the Island. Freshly converted into a limited company, with large numbers of local shareholders, the business, under its new managing director, Tom Heron, enjoyed a brief period of considerable renown on both national and international stages, with Walker's novel designs winning considerable acclaim in artistic circles. Indeed, Paul Nash was moved to comment, in 1926, when Walker was intimately involved not only in the design of the textiles but also in all aspects of the printing process, "I think this is the most complete independent achievement of our time." [700]

The printing of textiles by the application by hand of carved wooden blocks coated in dye enjoyed a brief period in the limelight in the couple of decades after 1915. It was a laborious process and considerable skill was involved in adapting patterns so as to be able to be printed by such method and in cutting the blocks. Once transfer printing was mastered, it soon fell out of fashion. The artist normally considered the pioneer of the hand block-printing movement was Phyllis Barron (1890-1964) who, having studied painting at the Slade School in 1911, embarked, in an essentialist spirit, on in-depth research into textile printing, dye stuffs and dye fixing. She cut her first block in 1915, held her first textile exhibition in 1917 and set up a small workshop at much the same time as Walker. Whilst she only used natural dyes during the 1920s, whilst Walker used synthetic ones, she did not produce her own fabric to print upon. In her designs, she tended towards geometrical patterns, whilst Dorothy Larcher (1882-1952), who joined her in 1923 and was her companion and partner for life, favoured flower motifs. However, albeit very successful and highly regarded, the designs of both women, whilst intricate and refined, now look rather tame in comparison with the vibrant, multi-coloured patterns produced by Walker, who was able to recreate on textiles the feel of a modernist painting. Accordingly, not only did he include local landmarks, naively but decoratively treated, but infused the designs with marks imitating brush strokes.

Fig. 10.47 Kay Earle and Alec Walker at the time of their engagement (Polly Walker)

---

700 Paul Nash, *Modern English Textiles*, Artwork, Vol 2, No 6, Jan-Mar 1926 at p.80.

## 10.5.2 Alec Walker and the establishment of Cryséde in Newlyn

Alec George Walker (1889-1964) was born at Mirfield, Yorkshire, and was the youngest of five children of the textile manufacturer, John Henry Walker and his wife, Emily (née Sykes), whose father had been a plush manufacturer and one time mayor of Huddersfield. His family, in fact, had been involved in industry in the West Riding since 1785 and, after his education at Epsom College, Alec joined the family firm. He later recalled, "In my early days I was always at work at 6.00 a.m. and went through every phase of mill life, thereby gaining a complete knowledge of textures, dyeing, the use of colour, weaving and so forth. Eventually I had charge of the mill and was responsible for the 'Vigil' silk, well known in the North." [701] Walker had taken over his own mill in 1912, at the age of just twenty-three, his father having recognised his ability. It was also in this year that he first visited Newlyn. Having advertised for a poster designer for the new 'Vigil Silk', one of the applicants, Kathleen Earle, who had been a student at the Forbes School, was so effusive about life in the colony that, the very same day, he travelled with her from London, where they had met, to Newlyn, so that he could see for himself. Welcomed by the artists, who encouraged his own artistic inclinations, he immediately felt at home, and, over the next few years, he returned, as and when he could, bringing parcels of velvets and silks for the female artists to make up into fashionable clothes. Seeing these against the background of grey and white cottages and the way that they contrasted with the dark clothes of the locals, gave him the idea of setting up a silk factory in Newlyn.

After the War, having married Kay Earle in 1918, Walker found that his own views as to how to tackle the slump, namely by keeping in direct contact with the public and controlling every aspect of the operation, did not accord with those of his father.[702] Accordingly, he decided to branch out on his own and to set up in Newlyn a small experimental factory producing textiles with more artistic designs. "My principle was to carry modern feeling, as expressed in modern design, into the fabrics themselves." [703] Having purchased, for their home, 'Myrtle Cottage', where many female art students had previously lodged, Walker acquired a neighbouring row of derelict fishermen's cottages, which he converted into a small works. Plant and machinery were brought down from Yorkshire, and local labour was trained. The name of Cryséde, inspired not from France, as everyone thought, but from Chaucer, was adopted in 1920.[704] To begin with, silk was sent down from the family business in the North, ready processed, and was printed with much the same designs of spots, checks and stripes as he had used before. However, Walker indicated, "The desire to get modern art - so alive and full of vitality - on to the fabrics soon became my one thought." [705] Accordingly, in 1923, he went to Paris to check out the latest French designs, meeting the sculptor Ossip Zadkine, who had been introduced to him by Ernest Procter, and, through him, Raoul Dufy, who had founded the Petit Usine for fabric printing. Soon realising that paying for designs made by the leading French artists would be prohibitively expensive, Walker, with encouragement from Dufy, decided to study hard so as to be able to make his own. His major influences, apart from William Morris, were Cezanne, Van Gogh and Gauguin. In an incredibly short period of time, Walker not only made considerable progress with his painting skills, but managed to transform motifs from his paintings into attractive textile designs. As Hazel Berriman commented, "Years of practical experience in handling textiles enabled him to visualise the repeated motifs, to adapt his designs to the scale required for dress or furnishing fabrics and to choose colour combinations which would be commercially successful, without compromising his artistic intentions." [706]

## 10.5 3 The Independent Gallery exhibition of 1925

In September 1925, Walker held an exhibition of his dresses, shawls and dress lengths at the Independent Gallery in Grafton Street, London, better known for its shows devoted to the works of Augustus John or the Post-Impressionists. There were twenty-four different designs.[707] Some were based on Cornish landscapes, such as 'St Buryan', 'Zennor' and 'Cornish Farm'; there was also a series inspired by

---

701 *St Ives Times*, 6/11/1925.

702 See *St Ives Times*, 21/5/1926.

703 *St Ives Times*, 6/11/1925.

704 Cryséde was felt by many to be a foreign name with a French flavour, but Walker confirmed that it was an adaptation of Chaucer's Criseyde in the tale of Troilus and Criseyde, best known from the the Shakespeare play, Troilus and Cressida. The latter, which had received little exposure previously, being seen as one of Shakespeare's 'problem plays', became very popular after the First World War, due to its cynical depiction of immorality and disillusionment during wartime. Walker felt that the name signified the "originality and distinctiveness", which he considered his attributes. See *St Ives Times* 21/5/1926.

705 *St Ives Times*, 6/11/1925.

706 Hazel Berriman, *Cryséde - the unique textile designs of Alec Walker*, Truro, 1993 at p.19.

707 The full list is Russian Ballet, Eden, St Buryan, Zennor, Storm, Yucca, Knitters, Passion Flower, Tennis, Jungle, Flowers of Lelant, Canterbury Bells, Dancer, Primitive, Grotesque, Lobster Supper, Flower, Entreacte, Cornish Farm, Gaiety, Pastoral, Dancing Flower, Flying Fishes and Matter.

the Ballet Russes, so popular at the time, such as 'Dancer', 'Pastoral', 'Entreacte' and 'Russian Ballet'. The critic of the *Manchester Guardian* was particularly taken with 'Pastoral' (Fig. 10.50). "Possibly the most modern and effective is 'Pastoral'. This is a design worked out on a Russian Ballet subject, with groups of full-skirted ballet dancers conventionalised into collections of fountains." [708] Another series was inspired by the interest of the Post-Impressionsists in the primitive and the exotic, and Walker confirmed that the design, 'Primitive', was based on a drawing by Gauguin, commenting, "In it out of the hands of his model, I produced the stigmata."[709] There was also a series depicting the more conventional subject of flowers, such as 'Flowers of Lelant', 'Canterbury Bells' and 'Dancing Flower', but, again, Walker's designs were innovative. Avoiding botanical correctness, he nevertheless captured the character of flower types, and would often concentrate on a single flower. In some of his designs, Walker's "puckish sense of humour" shone through, as forms were made deliberately ambiguous, so that, for example, flowers looked like dancers, and vice versa.

Fig. 10.48   Alec Walker/Cryséde   *Gaiety* design (Royal Cornwall Museum, Truro)

The show caused a sensation. Not only were the novel and colourful designs felt to reflect "an important current of taste and feeling in European Art", and to rival the work of any of the French designers who dominated the industry, but the enterprise was seen to match artistic flair with commercial practicality, something which most craft operations of the time lacked.[710] It had solved the much-debated problem of bringing "fine art into everyday life" on a commercial basis.[711] Furthermore, the critics were quick to emphasize that everything used in the manufacture of the material was English, with the silk even being spun in England. "There need be no fear of German competition if all designers and craftsmen were as well equipped as Mr Alec Walker", trumpeted one critic, whilst another said, "Paris had better look to her self. She has held the field for so long for exclusive printed dress silks, and now she has to face a real English challenge." [712]

### 10.5.4  The appointment of Tom Heron

The success of the Independent Gallery exhibition, coupled with Walker's inclusion in the British Institute of Industrial Art Exhibition at the Victoria and Albert Museum that year, cemented his reputation, and the business, which had already established a number of branch shops and a mail order operation, took off. The extent of his success not only took Walker by surprise, but was unwelcome. In an interview in November 1925, he passed the comment that he did not intend to make a commercial proposition of his work, preferring to continue with his researches and experiments. In short, he was much more interested in the design aspects than the management ones. Accordingly, he sent an S.O.S. to an old friend, Thomas Milner Heron (1890-1983), saying, "If you don't take Cryséde off my back, I will sell it or give it away or close it down." [713]

---

708 *Manchester Guardian*, 12/9/1925.

709 *St Ives Times*, 6/11/1925.

710 Sir Michael Sadler, in the Foreword to the exhibition catalogue.

711 *Daily Chronicle*, 10/9/1925.

712 Quoted in *St Ives Times* 21/5/1926.

713 John Pearl-Binns & Giles Heron, *Rebel and Sage - A Biography of Tom Heron (1890-1983)*, Bishop Auckland, 2001 at p.41.

Born in Bradford, Tom Heron was the son of Edmund Heron, a manufacturers agent and stuff merchant and, having worked in the family trade for a while, he set up, in 1913, a blouse making business, T.M.Heron Company, with his uncle Joshua Milner, which bought silk off the Walker family and went on to employ two hundred people. However, Heron's proposal, in the early 1920s, as sales dwindled, that the Company should cut out the middle man and open their own shops, had been rejected by his uncle, leading to Heron being bought out. He had then set up the Company of English Merchants, a retailing venture that incorporated the principles of the National Guilds League, of which he was a member, but, as this was losing money, he was grateful for the chance to work with Walker, whom he had known from the age of sixteen. Although not an artist himself, Heron had been a member from 1911 to 1924 of the radical Leeds Arts Club, whose founder was Alfred Orage, at a time when it was led by Michael Sadler, Vice Chancellor of Leeds University and an avid collector of Post-Impressionist paintings, and the art critic, Frank Rutter, then Curator of Leeds Art Gallery, both of whom had a significant interest in the avant-garde and proved strong supporters of Walker's enterprise. Heron had also frequently attended Orage's soirées at the Café Royal in London. Accordingly, not only was he in tune with Walker's art, but he came from a substantially similar background, had considerable management experience of running a factory, and shared Walker's views on quality as a pre-requisite and the need for direct outlets. He was perfect for the job.

### 10.5.5 The transfer to the Island Factory, St Ives

Heron was in no doubt that the business needed to expand and that it needed better, bigger premises and more capital. When efforts to obtain larger premises in the Penzance area fell through, the firm was considering a move to Dorset, until Martin Cock, of James Lanham Limited, appalled at the idea of the area losing such a business at a time of high unemployment, suggested that the old Western Pilchard cellar at the base of the Island, in St Ives, which had lain empty for some twenty years, would make a suitable site.[714] Accordingly, in December 1925, Cryséde took a fourteen year lease of the property, which covered more than an acre of ground and comprised a quadrangular building, with a large central courtyard, of two storeys - the ground floor having been used for the fish presses and brine tanks, and the first floor for storing net and gear. It appears that Walker and Heron, with their intimate knowledge of factory layouts, drew up the plans for the conversion themselves, and employed local men to do the work, with W.Batten as foreman. J.H.Daniel and Son carried out the plumbing and J.Slade, of the Maritime Recovery Company, supplied and installed the boilers and engines. With all parties working most efficiently, the premises were largely completed by the end of March 1926, and equipment could then be transferred across from Newlyn. A local reporter, 'Lanyon Cromlech', described the internal layout, "Although the exterior wall seems low, the ground dips, so that one enters really on the top floor and comes at once to the offices, the stockrooms, thence to the mail-order department, the packing room, the machine knitting, sewing and cutting departments, the hand-printing benches, chemist's laboratory, Mr Walker's room, etc, and back to the front entrance, the whole being in one unbroken run." [715] On the ground floor, which was reached by a set of steps, the dyeing and finishing of the silk was carried out, some of the old pilchard tanks being adapted for the purpose. Space was set aside for installing silk weaving plant, should this be decided upon later. The central court afforded a fine open-air drying ground, where the sun and sea air would provide a good means of testing the permanence of the colours. Excellent facilities, including a canteen, were provided for the use of the staff. The old fish cellar had, accordingly, been turned into a model factory, with new roof lights and windows all round the sides of the courtyard, central heating, and with electricity for lighting and power being provided by a generator on the premises. The contrast with the Leach Pottery could not be more stark.

In order not to lose the workers that had been trained up in Newlyn, the firm bought a Lancia charabanc to bring them to and from work. In between, in order to pay for itself, the vehicle provided a daily public service between St Ives and Penzance, whilst, dovetailed ingeniously into that timetable, it ran afternoon trips, principally for tourists, from St Ives to Gurnard's Head. Norman Gilbert, who had been Walker's first trainee in Newlyn, had acquired such skill as a printer that he became head of that department on the move to St Ives.

### 10.5.6 The formation of Cryséde Limited

The factory was formally opened on Whit Tuesday in the middle of May. At much the same time, a limited company, Cryséde Limited, was formed and, in June 1926, a prospectus was published offering shares in the company. In addition to Walker and Heron, the directors were John Williams Horton Bolitho J.P., a businessman from Falmouth, and Alfred Whitaker, a Chartered Accountant from Penzance. The initial issued share capital was 12,300 ordinary shares of £1 and 25,000 7.5% cumulative preference shares

---

714 See *St Ives Times* 28/3/1926.
715 *St Ives Times* 28/3/1926.

of £1. The ordinary shares were not available to the general public, 6,500 having been allotted to Walker as consideration for the business, and the balance having been taken up by the initial subscribers to the company. The prospectus revealed that profits in the year to 31st October 1924 had been £1,203, but had risen dramatically to £7,020 in the sixteen months to 28th February 1926. The mail order business, which had only been set up in 1923 and had attracted 3,000 customers in its first year, was now run by Heron's brother-in-law and was expected shortly to have a following of 7,000. It was also envisaged that further direct selling outlets would be added to the nine already opened in Newlyn, Penzance and St Ives (1921), Paignton, Newquay and Falmouth (1924) and Bournemouth, Bath, and Launceston (1925).[716] Turnover, it was estimated, would increase to £100,000 per annum. With regular glowing reports in the local paper, a large number of residents in the town decided to make an investment. So too did many of the mail order customers, something perceived as a tremendous vote of confidence in the company.

### 10.5.7 Alec Walker's designs

Tom Heron, in his first report to shareholders in 1927, commented that the old business in Newlyn had "depended almost entirely on Mr Walker's personality". His own appointment and the move to St Ives now meant that Walker was "set free to design", and the company arranged for part of the old premises at Newlyn to be converted into a studio for him.[717]

Unfortunately, the precise influences on Walker as an artist are not known. Berriman speculates that, like Heron, he will have attended at Leeds Arts Club, whilst sketches done on Café Royal notepaper indicate that he may well also have attended Orage's soirées there, on the occasions that he visited his London shop. He seems to have had some connections with the Vorticists, with whom Rutter and Orage were closely involved, for he commissioned Edward McKnight Kauffer to produce innovative posters for 'Vigil Silk' in 1917, 1919 and 1921. Key figures in the Vorticist movement, Wyndham Lewis and Edward Wadsworth, were visitors to Walker's home in Newlyn, and he was involved in the attempt to re-launch Vorticism, under the name Group X, in 1920, taking the exhibition to Yorkshire. Berriman also believes that Walker will have known about the experimental work at Roger Fry's Omega Workshops, where attempts were made to remove the distinction between fine and decorative art by applying the Post-Impressionist use of rich colour and strong design to furniture, textiles and rugs.[718]

Figs. 10.49 and 10.50  Alec Walker/Cryséde
*Hound and Tree* and *Pastoral* designs
(Royal Cornwall Museum, Truro)

---

716 Berriman lists the branches in Bournemouth, Bath and Launceston as having opened in 1926, but then admits that all are recorded as in operation by February 1926. Given the moratorium on opening new branches that seems to have been put into place whilst the company was incurring the cost of the transfer of the business to St Ives, it seems much more likely that these three branches were established in 1925.
717 *St Ives Times*, 27/5/1927.
718 See Hazel Berriman, *Cryséde - the unique textile designs of Alec Walker*, Truro, 1993 at p.11-2.

Walker indicated that, in making his designs, his first principle objective had been "to secure freedom". He explained, "The old idea was to design in squares. Obviously, there is little freedom allowed in a design confined to the conventional limits. Convention, too, demanded a rose or a flower, or something of that sort. I say you can take the most simple things in everyday life as did the old masters, and turn it into one of the most beautiful things, merely through a sense of design." [719] However, the sort of simple things that Walker used in his designs were very novel. Indeed, the very first of his 'new' designs in 1923 had been inspired by the sight of a lobster supper laid out for him by his wife, Kay, to welcome him home from his meeting with Dufy in Paris. Friends invited round for the evening, such as Cedric Morris, Lett Haines, Gladys Hynes and Dod Procter, were a little bemused to have Walker shout at them as he came into the kitchen, "Wait, just wait and don't touch a bloody thing", whilst he went off to get his sketch book![720] He found inspiration in the most unusual places. As he admitted, "Most people would ridicule the idea of putting a race meeting on a design, yet this one, which I call 'St Buryan' was suggested to me by a small country sports in Cornwall."[721] Whilst his designs were very fluid and often appeared abstract, he commented, "In my designs I have always gone on something definite. It is only in such a way that you can get vitality." [722] Nevertheless, his designs tended "to express a mood rather than a fact".[723]

Fig. 10.51 Alec Walker/Cryséde
*Zennor* design
(Royal Cornwall Museum, Truro)

Unfortunately, an example of the 'St Buryan' design has not been located, but his 'Zennor' pattern comes from the same period, and this was specifically mentioned by Frank Rutter, when outlining Walker's working practices. "Alec Walker, who in his paintings displays his sympathy with modernist aims, is equally progressive in the creation of his designs. These are invariably based on his own paintings and for this very reason they have a unity and distinction which give them unique decorative value. Thus Mr Walker goes to Zennor (nr St Ives) and there paints a picture. The painting finished, he returns to his studio and ponders over its possibilities as a design. He conventionalises the forms therein, re-organises it into a rhythmical repeating pattern, and arbitrarily disposes the shapes and colours to suit his ends. And the result is the 'Zennor' design, quite different from the painting, though in the design also the leading motives such as the church, the winding road, the bridge, trees and houses, are clearly recognisable...Almost anybody can paint a landscape nowadays, but it requires an artist of uncommon gifts, real talent and fertility to produce a series of genuinely personal and distinguished designs." [724] Sadly, the painting from which the design was drawn has not been located.

It is a little surprising that Rutter, who paid a visit to Cornwall in the spring of 1927, should have singled out the 'Zennor' design for specific comment, as it is by no means the most successful of his early efforts, being too cluttered with motifs and limited in colour interest. After Heron's appointment, Walker, freed from management responsibility, was able to devote more time to his painting and designing, with the result that there was a marked improvement in quality. Indeed, Heron recorded that Rutter, during his visit, had no difficulty in picking out the later work, being more mature, more complex and bearing witness to Walkers' reflective nature.[725]

---

719 *St Ives Times*, 6/11/1925.

720 For the full account of this seminal moment, see Hazel Berriman, *Cryséde - the unique textile designs of Alec Walker*, Truro, 1993 at p.31-2.

721 ibid.

722 ibid.

723 See *Art in Industry*, *St Ives Times*, 15/12/1933.

724 *The Studio*, 1928 Vol. 96, p.278-9.

725 See report of Annual Meeting in 1927 *St Ives Times*, 27/5/1927.

Fig. 10.52  Alec Walker     *Ding Dong Mine*
(Polly Walker/ Royal Cornwall Museum, Truro

As Walker enjoyed painting local subjects, he continued to produce designs that incorporated local landmarks or aspects of the Cornish countryside. Naturally, these proved particularly popular in Cornwall, with many feeling that he had caught the spirit of the Duchy in a number of his designs - "the soft blue of the Cornish sky and sea in spring was blended with the brightness and gaiety of the summer flowers and the browns of late autumn foliage." [726]  In a number of cases, the original paintings upon which the designs were based have survived, so that a comparison can be made. It is fascinating to see how the quality of the painting as a work of art normally bears little resemblance to the magnificence of the design, and just what motifs and colours Walker lifts from the painting to incorporate into his pattern. For example, Walker's painting, *Ding Dong Mine*, is an undistinguished effort; the block-like shape of the mine is set in the middle of the picture against a plain sky, with the vegetation, on the side of the road leading to the building, very roughly depicted by green, yellow, cream and orange sweeps of the brush. In the textile design, however, the mine itself plays an insignificant part, albeit its shape is included several times. Instead, Walker has concentrated on transforming the green, yellow, cream and orange brushstrokes into a colourful and most effective abstract pattern.

Fig. 10.53  Alec Walker/Cryséde     *Ding Dong* design
(Royal Cornwall Museum, Truro)

---

726 Quoted in Cyril Noall, *St Ives Times and Echo*, 27/5/1983.

Fig. 10.54  Alec Walker    *Men working in the Violet Fields, Trembath*
(Penlee House Gallery & Museum, gift of Polly Walker
- photo - Royal Cornwall Museum, Truro)

Fig. 10.55  Alec Walker    *Trevaylor Woods* (formerly known as *Zennor Woods*)
(Bridget Walker - photo - Royal Cornwall Museum, Truro)

Fig. 10.56 Alec Walker/Cryséde
*Trembath* design
(Royal Cornwall Museum, Truro)

Another interesting comparison can be made between his painting *Men working in the violet fields at Trembath*, which is dated 1927, and his design 'Trembath'. Here, he has selected from the painting, as the principal motif in the design, the spiky tree forms, but he has decided to omit the men bending over in the fields and has turned the busy patch of violets in the foreground into a neat decorative pattern of rows of distinct flowers. The orange seen in the bare winter treescape has been used as a vivid contrast against the background green in the design. A masterful design has again been drawn from a fairly ordinary painting. However, another painting of the same year, *Trevaylor Woods*, (formerly called *Zennor Woods*) is far more successful. It again features spiky trees, but has tremendous atmosphere, with its brooding sky, and is immensely colourful, with the green of the vegetation, contrasting with the orange of the paths and the blue of the springtime flowers. It shows the clear influence of Van Gogh. Walker seems to have worked on a design using merely the tree shapes, but, on this occasion, it is less successful than the painting.

One of his most interesting designs from the late 1920s is 'Godrevy' (Fig. 10.66), a vast panorama of St Ives Bay, featuring a range of selected motifs. The lighthouse, on its curved mound, takes centre stage, with, somewhat surprisingly, Tregenna Castle Hotel and its adjoining woods immediately to its right. In this way, Walker connects the Hotel with the most recognisable landmark seen from it. With the Island on the left, boats and fish scurry across the waters of the Bay, with the fish often being bigger than the boats. A church, which I cannot place, also features prominently in the design. This assembly of motifs decoratively arranged makes one wonder whether Alfred Wallis might have been an influence. Full of curved shapes, the whole resulted in a delightful design. Walker, however, seemed to move away from such large scale patterns, as more complex dress designs came into fashion, which lent themselves better to smaller motifs.

### 10.5.8 Cryséde fabrics

Walker proclaimed that aesthetic design required aesthetic texture, and the principal fabrics used by Cryséde were a very heavy *Crêpe-de-Chine*, supplied by Walker's family firm, which was used for plain and printed dresses, a plain weave silk cloth, which was also very heavy, and silk georgette, a loose woven cloth with a 'crinkle'. The raw silk would arrive at the factory and have to be de-gummed, before it was then rinsed and dried, bleached with Hydrogen Peroxide and left 'natural' or dyed. All these processes were carried out at Cryséde by passing the cloth, in rope form, over a winch in a large wooden trough. In 1928, Tom Heron introduced, in addition, a very heavy linen cloth for beachwear.

Fig. 10.57 Hand block-printing at the Island Works, St Ives.
Norman Gilbert, head of the printing department, is in the foreground.
The printer's assistant, with the trolley, was known as the 'wiper'
(Royal Cornwall Museum, Truro)

The firm used a version of the 'discharge method', which Walker indicated that he had invented himself, which meant that, by the use of a bleaching agent in the printing process, the original hue of the material was removed, enabling the colours of his design to be seen to best advantage. Clearly, the dyes used in the design had to be impervious to the bleach.[727]

### 10.5.9 The hand block-printing process

The hand block-printing process used by Cryséde required considerable skill. Each wooden block varied in size, dependent on the pattern, but, for ease of handling, did not exceed 15" x 12". The bottom layer, which was carved for printing, was made of apple, cherry or sycamore. All but the parts to be printed were cut away, and fine lines and detail were made by driving brass strip or metal shapes into the recessed parts. One block was made for each colour in the design, and, accordingly, for practical purposes, the number of colours in a design did not exceed six, and was often kept to three or four. The size of the block imposed a maximum dimension for the 'repeat' in the design. Accordingly, a huge amount of time was spent working out how best to transfer Walker's designs on to blocks. In some, as many as thirty-nine different blocks were required to be made, each one a work of art in its own right.[728] For Walker, though, what made the hand block-printing process attractive was the depth that could be achieved, for the colour on the blocks was driven in to the material with a mallet. No machine could replicate this.[729]

Fig. 10.58 Keith Ross carving a printing block, watched by
Tom Heron (Royal Cornwall Museum, Truro)

---

[727] For further information on this section, please see *Appendix One - Technical Information - Fabrics and Printing* in Hazel Berriman, *Cryséde - the unique textile designs of Alec Walker*, Truro, 1993 at p.43-4.

[728] 39 blocks were required for the design 'Deer' - see *Art in Industry, St Ives Times*, 15/12/1933.

[729] For further information on this section, please see *Appendix One - Technical Information - Fabrics and Printing* in Hazel Berriman, *Cryséde - the unique textile designs of Alec Walker*, Truro, 1993 at p.43-4.

The dyes used by the firm were all synthetic, most coming from Britain, but some from Germany and Switzerland, but all were subjected to rigorous testing as to fastness to light and washing. A resident chemist, John Sherlock, was employed in this connection, and as, by 1933, the company's products were being distributed in such hot places as India and Egypt, fastness was of supreme importance. The company's reputation on this aspect was much prized.[730]

The colours that Walker used in his designs were often difficult to replicate and Tom Heron commented at the 1927 Annual Meeting, "It is not easy to follow the flight of an artist like Mr Walker and the demands he makes for colours. The dyeing and printing are the foundations of the business, and the work of reproduction of Mr Walker's designs have not been easy. We are now beginning to feel the benefit of the hard work which Mr Sherlock and his workers have put into it." [731]

The laborious process involved in converting Walker's designs into blocks for printing meant that the company fell behind in getting all his designs available. At the Annual Meeting in 1928, Heron commented, "The best thing that Cryséde has obtained this year has been the new series of designs which Mr Walker has provided. We have not been able to make the fullest use of the old designs yet. It is amazing the way in which his output of last year has been repeated this year; nothing will stop him from designing." However, Walker, seemingly happy to leave all management matters to Heron, had little else to do but paint and design. One can easily see, therefore, how some friction might have arisen as a result, for Walker will have been keen to see his latest designs in production as soon as possible, whilst Heron and his team were left with the task of working out repeat patterns, cutting blocks, choosing appropriate dyes etc. If, as had started to happen by 1929, they dared suggest that a design needed modification, Walker was not happy. Nevertheless, when members of the St Ives Society of Artists had a tour of the factory in 1933, it was recorded that Cryséde had on offer no fewer than three hundred and fifty different designs - an astonishing achievement, which backed up the company's claim in its literature that "we produce a larger variety in style and design than any other firm in the world".[732]

Figs.10.59 - 10.62
Alec Walker/Cryséde
Top right : *Cherry Tree*
Middle right : *Madron Carn*
Bottom right : *Sacred Pool*
Bottom left : *Birds of Paradise*
(Polly Walker/
Penlee House Gallery and Museum)

---

730 See *Art in Industry*, *St Ives Times*, 15/12/1933.
731 *St Ives Times*, 27/5/1927.
732 Quoted in Hazel Berriman, *Cryséde - the unique textile designs of Alec Walker*, Truro, 1993 at p.37. Only 74 of such designs are listed in Berriman's book, and examples of a number of these had not been located. In the Programme devised for STISA, the following designs, not listed by Berriman, are mentioned: Pleasure Grove, Daisy, Cornflowers, Drift Valley, Summer Showers, Seagull, Floral, Shadow.

Fig. 10.63 Cutting room at the Island Works c.1931
(Royal Cornwall Museum, Truro)

### 10.5.10    A wonderful place to work

The advent of Cryséde in St Ives was a complete novelty. Never before had the town been host to a modern factory. Whilst most will have realised that the job opportunities it offered were precious, there will have been some who were worried about the impact that such an industrial venture would have on the ambience of the old town, particularly as it was situated in such a prominent position at the back of Porthmeor Beach. No doubt many of the artists who had studios fronting the beach were a little concerned. Whilst a new tall chimney probably elicited some grumbles, great emphasis was placed in public announcements on the fact that the business would only use smokeless fuel. Otherwise, the design of the building did not cause offence, given that it replaced what was becoming an eyesore. Even the sound of the factory hooter was soon welcomed, as people were able to set their clocks to it. The discharge of dye into the sea might be frowned upon these days, but, for those with artistic eyes, it provided a fascinating sight, as the dye stayed in the waves for hours.

Any misgivings amongst the locals were soon forgotten as word went round that it was a great place to work. Indeed, Emily Woolcock, step-great-grand-daughter of Alfred Wallis, commented, "If you got in at Cryséde, you were 'it' ".[733] However, Heron found that, without any tradition in the locality of the discipline required for machine working, it was much harder teaching employees the requisite skills than it had been in the North, but he did notice that the girls had a better eye for colour. For girls leaving school, there were opportunities in the finishing section, where they learnt to finish seams and hems and make perfect button holes by hand. Others became machinists and a few became cutters, working alongside the men on special orders and stock lines for the shops. At every stage, the work was checked as quality was paramount.

Heron was greatly liked by the workforce. Emily Woolcock recalled, "He was a beautiful man, very upright, very dark beautiful beard, very erect. He always walked with his hands behind his back. He was a marvellous boss but a very strict boss. He would always stop and listen to you. The discipline in that place was marvellous. When Mr Heron used to walk from the office down through there, you could here a pin drop. We were allowed to sing but not to speak. So you can just imagine what hundreds and hundreds of machines were going like, and we singing....They were wonderful people to work for. It was really a happy place, very very happy and I remember the day I left, I broke my heart. We were never laid off. Never, never laid off. They always found something for us to do." [734]

Heron's attitude to staff relations was very different to other employers of the period, and was influenced by his strong socialist views, which had led him to join the Labour Party and the Fabian Society.[735] He believed in the vital nature of human fellowship, and the need for freedom in labour and joy in the performance of it. The world, he felt, should value beauty over riches. Walker shared these views, although he perhaps strayed rather more than Heron into the realms of idealism. Speaking at the

---

733 Extract from an interview with Roger Slack, quoted in John Pearl-Binns and Giles Heron, *Rebel and Sage : A Biography of Tom Heron 1890-1983*, Bishop Auckland, 2001 at p.42.

734 Extracts from an interview with Roger Slack, quoted in John Pearl-Binns and Giles Heron, *Rebel and Sage : A Biography of Tom Heron 1890-1983*, Bishop Auckland, 2001 at p.42.

735 Heron became great friends with Will and Ka Arnold-Forster and supported Will's election campaign in 1928 as the first Labour candidate to stand in St Ives. For five months during the winter of 1927-8, the Arnold-Forsters allowed the Herons to live in their home, 'Eagle's Nest', near Zennor - Patrick Heron's first experience of the property that was to be his home for many years.

1929 Annual Meeting, he commented, "The aim of Cryséde is not power but beauty. Growing and developing in a beautiful county, we are using our brains and energy to give every worker high or low a decent standard of comfort and reasonable hours of work. The industrial workers of England and the world are being and have been made ugly by overwork, too long hours and work in degrading and ugly surroundings. Ugliness creates more ugliness, just as beauty creates more beauty and it is the firm policy of Cryséde to allow nothing ugly to be made in her works. We are going to prove to the world that beauty and ideals, far from being an impractical proposition, are today the only practical and paying proposition and the only policy leading to happiness and a decent standard of living." [736]

The result of this enlightened approach to the workforce was that they developed an immense sense of pride in their work and in the success of the company. Irene Dale, in recounting how tours of the factory became a tourist attraction, specifically states that visitors found that the employees' "work satisfaction and pride in the finished product were both enormously refreshing and somehow moving".[737] Few visitors left without making a purchase.

### 10.5.11 Expansion

The transfer of operations from Newlyn to St Ives meant that Tom Heron could immediately put his own stamp on the business. In new premises and with many new staff amongst the hundred employees, he could initiate his own procedures and set his own standards. He also could implement his own vision for the business.

As the business expanded, more people were taken on and, by 1929, the number of employees was one hundred and fifty, of whom one hundred and twenty worked in the factory. An important new recruit was the fashion designer, George Criscuolo, a friend of Walker, who had worked extensively in the theatre and designed for Pavlova. He created many beautiful new styles and made any special orders. The main lines, in addition to a range of frocks, included silk blouses, finely styled with pin tucks, tennis dresses in ivory, striped silk pyjamas, scarves, ties, handkerchiefs etc, whilst dress fabrics were available by the yard. A new department for the printing of curtains was set up in 1927, whilst, the following year, with the aid of a further share issue, a new linen department was established to produce beach and leisure wear. This caught on immediately and the company was soon able to boast that its linen coats and frocks had been seen "along every water's edge from Le Touquet to the Lido".[738] It proved a particularly popular and profitable range, and, when members of the St Ives Society of Artists had a tour of the factory in December 1933, they witnessed a thirty yard length of linen being printed with the design *Sacred Pool* Fig. 10.62), part of an order for *twelve thousand* yards from a hotel company.[739]

Fig. 10.64 George Criscuolo fitting a silk evening gown c.1927
(Royal Cornwall Museum, Truro)

---

736 *St Ives Times*, 19/7/1929.

737 Extract from an interview with Roger Slack, quoted in John Pearl-Binns and Giles Heron, *Rebel and Sage : A Biography of Tom Heron 1890-1983*, Bishop Auckland, 2001 at p.43.

738 Mail-order catalogue 1931.

739 See *Art in Industry*, *St Ives Times*, 15/12/1933.

The company also gradually built up its international business. Whilst initial enquiries from American retailers were rebuffed because of the commitment solely to direct outlets, experimental exhibitions of the company's textiles were held in South Africa and Australia in 1928 and it was reported in 1933 that the company's products were available not only in South Africa, but India and Egypt as well.[740]

Within a year, the output from the factory showed an increase of over fifty per cent, at a time when other textile companies were reporting a slump in demand. However, the expenditure involved reduced the gross profit from £12,178 to £3,400 net in 1927, and from £15,025 to £5,879 net in 1928. Given all the other expenses incurred, the policy of expanding the number of direct selling outlets was put on hold for a couple of years, with the only new one being in Torquay (1927).[741] However, Heron reiterated the benefit of such outlets at the Annual Meeting in 1928, if sales were to increase significantly, and suggested the establishment of a shopfitting department, so that new ones could be opened more economically. Subsequently, further ones were opened at Oxford (1928), Cheltenham, Exeter and Plymouth (1929), and Bristol, Eastbourne and Tunbridge Wells (1930). The network was expanded still further in the 1930s. Heron also recommended the construction of a new dye-house, which he felt would more than treble output, and again a share issue was made to enable this to happen. Despite difficult financial conditions, Cryséde, with its colourful and novel designs, quality fabric and reasonable prices, seemed to have found a niche market.

### 10.5.12 Breakdown

The manner in which the heyday of Cryséde came to an end is a sorry tale. It was largely the result of Alec Walker suffering a mental breakdown, brought on by personal problems. With the factory being run so efficiently by Heron, Walker's presence in St Ives was not often required. Accounts by workers of their Cryséde experiences mention Walker surprisingly little. Irene Dale, for instance, commented, "During my three years at Cryséde, I saw Alec Walker but rarely - certainly not more than six times. I seem to remember that one of these visits I missed. I was told that Walker turned up at the factory startling everybody by leading in a horse or a pony he had just bought." [742] With free time on his hands and enjoying the kudos that the company's success was bringing, Walker took to the riding and hunting lifestyle of the local dignitaries. He then fell in love with a colonel's daughter, a romance that he pursued for two years, before being rejected.

Fig. 10.65  Frances Ewan
*Catherine Richards in a Cryséde dress*
(Bushey Museum and Art Gallery)

---

740 See *Art in Industry*, St Ives Times, 15/12/1933.

741 Berriman notes this as opened in 1931, but Heron's report to the Annual Meeting in 1927 records that it had opened that year. *St Ives Times*, 27/5/1927.

742 From an interview with Roger Slack, quoted in John Pearl-Binns & Giles Heron, *Rebel and Sage - A Biography of Tom Heron (1890-1983)*, Bishop Auckland, 2001 at p.43.

Fig. 10.66  Alec Walker/Cryséde    *Godrevy* design
(Royal Cornwall Museum, Truro)

Fig. 10.67   Dressing Gown
in *Godrevy* design
(Penlee House Gallery & Museum)

Aware that Walker's marriage was falling apart, Heron, as an old friend, tried to help. He himself had found great inspiration from the ministry of Bernard Walke at St Hilary, and wondered whether Walker might find comfort there. He eventually got Alec and Kay to meet at his home in Lelant, so that they could at least talk things through. It proved their final discussion. Walker came to resent Heron's interference in his personal life, but this resentment turned to jealousy, as he heard from all sides what a wonderful job Heron was doing. Heron's plans for ever greater expansion were taking the business far beyond the little experimental craft workshop that Walker had initially envisaged. Whilst his designs were still key, the business was now very much Heron's.[743] By this juncture drinking heavily due to his personal problems, Walker suddenly announced that he wanted Cryséde back, all for himself, telling Heron, "I am responsible to God alone for this business. *You* are responsible to *me*."[744] In June 1929, Heron and Walker met on Smeaton's Pier to see if they could come to some arrangement but, after pacing up and down for ages, Heron told his wife, Eulalie, "It's no good; we shall have to go. I can't keep my self-respect and work under the conditions that Alec proposes."[745] Accordingly, the Board, believing that they might be able to get a new manager, but realising that they could not replace their unique designer, who was, in any event, a majority shareholder, reluctantly had to give Heron the sack and paid him six months' salary in lieu of notice.

Walker, however, was in no fit state to run the company, and he despised the 'professional' Board members, particularly after one of them suggested that he ought to make his designs more comprehensible to the general public. Accordingly, he locked himself away in the Tregenna Castle Hotel, where he painted feverishly. When his friends, Dod Procter and Mary Jewels, visited him, they found his suite looking "more like a Chelsea studio at its worst than hotel rooms", particularly as he had painted the walls with a large panoramic view of St Ives Bay.[746] Mary Jewels, who wanted to strip it off and take it away, recalled, "It was huge, you felt that you were a bird flying over the houses and the sea - all the fish looked more like whales than mackerel - better than anything that Van Gogh or that Alfred Wallis did."[747] Walker was eventually persuaded to live with Mary Jewels, her sister, Cordelia Dobson and their mother, Mrs Tregurtha (Fig. 10.68) at Vine Cottage, Newlyn, but he decided to leave Cornwall later that year. Accordingly, the Board of Cryséde Limited was left with little choice but to dismiss him on health grounds. In 1930, they attempted to persuade Heron to return, but he had set up, by then, Cresta Silks, which was to prove a

---

743 Tom Heron's biographers also suggest that Walker "had become aware of his own limitations as a painter" and was jealous of the talent shown by the young Patrick Heron. He also envied the circle of artist friends that Heron was developing. See John Pearl-Binns and Giles Heron, *Rebel and Sage : A Biography of Tom Heron 1890-1983*, Bishop Auckland, 2001 at p.45.

744 John Pearl-Binns & Giles Heron, *Rebel and Sage - A Biography of Tom Heron (1890-1983)*, Bishop Auckland, 2001 at p.45.

745 ibid..

746 Quoted in Hazel Berriman, *Cryséde - the unique textile designs of Alec Walker*, Truro, 1993 at p.29.

747 ibid.

very successful business. Between 1931 and 1933, Walker entered into various new contracts with the company to produce designs and even, on one occasion, to become General Manager, but his inherent instability always led to problems. In June 1932, however, he held an exhibition of thirty-nine paintings at the Lucy Wertheim Gallery, with *The Times*, in an enthusiastic review, commenting, "Mr Alec Walker...is to be commended for having grasped the fact, overlooked by many, that the Cornish landscape runs to pattern rather than atmospheric effects." [748] It was, of course, just this aspect of the Cornish landscape that he had captured so tellingly in his designs. In 1933, having finally broken with the company, he remarried and turned to farming beef cattle in Yorkshire. Cryséde struggled on until 1939, when it was put into liquidation.[749]

Fig. 10.68  Alec Walker
*Mrs Tregurtha*
(Polly Walker)

It is hard to improve upon the summary of the Cryséde story written by Tom Heron's son, Giles. "The rise and fall of Cryséde reads like a Greek tragedy. It is a story of brilliant promise undermined by a flaw in the personality of its founder that grew like a cancer to destroy the firm and its central characters, including Walker himself. His had been the germinal inspiration and his designing talent its greatest original asset. Alas, his too was the instability, the inner conflict of ambitions and, finally, the destructive jealousy. He blew out his own glittering candle." [750]

### 10.5.13  Craft or Industry

The designs of Alec Walker and the brief success of Cryséde receive very little attention in histories of the craft movement. This will be partly because, prior to Hazel Berriman's book in 1993, there was little information to work from. However, even at the time, there was a quandary as to whether to treat Cryséde as a large craft workshop or an industrial enterprise. Clearly at the time of the 1925 exhibition at the International Gallery, Walker's business was seen as a pioneering craft workshop that was one of those rare animals that might actually be commercially viable. However, once new works able to satisfy the huge demand were built, the business seemed to be designated an industry. Accordingly, one does not find Cryséde textiles being shown in exhibitions alongside those of Barron and Larcher, whose workshop only ever employed a handful of people. Whilst Bernard Leach became a great friend of Tom Heron, sharing his socialist views and his enjoyment of the ministry of Bernard Walke, there is no record of him ever sharing an exhibition with Cryséde, as he frequently did with Barron and Larcher. This was despite admitting in a letter to Eulalie Heron, in 1930, that the gap between his pottery and Tom's textile business was not great, "You say I'm an individual potter for individuals. Tom an industrialist for the populace. I say I want to promote decent pots for ordinary folk and I believe he can do the same with textiles, although he works with a small factory and I with a large studio." [751]

What did change in the nature of Cryséde's business on the move to St Ives? Clearly, one major difference was that Walker was not now in control of all aspects, as he had been before the appointment of Heron. However, such complete control was only possible in a fledgling business, and turnover had grown to such a size that this was impracticable. He was also not cutting his own blocks, as Barron and Larcher did. Nevertheless, in true workshop tradition, specialist craftsmen were being trained up to perform this skilled task, and the application of the blocks continued to be by hand, not by machine. Whilst Cryséde had always used synthetic dyes, which the likes of Ethel Mairet and Bernard Leach would have labelled a compromise, Barron and Larcher ended up by doing the same in the 1930s, as they found natural dyes too limiting and less durable. However, they rarely used more than two colours in comparison with the six that Walker's designs could demand. What is more, Cryséde made their own silk, which Barron and Larcher never had the expertise to contemplate. It seems clear, therefore, that Cryséde should really be considered as a large, highly skilled craft workshop, rather than an industrial enterprise, and that it demonstrated, more than most craft enterprises of the time, an ability to be a considerable commercial success. Albeit the story ended sadly after a relatively short time, it was still an extraordinary achievement.

---

748 *The Times*, 5/6/1932.

749 The Island Works were used for making camouflage nets and string vests for the troops during the War. It then became a mattress factory, before being destroyed in a fire. St Nicholas Court now stands on the site.

750 John Pearl-Binns & Giles Heron, *Rebel and Sage - A Biography of Tom Heron (1890-1983)*, Bishop Auckland, 2001 at p.45.

751 Quoted in John Pearl-Binns & Giles Heron, *Rebel and Sage - A Biography of Tom Heron (1890-1983)*, Bishop Auckland, 2001 at p.44.

# SEEKING A NEW IDENTITY

## 11.1 Introduction

Despite the good work being produced by a wide range of resident and visiting artists, the colony lacked, during this period, a definite identity, such as it had enjoyed in the pre-War years, when it had been recognised, both nationally and internationally, as a centre for the practice and teaching of marine and landscape painting. Furthermore, despite the successes of several resident artists at the Royal Academy and in Paris, there was no regular group of artists enjoying significant acclaim at major exhibition venues to lead to any talk of a St Ives School or a St Ives style. With the heyday of the rural art colony over, St Ives needed to find a new identity and its artists a common purpose.

## 11.2 London, Paris and Pittsburgh

The reputation of the colony in the pre-War years had been forged principally at the Royal Academy in London, at the Salon de la Societe des Artistes Francais in Paris and, latterly, at the Carnegie International Exhibitions at Pittsburgh, and, unsurprisingly, as the colony emerged from the War, thoughts turned again to the submission of works to these major exhibitions.

The War had been a difficult time for the Royal Academy, and the 1917 exhibition had been universally condemned. Indeed, the *St Ives Times* indicated that it was uncertain whether to offer, to those few local artists that had been hung, congratulations or condolences, and reproduced the comment of leading art critic, Paul Konody, that "The majority of the pictures have the same relation to the art of painting that Madame Tussaud's waxworks have to the art of sculpture." [752] Matters did not improve overmuch during the 1920s. The Hanging Committees were slow to embrace any form of modernism, and Royal Academy Illustrated seems packed with interminable portraits, frequently of military figures. With some justification, Frank Rutter declared in 1927 that recent Academy shows revealed few signs of change from those held thirty-five years before.[753] Such conservatism should have favoured members of the 'Old Guard', but, whereas Moffat Lindner and Alfred Hartley continued to enjoy considerable success, Arthur Meade and Fred Milner often had works rejected. As graphically illustrated by Fred Milner's letters to Ethel Brumfit (see Chapter 4.3), such rebuffs rankled, even with established artists, as the Academy was still seen as the primary shop window to gain national recognition and to secure significant sales. Whilst some younger members of the colony, such as Charles Simpson, John Park, Borlase Smart and Helen Stuart Weir, were gradually building reputations at Burlington House, St Ives ceased to have that unmissable presence at Academy shows that it had enjoyed in the pre-War era, whilst a number of the artists producing the most innovative work, such as Louis Sargent, Claude Francis Barry and Frances Hodgkins, were considered too modern for the Academy and found the International Society more welcoming.

One might have imagined that, if the St Ives artists were experiencing difficulty getting works hung at the Academy, their chances of being recognised in Paris were minimal, and yet, as indicated in Chapter 5.1 and 5.9 above, many members of the colony had work hung at one or more of the Salons during the 1920s, and artists such as Annie Falkner, Leslie Hervey, Reginald and Hettie Tangye Reynolds, Percy Ballance and others enjoyed considerably more success in Paris than in London. Unfortunately, very few of these works have come to light and so it is difficult to comment on this phenomenon, but it needs to be noted, for histories of the colony in the past have singularly failed to focus on the successes of St Ives artists abroad. However, whereas in the pre-War era, the continued success of St Ives artists in Paris had led to visits by art students of all nationalities who had based themselves there, this does not happen during the 1920s.

Unsurprisingly, the St Ives artists did not forget the acclaim that they had enjoyed at Pittsburgh prior to the War and, as Julius Olsson, albeit not Elmer Schofield, was again on the jury of award in 1920, there were a number of submissions that year. It was presumably Olsson, therefore, that Frances Hodgkins was referring to in a letter to her mother in November 1919, when she indicated that she had been contacted by a "Director of the Carnegie Institute" who had seen her work *Seaside Lodgings* at the

---

752 *St Ives Times*, 11/5/1917.
753 Frank Rutter, *Since I was Twenty-Five*, London, 1927, Chapter 1.

International and had specially invited her to send it to Pittsburgh.⁷⁵⁴ Olsson also encouraged Charles Simpson, John Park, Fred Milner, Moffat Lindner, Alfred Hartley and Louis Sargent to submit work to Pittsburgh that year as well. The result, however, was disappointing, as, from St Ives, only Hodgkins and Lindner had work hung. On the other hand, Algernon Talmage won an award for *By the Cornish Seas* and Olsson had two works hung. Lindner, who had enjoyed as much success at Pittsburgh as any of the other artists, had five works hung in the years 1920-22, but Simpson, Park and Borlase Smart experienced further rejections. In 1921, a change of Director at the Carnegie Institute led to a complete culture shift and a revamp of the selection process, and, after 1925, when John Park had one last success, the Pittsburgh show dropped out of the St Ives calendar.

### 11.3 Exhibitions outside Cornwall

In the early years of the Cornish art colonies, the artists from St Ives, Newlyn and Falmouth had banded together to put on major exhibitions promoting Cornish art at Dowdeswells in 1889, Nottingham Castle Museum in 1894 and Whitechapel Art Gallery in 1902. Since then, Cornish art had become so well-known at the Academy and in regional Art Galleries, that there had been no need for such shows. During the War, however, the situation had become desperate. In St Ives, Show Day was cancelled in 1917 and 1918, whereas no exhibitions were held at Newlyn between 1914 and 1920 and at Falmouth between 1913 and 1920. Accordingly, the artists gladly accepted the invitation of T.V.Hodgson, the Curator of Plymouth City Art Gallery, to hold an exhibition there in November and December of 1917. Although the majority of exhibits came from St Ives, the colonies at Newlyn (Forbes, Langley, Heath, Gotch, Norman and Alethea Garstin, Robert and Eleanor Hughes, Harold and Gertrude Harvey, and Annie Walke) and Lamorna (Lamorna Birch, Harold and Laura Knight, Alfred Munnings, Algernon Newton) were well represented. The show comprised one hundred and twenty works, which were hung by Moffat Lindner and Lamorna Birch, who, presumably, therefore, were the principal organisers. The artists agreed that twenty-five per cent of all sale proceeds should be donated to the Red Cross Fund. The advance notices indicated, "Most of the pictures are painted direct from Nature and reflect the local colouring and crisp freshness of the Cornish atmosphere. Impressionism is a feature, but it is not the sort of Impressionism, except in a few cases, which leads the artist to lose touch altogether with Nature." ⁷⁵⁵ The venture was described as an experiment, which it was hoped to be the forerunner of many more such shows in the future. A reviewer commented, "Landscapes and seascapes abound, portraiture is meagre in quantity; figure and still life subjects are numerous, and there is a remarkable paucity of works that tell a story." ⁷⁵⁶ The lack of typical Victorian narrative paintings demonstrated some advance, and the most commented upon works were those that displayed distinct originality, such as the symbolist works of Emile Fabry, the pointillist experiments of Claude Francis Barry and the babies of Frances Hodgkins. The most highly priced works from the St Ives contingent were Arthur Meade's *The Mill Stream* (300 gns), Louis Grier's *The New Moon* (£300), Moffat Lindner's *The Approaching Storm, Holland*, Charles Simpson's *Sea Gulls* and an Alfred Hartley landscape *At Low Tide* (all £150), and Fred Milner's *A Dangerous Corner* and Claude Barry's *'The Twilight of the World'* (both £105). Given the still uncertain state of the War, it would be surprising if such a venture proved a commercial success, and it was five years before a repeat show was organised.

The list of exhibitors at the 1922 exhibition at Plymouth, which comprised eighty-eight works, demonstrates just how much the St Ives colony had changed in the interim period, with the departure of artists of the standing of Emile Fabry, Louis Reckelbus, Frances Hodgkins, Marcella Smith, Claude Barry and Louis Sargent. On this occasion, in addition to works from Newlyn and Lamorna artists, there were contributions from Herbert Butler from Polperro and Garstin Cox from the Lizard. The exhibition received some good reviews. "The teaching is direct from Nature, there being no slavish adherence to this or that master, or style, or technique." ⁷⁵⁷ Each work was felt to represent the temperament of the artist and his own personal reaction to his subject and, as a result, there were some daring and novel attempts. In the main, though, these were contributed by Newlyn artists, such as Harold Harvey and Ernest Procter, and the Newlyn section, which also included work by Stanhope and Maude Forbes, Thomas Gotch, Frank Heath, Baragwanath King, and Norman and Alethea Garstin, gained greater coverage. Works from the St Ives artists singled out for mention included Arthur Meade's *The Flooded Fields*, which was considered "quite one of the best canvases on view", William Fortescue's *Off to Sea* and Edmund Fuller's *A September Morn* and a large old seascape *Clodgy Point* (RA 1904). Moffat Lindner's "quite unconventional" watercolour of Naples was considered one of the best in that section and there were a group of etchings by Alfred Hartley, George Turland Goosey and Frank Moore. As a tribute to the late Louis Grier, his masterpiece, *The Night Watch*, was also included. Borlase Smart's

---

754 Letter dated 18/11/1919 - Ed. L. Gill,*The Letters of Frances Hodgkins*, Auckland, 1993 at p.344.
755 *Western Evening Herald*, 5/11/1917.
756 *Western Evening Herald*, 5/11/1917.
757 *Western Morning News and Mercury*, reproduced in *St Ives Times*, 24/2/1922.

depiction of Jordan's Barn in Buckinghamshire, which was reputed to have been constructed from the wood of the original Mayflower, was acquired from the show for the Gallery's permanent collection. However, it is probably fair to conclude that, on this occasion, nothing terribly novel emanated from St Ives. It is not known how successful the exhibition was in terms of visitor numbers or sales, but no further group exhibitions were organised at the Art Gallery in Plymouth, although it did hold certain one man shows, including memorial exhibitions for William Fortescue (1924) and William Cave Day (1925). Thereafter, exposure in Plymouth tended to be through the art dealers, Harris and Sons.

The next exhibition that the St Ives artists mounted at a provincial Gallery - that at Cheltenham Art Gallery, in April and May 1925 - proved, in a number of respects, to be unique. It was the first - and only - time that the St Ives artists exhibited outside Cornwall without their Newlyn counterparts, and it was the first - and only time in the next twenty-five years - that a Cornish painting exhibition included a pottery section. The reasons why the St Ives artists decided to go it alone and not involve artists from the other Cornish art colonies are not known, but the decision is intriguing. Did they feel that their work would be overshadowed not only by the great master, Stanhope Forbes, but also by the new generation of Newlyn and Lamorna artists, such as John Lamorna Birch, Harold Harvey, Frank Heath and Dod and Ernest Procter, who were making significant reputations for themselves? Although Alfred Munnings and Laura and Harold Knight had moved away after the War, their presence in Lamorna and Newlyn during the previous decade had certainly changed the hegemony amongst the Cornish colonies, with St Ives in danger of falling into third place. Were the St Ives artists acutely aware of this and, therefore, were they trying to establish a new and separate identity for St Ives so as to attract new visitors, new art students and, of course, new patrons? Certainly, the introduction to the catalogue, written by Moffat Lindner, makes great play of the colony's distinguished past. The names of Hook, Whistler and Sickert are mentioned from the pre-colony days, whilst most of the principal artists from the pre-War days are listed, as well as Anders Zorn and a clutch of famous American visitors. Indeed, the exhibition was not restricted to works by current residents, and some effort was made to include paintings by artists, who had left St Ives many years previously, such as Julius Olsson, William Titcomb, Algernon Talmage and the Australian, David Davies, or those who had died, such as Louis Grier and Thomas Millie Dow. Nevertheless, it will have been a brave decision by the enterprising Curator at Cheltenham, Daniel Herdman, to put on such an exhibition, with Henry Tuke being the only non-St Ives artist included.

The choice of Cheltenham clearly resulted from quite a number of the St Ives artists having Cheltenham connections. Fred Milner had lived in Cheltenham before moving down to St Ives in the late 1890s and had retained his connections there. He painted regularly in the Cotswolds and art students from Cheltenham, such as Lil Godfrey, came to study under him in St Ives. Richard Heyworth, who had

Fig. 11.1  George Bradshaw     *Smeaton's Pier, St Ives*     (Private Collection)

# SEA CHANGE : FINE AND DECORATIVE ART IN ST IVES 1914-1930

Fig. 11.2  Julius Olsson    *Sunset on the Cornish Coast*    (David Messum Fine Art Ltd)

Fig. 11.3  Julius Olsson    *Moonlight on the Cornish Coast*    (David Messum Fine Art Ltd)

studied in St Ives under David Davies in the early years of the century and who had been based for a while in Falmouth before the War, now lived in Charlton Kings in Cheltenham and was well-known to Herdman. It was clearly Heyworth who arranged for David Davies, then living in Dieppe, to be well-represented in the show, for Davies and he had kept in contact and visited each other on a regular basis.[758] However, the person who seems to have played the major role in organising the exhibition was Moffat Lindner, who had a brother who lived in Cheltenham, and one can imagine Lindner floating the idea to Herdman on one of his visits. Certainly, it was Lindner who opened the exhibition and speeches were also made by W.A.Rixon, a Cheltenham artist, who had been a guest of Lindner at the Arts Club in 1899, and Heyworth, who had helped to hang the exhibition.

The largest of the sixty-five paintings exhibited was Heyworth's massive canvas *Teignmouth*, a painting that had been hung more than a decade before at both the Royal Academy and the Paris Salon. Heyworth later donated this to Cheltenham Art Gallery and it now hangs in Cheltenham Town Hall. Other works priced over £200 included Millie Dow's *Springtime in Cornwall* and Fred Milner's *September in the Cotswolds* - a work painted at Upper Swell in 1914. Other paintings that had already been exhibited at the Paris Salon were John Park's *When The Boats Are In* and Borlase Smart's *Cornish Cliffs* (Fig. 5.39). Charles Simpson contributed two works from his *Herring Season* series, and Olsson sent a typical pair of Cornish seascapes (see Figs. 11.2 and 11.3). Arthur Hayward was represented by two recent Royal Academy successes *The Crinoline* and *In A Sunlit Garden* (Fig. 5.47), whilst Algernon Talmage's *Winter Pastures*, which showed cattle grazing on snow-flecked grass under a grey sky, was considered to be "sheer mastery in composition, tones and handling".[759] However, it was Moffat Lindner's *Golden Autumn* that was acquired for the Gallery's permanent collection - probably more a reflection of his input into the exhibition than of its innate quality.

The exhibition coincided with the boom in the etching market and Alfred Hartley, the acknowledged 'black and white' master in the colony, showed twelve prints, including the aquatints *Evening in a Shropshire Valley* (V & A) and *Landing Place, Lake Como* and *In Old Bordighera* (both British Museum). As mentioned above, it is surprising that, apart from two etchings by Bernard Leach, none of the other printmakers in the colony were represented.

It is, however, the inclusion of twenty-eight of Leach's pots, including Stoneware, Galena Slip-ware and Raku work, that makes this exhibition of some historical interest, for this is two years before Ben Nicholson invited the potter, William Staite Murray, to exhibit with the Seven & Five Society, an event normally given great significance, in light of the then prevailing prejudice against including handicraft in Fine Art exhibitions. For reasons discussed in Chapter 10.3.21, this proved to be a one-off occasion, but the original invitation to Leach again demonstrates that the St Ives artists had a broader outlook than they are normally given credit for.

## 11.4  The formation of the St Ives Society of Artists

Although the artists managed to secure that the Cheltenham Exhibition was reviewed in *The Studio* and a number of works were illustrated, it is doubtful if the aims of the exhibition were fully realised. Certainly, just eighteen months later, the artists in the colony were despondent, feeling that it had become moribund and that an air of apathy pervaded the town. It was considered that the exhibitions at Lanham's had declined in quality alarmingly, partly because the most well-known artists were not sending in their best work, and that there was a lack of 'esprit de corps', resulting in students and younger artists receiving no advice and encouragement and no constructive criticism from their peers. This was a general malaise, but the situation had certainly not been helped by the departure of two particularly dynamic figures - Charles Simpson in 1924, with the resultant closure of his School of Painting, and Borlase Smart in 1925. It was not only the energy and enthusiasm of the latter that was missed, but also his well informed and tactful critiques of exhibitions.

George Bradshaw and new arrival, Herbert Truman, who had just spent fourteen years in Egypt as chief inspector of art and trade schools, were two artists who were particularly dismayed at the state of the colony. At the annual meeting to elect the Lanham's Galleries' Hanging Committee in November 1926, which only seventeen artists attended, Bradshaw suggested that the election should be postponed so that "the present state of the St Ives Arts Colony might be discussed and suggestions brought forward to raise the Colony from its present unimportant position in the Arts World."[760] After several meetings, involving wide-ranging discussions of the problems faced and potential solutions, Bradshaw and

---

758 Worcester Art Gallery have a painting by Davies of Cheltenham, whilst both Worcester and Cheltenham Art Galleries have paintings of Dieppe by Heyworth.

759 *Gloucestershire Echo*, reproduced in *St Ives Times* 10/4/1925.

760 Minutes of meeting, as transcribed by the St Ives Society of Artists.

Fig. 11.6 Borlase Smart painting on Westcott's Quay in the early 1930s
Smart's vision and self-less industry were hugely important in STISA's success

Truman put together a set of proposals in January 1927, which included the formation of a new Society and/or the establishment of a St Ives group of artists with common principles and aims, the forging of stronger links with the other art colonies in West Cornwall, the establishment of a St Ives School of Painting, with members of the colony giving lectures on their specialities, and the development of a common publicity initiative. Furthermore, they suggested that arrangements should be made for outside artists to give constructive criticism of work exhibited and, if requested, for members of the Lanham's Hanging Committee to visit individual studios to give critiques.[761]

In the course of these discussions, Herbert Truman felt it important to emphasize the principal attractions that St Ives still retained as an art colony. "The advantages possessed by St Ives, as a centre for artists, are many. The great variety of subject matter includes cottage architecture, harbour and coast scenery, seascape, moorland, boat and figure subjects in correct environment. The town is splendidly equipped with large well-lighted studios, situated to give excellent view points. There is a brilliance of light and colour, even on grey days. The weather effects are beautiful especially during winter and the climate is healthy and mild, making sketching possible during the greater part of the year. It is served by an agent for the transport of pictures to and from London and provincial exhibitions and also for artists' materials. Lanham's Gallery, though small, is well known and a great asset. Perhaps the one disadvantage is its distance from London."[762] Despite the heyday of the rural art colony having passed, these were very real attractions that should draw other artists down to the colony, if its vibrancy could be re-developed.

At the subsequent meeting in late January, the decision was taken to form a new Society, to be known as 'The St Ives Society of Artists', but, with one of the fundamental problems being the lack of artists of stature in the colony, there was no great belief that this would transform the position. The first year of the Society proved difficult, with attendances at its monthly meetings poor, and the only significant achievement was the mounting of a Retrospective Exhibition, drawn from local collections, aimed at highlighting the famous names of the past who had secured for the colony its initial reputation. At

---

761 For the fullest account of the meetings and discussions leading up to the formation of STISA, see David Tovey, *George Fagan Bradshaw - Submariner and Marine Artist - and the St Ives Society of Artists*, Tewkesbury, 2000 at pp.67-73.
762 *St Ives Times*, 14/1/1927.

the end of the year, the new Society very nearly folded and Bradshaw, who had been joint Secretary with Francis Roskruge, resigned. However, in 1928, a Committee with a more positive mindset was elected. This comprised Moffat Lindner (President), Alfred Cochrane (Secretary), Francis Roskruge (Treasurer), Herbert Truman, Pauline Hewitt, Arthur Hayward and Hugh Gresty, with John Douglas as librarian and Martin Cock representing the associate members. One of its first achievements was to secure for the Society its own Gallery - No 5 Porthmeor Studios - and so, for the first time since the colony's inception, the artists had artistic control over their own exhibitions in St Ives. In general, the arrangements at Lanham's Galleries had worked reasonably well but, in recent years, serious concern had been expressed, most strongly by Alfred Hartley, at the use of the Galleries for commercial purposes unconnected with art. As mentioned above, the constant display of cheaper handicraft items in one of the Lanham's Galleries was probably also felt to impact on sales of paintings in difficult economic times. The proposed new Gallery also offered a communal meeting place, which it was hoped would foster discussions on art and technique, and the artists set about, with enthusiasm, the redecoration and refurbishment of the old studio, which involved the installation of gas for both lighting and heating.

The new Committee, primarily through Moffat Lindner, also made a more concerted attempt, than had been made at the time of the Cheltenham exhibition, to involve some of the major artists, who had established their reputations in St Ives. Accordingly, Adrian Stokes, Arnesby Brown, Julius Olsson, Algernon Talmage and Terrick Williams were invited to become members of the new Society. Invitations to exhibit were also extended to Newlyn and Lamorna artists, such as Stanhope Forbes, Lamorna Birch, Harold Harvey and Dod and Ernest Procter. Unsurprisingly, the quality of the St Ives exhibitions soon improved dramatically, sparking greater interest from residents and visitors.

More attention was also given to publicity, particularly after Borlase Smart's return to the colony during 1928. The power of the Press was acknowledged and engaged, with reporters having private tours of studios on Show Day, so that styles and trends could be explained and the desired message imparted. Programmes were also produced and a quirky map of the studios was drawn by Francis Roskruge. Whilst plans for the formation of a new School of Painting were not realised for a decade, some attempt was made to encourage artists to lecture on their specialities, either at the Arts Club or at the Gallery, and Pauline Hewiit started a drawing class in the Gallery.

Fig. 11.5  Terrick Williams  *Low Tide, St Ives*  (Touchstones Rochdale)

Fig. 11.4  Alfred Cochrane    *The Harbour, St Ives*    (Private Collection)
Cochrane was Secretary of STISA from 1928-1933

The consequence of all these initiatives was that artists' mindsets changed. Gone was the apathy and torpor that had beset the colony in the mid-1920s; in its place was a real unity of purpose - a feeling that by working together to raise standards and to promote St Ives as a vibrant artistic centre, benefits would flow through to all, as other artists, collectors and visitors were encouraged down to the town. Accordingly, senior artists began to dispense constructive criticism to students and others making their way uncertainly, whilst lesser artists were inspired to work harder to try to emulate their superiors. Soon the number of artist members of the Society rose significantly and, as the new found enthusiasm spread through the town, many more residents, who were interested in art, applied to become associate members. Such members not only swelled the coffers of the Society, but were likely purchasers. The colony had found a common purpose.

# - 12 -
# BLUEPRINT FOR THE FUTURE

1930 might seem an odd date to close this survey. It was a pretty bleak year. The Wall Street Crash in late 1929 had resulted in financial melt-down in the Western World. If artists had thought the 1920s was a difficult economic climate in which to make sales, the widespread losses incurred on the stock markets during and after the crash meant that many previously well-to-do families were reduced to penury. Even the most well-known artists found making ends meet extremely difficult, and certain areas of practice, such as etching, were so badly hit that they took decades to recover. The future of the colony seemed far from assured. The initial impetus given by the formation of STISA might have raised hopes initially, but could it survive a downturn of this magnitude? The future of the Leach Pottery was also most uncertain. Rescued from closure by the generosity of Leonard and Dorothy Elmhirst, Leach was planning to move it to Dartington, where he was now teaching. Cryséde Limited too was in trouble, after the rows that had led to the dismissal the previous year of both Alec Walker and Tom Heron. Accordingly, St Ives' brief flirtation with the Decorative Arts looked certain to end in disappointment. Furthermore, with Christopher Wood's suicide that year, the Nicholsons' marriage breaking up and Jim Ede suffering a mental breakdown, there seemed little prospect of Alfred Wallis' paintings gaining wider recognition, whilst Nicholson himself had, following Wood's death, given up his own attempts at developing a naive style and had little reason to return to St Ives. The outlook was indeed glum.

1930, however, saw one good piece of news. This resulted from the visit to Cornwall that year of E.W.Payton, the former director of the Elam School of Art in Auckland, who had been sent to Europe by the Mackelvie Trustees (a charitable fund linked to Auckland Art Gallery), with authority to spend up to six thousand pounds on buying the best of European art. A strong critic of the Victorian narrative and history paintings acquired on behalf of the Trustees previously, Payton was determined to buy work "by the foremost workers of the day" in Scotland, England and France. However, Borlase Smart, who gave him a guided tour of the studios in West Cornwall, persuaded him to buy an extraordinary number of works by members of STISA. Accordingly, he returned to New Zealand with three works by Arthur Meade and Lamorna Birch, two works by each of Moffat Lindner, Fred Milner, John Park, George Bradshaw, Arthur Hayward, Hurst Balmford and Arthur Hambly, major works by Stanhope Forbes, Julius Olsson, Borlase Smart and Dorothea Sharp and a watercolour of The Sloop Inn by Miss E. M.Willett. His acquisitions in London also included works by Terrick Williams, John Littlejohns and Will Ashton, all STISA members. The Cornish artists could not believe their luck; the Mackelvie Trustees were a little bemused.[763]

Whilst these sales were most welcome and engendered a measure of additional confidence, it was the decision, taken bravely in the uncertain economic conditions of 1931, to put on a series of touring shows around the country, which transformed STISA into a nationally acclaimed body of artists. The brainchild of Borlase Smart, this decision again reflected the experience of the Cheltenham exhibition, which was able to be quoted as a precedent to curators doubting the wisdom of an exhibition devoted solely to a single regional art group. Whilst the Academicians within the membership were no doubt used by Smart to sell the concept, it is fascinating that the works bought from these touring shows, for the permanent collections of the Galleries that hosted them, tended to be the productions of the younger contemporary artists, such as Bernard Ninnes and Thomas Maidment, which were more in tune with current tastes. However, as was invariably the case with early St Ives art, there was an extraordinary range of styles on display, as new influences, such as Art Deco and the flat colour and decorative pattern of poster art, began to hold sway. Whilst, by 1936, the local initiatives had nearly doubled visitor numbers to the exhibitions in St Ives to four thousand five hundred, this figure was dwarfed by the *seventy-five thousand* visitors to just one of the Society's touring shows that year. Over the course of the 1930s and 1940s, over twenty-five public art galleries hosted shows by STISA and, in 1947, it was even invited to send a touring exhibition to South Africa. With STISA offering membership to any artist who had at some juncture worked in Cornwall, it was able to boast by the mid-1930s that Royal Academy shows regularly contained more than seventy works by its members. The colony was now identified with STISA, and St Ives art had never enjoyed such wide exposure before.[764]

---

763 See further David Tovey, *Creating A Splash : The St Ives Society of Artists (1927-1952)*, Tewkesbury, 2004 at pp.29-30. Appendix D on p.299 lists the works bought on behalf of the Mackelvie Trustees both on this visit and at other times.

764 The runaway success of the Society is the story told in my earlier book, *Creating A Splash - The St Ives Society of Artists 1927-1952*.

The formation of STISA in 1927 was, accordingly, a key feature in the revival in the colony's fortunes over the course of the next two decades. However, by 1930, other events had occurred, which, in due course, would shape the course of the colony for the whole of the rest of the century. The Leach Pottery may have been in desperate straits at the end of the 1920s, but it did survive, and the proposed move to Dartington, mooted for much of the 1930s, never came off. The employment by the Elmhirsts of Harry Davis to run the Pottery in the early 1930s ensured that it was better organised, and their funding of David Leach's training in production techniques at the North Staffordshire Technical College, contrary to the wishes of Bernard, demonstrated considerable foresight for, when there was an extraordinary surge in demand for the Pottery's tableware after the Second World War, the Pottery was, miraculously, not only still in existence, but also sufficiently well organised to be able to cope. Freed to a considerable degree from the business aspects of the Pottery, Bernard Leach was able to utilise his eloquence to become the sage for the new studio pottery movement, and *A Potter's Book*, first published in 1940, became the 'bible' for the next generation of potters. Accordingly, the Leach Pottery has been an important feature of the colony ever since, ensuring, firstly, that handicraft has made a distinctive contribution to the furtherance of the colony's reputation, and, secondly, that the colony has maintained important links with Japan and the Far East. Its recent refurbishment as both a display area and a working pottery should ensure that it continues to play an invaluable role.

By contrast, Crystéde Limited did not survive the 1930s. Given the extraordinary order for twelve thousand yards of linen from a hotel chain witnessed by members of STISA on their tour in 1933, the business may have had occasional bursts of profitability during the decade, but the market was difficult and it lacked the sort of inspired leadership that Heron had given it, so that it limped into liquidation in 1939. After being neglected for many decades, Crystéde Limited has seen, since Hazel Berriman's book in 1993, a surge of interest in its story and in the remarkable designs that Walker produced, which seem as vibrant and resonant now, as they did when they became the height of fashion in the 1920s. Largely due to the generosity of Alec Walker's daughter, Polly, both Penlee House Gallery and Museum, Penzance, and the Royal Cornwall Museum, Truro, have extensive collections, which are often on display.

It is probably unlikely that Ben Nicholson would have considered a move to St Ives, had it not been for the outbreak of the Second World War. With newly born triplets, somewhere safer than London was required, and having lodged initially with his friend, the art critic, Adrian Stokes, at 'Little Parc Owles', Barbara Hepworth and himself also took property in Carbis Bay. Writing to his first wife, Winifred, shortly after his return, he told her how he was seeing the place through his memories of eleven years earlier. This inspired him to return to landscape painting and to think again of Wallis' art. However, his Cubist-style still lifes, set against Cornish landscape backgrounds, were far more sophisticated and successful than the paintings that had resulted from his visit in 1928. Accordingly, Nicholson was in St Ives at the time of Wallis' death in 1942, and he was able to ensure that this unique painter was feted by the group of young artists that gathered round him during and after the War years, so that Wallis became a touchstone for the whole of the St Ives modernist movement. Coupled with his most unusual background, Wallis' unique vision has proved of timeless appeal. However, the presence in the colony later in the century of Bryan Pearce (1929-2007), who possessed an equally extraordinary and novel naive vision, has led to the colony having a matchless reputation as a centre for 'primitive' or naive art.

The group of artists with an interest in non-representational art, who gathered round Nicholson during the 1940s, such as Peter Lanyon, Wilhelmina Barns-Graham, Bryan Wynter, Terry Frost and Patrick Heron, went on to secure significant reputations in their own right, both nationally and in America. Accordingly, St Ives during this period developed a new identity as a centre of modernism. David Brown's seminal exhibition in 1985, *St Ives 1939-1964*, not only celebrated this further extraordinary chapter in the history of the colony, but also led indirectly to the establishment of Tate St Ives in 1993. If Nicholson had not met Wallis in St Ives in 1928, would this chain of events have occurred?

The period covered by this book may be one of transition, but, contrary to the experience of many other rural art colonies that had flourished before the War, it was one in which the continued existence of the colony in St Ives was assured, whilst events that occurred during this period can be seen to have shaped its long-term future. However, the period also demonstrates that, however dire the economic and political backdrop, St Ives always attracts talented artists and inspires them to produce seminal works.

# APPENDIX A

# BORLASE SMART WAR DRAWINGS

## TABLE A — AT THE IMPERIAL WAR MUSEUM

| TITLE OF DRAWING | IWM NO | FAS NO |
| --- | --- | --- |
| All That Was Left of Péronne | 4 | 25 |
| Arras Under Shell Fire | 5 | 20 |
| The Somme Offensive, as seen from the Madagascar Dump, Arras Road | 6 | 12 |
| A Derelict Tank Caught on the Edge of a Shell Hole ; Near Bouleaux Wood | 7 | 17 |
| The Ruins of the Sugar Refinery, Vimy | 8 | 21 |
| Near Vimy | 9 | 15 |
| Arras in Flames | 10 | 31 |
| A Dug-Out | 4463 | 27 |
| Ruins at Neuve Chapelle | 4464 | 37 |
| Ruins of the Chateau Vermelles | 4465 | |
| Beaumont Hamel | 4466 | 35 |
| Thelus, Vimy Ridge, Forward German HQ, Opposite 60th London Div. | 4467 | |
| Vimy Ridge from the Labrynthe | 4468 | |
| Ruins of Ypres from the Menin Road | 4469 | |
| Ruins of Cloth Hall (charcoal only) | 4470 | |
| Fricourt | 4471 | |
| Ruins Chateau Armentieres | 4472 | 19 |
| 'No Thorough Fare' - A shell-swept road near Arras | 4473 | |
| Ruins in the Champagne District | 4474 | |
| With the Machine Gun Corps near Vimy Ridge | 4475 | 16 |
| Ruins near the Somme | 4476 | |
| Ruins of the Fort Péronne | 4477 | 2 |
| The Germans Fired a Mine the Afternoon We Took Over. S. of Vimy | 4478 | 36 |
| Ruins of Cloth Hall, Ypres | 4479 | |
| Ruins at Béthune | 4480 | |
| Old French Communication Trench. S. of Vimy | 4481 | |
| A Church nr the Somme Untouched by Shell Fire amid the Village Ruins | 4482 | |
| Ovillers | 4483 | |
| Hindering Our Transport; A Road near Arras Traversed by German Fire | 5598 | |
| 'Grandmother' | 5599 | |
| The Huns Fired a Mine the Afternoon We Arrived (original sketch) | 6340 | |
| Portrait of a W.A.A.C. | 15854 | |

## TABLE B — AT PLYMOUTH CITY ART GALLERY

| TITLE OF DRAWING | PCAG NO |
| --- | --- |
| 'Grandmother' prepares to distribute her cough lozenges | 1917.201 |
| Ruins of Ecurie, North of the Somme | 1917.202 |
| German retaliation on the Lille road | 1917.203 |
| Shell-swept road, North of Arras | 1917.204 |
| Calvary at Etrun | 1917.205 |
| Old French Big Gun Emplacement | 1917.206 |
| Chaos | 1917.207 |
| Morning Hymn of Hate - or - A Little Liveliness North of Arras | 1917.208 |
| Moonlight at Marueil | 1917.209 |
| Madagascar Dump after a day's rain | 1917.210 |
| Ruins of the Cloth Hall, Ypres | 1918.147 |
| Ruins at Ypres | 1918.148 |
| Ruins of the Sugar Refinery, Vimy | 1918.149 |
| Munitions | 1918.150 |

# APPENDIX B

## ARTISTS EXHIBITING LOCALLY

Key:  CH = Cheltenham Exhibition    FA = Falmouth Exhibition    LG = Lanham's Galleries
      OS = Own show at Lanham's    PL = Plymouth Exhibition    PS = St Ives Print Society
      SD = Show Day                SE = Studio Exhibition

Note: The information for this Appendix is taken, in the main, from newspaper reviews, which, whilst of great interest, are haphazard in what exhibitions they report and which artists they feature.

**TABLE A       1914-1920**

| ARTIST | 1914 | 1915 | 1916 | 1917 (No SD) | 1919 | 1920 |
|---|---|---|---|---|---|---|
| Beale Adams | | | | | SD | SD, LG |
| Herbert Babbage | SD, LG, SE | SE | | | | |
| Alfred Bailey | SD | SD | SD | PL, LG | SD, LG | SD, LG, FA |
| Marjorie Ballance | | | | | LG | SD, LG |
| Percy Ballance | | | | | LG | SD |
| J Noble Barlow | SD, LG | SD | SD | [SE] | [SE, LG] | [SE] |
| Lilas Barrett | | | | LG | | LG |
| Claude Barry | | | | PL, LG | SD, LG, SE | SD, LG, SE |
| Doris Barry | | | | | SD, LG, OS | SD, LG, SE |
| Frederick Beaumont | | | | PL, LG | | |
| Lucy Bodilly | | | | | OS | LG, FA |
| Vera Bodilly | | | | | | LG, FA |
| John Bromley | | | | PL, LG | | |
| C Brownlow | | | SD | LG | | |
| Winifred Burne | | | | | | LG |
| Miss F M Campbell | SD | | | | | SD |
| Bertha Cockerham | SD, LG | SD | SD | | | SD, LG |
| Dorothy Cooke | | | SD | | | LG |
| William Cave Day | | | | | | SD, LG |
| Mabel Douglas | SD, LG | SD | | | SD, LG | SD |
| Emile Fabry | | | SD | PL | SD | |
| Annie Falkner | | | SD | LG | | |
| John Farquharson | LG | | | | | LG |
| Herbert Fitzherbert | SD, LG | | | | | LG |
| William Fortescue | SD, LG | SD | SD | PL, LG | SD, LG | SD, LG, FA |
| A Moulton Foweraker | LG | | | PL | | |
| Edmund Fuller | SD | SD | SD | PL, LG | | LG |
| Edith Gibson | SD, LG | SD | SD | | | |
| Louis Grier | | | | PL, LG | SD, LG | SD, LG |
| Alfred Hartley | SD, LG | SD | SD | PL, LG | SD, LG | SD, LG, OS, FA |
| Nora Hartley | SD, LG | | SD | PL, LG | SD, LG | SD, LG |
| Pauline Hewitt | LG | | SD | | | |
| Frances Hodgkins | | SD | SD | PL, LG | SD, LG | FA |
| Maud D Hurst | SD | | | | SD | SD |
| Robert Langley Hutton | SD, LG | SD | | PL, LG | SD, SE, LG | |
| Caroline Jackson | SD, LG | | SD | | | SD |

294

# APPENDICES

| ARTIST | 1914 | 1915 | 1916 | 1917 (no SD) | 1919 | 1920 |
|---|---|---|---|---|---|---|
| Helen Knapping | LG | | | | | FA |
| Augusta Lindner | | | | | LG | SD |
| Moffat Lindner | SD, LG | SD | SD | PL, LG | SD, LG | SD, LG, FA |
| Evelyn Evans Linton | SD, LG | SD | | | | |
| Frances Lloyd | | | | | LG | SD |
| Sara Maclean | | | SD | LG | | |
| Arthur Meade | SD, LG | SD | SD | PL, LG | SD | SD, LG |
| Fred Milner | LG | SD | SD | PL, LG | SD, LG | SD |
| Frank Moore | SD, LG | SD | | | | |
| Julius Olsson | LG | | | LG | LG | LG |
| William Parkyn | SD | SD | SD | PL, LG | SD, SE | SD, LG |
| Lynn Pitt | SD | SD | SD | | | |
| Louis Reckelbus | | | SD | PL | | |
| James Elgar Russell | | SD | SD, SE | | SD | |
| Louis Sargent | | | SD | PL, LG | LG | OS |
| Katharine Sargent | | | | LG | LG | |
| Edith Sealy | SD | SD | | LG | | |
| Mabel Shone | | | | | SD | SD |
| Charles Simpson | LG | SD | | PL, LG | SD, OS, SE | SD, LG, SE. PL |
| Ruth Simpson | | | | PL | LG, OS, SE | SD, LG, SE, PL |
| Edgar Skinner | SD, LG | | | | SD | |
| Borlase Smart | | | | | LG, OS | SD, LG, PL, FA |
| Frances Tysoe Smith | | | | | | SD. LG |
| Marcella Smith | | SD | SD | PL, LG | SD, LG | SD, LG, SE |
| Francis Raymond (Spenlove) | | | | LG | | SD, SE |
| William Spittle | SD | | SD | | | |
| A G Folliott Stokes | SD | SD | SD | | LG | |
| Betty Thompson | | | | LG | SD, LG | |
| John H Titcomb | SD, LG | SD | | | | LG |
| Frank Ver Beck | | | SD | | LG, SE | |
| Helen Stuart Weir | | SD | | | LG | |
| Nina Weir Lewis | | SD | | PL | | |
| Arthur White | SD, LG | SD | SD | PL, LG | SD, LG | LG, FA |
| Daisy Whitehouse | SD | SD | SD | PL | SD | LG |
| Lizzie Whitehouse | SD, LG | SD | SD | PL, LG | SD | |
| Mary F A Williams | | | | | | SD, LG |
| John Yabsley | SD | | SD | | SD | SD, LG, FA |

Also

1914 Arthur Beaumont SD, LG, D Lovett Cameron SD, Garstin Cox SD, LG, Mr Huttch SD, Frank Innes LG, Guy Kortright SD, R Hayley Lever LG, William Evans Linton SD, Evelyn Harke LG, Charles Mottram LG, Alice Nicholson SD, Ida Sawyer LG, Charles Tracy SD, Hanna Rion Ver Beck SD, Terrick Williams LG.
1915 Arthur Lyons SD, Ethel Rawlins SD.
1916 Leslie Hervey SD, Mrs L Scott Bower SD, Gertrude Talmage SD.
1917 T Millie Dow LG, Robert Morton Nance PL, Charles Bryant LG.
1918 (No SD). No art reviews at all except Marcella Smith SE and Claude and Doris Barry SE.
1919 Lowell Dyer SD, Vernon Ellis SD, Archibald E Haswell Miller LG, Sylvia Bowen LG, J Sutcliffe LG, Miss Townsend SD, LG, Dr A Watkinson LG, Ruth Davenport OS (Needlework).
1920 John Douglas SD, Allan Deacon SD, Nora Warleigh SD, LG, Dr Adam McVie SD, Ida Praetorius LG, David Murray Smith LG, Miss G M Evans LG, Minnie Agnes Cohen FA, Mary Grylls FA, Miss E Tewsley FA.

# SEA CHANGE : FINE AND DECORATIVE ART IN ST IVES 1914-1930

**TABLE B      1921-1927**

| ARTIST | 1921 | 1922 | 1923 | 1924 | 1925 | 1926 | 1927 |
|---|---|---|---|---|---|---|---|
| Beale Adams | SD | SD, PL | | SD | | | |
| Edith Meta Alexander | SD | SD | SD | SD | | | |
| Emily Allnutt | | | LG | | SD | SD | SD |
| W Donald Angier | | | | | SD, LG | SD | OS |
| Alfred Bailey | SD | SD, PL | SD | SD | SD, CH | SD | SD |
| Marjorie Ballance | SD | SD | SD, PS | SD, PS | SD, LG | SD | |
| Percy Ballance | SD, LG | SD, PL | SD, LG, OS | SD, OS | SD, CH, LG | SD | |
| Lilas Barrett | LG | | SD | | | | |
| Lucy Bodilly | | | | | SE | | |
| Vera Bodilly | | | | | SD, CH, SE | SD | |
| George Bradshaw | | SD, LG | SD, LG | SD | SD, CH, LG | SD | SD, LG |
| Kathleen Bradshaw | | LG | | | SD | SD | SD, LG |
| John Bromley | | PL | | | CH | SD | SD |
| Annie Bryant | | SD | | SD | | | |
| Winifred Burne | SD | SD | SD | SD | SD | | SD |
| Dorothy Cooke | | SD | SD, PS | PS | SD, LG | SD | |
| Elizabeth Cork | | SD | SD | SD | | | |
| Nell Cuneo | | SD | SD, LG, SE | SD | CH, SE | | |
| Shallett Dale | | | | | | SD | SD |
| Ruth Davenport | SE | | | SD | SD | SD | SD |
| William Cave Day | SD | SD, PL | SD | SD, OS | PL | | |
| John Douglas | | | | | | SD | SD |
| Mabel Douglas | SD | SD | SD | | | SD | SD, LG |
| Lowell Dyer | SD | PL | | | CH | LG | |
| Frances Ewan | SD | SD, PL | PS | PS | | | |
| William Fortescue | SD | SD, PL | LG | OS, PL | | | |
| E Charlton Fortune | | SD | SD | | | | |
| Helen Overbury Fox | | | SD | | | SD | |
| Ellen Fradgley | | | SD | | SD | SD, LS | SD |
| M Winifred Freeman | | | LG | | | SD | |
| Edmund Fuller | | PL | PS | PS | | | |
| George Turland Goosey | SD | SD, PL | SD | SD | | | LG |
| Hugh Gresty | | | | | | LG | SD, LG |
| Mary Grylls | SD | SD | SD | SD | SD | SD | SD, LG |
| Alfred Hartley | SD, LG | SD, PL | SD, PS | SD, PS | SD, CH, LG | SD, LG | SD |
| Nora Hartley | SD | SD | SD, PS | SD, PS | SD, CH, LG | SD | SD, LG |
| Arthur Hayward | | | LG | | SD, CH | | SD, LG |
| Pauline Hewitt | LG | SD, PL | SD, LG, SE | SD | SD, CH, SE | SD | SD, LG |
| Miss A H Holt | | | SD | SD | | | |
| Winifred Humphery | SD | SD, PL, LG | SD | | | SD | |
| Constance Jeayes | | | SD | | | | SD |
| Helen Knapping | SD | SD | SD | SD | SD | SD | SD |
| Bernard Leach | SD | SD, OS | SD, OS, PS | SD, OS, PS | CH | SD, OS | |
| Augusta Lindner | SD | SD | | SD | SD, CH | SD | SD |
| Moffat Lindner | SD | SD, PL | SD | SD | SD, CH | SD, LG | SD, LG |
| Averil Mackenzie-Grieve | SD | | LG | SD, PS | | | |

# APPENDICES

| ARTIST | 1921 | 1922 | 1923 | 1924 | 1925 | 1926 | 1927 |
|---|---|---|---|---|---|---|---|
| Patrick McMahon | | | | | SD | | SD |
| Dr Adam McVie | | SD, PL | | | | | |
| Arthur Meade | SD | SD, PL | SD | SD | SD, CH, LG | SD | SD |
| Fred Milner | SD | SD, PL | SD, PS, LG | SD, PS | SD, CH, LG | SD, LS | SD, LG |
| Frank Moore | | SD, PL, SE | SD, PS, LG | SD, PS | | | |
| Julius Olsson | | | | | CH | | LG |
| John Park | | SD, PL, LG | SD | SD | SD, CH, LG | SD | SD, LG |
| William Parkyn | SD | | | | LG | | |
| Francis Roskruge | | | SD, PS | SD, PS | SD, LG | SD | SD |
| Miss M T Rowse | | SD | | SD | | SD | |
| Helen Seddon | | | SD | SD | | SD | |
| David Segaller | | | | SD | SD | | |
| A Shearer Armstrong | | | | SD | SD | SD | SD, LG |
| Mabel Shone | | SD | | SD | | SD | |
| Charles Simpson | SD, LG | SD, PL, LG | SD, PS, SE | SD, PL, PS | LG, CH, OS | | |
| Ruth Simpson | SD | SD, PL, LG | SD | | | | |
| Borlase Smart | SD, LG | SD, PL | SD | SD, PS | SD, CH, LG | | |
| Annie Bliss Smith | SD | SD | SD, PS | PS | | | |
| Frances Tysoe Smith | SD | SD | SD | SD | SD | SD | |
| Marcella Smith | SD | | | OS (Hats) | OS (Hats) | | |
| F Raymond (Spenlove) | SD, LG | SD, PL | | SD | OS | SD | SD |
| John H Titcomb | SD | SD, PL | SD, LG | | CH | | |
| Herbert Truman | | | | | | SD, LS | LG |
| Reginald Turvey | | | | | SD | SD | |
| Frederick C Uren | SD | | SD | SD | SD | | |
| Miss D G Webb | | | SD, PS, LG | SD, PS | | | |
| Helen Stuart Weir | | PL, OS | SD, LG | | | | |
| Nina Weir Lewis | | OS | SD | | | | |
| Arthur White | SD | SD, PL | SD | SD | | SD | SD |
| Mary F A Williams | SD | SD, PL | SD, LG | SD | SD, CH | | |
| John Yabsley | SD | SD, PL | SD | SD | SD | SD | SD |

Also

1921 Claude Barry SD, Lynn Pitt SD, Louis Grier (dec'd) SD, Fanny Lloyd (dec'd) SD, Minnie Agnes Cohen SD, Daphne Allen SD, Miss Ffennell SD, Miss G M Evans SD, Miss Akers SD, Ackland Richings SD, Louis Sargent LG.

1922 Miss M Whalley SD, Millie Dow (dec'd) PL, Louis Grier (dec'd) PL, Reginald Dick PL, Ethel Brand LG, Mrs Wright LG, Miss Opie LG, Iris Cooke LG.

1923 Vernon Ellis SD, John de Walton SD, Mrs Fenn SD, Mrs Sharpe SD, J J Hart SD, Edith Walters PS, L S Edmonds LG, Doris Barry SE (Fashion).

1924 Ernest and Esther Borough Johnson SD, Robert Morson Hughes SD, T Matsubayashi SD, P Lambe SD, Miss Bucknill SD, L S Edmonds SD, Donald Currie SD, E Sykes PS.

1925 Mary McCrossan SD, CH, Selina Bromley SD, Terence Cuneo SD, Sara Maclean (dec'd) OS, David Davies CH, T Millie Dow (dec'd) CH, Louis Grier (dec'd) CH, Richard Heyworth CH, Algernon Talmage CH, William Titcomb CH, Henry C Wilkie LG.

1926 Hurst Balmford SD, Mr Lockwood LG.

1927 Georgina Bainsmith SD, Alfred Cochrane SD, W Emery SD, Eliza Tudor Lane SD, Hampden Minton SD, Robert Enraght Moony LG.

Note : For artists involved with STISA post-1927, see David Tovey, *Creating A Splash - The St Ives Society of Artists (1927-1952)*, Tewkesbury, 2004.

# ACKNOWLEDGEMENTS

My first thanks are due to Alison Bevan, the Director of Penlee House Gallery and Museum, Penzance, for agreeing to mount an exhibition on this period of St Ives art in the autumn of 2010. When I decided to end my book *Pioneers of St Ives Art at Home and Abroad* in 1914, I was not at all certain whether the period 1914-1927, being the one period of early St Ives art that I had not written about previously, would warrant separate treatment, but her enthusiasm for the exhibition led me to proceed with the further research, which has revealed the fascinating story told in this book. She also suggested the name 'Sea Change'. Katie Herbert, in her exceptionally efficient way, has organised the exhibition itself, and has been very long-suffering, when I have altered my exhibit preferences, as new research revealed further gems.

As St Ives art always has an international dimension, I am very reliant, due to the lack of any funding for research trips, on the goodwill of art historians and art dealers abroad. For this book, my most sincere thanks are due, in New Zealand, to Pamela Gerrish-Nunn for assistance with the section on Frances Hodgkins, and in particular for the provision of her notes for an excellent lecture on Hodgkins' time in Cornwall that she gave at St Ives Arts Club in 2008. She also recommended various other persons to consult, of whom Jonathan Gooderham of Jonathan Grant Galleries, Auckland has been exceptionally helpful, not only in relation to Hodgkins, but also as regards other New Zealand artists working in St Ives, such as Beatrice Wood, Francis McCracken and Elizabeth Kelly. Mary Kisler of Auckland Art Gallery, Genevieve Webb of Dunedin Public Art Gallery and Tim Jones of Christchurch Art Gallery have also, once again, been most supportive and helpful.

In Belgium, I am totally indebted to Jacqueline Guisset for biographical information and the supply of images relating to Emile Fabry. One of the most exciting discoveries of all was Fabry's huge mural *War and Peace* at Galerie Patrick Lancz, Brussels, here illustrated in a book for the first time. In Holland, I am grateful to Singer Laren for drawing my attention to the biography of Dirk Smorenberg (and to Els Strandberg of the Newlyn School Gallery for translating it). In America, I am grateful to Helaine Glick of Monterey Museum of Art in relation to the letters and paintings of Euphemia Charlton Fortune, an artist of immense talent previously ignored in St Ives, and to Carolyn MacHardy in relation to the etchings of Donald Shaw MacLaughlan. I am also indebted to various American auction houses for the supply of images, particularly Freeman's of Philadelphia, Eldred's of East Dennis, Doyle's, New York, Harlowe-Powell Auction Gallery of Charlotteville and Bonhams and Butterfield of San Francisco.

Without doubt, the person, who put herself out the most to help me, was Julia Twomlow of the Leach Pottery. She responded positively to every request, however tedious, and I owe her a huge debt of gratitude. Jean Vacher at the Craft Study Centre at the University for the Creative Arts in Farnham also spent a day helping me with my research. I am also grateful for the advice of John Edgeler of the Long Room Gallery, Winchcombe, who dealt patiently with someone who started out as a complete novice on the art of pots. Leach's principal biographer, Emmanuel Cooper, was most generous in his supply of images.

Another exciting discovery was the Smart War drawings at the Imperial War Museum, and I am obliged to Jenny Wood for locating most of them for my visit, which resulted in the insertion of a whole new Chapter. Graham Sacker was most helpful as regards Smart's time in the Machine Gun Corps. Chris Stephens of the Tate Gallery made a number of helpful suggestions as regards Ben Nicholson paintings to be included in the book/exhibition, but, unfortunately, lenders to his major Nicholson exhibition were not prepared to lend again and DACS's fees ensured images were kept to a minimum.

As always, I have been assisted by a large number of private collectors and by relatives of artists, many of whom have given copyright consent as well. In particular, I would like to mention Polly Walker (Alec Walker), Brian and Genie Smart (Borlase Smart), Nik Halliday (Lindner), Bill Lloyd (Fanny and Will Lloyd), Innis Ellis Jones (Hutton and Roskruge), David Capps and Robert Mitchell (Barry), Jean Starling and Lynda Holland (Marcella Smith), Austin Wormleighton (John Park), Annie Coultas and John Branfield (Charles Simpson), Gerald Mayne (Hutton), Sue Halliday (Leach), Seth Cardew, Corisande Percival-Smith (Sharp), Richard Read (Stuart Weir), Priscilla Fursdon (Ver Beck), George Yeager and Clement C Moore II (Irvine). I am also indebted to Marie Keeling for photos of the St Ives Arts Club works and to Marion Whybrow for the use of several photos.

The following art dealers have also been immensely helpful - David Messum of Messum Fine Art Ltd, Richard Green, Els Strandberg of the Newlyn School Gallery, Penzance, Douglas Chome-Wilson of Chome Fine Art, Bath, Viv Hendra of the Lander Gallery, Truro, Denys Wilcox of The Court Gallery, Somerset, Stephen Paisnel of the Paisnel Gallery, John Noott of the Noott Galleries, Broadway, and Anthony Hepworth Fine Art, Bath. I am also indebted, as usual, to the Penzance auctioneers David Lay of the Penzance Auction House and Graham Bazley of W H Lane & Son and also to Richard Kay of Lawrence's, Crewkerne, and Eva Van Geldorp of Sotheby's, Amsterdam.

Once again, Joe Frost of Joe Frost Design has worked wonders with the images and assisted with the design of the cover. Finally, Austin Wormleighton valiantly offered to read through a draft and corrected numerous errors. Any remaining ones, however, are my sole responsibility.

# SELECTED BIBLIOGRAPHY

Peter Barnes, *Alfred Wallis and His Family - Fact and Fiction*, St Ives, 1997
Sven Berlin, *Alfred Wallis - Primitive*, London, 1949
Hazel Berriman, *Crysède - the unique textile designs of Alec Walker*, Truro, 1993
Jon Blackwood, *Winifred Nicholson*, Cambridge, 2001
John Branfield, *Charles Simpson - Painter of Animals & Birds, Coastline and Moorland*, Bristol, 2005
Virginia Button, *Christopher Wood*, London, 2003
Katie Campbell, *Moon Behind Clouds - An Introduction to the life and work of Sir Claude Francis Barry*, Jersey, 1999
Michael Cardew, *Bernard Leach - Recollections* in *Bernard Leach - Essays in Appreciation,* Wellington, 1960
Michael Cardew, *A Pioneer Potter*, London, 1988
A. Cariou and M. Tooby, *Christopher Wood - A Painter between Two Cornwalls*, London, 1996
Sarah Jane Checkland, *Ben Nicholson - the Vicious Circles of his Life & Art,* London, 2000
Garth Clark, *Michael Cardew - A Portrait*, London and Boston, 1978
Judith Collins, *Winifred Nicholson*, London, 1987
Emmanuel Cooper, *Bernard Leach - Life and Work*, London and New Haven, 2003
Edmund de Waal, *Bernard Leach*, London, undated
Joanne Drayton, *Edith Collier - Her Life and Work 1885-1964*, Christchurch, 1999
John Edgeler, *Michael Cardew and the West Country Slipware Tradition*, Winchcombe, 2007
Euphemia Charlton Fortune papers, Monterey Peninsula Museum
Matthew Gale, *Alfred Wallis*, London, 1998
Ed. L Gill, *Letters of Frances Hodgkins*, Auckland, 1993
Jacqueline Guisset, *Emile Fabry 1865-1966*, Brussels, 2000
Harbor Gallery, *Donald Shaw MacLaughlan 1876-1938 - A Re-Introduction*, New York, 1986
Tanya Harrod, *The Crafts in Britain in the Twentieth Century*, Yale, 1999
Richard Ingleby, *Christopher Wood - An English Painter*, London, 1995
Wilson Henry Irving papers, Archives of American Art, Smithsonian Institution
Robert Jones, *Alfred Wallis - Artist and Mariner*, Tiverton, 2001
Richard King, *The Etchings of Sydney Long, the Richard King Collection*, Goulburn, 1990
Bernard Leach, *A Potter's Outlook*, London, 1928
Bernard Leach, *Hamada Potter*, Tokyo and New York, 1975
Bernard Leach, *Beyond East and West*, London, 1978
Bernard Leach, *A Potter's Book*, London, 1940
Bettina MacAulay, *Songs of Colour - The Art of Vida Lahey*, South Brisbane, 1989
Averil Mackenzie-Grieve, *Time and Chance*, London, 1970
E.H. McCormick, *Portrait of Frances Hodgkins*, Auckland, 1981
Fred Milner papers, Tate Gallery Archive
Monterey Peninsula Museum, *Colors and Impressions - The Early Work of E Charlton Fortune*, Monterey, 1990
Eric Newton, *Christopher Wood 1901-1930,* Redfern Gallery catalogue, London, 1938
Winifred Nicholson, *Kit - An Unpublished Memoir*, Tate Gallery Archive
Nicholson papers, Tate Gallery Archive
John Pearl-Binns & Giles Heron, *Rebel and Sage - A Biography of Tom Heron (1890-1983)*, Bishop Auckland, 2001
Emke Raassen-Kruimel and Jan de Ruijter, *Dirk Smorenberg - In de ban van de natuur*, Laren, 2005
Sarah Riddick, *Pioneer Studio Pottery : The Milner White Collection*, London, 1990
Scottish Arts Council, *Alfred Wallis - Christopher Wood - Ben Nicholson*, Kilmarnock, 1987
Charles Simpson, *Animal and Bird Painting*, London, 1939
Charles Simpson, *El Rodeo*, London, 1924
Dr Roger Slack - tape-recorded interviews - St Ives Trust Archive Study Centre
Harold Spencer, *Wilson Henry Irvine and the Poetry of Light*, Old Lyme, 1998
Ed. Chris Stephens, *A Continuous Line - Ben Nicholson in England*, London 2008
*St Ives Times* - passim
C.E. Vulliamy, *Calico Pie*, London, 1940
Lucy Carrington Wertheim, *Adventure in Art*, London, 1947
Marion Whybrow, *St Ives 1883-1993 - Portrait of an Art Colony*, Woodbridge, 1995
Terrick Williams, *The Art of Pastel*, London, 1937
Christopher Wood letters, Tate Gallery Archive
Austin Wormleighton, *Morning Tide - John Anthony Park and the Painters of Light - St Ives 1900-1950*, Stockbridge, 1998

# INDEX

Note : This Index refers to the main text only. Please also see Appendix B

## A

Abell, Theresa  15, 48, 49, 73
Akerbladh, Alexander  93, 196
Alexander, Edith Meta  142
Angier, W Donald  132, 135-6
Arnold-Forster, Will  6, 11, 256, 278
Ashton, Will  143, 291

## B

Babbage, Herbert I  16, 18, 19, 149, 263
Bailey, Alfred C  130-2
Ballance, Marjorie  93, 172, 176, 261, 266
Ballance, Percy  93, 132-3, 283
Balmford, Hurst  133-5, 291
Barker, Miss  146
Barlow, John Noble  7, 73, 75-6, 89, 93, 143
Barns-Graham, Wilhelmina  292
Barrett, Joan  31
Barron, Phyllis  267, 282
Barry, Claude F  7, 11, 52, 59, 60-2, 93, 169, 283-4
Barry, Doris  92, 261-3
Beaumont, Arthur  15
Beaumont, Frederick  74, 76, 230
Bergen, Henry  237, 239-242, 251, 260
Birch, S J Lamorna  14, 223, 284-5, 289, 291
Blumberg, Gen Herbert  11
Bodilly, Lucy  82, 256, 261-4
Bodilly, Vera  93, 261-4
Braden, Nora  240, 251-2
Bradshaw, George  8, 11, 14, 28-9, 93, 116, 142, 156-7, 256, 285-91
Bradshaw, Kathleen  142, 155-6, 256, 261, 266
Bromley, John  92, 162, 196
Brown, J A Arnesby  7, 14, 93, 120, 149, 188, 289, 292
Bryant, Annie  261
Bryant, Charles  12-3, 28, 30, 185-6
Budgen, Frank  64-5
Burgess, Arthur  52
Burne, Winifred  170
Butler, Herbert  284

## C

Cardew, Michael  5, 10, 231-260, 265
Chadwick, Wm  16, 33, 71-2, 160
Chapman, Evelyn  145
Cochrane, Alfred  289-90
Cock, Martin  108, 186, 266-7, 270, 289
Collier, Edith  8, 40, 143, 148-51
Cooke, Dorothy  13, 142, 169, 172, 176, 256

Cox, Garstin  75, 284
Crossley, Cuthbert  76
Croxford, William E  76
Cuneo, Nell T  140-1, 169, 176, 261
Cuneo, Terence  176
Cuningham, Phyllis  154-5
Cuningham, Vera  154-5
Currie, D  156

## D

Darmady, Stewart  159, 256
Davenport, Ruth  261, 265
Davies, David  285, 287
Davis, Harry  258, 260, 292
Day, William Cave  88, 91, 285
Deacon, Allan  89
Dismorr, Jessica  13
Dobson, Cordelia  208, 281
Dobson, Frank  199
Dougherty, Paul  10, 15, 183
Douglas, John  17-8, 92, 183, 289
Douglas, Mabel  73, 92, 261
Dow, T Millie  18, 82, 89, 285, 287
Du Deney, Mary  31
Dunn, George  228, 230, 240, 243
Dyer, Lowell  15, 18, 92, 183

## E

Ede, H S (Jim)  212-8, 291
Ellis, E Joan  176
Ellis, Vernon  188
Elmhirst, Leonard and Dorothy  206, 256, 258, 291
Eumorfopoulos, G  239-41
Ewan, Frances  172, 176, 280

## F

Fabry, Emile  7, 33, 44-54, 59, 93, 143, 284
Falkner, Annie  93, 141, 256, 283
Faulkner, Herbert  186, 256
Findlay, Anna  176
Findlay, James  11
Finn, Herbert J  76
Fitzherbert, Herbert  16, 31
Forbes, A Stanhope  14, 17, 93, 97, 129, 157, 268, 284-5, 289, 291
Forbes, Maude  284
Fortescue, William  7, 90-1, 256, 284-5
Fortune, E Charlton  12-3, 177-9
Foweraker, A Moulton  39
Fowler, W H  82, 157
Fradgley, Ellen  93, 256
Frier, Harry  76
Frost, Terry  292
Fry, Roger  219, 245, 271
Fuller, Edmund  19, 92, 169, 172, 176, 195, 221, 263, 284
Fuller, Leonard  21, 123, 157

## G

Garnier, Geoffrey  174, 176
Garstin, Alethea  212, 284
Garstin, Crosbie  116
Garstin, Norman  33, 212, 284
Gibson, E (Bessie)  143, 148
Gill, Eric  219, 234, 244
Gillett, Rosie  221-2
Goosey, G Turland  93, 135, 137-8, 169, 176, 284
Gotch, Thomas  284
Greenslade, Sidney  235, 240, 260
Gresty, Hugh  138-140, 142, 157, 176, 289
Grier, Louis  8, 19, 28, 30-1, 82, 89, 130, 143, 152, 284-5

## H

Haines, A Lett  43, 146, 272
Hamada, Shoji  226-260
Hambly, Arthur  176, 291
Hamilton-Jenkin, Kenneth  250, 252
Hamilton-Jenkin, Luned  252, 261, 264-5
Harvey, Gertrude  157, 284
Harvey, Harold  157, 284-5, 289
Hartley, Alfred  7, 13, 18, 66, 74, 92, 143, 159-65, 168, 172, 176, 189, 195, 283-4, 287, 289
Hartley, Nora  92-3, 189
Hayward, Arthur  31, 93, 129-30, 135, 153, 157-8, 287, 289, 291
Heath, Frank  284-5
Hellwag, Annie  188, 219
Hellwag, Rudolf  188
Henderson, Miss  143
Heron, Patrick  278, 292
Heron, Tom  267, 269-282, 291-2
Hervey, Leslie  93, 141, 283
Hewitt, Pauline  142, 256, 261, 289
Heyworth, Richard  82, 285, 287
Hilliard, F John  183
Hodgkins, Frances  6-9, 13, 16-8, 31, 33-44, 68, 73-4, 82, 84, 89, 93, 143-52, 158, 185, 190, 195, 217, 283-4
Holmes, Dora  196
Horne, Frances  9, 48-9, 195, 220-2, 226-7, 230, 239, 248, 254, 256, 258, 264
Horne, Margery  221-2, 230, 239, 241, 247-8, 250
Howell, Felicie W M  16
Hoyle, William  51, 227, 259
Hughes, Eleanor  153, 284
Hughes, Robert  153, 284
Humphrey, Winifred  116, 153, 156
Hunter, M Sutherland  196
Hutton, Robert Langley  52, 66-7
Hynes, Gladys  272

# INDEX

**I**

Irvine, Wilson Henry  10, 12, 92, 131, 180-4

**J**

Jack, Richard  27
Jenner, Henry  11, 82, 179, 248, 250
Jewels, Mary  208, 281
John, Augustus  199, 202, 223, 268
Johnson, Ernest Borough  33, 93, 195-6, 247
Johnson, Esther Borough  93, 195-6
Jonsson, Rolf  17
Judson, Charles C  16, 33, 73, 186
Judson, Helen  16, 33, 73, 186

**K**

Keasbey, Henry  15
Kelly, A Elizabeth  191
Kelly, Cecil  191
Kemp-Welch, Lucy  12, 93, 193-5
King, Baragwanath  284
Knapping, Helen  82, 265
Knight, Harold  74, 284-5
Knight, Laura  18, 38, 74-5, 130, 284-5
Knox, Wilfred  76
Krauss, Eliza  144

**L**

Lahey, Vida  8, 41, 148-9
Lanyon, Herbert  52, 73, 123, 263
Lanyon, Lilian  92
Lanyon, Peter  292
Larcher, Dorothy  267, 282
Larisch, Count  17
Leach, Bernard  6, 9, 13-4, 19, 49, 51, 141, 172, 176, 195, 215, 218-9, 221-261, 264-5, 270, 282, 287, 291-2
Leach, David  258, 292
Lever, R Hayley  7, 186
Lewis, Frank  76
Lindner, Moffat  7, 9, 18, 31, 33-41, 57, 77-83, 144, 157, 252, 283, 285, 287, 289, 291
Littlejohns, John  196, 291
Lloyd, Frances  15, 52-6, 143
Lloyd, Will  15, 17, 31-2, 252
Long, Sydney  13, 143, 165-6
Ludlow, W H  196
Lyons, Arthur  16

**M**

Mackenzie-Grieve, A  77, 159, 168, 174-6, 256
MacLaughlan, Donald S  13, 167-8
Maclean, Frank  81-2, 124-5
MacSymon, John  196
Mairet, Ethel  234, 243, 252-3, 265, 282
Matheson, Greville  6, 11, 92, 256
Matsubayashi, T  195, 246-8, 259-60
McCracken, Francis  12, 189-91
McCrossan, Mary  12, 93, 141-2
McNab, Robert  157
Meade, Arthur  7, 35, 77, 88-9, 283-4, 291
Miller, Richard E  15
Milner, Fred  7, 15-7, 68, 71, 84-8, 143, 168, 172, 176, 283-5, 287, 291
Milner-White, Eric  233, 238, 240, 254-5
Mole, Frank  196
Moore, Frank  168, 171-2, 176-7, 284
Morris, Cedric  13, 43, 146, 199, 201-2, 204, 212, 272
Morris, Edith  76
Morris, William  219, 224, 234, 242, 268
Mortimer, Lewis  196
Munnings, Alfred  284-5
Munster, Frosca  8, 201, 205-7
Murray, William Staite  204, 227, 232, 237, 240-2, 256-8, 260, 287

**N**

Nance, Ernest Morton  239, 248, 256
Nance, Robert Morton  6, 11, 197, 231, 241-2, 248-50, 259
Naper, Ella  115, 153
Nevinson, Christopher  13, 143, 168, 189
Nicholson, Ben  6, 13-4, 44, 93, 196-7, 199-218, 257, 287, 291-2
Nicholson, William  196, 203
Nicholson, Winifred  6, 13, 44, 197, 199-218
Norris, Walter  186
Norsworthy, Harold  19, 227

**O**

Olsson, Julius  7-8, 12, 14, 18, 22, 28, 31, 54, 56, 93, 120, 23, 125, 142-3, 148, 52, 157, 185-6, 188, 283-7, 289, 291
Orage, Arthur R  219, 270-1

**P**

Park, John  6, 12, 93, 123-9, 135, 138, 142, 157-8, 185, 195, 227, 261, 283-4, 287, 291
Parkyn, William  8, 30-1
Payton, E W  291
Pearce, Bryan  292
Pearson, W H  76
Peters, Rollo  115, 153
Pitt, Lynn  34
Pleydell-Bouverie, Katharine  230, 240, 243, 245-8, 51-2, 258, 260
Polderman, Dr  51
Potter, Will  11, 15
Powell, Arthur  184
Procter, Charles  128, 130
Procter, Dod  157, 272, 281, 285, 289
Procter, Ernest  157, 268, 284-5, 289

**R**

Raymond, Francis (see Spenlove)
Read, E H Handley  21
Reckelbus, Louis  7, 33, 36, 44, 47, 52-7, 66, 93, 125, 143, 284
Reynolds, H Tangye  93, 141, 283
Reynolds, Reginald  93, 141, 283
Rheam, Henry M  76
Rice, Helen  49
Ritchie, Hannah  145, 147
Roskruge, Francis  11, 13, 118, 170-2, 176, 256, 289
Rutter, Frank  38, 44, 204, 270-2, 283

**S**

Sargent, Louis  7, 11, 38, 52, 59, 62-66, 93, 120, 125, 261, 283-4
Sargent, Katharine E  64
Saunders, Dorothy Jane  145, 147
Schofield, Elmer  7, 16, 76, 185-6, 283
Sharp, Dorothea  12, 71, 93, 129, 194-5, 254, 265, 291
Shearer Armstrong, A  142, 176, 256
Sidgwick, Alfred & Cecily  153
Simpson, Charles  6, 8, 11-2, 31-2, 72-3, 93-113, 118, 120, 123, 126, 152-7, 172, 176, 195, 266, 283-4, 287
Simpson, Ruth  8, 12, 31-2, 72, 93, 114-6, 118, 152-7
Skinner, Edgar  6, 35-6, 41-2, 49, 52, 69, 76, 145, 188, 230-1, 235, 240-1, 245, 251, 256, 260
Skinner, Edith  18, 31, 35, 41-2, 221, 230, 235
Slatter, Kathleen (see Bradshaw)
Smart, E Rowley  196
Smart, R Borlase  6-7, 12-3, 19-27, 31, 56, 59, 64, 68, 71, 87, 89, 91, 93-4, 104, 107, 114-123, 138, 140, 156-7, 159, 162, 164, 168-9, 172-5, 177, 185, 189, 263, 283-4, 287-9, 291

SEA CHANGE : FINE AND DECORATIVE ART IN ST IVES 1914-1930

Smith, Annie Bliss  170, 172, 176
Smith, David Murray  188-9
Smith, Frances Tysoe  92
Smith, Marcella  14, 16, 33, 66-70, 93, 124, 129, 132, 138, 143, 158, 168, 195, 261, 265-6, 284
Smorenberg, Dirk  7, 33, 57-8
Snell, Florence  15
Snell, Henry B  8, 12, 15-6, 69
Soper, George  196
Spenlove, Francis Raymond  93, 138, 158
Spittle, William  74
Stafford, Eva  143
Stoddart, Margaret  33
Stokes, Adrian  14, 120, 218, 289, 292
Stokes, A G Folliott  62, 64, 73, 159, 162
Sully, Frank  196
Sykes, E  174
Symons, G Gardner  15, 84-5, 186

**T**

Talmage, Algernon  7-8, 142-3, 152, 157, 284-5, 287, 289
Thompson, M E (Betty)  52, 143
Titcomb, John H  92
Titcomb, William  89, 285
Trew, Harold  196
Truman, Herbert  14, 157, 287-9
Turner, Dorothy  222
Turner, Irene  222, 261, 264-5
Turvey, Reginald  223-4, 227, 258
Tylee, Marion  196

**U**

Uren, Frederick C  89, 157, 227

**V**

Ver Beck, Frank  15, 18, 33, 36, 57, 72-3, 93, 114
Ver Beck, Hanna Rion  15, 33, 49, 73, 93
Vivian, Beatrice  176
Vyse, Charles and Nell  237

**W**

Wagner, Gerard  158
Walker, Alec  6, 14, 267-282, 291-2
Wallis, Alfred  6, 13-4, 85, 87, 93, 196-7, 201, 204-218, 275, 278, 281, 291-2
Wallis, Katherine  146
Walters, Edith  172, 174
Ward, Charles D  196
Ward, Charlotte Blakeney  195
Webb, D G  172, 176
Weir, Helen Stuart  15, 68, 70, 93, 142-3, 168, 283
Weir-Lewis, Nina  15, 35, 68, 143-4

Welch, Florence  221-2, 261, 264
Wells, Reginald  237
Wertheim, Lucy C  42, 217-8, 282
White, Arthur  66, 92, 158
White, Herbert Thirkell  11
Whitehouse, S E (Lizzie)  74-5
Wiggins, Guy C  15, 180, 184
Willett, E M  291
Williams, Madeline  148
Williams, Mary F A  93, 141, 256
Williams, Terrick  9, 12, 82, 186-7, 289, 291
Winthrop, Miss  143
Wolmark, Alfred A  196
Wolter, Hendrik Jan  13, 190-2
Wood, Beatrice  8, 41, 146-7
Wood, Christopher  6, 8, 13-4, 44, 93, 196-210, 214-8, 291
Wyllie, William L  12, 196
Wynter, Bryan  292